The American Class Structure in an Age of Growing Inequality

Tenth Edition

Sara Miller McCune founded SAGE Publishing in 1965 to support the dissemination of usable knowledge and educate a global community. SAGE publishes more than 1000 journals and over 800 new books each year, spanning a wide range of subject areas. Our growing selection of library products includes archives, data, case studies and video. SAGE remains majority owned by our founder and after her lifetime will become owned by a charitable trust that secures the company's continued independence.

Los Angeles | London | New Delhi | Singapore | Washington DC | Melbourne

The American Class Structure in an Age of Growing Inequality

Tenth Edition

Dennis L. Gilbert
Hamilton College

Los Angeles | London | New Delhi
Singapore | Washington DC | Melbourne

FOR INFORMATION:

SAGE Publications, Inc.
2455 Teller Road
Thousand Oaks, California 91320
E-mail: order@sagepub.com

SAGE Publications Ltd.
1 Oliver's Yard
55 City Road
London EC1Y 1SP
United Kingdom

SAGE Publications India Pvt. Ltd.
B 1/I 1 Mohan Cooperative Industrial Area
Mathura Road, New Delhi 110 044
India

SAGE Publications Asia-Pacific Pte. Ltd.
3 Church Street
#10-04 Samsung Hub
Singapore 049483

Acquisitions Editor: Jeff Lasser
Editorial Assistant: Adeline Wilson
Content Development Editor: Sarah Dillard
Production Editor: Karen Wiley
Copy Editor: Beth Ginter
Typesetter: C&M Digitals (P) Ltd.
Proofreader: Annette Van Dwsen
Indexer: Sylvia Coates
Cover Designer: Candice Harman
Marketing Manager: Kara Kindstrom

Printed in the United States of America

ISBN: 978-1-5063-4596-3

This book is printed on acid-free paper.

17 18 19 20 21 10 9 8 7 6 5 4 3 2 1

Contents

About the Author

Dennis L. Gilbert holds a PhD from Cornell University and has taught at Cornell; the Universidad Católica in Lima, Peru; and Hamilton College, where he is Professor of Sociology Emeritus. He is also the author of *The Oligarchy and the Old Regime in Latin America, 1880 to 1970* (2017), *Mexico's Middle Class in the Neoliberal Era* (2007), *Sandinistas: The Party and the Revolution* (1991), and *La Oligarquía Peruana: Historia de Tres Familias* (1982).

Preface

This tenth edition of *The American Class Structure* answers three questions. Does class make a difference in our lives? Are class inequalities widening in American society? If so, why? I was 12 years old when the first edition was written in 1955. The author was Joseph Kahl, an unemployed Harvard PhD then living cheaply in Mexico. His book, which helped define the emerging field of social stratification, remained in print, without revision, for 25 years. It earned this long run by presenting a lucid synthesis of the best research on the American class system. Each study was lovingly dissected by Kahl, who conveyed its flavor, assessed its strengths and weaknesses, summarized its most significant conclusions, and explained how they were reached.

The American Class Structure was not a theoretical book. Kahl created a simple conceptual schema with a short list of key variables drawn from the work of Karl Marx and Max Weber. Kahl admitted that he had settled on this framework for the good and practical reason that it allowed him to draw together the results of disparate research reports. But the variables were interrelated, and Kahl believed that they tended to converge to create social classes in a pattern he called the American class structure. At the same time, he recognized that classes and class structure are abstractions from social reality—tendencies never fully realized in any situation but discernable when one stepped back from detail to think about underlying forces.

Sometime around 1980, Kahl invited me to collaborate on a new version of *The American Class Structure*. He was then professor of sociology at Cornell, and I had recently completed a PhD under his guidance. The book we published in 1982 encompassed a body of stratification research that had grown enormously in sophistication and volume since the 1950s. *The American Class Structure: A New Synthesis* consisted almost entirely of fresh material but preserved the general framework of the original edition and its analyses of classic studies of the American class system. That edition and two subsequent editions, which Kahl and I produced together, proved popular with a new generation of sociologists and sociology students.

But when our publisher asked for yet another edition, Kahl, who had retired to Chapel Hill, North Carolina, said he'd rather be listening to opera or playing golf than reading page proofs again. And since he would not be contributing to the new edition, he asked that his name be taken off the cover. Thus, the subsequent editions have been published under my name.

Although there is now only one official author, the authorial "I" reverts to "we" after this preface. Much of this book is the product of a long collaboration, and I am often at a loss to recall who wrote (or perhaps rewrote) a particular passage. Retaining the "we" of earlier editions seemed perfectly natural. That said, I want to stress that I bear sole responsibility for every word included in this edition.

I am, in particular, responsible for the theme that runs through the recent editions and is reflected in the revised subtitle: *In an Age of Growing Inequality*. This theme was inspired by data on trends in earnings, income, wealth, and related variables that reveal a remarkably consistent pattern of rising inequality since the mid-1970s—a pattern that contrasts sharply with the broadly shared prosperity of the 1950s and 1960s. We need to understand why this is happening.

Like its predecessors, this edition is not an encyclopedic survey of stratification research, nor is it an exercise in class theory. It focuses on the socioeconomic core of the class system. It emphasizes the effects of class differences on our everyday lives. Gender and race are treated in relation to class, rather than as parallel dimensions of stratification. The book looks at economic disparities between men and women and among whites, blacks, and Hispanics. More profoundly, it considers the effects on the class system of developments such as women's changing economic role, new patterns of family life, and occupational differentiation among African Americans. A guiding assumption is that the experience of class is inextricably bound up with gender and race.

For this edition, I have made substantial revisions to nearly every chapter, adding fresh material on income, wealth, earnings, jobs, poverty, politics, marriage, and other topics—especially as they are relevant to the theme of growing inequality. I have taken a fresh look at the effects of technological change and globalization on our class system and added material comparing the United States with other wealthy countries on poverty and social mobility. This book was written in the wake of Donald Trump's election to the presidency with the support of a majority of white working-class voters—a first for a Republican presidential candidate. I consider how growing inequality and racial antagonism contributed to this result.

I have retained two features of recent editions. One is the Glossary, added to make life easier for readers who are puzzled by Marx's use of the term "ideology," uncertain about the exact meaning of "net worth," or unable to recall how the text defined "postindustrial society." Readers will find a list of relevant glossary terms at the end of each chapter. The other is the streamlined citation of government statistics. In order to produce a less cluttered text, I have eliminated most references to standard statistical series on income, poverty, employment, and related topics. On this feature, see the "Notes on Statistical Sources" at the end of the book. There are a lot of tables in this book. Readers can be assured that table columns or rows that end in 100 percent (or 100.0 percent) cover all the individuals in the relevant category, even though they occasionally add up to 101 percent or 99 percent. The difference is the result of so-called "rounding errors" and can be ignored.

* * * *

Joe Kahl passed away on January 1, 2010. I remember him as an accomplished scholar, a fine teacher, a generous friend, and still my coauthor.

Dennis Gilbert
Washington, DC

CHAPTER 1

Social Class in America

All communities divide themselves into the few and the many. The first are the rich and well-borne, the other the mass of the people. . . . The people are turbulent and changing; they seldom judge or determine right. . . . Give, therefore, to the first class a distinct, permanent share in the government. They will check the unsteadiness of the second, and as they cannot receive any advantage by a change, they therefore will ever maintain good government.

Alexander Hamilton (1780)

On the night the *Titanic* sank on her maiden voyage across the Atlantic in 1912, social class proved to be a key determinant of who survived and who perished. Among those who lost their lives were 40 percent of the first-class passengers, 58 percent of the second-class passengers, and 75 percent of the third-class passengers. The class differences were even starker for women and children (who were given priority access to the lifeboats): Just 7 percent of first-class, but over half of third-class passengers, went down with the *Titanic* (U.S. Senate 1912).

The divergent fates of the *Titanic's* passengers present a dramatic illustration of the connection between social class and what pioneer sociologist Max Weber called **life chances**.[1] Weber invented the term to emphasize the extent to which our chances for the good things in life are shaped by class position.

Contemporary sociology has followed Weber's lead and found that the influence of social class on our lives is indeed pervasive. Table 1.1 gives a few examples. These statistics compare people at the bottom, middle, and top of the class structure. They show, among other things, that people in the bottom 25 percent are less likely to be in good health, less likely to own their home, more likely to have physically punishing jobs, and more likely to be the victims of violent crime. Those in the top 25 percent are healthier, safer, more likely to send their kids to college, and more likely to find their lives exciting.

Thoughtful observers have recognized the importance of social classes since the beginnings of Western philosophy. They knew that some individuals and families had more money, more influence, or more prestige than their neighbors. The philosophers also realized that the differences were more than personal or even familial, for the pattern of inequalities tended to congeal into strata of families who shared similar positions. These **social strata** or classes divided society into a hierarchy; each stratum had interests

Table 1.1 Life Chances by Social Class[a]	Bottom	Middle	Top
In excellent/very good health[b]	40%	52%	69%
Victims of violent crime per 1,000 population[c]	33.6	17.0	11.6
Own home (household heads 35 to 54)[d]	34%	63%	85%
College grad by age 24[e]	12%	28%	58%
Job requires lifting, pulling, pushing, bending[b]	71%	49%	33%
Find life "exciting" (not "routine" or "dull")[b]	46%	47%	67%

a. Classes defined by income: bottom 25 percent, middle 50 percent, and top 25 percent.

b. General Social Survey 2010. Computed for this table.

c. U.S. Department of Justice, Bureau of Justice Statistics 2015.

d. www.Zillow.com.

e. Pell Institute 2017. By Parents' income.

---

[1] Terms that appear in bold print are defined in the Glossary at the end of the book.

or goals in common with equals but different from, and often conflicting with, those of groups above or below them. Finally, it was noted that political action often flows from class interests. As one of the founding fathers, Alexander Hamilton, observed, the rich seek social stability to preserve their advantages, but the poor work for social change that would bring them a larger share of the world's rewards.

This book is an analysis of the American class system. We explore class differences in income, prestige, power, and other key variables. We will point out how these variables react on one another—for instance, how a person's income affects beliefs about social policy or how one's job affects the choice of friends or spouse. And we will explore the question of movement from one class to another, recognizing that a society can have classes and still permit individuals to rise or fall among them.

We begin by consulting two major theorists of social stratification, Karl Marx and Max Weber, to identify the major facets of the subject. Marx (1818–1883) and Weber (1864–1920) established an intellectual framework that strongly influenced subsequent scholars. (**Social stratification**, by the way, refers to social ranking based on characteristics such as income, wealth, occupation, or prestige.)

Karl Marx

Although the discussion of stratification goes back to ancient philosophy, modern attempts to formulate a systematic theory of class differences began with Marx's work in the nineteenth century. Most subsequent theorizing has represented an attempt either to reformulate or to refute his ideas. Marx, who was born in the wake of the French Revolution and lived in the midst of the Industrial Revolution, was both a radical activist and a scholar of social and political change. He saw the study of social class as the key to an understanding of the turbulent events of his time. His studies of economics, history, and philosophy convinced him that societies are mainly shaped by their economic organization and that social classes form the link between economic facts and social facts. He also concluded that fundamental social change is the product of conflict between classes. Thus, in Marx's view, an understanding of classes is basic to comprehending how societies function and how they are transformed.

In Marx's work, social classes are defined by their distinctive relationships to the **means of production**. Taking this approach, Marx defined two classes in the emerging industrial societies of his own time: the capitalist class (or **bourgeoisie**) and the working class (or **proletariat**). He describes the bourgeoisie as the class that owns the means of production, such as mines or factories, and the proletariat as the class of those who must sell their labor to the owners of the means to earn a wage and stay alive. Marx maintained that in modern, capitalist society, each of these two basic classes tends toward an internal homogeneity that obliterates differences within them. Little businesses lose out in competition with big businesses, concentrating ownership in a small bourgeoisie of monopoly capitalists. In a parallel fashion, gradations within the proletariat fade in significance as machines get more sophisticated and do the work that used to be done by skilled workers. As the basic classes become internally homogenized, the middle of the class structure thins out and the system as a whole becomes polarized between the two class extremes.

But notice that these broad generalizations refer to long-range trends. Marx recognized that at any given historical moment, the reality of the class system was more complex. The simplifying processes of homogenization and polarization were tendencies, unfolding over many decades, which might never be fully realized. Marx's descriptions of contemporary situations in his writings as a journalist and pamphleteer show more complexity in economic and political groupings than do his writings as a theorist of long-term historical development.

We have noted that Marx defined the proletariat, bourgeoisie, and other classes by their relationship to the means of production. Why? In the most general sense, because he regarded production as the center of social life. He reasoned that people must produce to survive, and they must cooperate to produce. The individual's place in society, relationships to others, and outlook on life are shaped by his or her work experience. More specifically, those who occupy a similar role in production are likely to share economic and political interests that bring them into conflict with other participants in production. Capitalists, for instance, reap profit (in Marx's terms, *expropriate surplus*) by paying their workers less than the value of what they produce. Therefore, capitalists share an interest in holding down wages and resisting legislation that would enhance the power of unions to press their demands on employers.

From a Marxist perspective, the manner in which production takes place (that is, the application of technology to nature) and the class and property relationships that develop in the course of production are the most fundamental aspects of any society. Together, they constitute what Marx called the **mode of production**. Societies with similar modes of production ought to be similar in other significant respects and should therefore be studied together. Marx's analysis of European history after the fall of Rome distinguished three modes of production, which he saw as successive stages of societal development: *feudalism*, the locally based agrarian society of the Middle Ages, in which a small landowning aristocracy in each district exploited the labor of a peasant majority; *capitalism*, the emerging industrial and commercial order of Marx's own lifetime, already international in scope and characterized by the dominance of the owners of industry over the mass of industrial workers; and *communism*, the technologically advanced, classless society of the future, in which all productive property would be held in common.

Marx regarded the mode of production as the main determinant of a society's **superstructure** of social and political institutions and ideas. He used the concept of superstructure to answer an old question: How do privileged minorities maintain their positions and contain the potential resistance of exploited majorities? His reply was that the class that controls the means of production typically controls the means of compulsion and persuasion—the superstructure. He observed that in feudal times, the landowners monopolized military and political power. With the rise of modern capitalism, the bourgeoisie gained control of political institutions. In each case, the privileged class could use the power of the state to protect its own interests. For instance, in Marx's own time, the judicial, legislative, and police authority of European governments dominated by the bourgeoisie were employed to crush the early labor movement, a pattern that was repeated a little later in the United States. In an insightful overstatement from the *Communist Manifesto* (1848), Marx asserted, "The executive of the modern State is but a committee for managing the common affairs of the whole bourgeoisie" (Marx 1978:475).

But Marx did not believe that class systems rested on pure compulsion. He allowed for the persuasive influence of ideas. Here, Marx made one of his most significant contributions to social science: the concept of **ideology**. He used the term to describe the pervasive ideas that uphold the *status quo* and sustain the ruling class. Marx noted that human consciousness is a social product. It develops through our experience of cooperating with others to produce and to sustain social life. But social experience is not homogeneous, especially in a society that is divided into classes. The peasant does not have the same experience as the landlord and therefore develops a distinct outlook. One important feature of this differentiation of class outlooks is the tendency for members of each group to regard their own particular class interests as the true interests of the whole society. What makes this significant is that one class has superior capacity to impose its self-serving ideas on other classes.

The class that dominates production, Marx argued, also controls the institutions that produce and disseminate ideas, such as schools, mass media, churches, and courts. As a result, the viewpoint of the dominant class pervades thinking in areas as diverse as the laws of family life and property, theories of political democracy, notions of economic rationality, and even conceptions of the afterlife. In Marx's (1978) words, "The ideas of the ruling class are in every epoch the ruling ideas" (p. 172). In extreme situations, ideology can convince slaves that they ought to be obedient to their masters, or poor workers that their true reward will eventually come to them in heaven.

Marx (1978) maintained, then, that the ruling class had powerful political and ideological means to support the established order. Nonetheless, he regarded class societies as intrinsically unstable. In a famous passage from the *Communist Manifesto,* he observed,

> The history of all hitherto existing society is the history of class struggles. Freeman and slave, patrician and plebeian, lord and serf, guild master and journeyman, in a word, oppressor and oppressed stood in constant opposition to one another, carried on an uninterrupted, now hidden, now open fight, a fight that each time ended either in a revolutionary reconstitution of society at large, or in the common ruin of the contending classes.
>
> In the earlier epochs of history, we find almost everywhere a complicated arrangement of society into various orders, a manifold gradation of social rank. In ancient Rome, we have patricians, knights, plebeians, slaves; in the Middle Ages, feudal lords, vassals, guild-masters, journeymen, apprentices, serfs; in almost all of these classes, again, subordinate gradations. . . .
>
> Our epoch, the epoch of the bourgeoisie, possesses, however, this distinctive feature: It has simplified the class antagonisms. Society as a whole is more and more splitting up into two great hostile camps, into two great classes directly facing each other: Bourgeoisie and Proletariat. (pp. 473–474)

As these lines suggest, Marx saw class struggle as the basic source of social change. He coupled class conflict to economic change, arguing that the development of new means of production (for example, the development of modern industry) implied the emergence of new classes and class relationships. The most serious political conflicts develop when the interests of a rising class are opposed to those of an established ruling class. Class struggles of this sort can produce a "revolutionary reconstitution of society." Notice that each epoch creates within itself the growth of a new class that eventually seizes power and inaugurates a new epoch.

Two eras of transformation through class conflict held particular fascination for Marx. One was the transition from feudalism to modern capitalism in Europe, a process in which he assigned the bourgeoisie (the urban capitalist class) "a most revolutionary part" (Marx 1978:475). Into a previously stable agrarian society, the bourgeoisie introduced a stream of technological innovations, an accelerating expansion of production and trade, and radically new forms of labor relations. The feudal landlords, feeling their own interests threatened, resisted change. The result was a series of political conflicts (the French Revolution was the most dramatic instance) through which the European bourgeoisie wrested political power from the landed aristocracy.

Marx believed that a second, analogous era of transformation was beginning during his own lifetime. The capitalist mode of production had created a new social class, the urban working class, or proletariat, with interests directly opposed to those of the dominant class, the bourgeoisie. This conflict of interests arose, not simply from the struggle over wages between **capital** and labor, but from the essential character of capitalist production and society. The capitalist economy was inherently unstable and subject to periodic depressions with massive unemployment. These economic crises heightened awareness of long-term trends widening the gap between rich and poor. Furthermore, capitalism's blind dependence on market mechanisms built on individual greed created an alienated existence for most members of society. Marx was convinced that only under communism, with the means of production communally controlled, could these conditions be overcome.

The situation of the proletarian majority made it capitalism's most deprived and alienated victim and therefore the potential spearhead of a communist revolution. However, in Marx's view, an objective situation of class oppression does not lead directly to political revolt. For that to happen, the oppressed class must first develop **class consciousness**—that is, a sense of shared identity and common grievances, requiring a collective response. Some of Marx's most fruitful sociological work, to which we will return in Chapter 9, is devoted to precisely this problem. What intrinsic tendencies of capitalist society, Marx asked, are most likely to produce a class-conscious proletariat? Among the factors he isolated were the stark simplification of the class order in the course of capitalist development; the concentration of large masses of workers in the new industrial towns; the deprivations of working-class people, exacerbated by the inherent instability of the capitalist economy; and the political sophistication gained by the proletariat through participation in working-class organizations such as labor unions and mass political parties.

What, in sum, can be said of Marx's contribution to stratification theory? His recognition of the economic basis of class systems was a crucial insight.

His theory of ideology and his conception of the connection between social classes and political processes, although oversimple as stated, proved a fruitful starting point for modern research. As for his conception of change, a series of twentieth century revolutions—including those in Mexico (1910), Russia (1917), and China (1949)—established the significance of class conflict for radical social transformation. However, social revolutions have typically occurred in peasant societies during early stages of industrialization under foreign influence rather than in the advanced industrial countries where Marx anticipated them. In the advanced industrial countries, the proletariat used labor unions and mass political parties to defend its interests, thus rechanneling the forces of class conflict into the legal procedures of democratic politics.

More than a century after his death, it is apparent that Marx was a better sociologist than he was a prophet. He identified many of the central processes of capitalist society, but he was unable to foresee all the consequences of their unfolding, and his vision of a humane socialist future has not been realized in any communist country.

Max Weber

The great German sociologist Max Weber, who wrote in the early years of the twentieth century, was interested in many of the same problems that had fascinated Marx—among them, the origins of capitalism, the role of ideology, and the relationship between social structure and economic processes. Weber frequently benefited from Marx's work, even while reaching rather different conclusions. In the field of stratification, his special contributions were (1) to introduce a conceptual clarity that was often lacking in Marx's references to social classes and (2) to highlight the subjective aspects of stratification, as expressed in everyday interactions.

Weber made a crucial distinction between two orders of ranking or stratification: *class* and *status*. Class had roughly the same meaning for both Weber and Marx. It refers to groupings of people according to their economic position. Class situation or membership, according to Weber, is defined by the individual's strength in economic markets (for example, the job market or capital markets), to the extent that these determine individual life chances. By life chances, he meant the fundamental aspects of an individual's future possibilities that are shaped by class membership, from the infant's chances for decent nutrition to the adult's opportunities for worldly success. (Table 1.1 at the beginning of this chapter provides other examples of life chances.)

Following Marx, Weber stressed that the most important class distinction is between those who own property (land, small businesses, corporate stock, etc.) and those who do not. However, he noted that many significant distinctions can be made within each of these categories. Among the propertied elite, for example, there are rentiers, who support themselves with income from stocks, bonds, and other securities, and entrepreneurs, who depend on profits from businesses they create, own, and operate. The propertyless can be differentiated by the occupational skills that they bring to the marketplace: The life chances of an unskilled worker are vastly different from those of a well-trained engineer. This suggests that the vast population of wage earners whom Marx lumped into the proletariat were really a highly differentiated group.

For Weber, a **social class**, then, becomes a group of people who share the same economically shaped life chances. Notice that this way of defining a class does not imply that the individuals in it are necessarily aware of their common situation. It simply establishes a statistical category of people who are, from the point of view of the market (and the sociologist), similar to each other. Only under certain circumstances do they become aware of their common fate, begin to think of each other as equals, and develop institutions of joint action to further their shared interests.

Status, the second major order of stratification defined by Weber, is ranking by social prestige. In contrast with class, which is based on objective economic fact, status is a subjective phenomenon, a sentiment in people's minds. Although the members of a class may have little sense of shared identity, the members of a status group generally think of themselves as a social community, with a common **lifestyle** (a familiar term we owe to Weber). In a classic essay on stratification, Weber (1946) outlined these distinctions:

> In contrast to the purely economically determined "class situation," we wish to designate as "status situation" every typical component of the life fate of men that is determined by a specific, positive or negative, social estimation of honor. . . .
>
> Status groups are normally communities. They are, however, often of an amorphous kind. . . . In content, status honor is normally expressed by the fact that above all else a specific style of life can be expected from all those who wish to belong to the circle. Linked with this expectation are restrictions on "social" intercourse (that is, intercourse which is not subservient to economic or any other of business's "functional" purposes). These restrictions may confine normal marriages to within the status circle and may lead to complete endogamous closure. . . .
>
> Of course, material monopolies provide the most effective motives for the exclusiveness of a status group. . . . With an increased enclosure of the status group, the conventional preferential opportunities for special employment grow into a legal monopoly of special offices for the members. . . .
>
> With some oversimplification, one might thus say that "classes" are stratified according to their relations to the production and acquisition of goods; whereas "status groups" are stratified according to the principles of their consumption of goods as represented by special "styles of life." (pp. 186–193)

In those passages, Weber specified many of the interrelations between class and status, between economy and society. Because of class position, a person earns a certain income. That income permits a certain lifestyle, and people soon make friends with others who live the same way. As they interact with one another, they begin to conceive of themselves as a special type of people. They restrict interaction with outsiders who seem too different (they may be too poor, too uneducated, too clumsy to live graciously enough for acceptance as worthy companions). Marriage partners are chosen from similar groups because once people follow a certain style of life, they find it difficult to be comfortable with people who live differently. Thus, the status group becomes an ingrown circle. It earns a position in the local community that entitles its members to social honor or prestige from inferiors.

Status groups develop the conventions or customs of a community. Through time, they evolve appropriate ways of dressing, of eating, and of living that are somewhat different from the ways of other groups. These ways are expressed as moral judgments reflecting abstract principles of value that separate "good" from "bad." The application of these principles to individuals establishes rankings of social honor or prestige. These distinctions often react back on the marketplace; to preserve their advantages, high-status groups attempt to monopolize those goods that symbolize their style of life—they pass consumption laws prohibiting the lower orders from wearing lace, or they band together to keep Jews or blacks out of prestigious country clubs. (Weber regarded invidious distinctions among ethnic groups as a type of status stratification.)

A status order tends to restrict the freedom of the market, not only by its monopolization of certain types of consumption goods, but also by its monopolization of the opportunities to earn money. If they can get the power, status groups often restrict entry into the more lucrative professions or trades and access to credit. For example, entry into the electricians' union might be restricted to sons of current members. The local bank might be more willing to grant a loan to a member of the country club than to a social nobody, especially if the bank officer is also a member of the club. More generally, birth into a high-status family gives children advantages of social grace and personal contacts that eventually help their careers.

Weber observed that, in theory, class and status are opposed principles. In its purest form, the class or economic order is universalistic and impersonal; it recognizes no social distinctions and judges solely on the basis of competitive skill or accumulated wealth. Status, in contrast, is based on particularistic distinctions: Some people are "better" than others.

But Weber recognized that, in practice, class and status are intertwined—at least in the long run. Historically, the status order is created by the class order; consumption, after all, is based on production. Although the established social elite might react against the status claims of the newly rich, it typically accepts their descendants if they have properly cultivated the conventions of the higher status group. On another level, the appearance of classes based on new sources of wealth—for instance, the emergence of an industrial bourgeoisie in Europe and America in the nineteenth century—signals a future restructuring of the status order as a whole.

Weber, like Marx, was interested in the relationship between stratification and political power. It would be accurate to say that for both men, stratification was essentially a political topic. But Weber was highly skeptical of the implication in Marx's work that all political phenomena could be traced back directly to class. For instance, Weber suggested that the institutions of the modern bureaucratic state exercise an influence on society that is not reducible to the control exercised by a single class. (In *The Eighteenth Brumaire*, Marx [1978:594–617] himself reluctantly adopted this view for a special circumstance but not Weber's corollary that a communist state might be grimly similar to a capitalist state, reflecting bureaucratic domination of society.)

Weber opposed what he called the "pseudo-scientific operation" of Marxist writers of his day, who assumed an automatic link between class position and class consciousness (Weber 1946:184). He noted that a shared economic situation can and sometimes does lead to an awareness of shared class interests and a willingness to engage in militant class action, but it need not. Indeed, the very notion of class interest was highly ambiguous for Weber. In his view, there are multiple classes in modern societies, and they are continually changing. Under such conditions, individuals may think of their own identities, and shared or conflicting interests with others, in varied ways. Someone whom sociologists would identify as working class might think of himself as white and middle class, because he believes he has nothing in common with minority workers and supposes himself to be a middle-income, average American. Or he might strongly identify with other workers, whatever their race, and become class conscious in the Marxian sense. Neither would surprise Weber.

Implicit in Weber's approach to stratification is the idea that status considerations can undermine the development of class consciousness and class struggle. For example, the politics of the American South has long been shaped by the tendency of poor whites to identify with richer whites rather than with poor blacks who share their economic position. Weber noted that political parties can develop around class, status, or other bases for conflict over power. The major American political parties are amorphous coalitions that have never been as clearly oriented toward the pursuit of class interests as have, for example, the working-class parties of Western Europe. Again, none of this would have surprised Weber.

In sum, Weber accepted Marx's idea of the underlying economic basis of stratification. But Weber's conception of social class was much more flexible than Marx's and probably better adapted to the complexities of modern societies. Weber also identified another order of stratification, by differentiating between class and status. He argued that the two interact with each other and with the political process in ways not fully recognized by Marx.

Three Issues and 10 Variables

Marx's and Weber's writings suggest three broad issues in the study of social class:

1. *Economic basis.* How do class distinctions arise from economic distinctions? And how, in particular, does economic change transform the class system? These were central concerns for both theorists.

2. *Social basis.* How are economic class distinctions reflected in social distinctions and social behavior? Weber's discussion of status groups is relevant here. He noted their tendency to become social communities with distinctive lifestyles and values. He was intrigued by the complex relationship between class and status.

3. *Political implications.* How does the class system affect the political system? How do economically dominant classes interact politically with the other classes in a society? For both Marx and Weber, class was ultimately a political topic.

These issues led us to organize our examination of the class system around a series of related sociological variables. With regard to the economic issue, we will be looking at occupation, wealth, income, and poverty; with regard to the social issue, at prestige, association, **socialization**, and social mobility; and with regard to the political issue, at power and class consciousness. These variables are more precisely defined in the appropriate chapters and included in the glossary at the end of the book, along with other terms we consider important. When they are discussed for the first time, they appear in **bold** print as a reminder that they can be found in the glossary. A list of pertinent glossary terms appears at the end of each chapter.

What Are Social Classes?

We define social classes as groups of families or households, more or less equal in rank and differentiated from other families above or below them with regard to characteristics such as occupation, income, wealth, and prestige.[2]

Our approach raises two questions: Why conceive of stratification in terms of *discrete classes?* And why think of classes as groupings of *families?* The first question arises because it is logically possible for a society to be stratified in a continuous gradation between high and low without any sharp lines of division. In reality, this is unlikely. The sources of a family's position are shared by many other similar families; there are only a limited number of types of occupations or of possible positions in the property system. One holds a routine position in a service, factory, or office setting; lives by manual skill or professional expertise; or manages people and money. People in similar positions have similar incomes and a tendency to mix with one another, to grow similar in their thinking and lifestyle. The similarities are shared within families and often inherited by children. In other words, the various stratification variables tend to converge and jell; they form a pattern within which social classes begin to form. (We say "tend to converge" because we are describing a general process with frequent inconsistencies.)

The pattern formed by the objective connections among the variables is heightened by the way people think about social matters because popular thought tends toward stereotypes. Doctors are viewed as a homogeneous group, and distinctions among them tend to be ignored. Similarly, the working poor tend to lump together all bosses, and the rich overlook the many distinctions that exist among those who labor for an hourly wage.

The second question arises because it is logically possible to study stratification of individuals rather than families. Why not define classes as

---

[2] At times we will use the terms *family* and *household* interchangeably. When discussing income, we will sometimes invoke the Census Bureau's more rigorous distinction between a group of related people residing together (family) and the broader concept that encompasses families, individuals residing alone, and unrelated individuals residing together (household).

discrete groups of *individuals* of equal rank? The simple answer, implied earlier, is that the members of a **household** live under the same roof, pool their resources, share a common economic fate, and tend, for all these reasons, to have a similar perspective on the world. This answer is not quite as persuasive as it was 30 or 40 years ago. What made it seem self-evident in the past was that families were largely dependent on income produced by a "male head of household." The sociologist could place the family in the class system on the basis of his occupation, which tended to be a good predictor of the family's economic condition and its political outlook. Women, of course, were largely ignored in this conception of the class order, but it was arguably a reasonable approach to a world in which women's public economic role was quite circumscribed.

In the last few decades, women's economic and family roles have changed radically. Single women head a growing proportion of households. Married-couple families increasingly depend on two incomes. Where do we place a family in the class hierarchy if two spouses, both employed in working-class jobs, produce a comfortable middle-class income? Suppose the husband is a janitor and the wife is a teacher. Again, where do we place them?

There are no fully satisfactory answers to such questions—the world is a complicated place. But there are, again, tendencies toward convergence and consistency. Family members (whatever disparities exist among them) still depend on common resources. They are viewed by outsiders as sharing the same position within the community. Husbands and wives typically have similar levels of education, and, as a result, there is a correlation between the jobs held by working couples. Although married-couple families have grown increasingly dependent on wives' earnings, husbands are still the most important providers in the majority of families. In the chapters that follow, we will repeatedly return to these issues, exploring the changing economic role of women in some detail. But we will continue to regard families as the basic unit of stratification analysis and define classes as groups of families or households.

At the same time, we will use the term **family** in the broadest possible sense to include households consisting of one person and larger domestic units "headed" by single females, single males, or couples (both heterosexual and homosexual). We will generally establish the class position of a family by the occupation of the family member who is the principal income earner. (In some cases, we will use household wealth or dependence on government payments to define class position.)

In sum, we will interpret the stratification system with the 10 variables mentioned earlier and discrete social classes composed of families. But we recognize that households may have inconsistent scores on the variables (for example, a high-income, low-prestige occupation), that the lines dividing classes may be inconveniently fuzzy, and that the class placement of some families may be ambiguous. The reason for all this incoherence is not so much the inadequacy of the variables or definitions we use as the vague, fluid character of the stratification system itself. This book emphasizes the tendencies toward convergence, toward crystallization of the pattern, despite the many disturbing influences, often the result of social change, that keep the patterns from becoming as clear-cut in reality as in theory.

An American Class Structure

Some readers will have concluded by now that there is more than a little art in the science of social stratification—and they are probably right. We can make factual statements about, say, the distribution of income or patterns of association. But efforts to combine such information into broader statements about the class system run up against the inherent inconsistencies of social reality and are inevitably influenced by the viewpoint of the author.

We will, for example, be examining several general models of the class structure. Each tells us how many classes there are, how they can be distinguished from one another, and who belongs in each class. Some class models are more convincing than others because they make better use of the facts and illuminate matters that concern us. Some are obviously worthless. But there is really no way to distinguish the one "true" model.

Our own model of the American class structure represents a synthesis of what we have learned writing this book. We summarize it here and reconsider it in greater detail in the last chapter. The **Gilbert-Kahl model**, diagrammed in Figure 1.1, stratifies the population into six classes and one subclass. The diagram shows the occupations and household income levels *typical* of each class. But our main concern, as we explain below, is not with the level of income but a family's principal *source* of income. We do not intend to define classes based on their income level.

Drawing from Marx, we distinguish a very small top class, whose income derives largely from return on assets—the **capitalist class**. These are people who own lucrative businesses, commercial real estate, and securities such as stocks and bonds. They may hold jobs—some are top corporate executives—but ownership is the key to their high incomes. Drawing from Weber, we recognize multiple class distinctions among the nonpropertied majority below the capitalist class. Most depend, not on income from assets, but income from jobs. We sort them into classes based on the occupation of the principal income earner in each household.

Below the capitalist class is an **upper-middle class** of well-paid, university-educated managers and professionals: people with responsible positions in business organizations, along with lawyers, doctors, accountants, and other specialists. At the very top of this class, we distinguish a small but growing stratum of very successful professionals (for example, physician-specialists, corporate lawyers), business owners, money managers, and mid-ranking corporate executives; they typically have incomes in the hundreds of thousands of dollars, sometimes higher. We call this subclass of the upper-middle class the **working rich** because their incomes would largely disappear if they stopped working.

Next are the two largest classes, the **middle class** and the **working class**. Among those we place in the middle class are lower level managers, insurance agents, teachers, nurses, electricians, and plumbers. Our working class includes unskilled factory workers, office workers without specialized training, and many retail sales workers. The boundary between these two classes cannot be sharply drawn. Note that we do not depend on the traditional blue-collar–white-collar (manual versus nonmanual) distinction; there are blue-collar and white-collar workers in both classes. Instead, we

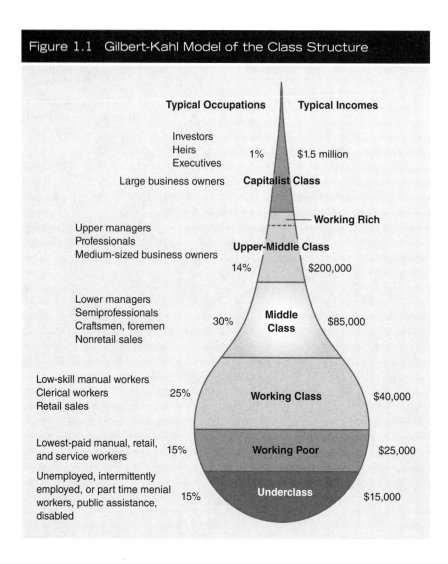

Figure 1.1   Gilbert-Kahl Model of the Class Structure

Typical Occupations   **Typical Incomes**

Investors
Heirs   1% $1.5 million
Executives
Large business owners   **Capitalist Class**

                                    —— **Working Rich**
Upper managers
Professionals   **Upper-Middle Class**
Medium-sized business owners
                         14% $200,000

Lower managers
Semiprofessionals   30%   **Middle $85,000**
Craftsmen, foremen   **Class**
Nonretail sales

Low-skill manual workers
Clerical workers   25%   **Working Class $40,000**
Retail sales

Lowest-paid manual, retail, 15% **Working Poor $25,000**
and service workers

Unemployed, intermittently
employed, or part time menial 15% **Underclass $15,000**
workers, public assistance,
disabled

have delineated the two classes based on the levels of skill or knowledge and independence or authority associated with occupations.

At the bottom of the class structure are the **working poor** and the **underclass**. The working poor are employed at very low-skill, low-wage, often insecure jobs that do not pay benefits such as health insurance. Fast-food workers, home health aides, maids, and janitors, and many unskilled construction workers fall into this class. Because their jobs are poorly paid, precarious, and devoid of benefits, their lives are marked by financial instability. Members of the underclass may have job income, but they are likely to work part-time or erratically. They may be dependent on public assistance or disability payments. A few draw income from criminal activities. As we will show in Chapter 10, the population receiving public assistance ("welfare") is much smaller than it was in the 1990s. On the other hand, the food stamp program is much expended and serves many working poor and underclass families.

Note that this model or map of the class system is based entirely on economic distinctions. We do not incorporate prestige differences (in Weber's terms, status distinctions) because we believe they derive, in the long run, from economic differences. Our model is built around *sources of income:* The top class draws income from capitalist property, the intermediate classes rely on earnings from jobs at differing occupational levels, and the bottom class depends on a mix of unstable job income and government payments. Again, the emphasis here is on the *source* rather than the *level* of income. In fact, there is inevitably some overlap in income level between classes as we have defined them. In the middle of the model, *occupation* is the decisive variable, separating those who depend on jobs into distinct levels.

A final observation: The distinction between middle class and working class—traditionally portrayed by division between office and factory—was long regarded as the critical dividing line in the class structure. But today many office jobs are simplified and routinized like jobs in the factory. We believe that the line separating the capitalist class and the upper-middle class from the classes below them has become the most important boundary. One reason is that economic returns on capitalist property and on the advanced education typical of the upper-middle class have grown rapidly in recent years, while rewards for lower levels of education or skill have stagnated or shrunk. With this in mind, we call the top two classes "the privileged classes."

Is the American Class Structure Changing?

We will return to this question repeatedly as we move from topic to topic in this book. In particular, we will want to find out how the transformation of the U.S. economy in the last 4 decades has affected the class structure. In recent years, increasing class inequality has become a national political issue. Critics argue that the United States is becoming a less egalitarian, more rigidly stratified society. They say that poverty is increasing, the middle class is shrinking, social mobility is declining, and wealth is becoming more concentrated. We examine data on wealth, income, jobs, mobility, poverty rates, political attitudes, and other factors to see whether the American class system is changing, and if so, how. Among the questions we ask are these: Is the gap between the rich and the rest of the population growing? Are opportunities to get ahead better or worse than they were in the past? Are neighborhoods becoming more segregated by social class? Is the balance of political power between classes shifting?

The charts in Figure 1.2 preview some of our findings. They tell a story of a disquieting reversal: Class inequalities, which fell through the 1960s and early 1970s, rose steeply after 1975. This turnaround is explicit in the three U-shaped curves. Individually, the charts in Figure 1.2 tell us the following about the years since the early 1970s: (a) wealth is increasingly concentrated in the hands of the richest 1 percent of households; (b) the share of income claimed by the top 1 percent has more than doubled; (c) the income advantage of the top 5 percent over the bottom 40 percent of families soared after the mid-1970s.

We take a second, more careful look at these trends and their consequences in the chapters that follow. For now, we want to drive home the lesson of what has been called "the great U-turn" and distinguish two periods in

Figure 1.2   From Shared Prosperity to Growing Inequality

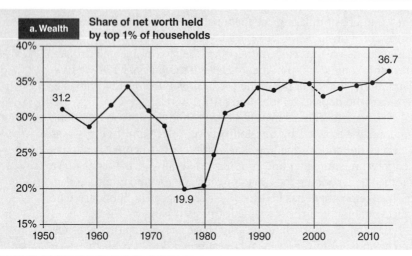

a. Wealth

**Share of net worth held
by top 1% of households**

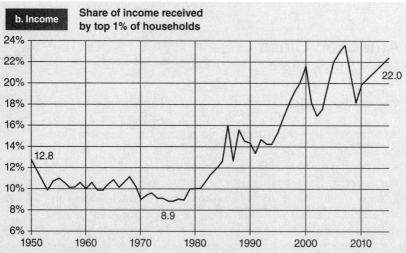

b. Income

**Share of income received
by top 1% of households**

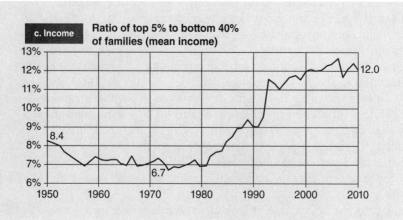

c. Income

**Ratio of top 5% to bottom 40%
of families (mean income)**

Sources: (a) Wolff 2002 and Wolff 2014, data points before and after 2000 not compatible. (b) Piketty and Saez 2003, data updated at http://elsa.berkeley.edu/~saez/, (c) U.S. Census, Current Population Survey. (See "Note on Statistical Sources.)

recent history. We will call the years after World War II, from 1946 to approximately 1973, the **Age of Shared Prosperity**, and the years since 1973, the **Age of Growing Inequality**.

Conclusion

We finish most chapters with a summary of the main points and some general conclusions. That's a little hard to do for this first chapter because it is actually a conceptual summary of the book. Much of what we will have to say about the American class system and the way we approach the subject are foreshadowed here. Our advice to serious readers is simply to reread this chapter. The effort will be rewarded as you move through the rest of the book.

At the end of each chapter, you will also find a list of the key terms that were used and that are defined in the Glossary, which begins on page 257. The list below is limited to concepts that were emphasized in this chapter.

KEY TERMS DEFINED IN THE GLOSSARY

Age of Growing Inequality
Age of Shared Prosperity
bourgeoisie
capital
capitalism
capitalist class
class consciousness
family
Gilbert-Kahl model of the
   class structure

household
ideology
life chances
lifestyle
means of production
middle class
mode of production
proletariat
social class
social status (see status)

social stratification
socialization
status
superstructure
underclass
upper-middle class
working class
working poor
working rich

SUGGESTED READINGS

Acker, Joan. 2006. *Class Questions: Feminist Answers.* Lanham, MD: Rowman & Littlefield.

Social class from a feminist perspective.

Bendix, Reinhard and Seymour Martin Lipset, eds. 1966. *Class, Status, and Power: Social Stratification in Comparative Perspective.* 2nd ed. New York: Free Press.

Crompton, Rosemary. 1998. *Class and Stratification: An Introduction to Current Debates.* 2nd ed. Cambridge, MA: Polity.

Thoughtful guide to controversies.

Grusky, David, ed. 2014. *Social Stratification: Class, Race, and Gender in Sociological Perspective.* 4th ed. Boulder, CO: Westview.

Anthology blending classic and postmodern readings.

Kingston, Paul W. 2000. *The Classless Society.* Palo Alto, CA: Stanford University Press.

Pakulski, Jan and Malcolm Waters. 1996. *The Death of Class.* Thousand Oaks, CA: SAGE.

Two provocative books, arguing that the concept of social class no longer corresponds to social reality and should be abandoned by students of social inequality.

Lenski, Gerhard. 1966. *Power and Privilege: A Theory of Social Stratification.* New York: McGraw-Hill.

Ambitious attempt to explain the development of stratification in each of several evolutionary stages, based on technology.

Manza, Jeff and Michael Sauder. 2009. *Inequality and Society and Society. Social Science Perspectives on Social Stratification.* New York: Norton.

Marx, Karl. 1978. *The Marx-Engels Reader,* edited by Robert C. Tucker. 2nd ed. New York: Norton.

Convenient collection of the writings of Marx and his partner, Friedrich Engels. Particularly relevant are "The German Ideology," Part I; "Wage Labour and Capital"; "Manifesto of the Communist Party"; and Engels' "Socialism: Utopian and Scientific."

Weber, Max. 1946. *From Max Weber: Essays in Sociology,* edited by H. H. Gerth and C. Wright Mills. New York: Oxford University Press.

A selection of Weber's most important sociological writings (except for his book The Protestant Ethic and the Spirit of Capitalism*). Especially relevant are "Class, Status, Party"; "Bureaucracy"; and "The Protestant Sects and the Spirit of Capitalism."*

2

Position and Prestige

America is a nation of tribes.

PBS, *People Like Us*

Prestige or status—the terms can be used interchangeably—is a sentiment in the minds of people that is expressed in social interaction. In almost any social setting, we note that some individuals are considered people of consequence, looked up to, and deferred to (though sometimes resented), while others are thought of as ordinary, unimportant, even lowly. Sociologists think of prestige as a ranking or scale based on degrees of social esteem. They find that groups of people similar in prestige tend to draw together and develop common lifestyles. Max Weber, whose views on stratification we examined in the last chapter, called them "status groups." We can call them prestige classes.

People Like Us

A few years ago, PBS aired a provocative documentary titled *People Like Us: Social Class in America*[1] that explored these themes. *People Like Us* probes the ways Americans experience prestige differences and offers revealing glimpses of the raw emotions lingering just beneath the surface when Americans, like those quoted below, talk about class.

Thomas Langhorne Phipps:	I am a member of the privileged American class known as the WASPs[2], the silver spoon people, the people who were handed things from an early age. . . . We stand better, we walk better, we speak better, we dress better, we eat better, we're smarter, we're more cultured, and we treat people better—we're nicer, and we're more attractive, and that was built into my sense of who I was growing up. . . . I got a phone call from somebody who decided he wanted to become a WASP . . . [and] would pay me [for] WASP lessons in style. And it was sad because the whole point is . . . *you either are it or you aren't, we believe.* That's the tribal belief, that you either have it or you don't.
Bill Bear, plumber:	I'm standing in line [waiting to pay a bill] and because of the way I'm dressed, I have a tendency to be overlooked, you know? [T]hey really don't want to deal with me. They want to deal with Mr. Suit-and-Tie. . . . I almost started a riot. . . . I had to make it known that I was next, not Mr. Suit-and-Tie. If you want to deal with the son of a bitch, make a date with him later, you know? But *just because I have on working clothes doesn't mean I can't afford to pay my bill, baby.* Well, then she got all embarrassed about that and the manager came

---

[1] Alvarez and Kolker 1999. See www.pbs.org/program/people-like-us/

[2] Literally White Angle-Saxon Protestant. Refers to the traditional American upper class.

out . . . and I just exploded. And uh, there was about four working-class guys in there, they all started applauding. 'Cause they felt the same way. You know? Because society does that automatically.

Barbara Brannen-Newton: I am from the middle class because that's where I was born and that's where I live. Socioeconomically, statistically *we are middle class. But we're black middle class*, and we will always have that word black in front of us until the day I die.

Ginie Polo Sayles: When I was in high school, I went to a country club with a girlfriend. . . . I had never been to a country club, and we went swimming in the summer, and she said, "Let's go over to the clubhouse and have some fried shrimp and charge it to my daddy." And I'd never had fried shrimp. And I thought, what is that, what will it taste like, what will it look like, will I use the right fork? And what really hit me then was that there were limitations. And that's what I didn't like. *I didn't like the idea of feeling less than, ignorant, eliminated, limited by a class.*

Tammy Crabtree [lives in a trailer that "embarrasses" her teenage son]: I was on welfare 18 years. And now, I work at Burger King, and I'm trying to make a living, and make a home for the kids. It ain't my fault 'cause I'm poor. I growed up poor. . . . Even when I'm walkin' to work or something, someone'll holler, "Ey! Trashy bitch! What're you doing?" I'm just walking to work [at Burger King]. All I want is just a life where I can be happy. But right now, I'm not because the way people treats me and the way my kids treat me. . . . *My son, he thinks he's high class and a preppie.* He's the best. He thinks he's better than me, better than his brothers. [All emphases added.]

People Like Us is often about respect and disrespect, from the blue-blood pride of Thomas Langhorne Phipps to the blue-collar anger of plumber Bill Bear. Barbara Brannen-Newton laments that an African American woman can never be fully middle class, however well brought up and educated she may be. Young Ginie Sayles is intimidated by the country club dining room. Hardworking Tammy Crabtree is made to feel like "trailer trash" by perfect strangers and her own son.

Respect and disrespect is another way of thinking about prestige. While the term *prestige* inevitably draws our gaze upward to the silver-spoon world of Thomas Phipps, respect and disrespect broadens our vision to include people in the middle and at the bottom, who may feel injured by class distinctions.

Some of the people who appear in the documentary are trying to claim respect with lifestyle choices. Tammy Crabtree's teenage son disapproves of the way his mother dresses—often in her Burger King uniform—and is seeking higher status with his own clothes. A man whom the documentary identifies as "a social climber" tells the camera that he would never drive a Ford or even a Volvo; they send the wrong signals. An affluent couple shows us around their elegantly remodeled kitchen, noting the influences of Tuscany, southern Italy, and "[perhaps] an old French country kitchen or an English farmhouse."

We tour an upscale kitchenware store with satirist Joe Queenan, who draws our attention to various esoteric cooking implements and a slim bottle mysteriously labeled "Al Sapone di Tartufo Bianco." Those who know what these things are and can afford them belong here, explains Queenan. But if "you, a working-class person," don't and can't, perhaps you should go to Wal-Mart, where everything is identifiable. The store's customers are defining a lifestyle by surrounding themselves with sophisticated possessions and, at the same time, asserting a superior class position.

A recurring theme of *People Like Us* is that we are, in the words of the narrator, "a nation of tribes." The members of our tribe, according to the documentary, are the people we live among and feel comfortable with. They share our background and our lifestyle. The documentary sometimes suggests that the boundaries defining tribes are fixed and well-defended, but it also provides ample evidence that people move from tribe to tribe.

Americans are famous for their ability to reinvent themselves. By the time we encounter Ginie Sayles, she has married a wealthy man and is wholly at ease in the country club settings that made her feel "ignorant" and "limited" as a teenager. We also meet Dana Felty, an ambitious young woman who left her working-class home in rural Kentucky to attend Antioch College and start a career as a journalist in Washington, DC. Tammy Crabtree's teenage son, growing up in a trailer in rural Ohio, seems to have similar ambitions. The wealthy crowd we see attending a polo game includes people who have made considerable (and probably recent) fortunes in Internet ventures, finance, fashion, and other fields. Perhaps the members of this success elite yearn to join Langhorne Phipps' old-money upper class. Perhaps they couldn't care less. Phipps' people cherish the myth that admission is by birth only. But, as we will see in Chapter 3, the history of the American upper class contradicts this notion.

The tribes of *People Like Us,* like the prestige classes we will examine in this chapter, are more amorphous and porous than they might initially appear. Their indefinite character contributes to the ambitions and anxieties chronicled in the film. Americans, the documentary reminds us, are uncomfortable with class distinctions, which seem undemocratic to them. At the same time, they are aware of a prestige hierarchy and may feel pressured to improve their own rank. Unsure of where they stand, they demand respect, cultivate their manners, remake their wardrobes, and remodel their kitchens.

W. Lloyd Warner: Prestige Classes in Yankee City

The talk of tribes in *People Like Us,* raises some intriguing questions. In particular, how do people create mental maps of the class system from their varied daily experiences of prestige distinctions? And can we turn their often vague and contradictory perceptions into coherent models of the class structure? One place we can look for answers is in early community studies conducted by W. Lloyd Warner and his students and colleagues. The first and most famous of these studies was done in a small New England town Warner called "Yankee City" (Warner and Lunt 1941; Warner et al. 1973).

Yankee City was once a famous seaport. It had a long history in New England commerce, having been a center of trade, fishing, and, more recently, manufacturing, especially of shoes and silverware. In many ways, its glory was in the past. In recent years, it had become merely a small city not too far from Boston, and many of its young people left for the more exciting life to be found in Boston and New York. Ethnically, the town was relatively homogeneous but not perfectly so. Some families had been there for 300 years. Half its inhabitants had been born in the community, and another quarter came from other parts of New England and the United States. But the remaining quarter was from French Canada, Ireland, Italy, and Eastern Europe.

Warner and his team began their research with the assumption that class distinctions people in Yankee City made among themselves would be determined by economic differences. The initial interviews tended to confirm this view. Their respondents spoke of "the big people with money" and "the little people who are poor." Property owners, bankers, and professionals were high status. Laborers, ditch diggers, and low-wage workers were low status.

However, after the researchers had been in Yankee City for a while, they began to doubt that social standing could so easily be equated with economic position, for they found that some people were placed higher or lower than their incomes would warrant. They noticed that certain doctors were ranked below others in the social hierarchy, even though they were regarded as better physicians, and that high prestige was associated with certain family names. Such distinctions were often made unconsciously, which made them all the more convincing to the researchers.

Warner discovered a hierarchy of prestige classes in Yankee City consisting of groups of people who were ranked by others in the community as socially superior or inferior. From his interviews and observations, he concluded that the place of individuals within this system was the result of a combination of economic and social variables that included wealth, income, and occupation but also patterns of interaction, social behavior, and lifestyle. People of the same class tended to spend time together and, as a result, developed similar attitudes and values. Their children were likely to marry one another. Warner's Yankee City research had, in other words, led him to a conception of social class close to Weber's idea of "status group"—a communal group bound by shared prestige, lifestyle, values, and patterns of association.

Some of the patterns Warner observed were based on kinship. Children were assigned the status of their parents, and certain families had a prestige position that was not entirely explainable by their current wealth or income and seemed to flow from their ancestry.

Warner noted that when a person had an equivalent rank on all the economic and social variables, people in Yankee City had no difficulty determining his or her prestige rank. But when someone had different scores on the several variables, ranking became problematic. This usually meant that the person was mobile and was changing position on one variable at a time. Consequently, time was an important factor in stratification placement. For example, if a man who started as the son of a laborer became successful in business, he would be likely to move to a "better" neighborhood, to join clubs of other business and professional men, and to send his children to college. However, if he himself did not have a college education and polished manners, he would never be fully accepted as a social equal by the businessmen who had Harvard degrees. His son, however, might well gain the full acceptance denied the father.

After several years of study by more than a dozen researchers, during which time 99 percent of the families in town were classified, Warner declared that there were six groupings distinct enough to be called classes (Warner and Lunt 1941:88):

Upper-Upper Class (1.4 percent). This group was the old-family elite, based on sufficient wealth to maintain a large house in the best neighborhood, but the wealth had to have been in the family for more than one generation. Generational continuity permitted proper training in basic values and established people as belonging to a lineage.

Lower-Upper Class (1.6 percent). This group was, on average, slightly richer than the upper-uppers, but their money was newer, their manners were therefore not quite so polished, and their sense of lineage and security was less pronounced.

Upper-Middle Class (10.2 percent). Business and professional men and their families who were moderately successful but less affluent than the lower-uppers. Some education and polish were necessary for membership, but lineage was unimportant.

Lower-Middle Class (28.1 percent). The small businessmen, the schoolteachers, and the foremen in industry. This group tended to have morals that were close to those of Puritan Fundamentalism; they were churchgoers, lodge joiners, and flag wavers.

Upper-Lower Class (32.6 percent). The solid, respectable laboring people, who kept their houses clean and stayed out of trouble.

Lower-Lower Class (25.2 percent). The "lulus" or disrespectable and often slovenly people who dug clams and waited for public relief. (The relatively high proportion of people in this category apparently reflects the difficult economic conditions of the Great Depression, when the study was conducted.)

Among the notable features of this schema of Yankee City classes are the following: (1) the distinction, at the top, between an old-money elite, the product of New England's long history, and a class of families with more recent fortunes; (2) the distinction between those who work with their hands—members of the bottom two classes, comprising more than half the population—and those who do not, in the higher classes; and (3) the attribution (presumably reflecting what Warner and his associates heard in Yankee City) of moral status to class position—the lower-lowers, are, for example, "disrespectable," while those above them have Puritan morals and are "respectable" or "clean."

Once the general system became clear to him, Warner said, he used clique and association memberships as a shorthand index of prestige position. Thus, among men, there were certain small social clubs that were open only to upper-uppers, the Rotary was primarily upper-middle in membership, the fraternal lodges were lower-middle, and the craft unions were upper-lower. It seems that in cases of doubt, intimate clique interactions were the crucial test: A repeated invitation home to dinner appeared to be, for Warner, the best sign of prestige equality between persons who were not relatives.

Prestige Class as a Concept

Warner maintained that the breaks between all these prestige classes were quite clear-cut, except for that between the lower-middle and the upper-lower. At that level, there was a blurring of distinctions that made placement of borderline families quite difficult. Of course, the placement of mobile families at all levels was difficult.

When Warner said that the distinctions between the classes were clear-cut, he did not mean that people in Yankee City could necessarily give a consistent account of them. Like many Americans, they were uncomfortable with the idea of social inequality. After all, the American creed says that we are born equal. Some Yankee City residents were quite aware of class differences and could describe them. Some denied that classes existed while acting as if they did. Social ranking was often an unconscious process.

But if ranking is unconscious, how can researchers learn about it? The answer, for Warner and his colleagues, was listening to what people said and observing their behavior over an extended period. As this suggests, Warner's version of Yankee City's class system is not a summary of what residents told him about it, nor is it a simple reflection of life in Yankee City. Instead, it is an abstraction from reality, based on systematic questioning, listening, and observation. Warner's analysis is a map of the prestige class system. Like any map, it is a simplification of complicated terrain, ignoring irregularities and focusing on what the mapmaker regards as major features.

The individual classes that Warner identified are not mere descriptions of the mental categories used by people in Yankee City and other small towns. They are abstract concepts, designed by the researcher to help organize a vast amount of data on attitudes and behavior. They are not identical with social reality but a useful way of understanding it.

How Many Classes?

Describing the structure of prestige classes in a community is inevitably problematic. The analyst wants to know how many classes there are and where boundaries between them are located but soon discovers that there is little consensus on these matters. One reason, according to a study of a small Southern town by three Warner colleagues, is that the class structure looks different from the perspectives of people at different class levels (Davis,

Gardner, and Gardner 1941). Their report, titled *Deep South,* demonstrated this phenomenon with a chart showing how the people at each level perceive the people at other levels. It is reproduced here as Figure 2.1.

Based on patterns of association and lifestyles, the researchers found six classes among the town's white population, similar to the Yankee City classes. The six boxes in the chart show how the class structure appeared to people in each of these classes. Think of them as windows, each of them showing the distinctive perspective from which a particular class views the class structure. Between the boxes, there are abbreviated labels delineating the classes described by the researchers (UU = upper-upper class, LM = lower-middle class, etc.). Within the boxes, horizontal lines indicate perceived class distinctions—with solid lines marking a distinct social cleavage and broken lines suggesting less social distance between adjacent classes.

A comparison between the upper-upper class window and the lower-lower class window in the chart reveals large gaps in perceptions. The lower-lowers lump the people in the top three classes into one big class ("Society or folks with money"). Similarly, the upper-uppers collapse the two bottom classes into one ("Po' whites"). People in both classes make more class distinctions at their own level. The labels they use for one another are quite different. For example, the lower-lowers describe the people at the top with phrases suggesting wealth and social pretense, while the upper-uppers describe themselves and nearby classes in terms emphasizing inherited position, social prestige, and respectability.

Some important conclusions about perceptions of the class structure in this Southern town and elsewhere can be drawn from the chart. (Like the chart itself, these points tend to underestimate the differences of perception *within* classes, while usefully highlighting the differences between classes.)

1. *Number of classes.* People at all class levels perceive class differences, but there is disagreement about the number of classes in the community. No class recognizes a structure of six classes, corresponding to the Warnerian classes. Instead, they see four or five.

2. *Perception and distance.* People make more distinctions among those close to themselves in the hierarchy than among those who are far away. That tendency emerged sharply in the mutual perceptions of the upper-uppers and lower-lowers described in *Deep South.*

3. *Coincidence of cleavages.* Despite class differences in the number of classes perceived at various levels in the hierarchy, the distinctions actually made by people from different classes coincide. For example, the line that the lower-lowers drew between "society" and the "way-high-ups but not society" was the same as the upper-uppers' distinction between "nice respectable people" and "good people but nobody." That is, when the researchers asked people about specific families, they found that the lower-lowers and upper-uppers placed them in the same one of these two groups.

4. *Basis of class distinctions.* People often agree about where individuals or families belong in the class hierarchy, but not about why they are there. In other words, they find different bases for class

Figure 2.1 The Social Perspectives of the Social Classes

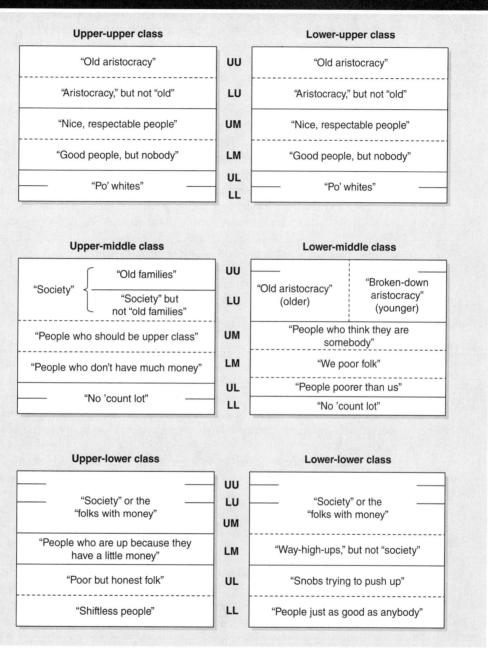

Source: Reprinted from page 65 of *Deep South: A Social-Anthropological Study of Caste and Class*, by Allison Davis, Burleigh B. Gardner, and Mary R. Gardner. Reprinted by permission of University of Chicago Press.

Note: UU = upper-upper class; LU = lower-upper class; UM = upper-middle class; LM = lower-middle class; UL = upper-lower class; LL = lower-lower class.

distinctions. For example, people at the top understand class position in terms of time; they distinguish between "old" families and "new" families. People in the middle make moral evaluations of how things "should be." People in the lower class view the system as a hierarchy of wealth.

From the analyst's viewpoint, perceptions of four or five rather than six classes or discrepancies in the perceived basis of class distinctions are not important as long as the breaks that people do make all fit together in a consistent way. Naturally, people make the finest distinctions regarding those whom they know best and tend to merge others into broader categories. Researchers can take this into consideration and, if they wish, can subdivide a group according to the views of those in and immediately adjacent to it. The practical problems in mapping the structure of prestige classes can be reduced to two: Do all observers put Albers above Jackson in the hierarchy, and if they distinguish between their ranks at all, do they all divide Jackson's group from Albers' at the same place in the hierarchy? These are the questions of *ranking* consistency and of *cutting* consistency.

Class Structure of the Metropolis

Several decades after the appearance of the original Yankee City report, two of Warner's former students, Richard Coleman and Lee Rainwater, published the results of their study of prestige classes in two metropolitan areas: Boston and Kansas City. Working in metropolitan areas, Coleman and Rainwater could not duplicate the detailed ethnographic investigation that Warner conducted in Yankee City. Nonetheless, their book *Social Standing in America* (1978) shows the influence of their mentor, to whose memory the book is dedicated.

Social Standing in America was an ambitious undertaking, involving 900 interviews in the two cities. The statistical procedures employed were designed to provide representative samples of adults in Greater Boston and Greater Kansas City. Interviews were standardized and followed a fixed schedule of questions in the style of a social survey, but many questions were open-ended, allowing respondents to describe the class system in their own terms.

The hierarchy of prestige classes that Coleman and Rainwater (1978) stitched together from their analysis of the interviews is rather complex, so we offer a simplified, schematic version in Table 2.1. (Note that the annual incomes were recorded in 1971 dollars. Multiplying these amounts by 6 will give roughly equivalent values in inflated dollars of recent years.) Inspection of the table shows that the basic structure of the hierarchy is parallel to the one found by Warner in Yankee City. For instance, in both studies, the upper-upper and lower-upper classes correspond to a distinction between established families and "new money," although the distinction might be noticed only by those who are themselves close to the top. In Boston, the upper-class respondents spoke of the former as "the tip-top—as close to an aristocracy as you'll find in America. . . . Yankee families that go way back; the WASPs who were here first . . . the bluebloods with inherited income—they live on stocks and bonds" (p. 150). The same respondents described the lower-uppers as

> a mix of highly successful executives, doctors, and lawyers with [very high] incomes. . . . They have help in the house, fancy cars, frequent and expensive vacations, and at least two houses. . . . They're not considered top society because they don't have the right background—they're newer money, with less tradition in their lifestyle. (p. 151)

At the other end of the class structure, Coleman and Rainwater delineated a bottom class characterized by dependence on irregular, marginal employment or public relief, often shifting from one to the other. As in Yankee City, Boston and Kansas City families in this class were regarded as less than respectable and described in terms suggesting that they were physically and morally "unclean." However, many of Coleman and Rainwater's respondents made a distinction, which was incorporated into the model, between families on the very bottom and a class of semipoor families who worked more regularly and were slightly more orderly in their lifestyles.

As portrayed by Coleman and Rainwater, then, the classes of "upper America" and "lower America" neatly parallel corresponding prestige groupings in Yankee City. The same would appear to be true of "middle America," where Coleman and Rainwater's middle class and working class are equivalent to Warner's lower-middle and upper-lower classes. However, it was in the middle range of the class structure that they had the hardest time organizing the views of Kansas City and Boston respondents into prestige categories. In judging prestige, city respondents at this level gave almost exclusive emphasis to income and standard of living and paid relatively little attention to other stratification variables, such as occupation and association that had seemed important to Warner.

Coleman and Rainwater reported that their middle-American respondents recognized three levels among themselves, often called "people at the comfortable standard of living," "people just getting along," and "people who aren't lower class but are having a real hard time" (pp. 158–159). But the two sociologists found these categories inadequate and insisted on a more traditional distinction between middle class and working class (each of which, they suggest, can be subdivided along income lines). The distinction the researchers made was essentially between **white-collar** and **blue-collar workers** (office workers versus manual workers). They decided to place the lowest paid white-collar workers in the working-class category. But there are no blue-collar workers, even the best paid, in their middle class. Thus, a highly skilled, well-paid electrician is working class in their schema (see Table 2.1).

How do Coleman and Rainwater justify substituting their own judgment here for their respondents' judgments? They argue that lifestyle and associational differences that emerged in the interviews show that the traditional middle-class/working-class distinction is more fundamental than any income distinction. For instance, among families at the same "comfortable" income level, they noted important differences in consumption patterns. The middle-class families at this level were likely to spend more on

Table 2.1 Coleman and Rainwater's Metropolitan Class Structure

Class	Typical Occupations or Source of Income	Typical Education	Annual Income, 1971	Percent of Families
I. Upper Americans				
Upper-upper Old rich, aristocratic family name	Inherited wealth	Ivy League college degree; often postgraduate	Over $60,000	} 2
Lower-upper Success elite	Top professionals; senior corporate executives	Good colleges; often postgraduate	Over $60,000	
Upper-middle Professional and managerial	Middle professionals and managers	College degree; often postgraduate	$20,000 to $60,000	19
II. Middle Americans				
Middle class	Lower level managers; small-business owners; lower status professionals (pharmacists, teachers); sales and clerical	High school plus some college	$10,000 to $20,000	31
Working class	Higher blue-collar (craftsmen, truck drivers); lowest paid sales and clerical	High school diploma for younger persons	$7,500 to $15,000	35
III. Lower Americans				
Semipoor	Unskilled labor and service	Part high school	$4,500 to $6,000	} 13
The bottom	Often unemployed; welfare	Primary school	Less than $4,500	

Source: From *Social Standing in America* by Richard P. Coleman and Lee Rainwater. Reprinted by permission of Basic Books, a member of Perseus Books Group.

Note: We adjusted percentages for undersampling of "Lower Americans," acknowledged by authors.

living room and dining room furniture and less on the television sets, stereos, and refrigerators and other appliances that were attractive to working-class families with similar incomes. The working-class families owned larger and more expensive automobiles and more trucks, campers, and vans. Moreover, income equality in middle America does not appear to produce social equality: Patterns of friendship, organizational membership, and neighborhood location parallel the differences in consumption patterns (pp. 182–183). Some respondents implicitly recognized these differences. A "comfortable" working-class man observed,

> I'm working class because that's my business; I work with my hands. I make good money, so I am higher in the laboring force than many people I know. But birds of a feather flock together. My friends are all hard-working people. . . . We would feel out of place with higher-ups. (p. 184)

The wife of a white-collar man was more explicit:

I consider myself middle class. My husband works for a construction company in the office. Many of the construction workers make a lot more than he does. But when we have parties at my husband's company, the ones with less education feel out of place and not at ease with the ones with more education. I think of them as working class. (p. 184)

The difficulties Coleman and Rainwater encountered in delineating the prestige hierarchy of middle America raise general, and by now familiar, questions about the way sociologists boil down what they hear and observe into coherent descriptions of the structure of prestige classes in a community. Coleman and Rainwater describe their approach to prestige measurement as close to Warner's. However, the metropolitan context of their research imposed an important limit on their ability to replicate his methodology. Warner's basic method involved matching the standing of one family against another on the basis of what others said about them and whom they associated with (Warner et al. 1949b). Because the respondents in Boston and Kansas City were unlikely to know or associate with one another, this approach was impractical. Synthesizing individual judgments of the class system was problematic for Coleman and Rainwater because their data consisted of verbal statements about general symbols rather than details about particular others in the community.

Coleman and Rainwater were clear that their version of the prestige hierarchy was not a mirror image of the system as understood in the community. There was, they recognized, no public consensus about the shape of class structure. But they were able to create a composite map of the class structure out of the sometimes inconsistent answers of respondents, each of whom viewed the system from an "inevitably narrow vantage point" (p. 120). Coleman and Rainwater assumed that people were most knowledgeable about the lives of people like themselves, so they gave particular weight to respondents' views concerning the social standing, lifestyles, and associations of those who were near their own level. They listened carefully for repeated references to cleavages in the social hierarchy, which might mark class boundaries.

Table 2.2 Three Class Models Compared						
Gilbert & Kahl (National, Contemporary)		Coleman & Rainwater (Metropolitan, Early 1970s)			Warner (Small City, 1930s)	
Capitalist	1%	Upper-Upper	2%		Upper-Upper	3%
		Lower-Upper			Lower-Upper	
Upper-Middle	14%	Upper-Middle	19%		Upper-Middle	10%
Middle	30%	Middle	31%		Lower-Middle	28%
Working	30%	Working	35%		Upper-Lower	33%
Working poor	13%	Semipoor	13%		Lower-Lower	25%
Underclass	12%	The Bottom				
Total	100%		100%			100%

How does the Coleman-Rainwater metropolitan model differ from the Gilbert-Kahl national model outlined in Chapter 1? (See Table 2.2.) There are some variations in class labels, but the main differences stem from the underlying bases of the models. Our model is based on purely economic considerations, in particular occupation and sources of income. Coleman and Rainwater, like their mentor Warner, have created a prestige model based on public perceptions of the class order, lifestyles, and patterns of association. For this reason, they make the distinction between old money and new money (in effect splitting our capitalist class) and they lean toward the traditional blue-collar/white-collar distinction to define the middle and working classes. Despite these differences, the three maps of the class system are broadly similar. This may, in some degree, reflect their common debt to the tradition of sociological thinking about class. But the real key to their similarities is that in Kansas City and Boston, as well as Yankee City, prestige is largely, though not quite wholly, derived from economic position.

Prestige of Occupations

Warner, Coleman, and Rainwater, and many other investigators, have stressed the importance of occupation for the prestige evaluations Americans make of one another. Especially in metropolitan settings, where people do not have a detailed knowledge of one another's income, family background, lifestyle, associations, and so forth, they are forced to fall back on a few shorthand indicators of personal prestige, such as occupation. They know, of course, that occupation is a fair indicator of two other sources of prestige: income and education. Physicians are typically affluent; not many janitors hold college degrees. People may also associate particular lifestyles and patterns of interaction with specific occupations or, more generally, with the distinction between blue-collar and white-collar workers. These expectations account for the emphasis they place on occupation in making prestige assessments. For the sociologist engaged in a large-scale research operation, occupation is especially useful: It is more visible than income, and it can be studied with census data as well as social surveys and qualitative field studies. Furthermore, because census data are available for earlier periods, we can use occupation as an indicator in historical research.

There have been numerous studies of **occupational prestige**, going back more than 50 years, but the best known are the national polls conducted under the auspices of the National Opinion Research Center (NORC) at the University of Chicago since 1947 (Hodge, Treiman, and Rossi 1966; Nakao and Treas 1990; Reiss 1961).

Table 2.3 presents a sampling of occupational prestige scores from a NORC survey. Respondents were asked to rate the "social standing" of each occupation. The scores were created by averaging their responses. Theoretically, the scale runs from 0 to 100, but in practice, scores seldom go above 80 or below 20. The results toward the top and bottom are consistent with what we have seen in the Warner group's community and the Coleman and Rainwater metropolitan studies (which, of course, are based on much more than occupation). The highest ranking occupations are professional and managerial (physician, professor, plant manager, hospital administrator), ordered by the level of expertise or administrative responsibility entailed. Virtually all assume a college education or better.

The lowest ranking occupations are unskilled, manual jobs, such as garbage collector, janitor, and farm worker. Between these extremes are the less demanding office or sales positions (bookkeeper, secretary, cashier in a supermarket) and the skilled manual jobs (electrician, plumber, welder). But note there is no clear distinction between white-collar and blue-collar jobs (in Warner's terms, lower-middle and upper-lower). The electrician ranks above the manager of a supermarket, the plumber precedes the post office clerk, and the assembly-line worker outranks the furniture and shoe salespeople. Obviously, when faced with this sort of task, respondents are interested in something more than just where someone works or the color of a shirt collar.

When interviewees in the first NORC survey were asked the main factor they had weighed in making their ratings, the most frequent replies were pay, service to humanity, education, and social prestige, but none of these criteria was volunteered by more than 18 percent of the sample (NORC 1953:418). Whatever the bases of their judgments, the surveys demonstrate that respondents did have a scale in mind on which they could place occupations with a rough consensus. Although there were significant differences among individuals in their relative ratings of occupations, sociologists were more impressed with the great consistency of the average ratings that were given to occupations by relevant subgroups of the population. The average ratings made by the prosperous and the poor, people in high- and low-prestige occupations, blacks and whites, men and women, residents of the Northeast and the South, and city and country dwellers were almost exactly the same. Even those who proposed different criteria for judging occupations did not differ in the way they ranked occupations. In other words, differences were largely idiosyncratic, reflecting personal views, rather than systematic variations by class, race, gender, or geography.

Table 2.3 NORC Prestige Scores for Selected Occupations

Higher Prestige Jobs		Medium Prestige Jobs		Lower Prestige Jobs	
Job	Score	Job	Score	Job	Score
Physician	86	Policeman	59	Barber	36
Lawyer	75	Construction superintendent	57	File clerk	36
College professor	74	Airplane mechanic	53	Assembly-line worker	35
Computer systems analyst	74	Electrician	51	House painter	34
Chemist	73	Computer operator	50	Cashier in supermarket	33
Dentist	72	Manager of a supermarket	48	Bus driver	32
Hospital administrator	69	Secretary	46	Furniture salesperson	31
Registered nurse	66	Bookkeeper	46	Carpenter's helper	30
Accountant	65	Insurance agent	46	Shoe salesperson	28
Public schoolteacher	64	Plumber	45	Garbage collector	28
General manager of manufacturing plant	62	Bank teller	43	Bartender	25
		Welder	42	Cleaner, private home	23
		Post office clerk	42	Farm worker	23
				Janitor	22
				Telephone solicitor	22
				Filling station attendant	21

Source: Nakao and Treas 1990. Occupations and Social Classes; General Social Survey 2000 files.

What systematic differences there were can be summed up in two principles: (1) People tended to raise in rank their own and closely related occupations, and (2) people agreed with each other more concerning occupations that were well known. However, even in the best-known fields, brief occupational titles of the sort employed in the NORC surveys are somewhat ambiguous. Confronted with "lawyer," the respondent does not know if the reference is to a small-town, general-practice lawyer or a partner in a major Wall Street firm. Of course, we can never capture with a survey the richness of detail that Warner reports from a community study because surveys force us to depend on a few simple categories. On the other hand, there is no substitute for the systematic knowledge a survey can provide. It is especially useful for making broad comparisons between different communities or different historical periods, but we must always remember that we are using social symbols about general types of jobs, leaving out a lot of concrete detail.

The consistency of prestige ratings across social subgroups is matched by their stability over time. Researchers noted that the ratings barely changed from one survey to the next over many decades. The consistency over time and across different social groups suggests that occupational ratings tap a very fundamental dimension of social consciousness.

Occupations and Social Classes

The NORC surveys reveal how the public places occupations on a continuum, but the surveys leave us in the dark about how people might cut that continuum into occupational classes. The problem is obviously similar to the one we raised earlier concerning the grouping of families in Yankee City or Boston into prestige classes. Some evidence on this question was gathered in a national survey of approximately 2,000 adults conducted by the University of Michigan's Survey Research Center (SRC) in 1975 (Jackman, 1979). The SRC questionnaire asked respondents to place a series of occupations into 1 of 5 class categories: poor, working class, middle class, upper-middle class, and upper class.

The researchers found that people did not have a difficult time associating occupations with social classes (there were few "don't know" responses) and that there was considerable popular agreement about where specific occupations should be placed in the five-class system that was suggested by the interviewer. Majorities of respondents agreed on the class placement of most of the occupations presented. But as we can anticipate by now, placing occupations was easier at the top and bottom of the scale than in the middle. There was, for example, strong agreement that high-ranking corporate officers are upper class and janitors and assembly-line workers are working class. However, there was less consensus about where to place a factory foreman or a plumber.

Conclusion: Perception of Social Rank and Prestige Classes

From the studies we have reviewed, three conclusions stand out: (1) In American society, there is a prestige hierarchy of both persons and occupations—this hierarchy or rank order is divided by most citizens into a few categories or classes; (2) there exists considerable ambiguity about just how to define and differentiate them; and (3) there is more agreement about rank order than about the criteria used in making ranking decisions, and more agreement about ranking than about division into classes. To recall our earlier language, there is greater **ranking consistency** than **cutting consistency** among respondents.

Some tentative principles seem to explain the variation we have encountered in perceptions of ranking and grouping:

1. People perceive a rank order.

2. They agree more about the extremes than about the middle of the prestige range.

3. They agree most about the top of the range and make more distinctions about the top than about the bottom. (Perhaps the top is just more conspicuous.)

4. People lump together into large groups those who are furthest from them.

5. People in the middle or at the bottom are more likely to conceive of class differences in financial terms.

6. Those at the top are more conscious of prestige distinctions based on family history ("old money") and style of life.

7. Mobility is a source of ambiguity in perception of the prestige order. People find it difficult to "place" mobile individuals. Perception of high rates of mobility leads to the conclusion that class boundaries are amorphous or nonexistent.

These principles connecting social facts with the way people perceive those facts are sufficient to explain why there is no straightforward answer to the question that is asked so often: How many social classes are there in America? The moment we try to answer the question with data that come from the views of ordinary citizens, we are confronted with ambiguities and contradictions. Coleman and Rainwater manage to stitch together a simplified but coherent schema of prestige classes for Boston and Kansas City out of these inconsistent materials. An alternative, taken by the authors of this book and many theorists before them, is to develop a model that does not claim to be based on perceptions of the class order. These alternative models are typically based on economic distinctions rather than prestige judgments. But they must also be fashioned out of inconsistent materials—drawn from history, economic data, and demography. Both approaches involve a combination of art and science. We can expect the analyst to know the facts and make convincing use of them to develop a map of the class system. The map may be more or less effective as a device to interpret social life. But in the final analysis, the class system is not like the solar system, an objective reality we can hope to discover. Our conceptions of it will always be provisional.

KEY TERMS DEFINED IN THE GLOSSARY

blue-collar workers	occupational prestige	ranking consistency
cutting consistency	prestige	white-collar workers

SUGGESTED READINGS

Aldrich, Nelson W., Jr. 1988. *Old Money: The Mythology of America's Upper Class.* New York: Vintage.   *Old money and not-so-old money. The ethos of the national upper class explained from within.*

Alvarez, Louis and Andrew Kolker. 1999. *People Like Us: Social Class in America* [Video]. Public Broadcasting Service.

How Americans experience social class. A provocative, revealing program, originally broadcast on Public Television.

Bowser, Benjamin P. 2007. *The Black Middle Class: Social Mobility—and Vulnerability*. Boulder, CO: Lynne Rienner.

African American class structure. The history and future of the black middle class.

Fiske, Susan and Hazel Rose Markus, eds. 2012. *Facing Social Class: How Societal Rank Influences Interaction*. New York: Russell Sage Foundation.

Essays on the social psychology of social class: How class shapes everyday encounters.

Graham, Lawrence Otis. 1999. *Our Kind of People: Inside the Black Upper Class*. New York: HarperPerennial.

Perceptive, engaging account by an insider.

Kahn, Shamus 2011. *Privilege: The Making of an Adolescent Elite at St. Paul's School*. Princeton: Princeton University Press.

Ethnographic account suggesting that the upper class has turned merit into a new ideology of privilege.

Ossowski, Stanislaw. 1963. *Class Structure in the Social Consciousness*. New York: Free Press.

A systematic account of competing basic conceptions of class structure in the history of Western social thought.

Veblen, Thorstein. 1934. *The Theory of the Leisure Class*. New York: Modern Library. (First published in 1899.)

This book introduced the idea that "conspicuous consumption" was the way to buy prestige in competitive America.

Warner, Lloyd W., et al. 1973. *Yankee City*. New Haven, CT: Yale University Press.

Handy abridgment of the entire series of volumes on Yankee City.

Social Class, Occupation, and Social Change

A post-industrial society, being primarily a technical society, awards place less on the basis of inheritance or property . . . than on education and skills.

Daniel Bell, sociologist

American business is about maximizing shareholder value. You basically don't want workers. You hire less, and you try to find capital equipment to replace them.

Allen Sinai, business economist

In 1924, sociologists Robert S. Lynd and Helen Merrell Lynd went to Indiana to describe a "typical" American town. For more than a year, the couple studied everyday life in a community of 35,000—Muncie, Indiana, which they called "Middletown." To establish a historical baseline for their work, the Lynds reconstructed life in 1890, when Middletown had only 11,000 people and was going through the first stages of industrialization. They returned in 1935 for a restudy. Thus, we have three points of observation: 1890, 1924, and 1935.

The Lynds' two books, *Middletown* (1929) and *Middletown in Transition* (1937), are classic studies of American life. They are especially valuable to us because they illustrate, in the miniature scale of a small town, how the American class structure was transformed by industrialization. Their narrative links social change, occupation, and social class—our key concerns in this chapter—and provides a historical backdrop against which we can understand the more recent social transformation associated with the emergence of a "postindustrial society."

Middletown: 1890 and 1924

In their first book, the Lynds reported that daily life in Middletown in 1924 was conditioned by a fundamental social distinction: the division of the population into working class and business class. Generally, members of the first class (70 percent of the population) supported themselves by working with *things*, while members of the second class (30 percent) made a living in activities oriented toward *people*. Being born on one side or the other of this cleavage was "the most significant single cultural factor" in the lives of Middletown's inhabitants, influencing matters as varied as whom they married, when they got up in the morning, how they dressed, and whether they drove Fords or Buicks and worshiped with the Holy Rollers or the Presbyterians.

The first volume emphasized changes in the work patterns of both classes between 1890 and 1924—changes, incidentally, that widened the gap between them. These changes flowed from three causes: larger population, more machinery, and an increasing emphasis on money.

Middletown in 1890 was a market town that was just beginning to turn to manufacturing. The work habits and values of its people were extensions of the traditions of their farmer parents, people who had conquered a wilderness. There had been land for all who would work it, and from such plenty, there emerged a society that lacked clear gradations of rank and privilege, a society that stressed individual initiative and progress, family solidarity, simplicity of manners and style of life, and equality among neighbors.

As trading and handicraft manufacturing succeeded farming as the base of livelihood, the old traditions could easily continue. A man earned whatever his own efforts deserved. True, there developed a gradation in income that extended from unskilled through skilled laborers to bosses (who were often former craftsmen) and a few professional people. But income and prestige, which were understood to be direct outcomes of competence at work, tended to rise with age and experience.

The spread of machine production began to change all this. The machine undermined the value of the traditional knowledge and skills of the master craftsman. It demanded speed and endurance. After a few weeks' experience with the machine, a 19-year-old boy could outproduce his 42-year-old father. The old apprentice system was gradually abandoned, and with its passing, the traditional distinction between skilled and unskilled workers was blurred.

There were basic changes within the business class as well. The old businessman was a small merchant or manufacturer, whose capital consisted mostly of his personal savings. He had started as a worker and had become a businessman. His relations with both employees and customers were personal, even intimate. The new businessman operated with bank credit, had too many employees and customers to know them personally, and had ties with other businessmen all over the country. Sometimes he was a branch manager for a national corporation from somewhere else.

Money had become the significant link between people. In the old days, families were more self-sufficient, producing much of their food and clothing at home. When they purchased things, they paid cash. Now they bought most of what they needed, sometimes on credit. The money nexus was becoming increasingly important as more spheres of life became parts of the commercial market. The result was that people began to use money as a sign of accomplishment, a common denominator for prestige.

Within the business class, friendships, social activities, church membership, and political principles were often viewed from the instrumental standpoint of their contribution to one's business success. In turn, social status in these other realms became dependent on financial status. Newcomers to Middletown were judged by material externals—where they lived, what kind of car they drove. "It's perfectly natural," a leading citizen told the Lynds. "You see, they know money, and they don't know you" (Lynd 1929:80–81).

Middletown Revisited

When the Lynds returned for a restudy in 1935, Middletown had grown larger. Its industrial base was more mechanized, more centralized into larger units, and more subservient to national corporations like General Motors, which owned plants in Middletown. Production was becoming so efficient that an industrial labor force that was only slightly larger could produce vastly more goods. As a result, new employment was flowing into the **service sectors** of the economy (such as finance, health, education) and the **occupational structure** was changing accordingly. There were more schoolteachers, more social workers, and more dental hygienists.

At work, the gap between worker and manager had widened. The managers were not so often self-made owner-businessmen but, increasingly, members of "the new middle class" of college-trained professionals and administrators, who worked for a salary.

The factories had become fewer and bigger. They hired more semiskilled machine tenders, fewer highly skilled manual workers, and growing numbers of specialists, like engineers and chemists. The latter came from outside rather than being promoted from the ranks.

Technological change was transforming Middletown's class structure. It could no longer be adequately described by the simple division into a business class and a working class, which had seemed sufficient in 1924. The Lynds described what they saw in 1935 with a schema of six classes, three manual and three nonmanual. Although based on occupational niches, their new conception of the class structure was quite like the one that Warner was describing about the same time for Yankee City, based on prestige, consumption style, and interaction networks.

At the top of the new class structure was an emergent upper class. The Lynds' account of one prominent family of this class, whom they call the "X family," illustrates the process by which new wealth is transformed into lifestyle symbols, interaction networks, personal prestige, and political power. Four brothers founded the family fortune at the end of the nineteenth century by starting a small glass-manufacturing plant with $7,000 in cash. The legends of Middletown contain many tales of the simplicity and humbleness of these business pioneers. When one of the brothers died in 1925, a newspaper recalled that "'he always worked on a level with his employees. He never asked a man to do something he would not do himself'" (Lynd 1937:75).

These men built an industrial enterprise that became world famous. They grew rich, contributed vast sums to local charities, bought a substantial interest in the local newspaper, and became politically powerful. Believers in high profits and low wages, they led the fight against unionization. The X clan did not run Middletown by itself. There were other powerful business interests, and the people of Middletown still voted. But, concluded the Lynds, "the business class in Middletown runs the city. The nucleus of business-class control is the X family" (1937:77).

Not until the second generation did the X family gain leadership in consumption affairs: Around the adult sons and daughters of the X clan, with their model farms, fine houses, riding clubs, and airplanes, there developed an exclusive younger set that was self-consciously upper class. These families were distinguished from lesser business folk by their residence in an exclusive neighborhood and elite patterns of leisure, symbolized by the annual horse show. In contrast, the men of the older generation had always been preoccupied with business and, by and large, disinclined to cultivate an opulent lifestyle.

The second generation of owners is bound to be different: They cannot have the motives of ambitious individuals born in poverty. They are born to the wealth that brings power, the income that brings luxury, and the values of those who have been reared to expect both; these values have been polished by attendance at universities with national prestige, rather than at the local college. They will be bound to seek the company of others like themselves. They will, in other words, create an upper class with links to the national elite.

Industrialization and the Transformation of the National Class Structure

The changes the Lynds chronicled in Middletown reflect the sweeping transformation of the United States into an industrial society. Although the process was underway in the 1840s and 1850s, it was consolidated after the

Civil War. Between 1870 and 1929, the national population tripled, but the output of the American economy grew tenfold, largely as the result of the colossal gains in **productivity** (output per worker or per hour worked) made possible by new industrial technologies. By 1900, the United States was the world's leading industrial nation.

Closely associated with this achievement were other developments of critical significance for the American class system, most of which we have seen played out on a small scale in Middletown. For instance, Americans changed from predominantly rural residents and farmers to city dwellers employed at urban occupations. In 1870, approximately three quarters of the population lived in rural places (under 2,500 inhabitants), and more than half the labor force was employed in farming. By 1930, most Americans lived in towns and cities, and nearly 80 percent of the labor force was engaged in nonfarm occupations (Ross 1968:26). During the same period, occupational tasks were becoming increasingly subdivided and specialized. Thus, the steelworker and the metallurgist were among the successors to the blacksmith.

As the industrial economy expanded, the country's labor requirements grew faster than the native population did. This labor deficit was met by encouraging immigration from abroad, a policy so successful that by 1920, 22 percent of the industrial labor force was foreign born.

Finally, the period saw a leap in the scale of economic organization. Large corporations emerged as the dominant force in the American economy. Industrial technology requires large enterprises, but it was the drive to control national markets and generate monopoly profits that produced such giants as Standard Oil (whose successors include Exxon), E. I. du Pont de Nemours, and General Electric through a wave of corporate mergers at the turn of the century.

In the next few pages, we will show how the class structure was affected by these changes. First, we will look at three broad class groupings (upper class, working class, and middle class) that were decisively transformed by industrialization. Then we will examine how the occupational structure was altered.

The National Upper Class

Our account of the upper class draws on the work of sociologist C. Wright Mills, whose best-known work, *The Power Elite* (1956), is examined in greater detail in Chapter 8. Writing of the history of the upper class in that book, Mills observed that the United States had never had a national aristocracy of the type known in Europe. Without a feudal past or a single national center of wealth, power, and prestige like Paris or London, an enduring "pedigreed" class never developed. But before industrialization, there had been a series of relatively stable and compact regional upper classes across America:

> Up the Hudson, there were patroons, proud of their origins, and in Virginia, the planters. In every New England town, there were Puritan shipowners and early industrialists, and in St. Louis, fashionable descendants of French Creoles living off real estate. In Denver, Colorado, there were wealthy gold and silver miners. And in New York City, as Dixon Wecter has put it, there was a class

made up of coupon-clippers, sportsmen living off their fathers' accumulation, and a stratum [of families] . . . trying to renounce their commercial origins as quickly as possible. (Mills 1956:48)

The prestige of these regional upper classes rested on old family fortunes, some on the Eastern Seaboard reaching back to colonial times. By gradually assimilating new moneyed families, the established families were able to keep prestige and wealth in close correspondence. But this system was overwhelmed in the decades after the Civil War. The postwar expansion of the industrial economy created unprecedented opportunities for rapid accumulation of new wealth. Before the war, millionaires were rare, but an 1892 survey found more than 4,000 (Mills 1956:101–102). The wealth of the Lynds' X family and the fortunes associated with names such as Rockefeller, Carnegie, Morgan, and Vanderbilt originated in this period.

The post-Civil War fortunes destroyed the neat coincidence of family lineage, wealth, and prestige. The established families initially resisted the social pretensions of the new rich, but this was not easy because the size and national scope of the new wealth dwarfed the older family fortunes.

Not by chance, this era produced one of the most famous attempts to define membership in upper-class society, Ward McAllister's "400" list. McAllister established himself as an arbiter of New York society on the basis of his close ties to the prestigious Mrs. John Jacob Astor. In the 1880s, he decided that there were "only about four hundred people in fashionable New York Society. If you go outside that number, you strike people who are either not at ease in a ballroom or else make other people not at ease" (Mills 1956:54).

But McAllister's defensive effort to specify the makeup of upper-class society was obsolete even before his list was published in 1892. A decade earlier, Mrs. Astor had overcome her disdain for Mrs. Vanderbilt's new railroad money and accepted an invitation from her to a fancy-dress ball. Gestures of this sort, Mills argued, have prevented the emergence of an American aristocracy. "Always in America, society based on descent has been either bypassed or bought-out by the new and vulgar rich" (Mills 1956:52).

In the late nineteenth and early twentieth centuries, the family fortunes built after the Civil War were merged with the old society to create a new prestige class, national in scope like the new economy and centered in major cities like New York, Philadelphia, Chicago, and San Francisco. The progress of this merger can be seen in the *Social Register*, an elite directory that first appeared during this era and proved to be the most successful and enduring effort to specify the socially elect. The first *Social Register*, published in New York in 1887, contained 881 families in a careful mix of new and old. Within a few years, registers were issued in other major cities. During the period 1890 to 1920, the rate of admissions to the *Social Register* was high, reflecting rapid assimilation of the new rich; thereafter, annual admissions declined to more modest levels (Baltzell 1958:20).

The Industrial Working Class

The economic transformation that forced a restructuring of the upper class also recast the lower levels of the American class structure. Factory production, limited before the Civil War to the textile mills of New England, spread across the country and created a modern industrial working class. By 1930, a total of 17 million workers were employed in the sectors most directly affected by industrialization: manufacturing, mining, and utilities and transportation.

Many of the new industrial workers were immigrants—notably Italians, Jews, and Slavs, who came after 1890. These recent arrivals were relegated to the least attractive manual-labor jobs, while native-born Americans, including the offspring of the earlier immigrants, dominated skilled occupations and supervisory positions. Thus, a close association grew up between stratification and ethnicity, with the highest positions being occupied by the members of the most culturally Americanized groups. This system was reinforced by active discrimination against immigrants and their children in schools and politics.

The working conditions and wages offered America's expanding working class were often dismal. In 1897, the average workweek in industry was nearly 60 hours. Long hours and the indifference of employers to safety conditions produced an appalling record of industrial accidents. More than half a million workers were killed, crippled, or seriously injured on the job in 1907. The Commission on Industrial Relations, appointed by President Wilson, concluded in 1915 that

> a large part of our industrial population are . . . living in conditions of actual poverty. . . . It is certain that at least one third and possibly one half of the families of wage earners employed in manufacturing and mining earn in the course of the year less than enough to support them in anything like a comfortable and decent condition. (Link and Cotton 1973:38)

The commission discovered that the children of the poor (many of whom were themselves employed in factories and sweatshops) were dying at 3 times the rate of middle-class children and that 12 percent to 20 percent of all children in six major cities were underfed and undernourished.

The early years of the new century saw some improvement in these conditions. State legislatures, over the determined opposition of employers, started to pass legislation controlling safety conditions, providing compensation for injured workers, prohibiting child labor, and regulating the labor of women. As industrial productivity increased, hours of work declined and wages increased. However, the life of the average worker remained unenviable.

The contrast between the conditions of the working class and the opulent lifestyles of the new rich convinced many Americans that class divisions were becoming sharper. This impression was reinforced by the conflict between the emerging industrial working class and its capitalist-class employers. The period from the Civil War to World War I saw the most violent labor confrontations in American history. For example, in 1877, after railroads cut the wages of their already overworked (15 to 18 hours per day) and underpaid workers, a wave of strikes hit the nation's rail system. State militia and federal troops (called out by officials sympathetic to the railroads to "maintain order") provoked bloody confrontations in which scores of people were killed or injured and millions of dollars of damage was done to company property. In 1892, at Homestead, Pennsylvania, a private army of 300 Pinkerton guards hired by management fired on striking employees of the Carnegie Steel Corporation. In the ensuing battle, three guards and seven workers were killed. A few days later, the company prevailed on the governor to send state militia to take over Homestead, which was under the (peaceful) control of a strike committee.

Multiple indictments against strike leaders, charging crimes from murder to "treason against the state of Pennsylvania" broke the strike, and the union itself, by depleting the union treasury with legal expenses. However, not all strikes ended in management victories. When textile workers in Lawrence, Massachusetts, struck in 1912, martial law was immediately declared, and three dozen strikers were arrested and summarily sentenced to prison. After several violent incidents, including an attack by police on a group of women and children from striking families, the strikers gained public sympathy and won concessions from employers.

In the wake of the 1877 rail strikes, E. L. Godkin, the prestigious editor of *The Nation*, wrote, "We have had an uprising not against political oppression or unpopular government but against society itself." These events should disabuse Americans of the illusion that "this was the one country in which there was no proletariat, no dangerous class." Godkin urged reinforcement of the army and militia and reduction of loose talk "about the laborer and his rights" (Litwack 1962:53–56).

If such violent incidents were exceptional, they were nonetheless symptomatic of the era. Workers who sought decent wages and working conditions had to contend with powerful companies, which could generally count on the support of state and federal governments; the courts; and, as Godkin's remarks suggest, the press. Only gradually did the federal government begin to assume a more balanced attitude toward labor conflicts. In 1930, the legal right of workers to form unions was still in question.

In the late nineteenth and early twentith centuries, the United States came as close as it ever has to Marx's conception of a capitalist society. Readers of the *Communist Manifesto* would recognize the emergence of a bourgeoisie and a proletariat in an era of rapid industrial development, the creation of a political and ideological superstructure beholden to the bourgeoisie, and evidence of violent class conflict. However, events did not take the course that the *Manifesto* anticipated. Despite Godkin's observation about an "uprising against society," American workers proved to be more interested in earning good wages than in creating a socialist society, and they used both their unions and their votes to help achieve their goals. In addition, two tendencies prevented stark polarization between two classes, a development that Marx regarded as a prerequisite to proletarian revolution. One was division within the working class among ethnic or racial groups and among workers at different skill and wage levels. These divisions kept the workers from developing a shared, militant class consciousness. The other was the expansion of the middle class, which offered the chance of advancement to workers or their children. Added to this were the long-term gains in the standard of living of most groups that appeared to absorb their attention more than did the differences between rich and poor.

The New Middle Class

For an understanding of the transformation of the middle class in industrializing America, we turn again to the work of C. Wright Mills. In *White Collar*

(1951), drawing on the earlier work of Lewis Corey (1935, 1953), Mills distinguished between two groupings he called **old middle class** and **new middle class**. The former is composed of small entrepreneurs: farmers, shopkeepers, self-employed professionals, and the like. The hallmark of this class is its independence, based on the entrepreneur's ownership of the property with which he or she works. The new middle class is composed of the salaried white-collar people whose emergence the Lynds chronicled in Middletown—a heterogeneous grouping of office workers, salespeople, and salaried professionals and managers. Early in the nineteenth century, the old middle class, as defined by Mills, comprised as much as 80 percent of the total population, but as the country's industrial society matured, the working class became the majority and the new middle class grew in proportion to the old. In particular, there were fewer farmers and many more salaried professionals, salespeople, and office workers.

The changing balance within the middle class, Mills observed, represented the decline of property and the rise of occupation as the principal basis of stratification. In the countryside, many small farmers were forced off the land or became tenant-farmers as agricultural prices fell relative to the prices of the urban products that farmers buy. Behind declining prices were advances in agricultural technology that enabled fewer farmers to feed an expanding urban population, competition from foreign agriculture, and the domination of national economic policy by the new industrialists and financiers of the Northeast.

In the cities, many businesspeople shared the financial plight of the small farmers. However, in this case the modest relative decline in the proportion of business owners in the labor force masked what was actually happening: Each year, millions of small-business enterprises collapsed, only to be replaced by millions of new enterprises, most of them doomed to the same fate. As corporate dominance of the economy expanded, small business was relegated to the highly competitive retail sector of the economy.

If the decline of the old middle class was evident in the fate of the farmer and small-business owner, the emergence of the new middle class was tied to the triumph of the corporation. As the operations of corporations grew in productive efficiency, financial magnitude, and geographic scope, a decreasing proportion of the workforce was required in the actual production of things, but an increasing proportion was needed to manage, design, sell, and keep account of production. Moreover, the growth of the corporate economy imposed new tasks on government, which grew in response. The rise of corporate and public bureaucracies fed the expansion of the new middle class.

Over time, however, as office employment increased, the social prestige and material advantage conferred by the white collar declined. At the bottom of large bureaucracies, routinized jobs began to approximate assembly-line employment. The wage gap between average white-collar and blue-collar employees shrank. Of course, the better-trained professionals and managers earned salaries well above blue-collar wages. But the line between blue collar and white collar was no longer the critical boundary in the class system, separating working class and "business class," which the Lynds found in Middletown in 1924.

The class system we have been describing in this and the preceding two sections has evolved in significant ways since the 1970s. In particular, (1) new wealth, often based on information technology or finance, is challenging the position of the established upper class; (2) the decline of manufacturing employment has eroded the economic basis of the industrial working class; and (3) the growing technological and organizational complexity of the economy has broadened opportunities for the well-trained professionals and managers who make up the upper-middle class. In the remainder of this chapter and subsequent chapters, we will explore these trends in greater detail.

National Occupational System

The Lynds' chronicle of Middletown and the parallel national accounts by Mills and others suggest that the post-Civil War transformation of the American class system can be viewed as a result of a series of shifts in the distribution of occupations. We know, for instance, that there was a proportional decline in the number of farmers and a proportional increase in the number of factory and office workers. Approaching social change this way has the advantage of being precise—we can count the number of people employed in different occupations at various points in time. It is also directly relevant to the technological and organizational shifts that have reshaped the economy.

The U.S. Census Bureau has been collecting information on the occupations of Americans for over a century, but analyzing these data requires a schema to reduce a shifting constellation of (literally) thousands of occupations to a manageable set of categories. Since the 1940s, the Census Bureau and independent researchers have been using variants of the schema described in Table 3.1, which groups occupations into a set of broad categories. Because this system, invented by a bureau official named Alba Edwards (1943), is commonly employed by ourselves and others, we take a good look at his handiwork, and urge readers to peruse the examples in the table.

Edwards based his schema on his own estimation of the nature of the work, skill and training, income, and general social standing associated with occupations. He maintained that his categories formed a "socioeconomic" hierarchy of earnings, education, and prestige, ascending together. This is mostly true. But there is some inconsistency, as we often find, in the middle. Edwards seems to have assumed that white-collar jobs consistently outrank blue-collar jobs. In fact, *skilled* blue-collar workers, on average, earn more than clerical workers and rank about the same on surveys of occupational prestige, even though they have lower levels of formal education. Other problems with the Edwards schema come from lumping diverse occupations into broad categories, especially in the upper categories. For example, the professional grouping includes doctors and engineers, who rank high on all three dimensions. However, the most numerous professionals by far are public schoolteachers, who occupy a more modest position. Another example is the managerial category, which is large enough to encompass the manager of a fast-food restaurant and the CEO of a major corporation.

The Edwards schema is less than perfect as a stratification measure. However, it would be hard to do much better without producing something infinitely more complex. The original purpose of Edwards' schema was to organize occupational data to make broad historical comparisons, and it serves well for that purpose.

Table 3.1   Major Occupational Groups, With Examples, 2011

(1) Professionals 16%	(6) Craft, precision production, & repair workers 8%
Doctors Public schoolteachers Computer systems analysts Registered nurses Librarians Engineers	Carpenters Masons Foremen in construction or manufacturing Machinists Telephone repair workers Auto mechanics
(2) Managers and administrators 18%	**(7) Operatives 9%**
Corporate executives Sales managers Public administrators Bar managers Owner-operators of retail enterprises Stockbrokers	Assembly-line workers in manufacturing Butchers Gas station attendants Truck drivers Bakers
(3) Technicians (often classified with professionals) 5%	**(8) Service workers 17%**
Medical laboratory technicians Dental hygienists Computer programmers Practical nurses	Waiters and waitresses Police and firefighters Child care workers Maids and janitors Domestic servants
(4) Sales workers 9%	**(9) Laborers (excludes farm) 3%**
Retail store clerks Telemarketers Cashiers Travel agents	Unskilled construction workers Freight and stock handlers Garbage collectors
(5) Clerical workers 13%	**(10) Farm workers 2%**
Bank tellers Bookkeepers Secretaries Hotel desk clerks Data entry operators	Farmers (owner-operator) Farm managers Unpaid farm-family laborers Migrant farm laborers

Note: U.S. Census. Occupational categories modified for this text. Percentages based on 2011 statistics. See "Note on Statistical Sources" on page 283.

The Transformations of the American Occupational Structure

Using Edwards' compilation and more recent census data, we have charted the evolution of the American occupational structure from 1870 to 2000. The results are assembled in Table 3.2. The occupational upheaval that first

Table 3.2 Occupational Structure of the United States: 1870 to 2000

Occupation	Percent of the Labor Force						
	1870	1900	1930	1950	1972	1990	2000
Professionals and technicians	3	4	7	9	14	17	19
Managers, officials, and proprietors	6	6	7	9	10	13	15
Sales workers	4	5	6	7	9	12	13
Clerical workers		3	9	12	16	15	14
Craftsmen and foremen	9	11	13	14	13	12	12
Operatives	10	13	16	20	16	11	9
Laborers, except farm	9	12	11	7	5	4	4
Service workers	6	9	10	10	13	13	12
Farmers and farm laborers	53	38	21	12	4	3	3
TOTAL	100	100	100	100	100	100	100
Number in labor force (millions)	12.9	29.0	48.7	59.0	81.7	117.9	136.2
Percent female	15	18	22	28	38	45	47

Sources: 1870 from Edwards 1943; 1900–1950 from U.S. Census Bureau 1975; 1972 from U.S. Census Bureau 1973; U.S. Department of Labor 1984; 1990 and 2000, from U.S. Department of Labor 2001b.

Note: The first three columns are consistent with the 1970 Census occupational classification; the last two are based on the 1980 classification. The column for 1972 is the average of the two classifications for that year, which were quite close.

transformed Middletown is reflected here. Following the percentages across the table, you will note that farm occupations have declined from more than half the labor force in 1870 to less than 3 percent at the beginning of the twenty-first century. As the percentage of agricultural workers declined, the proportion of operatives, the grouping that includes most factory workers, rose steadily until it became the single largest occupational category, accounting for 1 in 5 workers in 1950. But after 1950, the proportion of operatives began to decline. This happened despite the steady increase in the volume of goods produced. The other two major blue-collar categories, craftsmen and nonfarm laborers, have followed a similar curved trajectory.

While the agricultural categories have continuously contracted and the blue-collar groupings first expanded and then contracted, white-collar employment has grown steadily, as it did in Middletown. By the 1970s, white-collar workers (professionals, technicians, managers, sales, and clerical workers) accounted for half the labor force. Two classifications within that group grew especially rapidly—professional/technical and clerical.

The more modest growth of a third white-collar grouping, the managerial occupations, obscures the radical transformation of this classification. The decline of the independent entrepreneur and complementary increase of salaried managers, noted by Mills in the period 1870 to 1940, has not abated. The proportion of managers who were self-employed dropped from more than half in the 1950s to a few percent 50 years later. The United States has truly become a nation of employees.

The **service worker** category has also changed as it has grown. At the beginning of the twentieth century, most of the workers falling under this rubric were domestic servants (or in the more neutral current language of the Census Bureau, "private household workers"). Recently, the largest and most rapidly expanding service occupations include hospital attendants, waiters and waitresses, janitors, and security guards. While making a hospital bed or washing windows in an office building may be no more satisfying than performing similar tasks in a private home, the change suggests a different kind of class relationship. Of course, there are still privileged American households where domestic chores are done by hired servants.

The statistics in Table 3.2 track broad shifts in the national occupational structure from 1870 to 2000. These trends, as we will see below, are critical for understanding the evolution of the American class system. For more recent occupational statistics, see Tables 3.1 or 3.3.

Unfortunately, the Census Bureau has changed its methods, so that these recent statistics are incompatible with the earlier numbers.[1]

From Agricultural to Postindustrial Society

There are several keys to these long-term patterns of occupational change. Earlier, we noted the growth of large bureaucratic organizations associated with the modern corporation and the expansion of government. This tendency increases the demand for managers; certain professionals, such as accountants; and, above all, clerical workers. The phenomenal expansion of clerical employment is also linked to the increasing participation of women in the labor force.

However, the fundamental cause of changes in the occupational structure since 1870 has been the transformation of the United States from an **agricultural** to an **industrial** and finally to a **postindustrial society**. These three stages are outlined in Figure 3.1. They are defined in terms of the predominant employment sectors of the economy. In 1870, agriculture was still the mainstay of the economy, and most working Americans were farmers. By 1900, the United States had become an industrial society, with most workers employed in manufacturing and related sectors of the economy. After 1970, the United States could be described as a postindustrial society, with most jobs in service-producing rather than goods-producing sectors of the economy. Of course, agricultural production and the output of manufactured goods continued to grow after employment shifted to the service-producing sectors.

These major economic shifts were conditioned by technological change. The transition to an industrial society was predicated on new technology, which substituted machine power for animal and human muscle. The emergence of a postindustrial society depended on continuing technological advances,

---

[1] For an explanation of these changes, see the "Note on Statistical Sources" on page 283.

Figure 3.1 From Agricultural to Postindustrial Society

Periods and Predominant Employment Sectors

Agricultural Society	**Industrial Society**	**Postindustrial Society**
1776–1900	1900–1970	1970–
Agriculture	Manufacturing	Retail and wholesale trade
Fisheries	Mining	Finance and insurance
Forestry	Construction	Real estate
	Transportation	Health care
	Public utilities	Education
	Communications	Government
		Legal services
		Business services
		Social services
		Lodging and restaurant
		Personal services

Source: Based on employment data from U.S. Census Bureau 1975.

which steadily increased productive efficiency and enabled a shrinking proportion of the labor force to meet the material needs of the rest. This dependence on technology, of course, has increased demand for scientific and technical personnel. Engineering, for instance, is one of the largest professional occupations.

As the proportion of the labor force employed in producing goods has declined, employment has expanded in retail, finance, law, hotels, health care, and education. (As this list suggests, most people employed in what are commonly referred to as "the service sector" are not occupationally "service workers.") The net result of these changes has been to move employment out of the sectors that require large numbers of blue-collar production workers and into those that depend more on workers in white-collar or service occupations. This tendency, as we see later, was reinforced by globalization, which brought growing dependence on imported manufactured goods.

Early assessments of postindustrial society ranged from sunny optimism to dark pessimism. Interpreters on the sunny side anticipated a world of prosperity, opportunity, and social mobility. The postindustrial economy would employ fewer low-skilled manual workers at dirty, back-straining jobs but require growing armies of professionals, technicians, and managers. One writer looked forward to the "white-collarization of America" (Wattenberg 1974:26). Another expected a "status upheaval" (Bell 1976:134).

Interpreters on the dark side, in contrast, predicted that postindustrial society would provide shrinking opportunities for most Americans and growing social inequality. The sons and daughters of factory workers were more likely to become janitors and food-service workers than engineers and computer systems analysts. These writers did not associate "white-collarization" with opportunity but with the declining prestige, shrinking rewards, and increasingly menial character of office work (Braverman 1974; Glenn and Alston 1975). Writers on both sides of the debate saw a parallel between the earlier Industrial Revolution and the contemporary shift toward a postindustrial society. Both anticipated another round of sweeping social transformation in the wake of economic change.

The changes we have examined in the occupational structure provide support for both sunny- and dark-side interpretations of postindustrial society. Fewer Americans are employed at dirty, back-straining jobs and more have professional, technical, and managerial jobs. But the job market has polarized. The fastest job growth has been in high skill, well-rewarded occupations for people with college degrees and in low skill, low wage service jobs with minimal education requirements. Job growth has been slowest in the middle, for people in mid-waged clerical, sales, craft, and operative occupations. Detailed statistics show that postindustrial society has required many more managers, electrical engineers, registered nurses, accountants, and computer specialists, but also growing numbers of janitors, home health aids, security guards, and food-service workers. It doesn't need as many people for routine jobs in the factory and the office, where computers and automation have reduced labor requirements (Autor 2010). Compared to the top and mid-level jobs, the service jobs commonly available don't just pay less; they are notable for unstable employment, unsafe and unpleasant work conditions, and few benefits, such as health insurance, sick pay, vacation time, or pensions.

The Loss of Manufacturing Jobs

The most consequential change that came with postindustrial society was the loss of manufacturing jobs. American industry is producing much more stuff with much less labor. As Figure 3.2 shows, by 2016, manufacturing output was, in rough terms, 3 times what it had been in 1972 and manufacturing employment had sunk to almost half. The opportunities today are even slimmer than these figures suggest for the unskilled workers who had traditionally found employment on the assembly lines. The national labor force has almost doubled in size since the early 1970s, and factories need better educated workers to fill many of the jobs in what has become a technologically sophisticated workplace.

Public discussion of these trends has centered on the good jobs being "exported to Mexico" or, more recently, China. Much of the production of certain basic goods (for example, apparel or consumer electronics) has shifted to Asia or Latin America. In some cases, whole factories have been moved abroad. The emergence of China, as a major exporter of manufactured consumer products, has devastated the competing American industries and communities where its effects were concentrated. The impact of what has been called "the China shock" is notable in Figure 3.2: The level of manufacturing employment, which had been stagnant since the 1980s, sank after 2000, the year China joined the World Trade Organization. But the

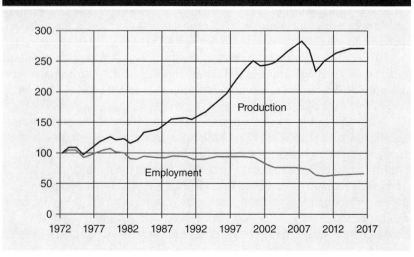

Figure 3.2 Manufacturing Production and Employment

Indexes: 1972=100

Note: Refers to total employment in manufacturing and real value of manufacturing output

Source: St. Louis Federal Reserve. https://stlouisfed.org

main force holding industrial employment down is, as Figure 3.2 suggests, rising industrial productivity. Economic research confirms that the effect of rising imports is small relative to that of improved methods of production. By one estimate, in 2010, American manufacturers were able to produce with 12 million workers what would have required 21 million at year 2000 levels of productivity (Acemoglu et al. 2016; Autor, Dorn, and Hanson 2016; Hicks and Devaraj 2017).

The stagnation and eventual decline of manufacturing employment had enormous consequences for American economic, family, and political life. The better paying jobs in this sector had enabled many workers, especially men with limited education, to support families at middle-income levels. Those who lost jobs in manufacturing or had never found them were likely to be channeled into poorly paid service jobs. The low **earnings** and unstable employment typical of such jobs strained working-class family life and, as Chapter 5 will show, contributed to rising numbers of unwed childbirths and single parent families. Shrinking employment in industry eroded the traditional base of labor union membership, which had political consequences we explore in Chapters 8 and 9. In one way or another, these processes all contributed to the growing inequality of the current era. They also contributed to the popular discontent that propelled the unconventional candidacies of Donald Trump and Bernie Sanders in 2016.

Women Workers in Postindustrial Society

A dramatic increase in the proportion of female workers has accompanied the development of postindustrial society. At the beginning of the twentieth century, women constituted only a tiny proportion of the paid labor force. As late as 1950, only 28 percent of the labor force was female, but in recent decades, women's labor force participation has accelerated, while the participation of men has begun to decline. By 2000, women constituted almost half the labor force.

Women workers have long been segregated into a relatively small number of **pink-collar occupations**—fields that are almost entirely female. Secretaries, cashiers, hairdressers, nurses, and elementary school teachers are among the pink-collar workers. Although some pink-collar jobs pay relatively well (registered nurses, for example), most offer lower wages, less prestige, and slimmer opportunities for advancement than positions in male-dominated fields requiring similar levels of education and training. But women workers have been moving out of the pink-collar ghetto.

In the twentieth century, women were drawn into the labor market by the ballooning demand for clerical workers and later for service workers. Beginning in the early 1970s, growing numbers of wives joined the labor force to bolster family incomes that were being eroded by the stagnating earnings and the rising unemployment rates of male workers. Increasingly, couples recognized that middle-class and upper-middle class living standards required two incomes.

The pull of economic forces was reinforced by the push of social forces: A declining birth rate, a rising divorce rate, and the increasing proportion of births to single mothers all led women to seek work outside the home. By 1970, the implicit marital compact that had tied men and women to sharply defined family roles in industrial society (husband as provider, wife as permanent housekeeper-caregiver) was collapsing. Attitudes toward working wives and mothers were shifting—encouraged perhaps by the women's movement, but also compelled by the new economic and marital uncertainties.

These changes were particularly felt by the women of the baby boom generation—the extra-large cohort of Americans born after World War II, from 1946 to 1965. Compared with their own mothers and grandmothers, the boomers were much closer to men in their educational achievement, late to marry, and more likely to be childless or to delay childbearing. As a result of these factors and others outlined earlier, boomer women were more likely to join the labor force, more career oriented, more inclined to work full time and continuously, and more like men in their occupations and earnings.

For example, in 1979, a woman employed full time, year round, earned, on average, 62 cents for every dollar earned by a similarly employed man. This figure had remained stubbornly unchanged for many years. By 2015, the relative pay rate had risen to 80 cents. In 1970 (the year Hillary Clinton entered Yale Law School), women were 5 percent of law school graduates; by 2011, they were 47 percent. Over the same period, the proportion of women among medical school graduates climbed from 8 percent to 48 percent, and the proportion of females among people classified by the Census Bureau as "managers" rose from 17 percent to nearly 46 percent. There was, however, little change in these statistics after 2000.

Women remain, on average, quite different from men in the marketplace. Even among baby boomers, women are less likely than men to work full time, year round. Their yearly earnings, although advancing, are therefore likely

Table 3.3 Occupational Distribution by Sex, 2011

Occupation	Percent	
	Males	Females
Managers	17.7	14.9
Professionals	15.7	20.5
Technicians	2.6	6.6
Sales	8.0	9.9
Clerical	6.6	20.5
Crafts	14.6	0.5
Operatives	13.2	4.3
Services	12.7	20.9
Laborers	5.2	1.1
Farm	3.7	0.8
Total	**100.0**	**100.0**
Number (millions)	**74.3**	**65.6**

Source: U.S. Census. Revised occupational categories.

to lag behind men's. As Table 3.3 indicates, women's occupational profile is different from men's. Women are more likely to be employed as clerical or service workers and less likely to hold one of the skilled blue-collar jobs. Although women appear to be well represented in the general category of "professionals," more detailed occupational data indicate that the majority of female professionals work in just three fields: nursing, teaching, and social work. It is still the case that the great majority of those working in the high-prestige, high-income professions, including law, medicine, engineering, and architecture, are men. Thus, the pink-collar phenomenon endures, though it is slowly fading.

Recently, one category of women workers has been outearning men: Single, childless women under 30 earn 8 percent more than men their age. The reason is that women are more likely to go to college. But their advantage vanishes for women over 30, especially if they have children. Women run up against what has been described as a discriminatory "maternal wall"—the apparent reluctance of many employers to hire or advance women who are mothers or likely to become mothers on the assumption that they are less committed to their careers (Noguchi 2013).

Both declining pink-collar employment and what might be called the Hillary Clinton/Michelle Obama phenomenon—ambitious, successful women married to ambitious, successful men—are of growing importance for the class system. The reason, as we will see in Chapter 4, is that U.S. households increasingly depend on women's earnings.

Transformation of the Black Occupational Structure

In his classic 1944 report on black America, Gunner Myrdal declared, "The economic situation of the Negroes in America is pathological. Except for a small minority enjoying upper or middle class status, the masses of American Negroes . . . are destitute." Even as Myrdal wrote, the situation he described was changing. From 1940 to 1980, the weekly earnings of the average full-time black worker (in inflation-adjusted "real" dollars) rose 400 percent. Because white wages were growing at a slower rate, the wages of black men advanced from 43 percent to 73 percent of the white male average over the same period (Smith and Welch 1989).

Table 3.4 reveals the transformation of the black occupational structure. In 1940, an estimated 80 percent of black workers were still concentrated in the three lowest occupational categories. In the decades that followed, the black occupational structure shifted decisively toward the higher categories, bringing it closer to the distribution of white workers. The change for black women was even more dramatic than this general picture for both sexes. As late as 1960, one third of employed black women cleaned white people's houses. Only a small percentage worked at the white-collar jobs that were typical of white women. By the 1980s, about half of black female workers held white-collar positions (Farley 1984:48–49).

Black workers were affected by the same broad processes of change that were altering the world of white workers, but in ways that were peculiar to an oppressed minority. In the 1930s and 1940s, under the pressures of new industrial unions and the needs of economic mobilization for World War II,

Table 3.4 Occupational Structure of Black Workers, 1940–2002

Occupation	Percent			
	1940	1960	1983	2002
Managers/proprietors	1	2	5	10
Professionals and technicians	3	5	12	15
Sales and clerical	2	8	23	25
Craftsmen and foremen	3	7	9	7
Operatives	10	21	17	13
Laborers	14	14	7	5
Service workers	34	34	25	23
Farm	32	8	3	1
Total	100	100	100	100

the discriminatory barriers that had kept blacks out of many manufacturing jobs began to fall.

The Civil Rights Movement of the 1960s produced antidiscrimination legislation and affirmative action programs in government and private industry, opening many new jobs to blacks. At the same time, blacks were closing the educational distance between themselves and whites. As a result, many young blacks were able to qualify for the more attractive white-collar jobs.

Despite the progress since 1940, a considerable occupational gap remains between blacks and whites. Compared with whites, blacks are still underrepresented at the top of the occupational structure and overrepresented at the bottom, most notably among service workers, which remains, by far, the largest single occupational category for blacks. There are, to take an extreme case, approximately two "health aides" for every practicing physician, but 15 black health aides for every black physician. Blacks are still much more likely than whites to have no job at all—especially in periods of economic stagnation. Toward the end of the recession year 2009, approximately 10 percent of whites and 16 percent of blacks were unemployed, according to official statistics.

One result of these diverse trends has been increasing class differentiation among African Americans. Although large numbers of young, well-educated black men and women have been moving into jobs that were open to few of their parents, the black underclass of low-wage or unemployed workers persists. Income inequality among blacks has been increasing since the mid-1970s.[2] By 1980, sociologist William J. Wilson (1980), an influential scholar of black America, was writing about a "deepening economic schism in the Black community" (p. 142).

The black-white pay gap, which had long been shrinking, began to expand after 1980. From 1980 to 2016, the median hourly wage of black men sank from 76 to 69 percent of white men's. For black women, who were near parity with white women in 1980, the retreat was even larger: from 90 to 80 percent.[3] (The wages of black women rose in this period, but white women's wages rose faster.) In part, these trends reflect larger changes in the American economy, which have especially affected people at lower levels in the labor market, where blacks are still disproportionally concentrated: falling employment in manufacturing, the decline of labor unions, the widening wage gap between college educated and less educated workers.

Hispanic Workers in Postindustrial Society

Hispanic workers are at a disadvantage relative to both whites and blacks in their occupations and wages. As Table 3.5 indicates, they are, like blacks, overrepresented among service workers and more likely than blacks to be employed in the two bottom categories as laborers or farm workers. In 2016, the median hourly wage of Hispanic men was 69 percent that of

---

[2] For evidence of this trend, see the Gini ratio series for black families available on the Census Bureau website. The Gini ratio is commonly used as a measure of income inequality.

[3] Policy Institute's State of Working America Data Library. www.epi.org/data.

Table 3.5 Occupational Distribution of All Workers, Blacks, and Hispanics, 2011

Occupation	Percent		
	All Workers	Blacks	Hispanics
Managers	16.4	10.8	8.8
Professionals	18.0	14.9	9.2
Technicians	4.5	4.7	2.9
Sales	8.9	9.0	8.3
Clerical	13.1	15.3	12.2
Crafts	8.0	4.8	11.7
Operatives	9.0	11.2	12.6
Services	16.6	24.3	22.5
Laborers	3.3	4.0	6.6
Farm	2.3	0.9	5.1
Total	100.0	100.0	100.0
Number (millions)	*139.9*	*15.2*	*20.4*

non-Hispanic white men. For Hispanic women the comparable figure was 80 percent.[4] Generalizations about those we call Hispanics should be read with the understanding that the term lumps together a diverse and changing population. It encompasses, for example, large numbers of people of Mexican, Puerto Rican, Cuban, and Central American origin, who have different histories of immigration to the continental United States and are concentrated in different parts of the country.

Wages in the Age of Growing Inequality

The shift from an industrial to a postindustrial economy nearly coincided with the transition, described in Chapter 1, from the Age of Shared Prosperity to the Age of Growing Inequality. We have labeled the quarter century after World War II the Age of Shared Prosperity because during these years the incomes of families at all levels were growing and becoming more equal. In that period, the wages of the typical worker rose in tandem with rising productivity. In other words, as output per worker increased, because of factors including better training, improved technology, and added machinery, wages also increased. But beginning in the early-1970s, wages became disconnected

---

[4] Policy Institute's State of Working America Data Library. www.epi.org/data

from the continuing gains in productivity, as shown in Figure 3.3. The benefits of economic progress were no longer shared with workers, but flowed disproportionately to those at the top of the labor market, along with business owners and stockholders. Wages became increasingly unequal among men and among women. The occupational polarization noted earlier was, as might be expected, paralleled by the polarization of earnings.

Table 3.6, which covers 4 decades of the Age of Growing Inequality, reveals a *widening gulf between a high-wage elite at the top of the labor market and workers near the bottom or in the middle*. Among men, wages dropped significantly at the 20th percentile and more or less stagnated at the 50th, but rose steadily and substantially at the 95th. In 1973, the wage at the 95th percentile was about twice that of the median wage. By 2015, it was 3 times as much. Among women, wages increased slightly at the bottom, rose notably in the middle, but jumped at the top. Here, too, the 95/50 ratio rose from about 2 to 3 times.

An especially discouraging feature of the Age of Growing Inequality has been the growing number of men working for what can be considered poverty wages. A 1992 Census Bureau report defined a "low-wage worker" as someone who worked full time, year round, without making enough to lift a family of four above the federal poverty line ($24,499 at 2015 price levels).[5]

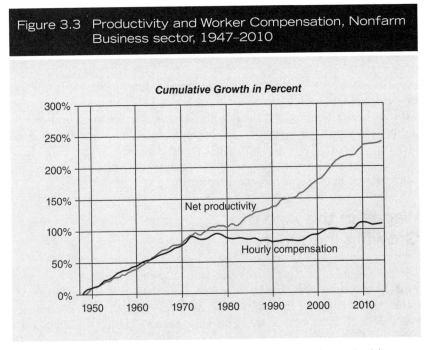

Figure 3.3 Productivity and Worker Compensation, Nonfarm Business sector, 1947–2010

Source. Fleck, S., Glaser, J., & Sprague, S. (2011). The compensation-productivity gap: a visual essay. *Monthly Labor Review*, January 2011, 59.

---

[5] These low-wage workers would not necessarily be "poor" under the federal poverty standard we will discuss in Chapter 10, since many men in this situation are not supporting families or are supporting families smaller than four, and/or have working wives who also contribute to the family income.

Table 3.6 Growing Inequality in Pay

	Real Hourly Wage by Percentile (in 2015 dollars)			Ratio of 95th to 20th	Ratio of 95th to 50th
	20th Percentile	50th Percentile (Median wage)	95th Percentile		
Men					
1973	$13.01	$19.89	$43.50	3.34	2.19
1989	$11.11	$18.57	$46.20	4.16	2.49
2007	$11.47	$19.21	$57.06	4.97	2.97
2015	$11.07	$18.94	$65.06	5.88	3.26
Women					
1973	$8.97	$12.47	$26.86	2.99	2.15
1989	$8.96	$13.71	$33.23	3.71	2.42
2007	$10.11	$15.50	$44.08	4.36	2.81
2015	$9.96	$15.67	$48.03	4.82	3.07

Source: Economic Policy Institute. www.epi.org/data.

The bureau found that from the mid-1960s to the mid-1970s—that is, during the Age of Shared Prosperity—the percentage of low-wage male workers dropped from about 17 percent to 7 percent, only to rise again in the 1980s (U.S. Census 1992). But poverty wages did not disappear along with rotary dial telephones and vinyl records. By a slightly different standard, more than 20 percent of working men and more than 30 percent of working women were earning poverty wages in 2015.[6]

At the other end of the job market, earnings have soared, especially among the **chief executive officers (CEOs)** of major corporations. From 1973 to 2014, the real earnings of CEOs at major corporations rose by over 1,000 percent—a remarkable increase in an era of stagnant wages. The gulf separating the typical CEO from the typical American worker has grown to colossal proportions. The average compensation of the CEO of a major corporation rose from about 22 times what a typical worker made in 1973

---

[6] These figures are author's estimates based on wage data from Table 3.6 for men and, from the same source, for women. Someone working full time, year round (FTYR) would need to earn $11.78/hour to reach the federal poverty line in 2015. That's more than the 20th percentile wage shown in the table or the 30th percentile figure for women (not shown in the table). Of course, low-wage jobs tend to be unstable and many do not provide a steady 40-hour work week over a year or more. The data used here (unlike the original Census statistics for "low-wage workers" in earlier periods) cannot distinguish FTYR workers from others and, therefore, only permit lower boundary estimates.

to 303 times in 2014 (Economic Policy Institute. www.epi.org/data). By one calculation, the CEO of Wal-Mart earns as much in 2 weeks as an average Wal-Mart employee might earn in a lifetime (Reich 2007:113).

Growing Inequality of Wages: Why?[7]

The contrast between the Age of Shared Prosperity and the Age of Growing Inequality is epitomized by the fate of a young man, recently graduated from high school, looking for work. A generation ago, he might have found a low-skill, blue-collar job in manufacturing—in the auto industry, if he was lucky—or construction that would enable him to support a family at a reasonable standard. Today, with the same qualifications, the young graduate would likely find a service or retail position that pays much less in real terms; he would have a tough time supporting a family on his own. Since the late 1970s, the earnings gap between high school and college-educated workers has widened. So have the gaps between skilled and unskilled and between younger and older workers. Obviously, the tide is running against our high school grad. He will likely earn less than his father did at the same age. He will need a working partner if he wants to have a family. But he is less likely to marry, or at least to stay married, than his father was.

In an era of growing inequality, the less educated, the less skilled, and the less experienced have been the biggest relative losers. But the phenomenon of wage polarization does not end with them. At the same time that high school graduates are falling behind college graduates, earnings inequality is increasing *among* high school grads and *among* college grads. In fact, such within-group inequality in earnings is rising among the members of virtually any definable group in the labor force: doctors, lawyers, waiters, carpenters, men, women, older workers, younger workers, workers in manufacturing, workers in service industries—even workers in specific firms. The only earnings gap that is closing is that between men and women.

Why is this happening? Consider the following:

1. *Economic Restructuring.* By definition, employment in a postindustrial society shifts away from manufacturing and related sectors and into the service-producing sectors of the economy such as restaurants and lodging, retail, health care, and finance (see Figure 3.1). The expanding sectors typically provide new opportunities for well-educated managers, professionals, and technicians, but fewer decent-paying jobs for workers with limited skills. In the health care sector, for example, there are ample rewards for doctors, nurses, hospital administrators, and data base managers, but meager pay and benefits for the unskilled armies of hospital janitors, food service workers, or home health aides.

---

[7] This section draws on the following sources: Acemoglu et al. 2016; Autor 2010, 2014, 2015; Blau and Kahn 2009; Duhigg and Bradsher 2012; Frank and Cook 1995; Freeman 1996; Gittleman 1994; Golden and Katz 2007; Harrison and Bluestone 1988; *In the Vanguard* 2011; Kodrzycki 1996; Koten 2013; Levy and Murnane 1992; Levy and Temin 2007; Liu and Grusky 2013; Mishel et al. 2012; Reich 2007; Rodrick 2011.

2. *Globalization.* In the Age of Shared Prosperity, foreign trade weighed little in the American economy. In 1960, for example, only 4 percent of the cars purchased in the United States were imported (Reich 2007:43). But from 1960 to the end of the century, total imports and exports climbed from 10 percent to 24 percent of GDP (Wright 2007:322). Not just goods, but also services are globalized. The United States "exports" financial services and "imports" call center services. This book may be copy-edited by someone in India. Globalization, which benefits the economy as a whole, nonetheless creates economic winners and losers. Imports of relatively cheap consumer goods produced by low-wage workers in developing countries constrict opportunities for the least skilled American workers.[8] At the same time, increased demand from abroad for high-value American products, from computer software to jetliners and sophisticated services in areas such as media and finance, creates high-paying jobs for American workers with advanced skills and education. Even high-tech products created and sold by American firms may be produced abroad. For example, Apple iPods and iPhones are designed, administered, and promoted from the company's headquarters in Cupertino, California, but assembled in China from components made in various Asian countries. Those who benefit most from the success of these devices are Apple's professionals, executives, and stockholders.

3. *Technological Change.* New technologies and modern communications also tend to displace unskilled workers while creating new jobs and rising wages for workers with relevant skills and education. Advanced digital technologies, robotics, and most recently 3-D printing have transformed manufacturing. A plant that might have employed thousands in the past can achieve the same output with hundreds of workers today. Likewise in the office, computer applications have displaced many of the middle-skilled workers who once would have performed routine clerical tasks, like basic bookkeeping. Among the winners are those with sophisticated skills who are best positioned to take advantage of these same technologies, including systems analysts, actuaries, engineers, financial analysts, logistics specialists, and marketing managers.

4. *Education.* Increasing rewards to education are implicit in the previous three points. An advanced economy, observes economist David Autor, "requires a literate, numerate, and technically and scientifically trained workforce to develop ideas, manage complex organizations, deliver healthcare services, provide financing and insurance, administer government services and operate critical infrastructure." In 1982, college graduates earned 50 percent more than high school graduates. By 2005, they earned twice as much

---

[8] These low-skilled workers benefit from cheap imports, but declining real wages at the bottom of the labor market tell us that their purchasing power has declined.

(Autor 2014:845–846). Over that period, the rising market value of education accounted for 65 percent of the increase in wage inequality, after other individual characteristics were controlled for (Goldin and Katz 2007:145). The advantage enjoyed by the educated is enhanced by the forces of supply and demand. Since 1980, the increasing demand for highly educated workers has outstripped the slowing growth of the educated labor supply.

5. *Weakened Wage-Setting Institutions*. Since the 1970s, "the invisible hand of the market" has gained influence over wages at the expense of institutions like labor unions, "internal labor markets," and **minimum wage** laws that previously shielded lower earning workers from market forces. Fewer workers are represented by labor unions and covered by collective bargaining agreements, which tend to boost the earnings of unskilled workers and limit wage differentials. Fewer corporations draw on internal labor markets (promoting existing employees from within rather than hiring outside the firm), a practice that also constrains wage differences. Over time, federal law has allowed inflation to erode the real value of the minimum wage, an important protection for the working poor. (These developments are treated in Chapters 9 and 10.)

6. *Deregulation*. The invisible hand of the market was also strengthened by the dismantling, beginning in the late 1970s, of the regulations that controlled large sectors of the American economy. By setting the price of a long-distance phone call or an interstate flight, regulatory agencies had limited price competition in these and other sectors. Deregulation unleashed competition and compelled companies to control labor costs. Consumers benefited, but deregulation undermined the wages and job security of truck drivers, telephone technicians, airline attendants, and other workers in regulated industries.

There is good evidence for the influence of all these factors—although their relative importance has been the subject of debate. By now, most thoughtful writers on the subject have concluded that multiple causes are at work. The very pervasiveness of the phenomenon of growing inequality in earnings undercuts simple explanations.

We conclude this chapter by examining two intriguing interpretations of the trends we have associated with the Age of Increasing Inequality: *The Great U-Turn*, by Bennett Harrison and Barry Bluestone, and *The Winner-Take-All Society*, by Robert Frank and Philip Cook. The first looks at developments affecting workers in the bottom half of the labor market, and the second looks at the very top.

Harrison and Bluestone: New Corporate Strategies

American corporations were in serious trouble in the early 1970s, according to Harrison and Bluestone (1988). Labor's share of national income was up.

The business share was down. Profits had been falling continuously since the mid-1960s. Corporate executives were contending with a demanding workforce, abrupt increases in the price of energy, rising taxation, growing government regulation, and accelerating inflation. But the central problem facing American business was rising competition from abroad. Producers in Europe, Japan, and newly industrializing countries such as South Korea and Taiwan were claiming large shares of the U.S. market for products from shoes and textiles to steel and automobiles.

According to Harrison and Bluestone, American capitalists responded to this challenge on three fronts: They adopted new strategies to reduce labor costs, they pursued short-term profit through speculative financial dealings, and they sought favorable government policy in areas from taxes to workplace safety rules. The authors suggest that all three have contributed to increasing inequality, but they particularly stress corporate labor strategies.

Corporations shrank their labor costs, say Harrison and Bluestone, by becoming lean and mean—that is, by reducing their labor force and cutting wages. Massive layoffs by major corporations, so-called **downsizing**, were commonplace in the 1980s and remained so in the 1990s. Industrial corporations took advantage of cheap labor abroad by opening plants in developing countries. Another strategy was **outsourcing**, buying components or finished products from low-wage companies at home and abroad. To reduce the cost of labor, companies imposed wage freezes (which depend on inflation to cut real wages over time), reduced benefits, and adopted **two-tier wage systems** providing lower pay scales for new hires.

After downsizing their permanent workforces, corporations increased their use of part-time, temporary, and "leased" employees, who typically worked at lower wages, often without benefits. Here's a recent example: In 2017, a janitor working at Apple's California headquarters, but employed by an outside contractor, earned $16.60 an hour. In the 1980s, a janitor at Kodak, a major technology firm of that era, earned about the same wage in inflation adjusted dollars. But the Kodak job came with benefits including a month of paid vacation, a yearly bonus, tuition support for part-time college study, and, perhaps most important, a chance to move up to better jobs in the corporation. Federal law requires corporations to provide all employees the same health and retirement matching benefits. By using contractors, companies evade this obligation toward their lower level workers, such as janitors and security guards, but also workers in routine white collar jobs (Irwin 2017).

Corporations also found ways to reduce, if not escape, the influence of labor unions. Often, unionized plants were closed and replaced by non-union plants in regions of the United States, especially the South, or in foreign countries unfriendly to union activity. The very threat of such action could be used to intimidate union members and their organizations.

Harrison and Bluestone's account incorporates most of the explanatory factors we listed earlier. In an analysis relevant to the first factor, they measured the effect of replacing manufacturing jobs with service sector jobs. They found that about one fifth of the increase in wage inequality can be attributed to these sectoral job shifts; they attribute the other four fifths to the changing wage distribution *within individual sectors* of the economy. In other words, the postindustrial shift toward the service sectors is important, but not as important as the growing wage inequality affecting all sectors. Their description of corporate strategies to hold down wage costs helps explain these broader developments. On the other hand, the authors have little or nothing to say about the role of technology in reducing opportunities for less-educated workers.

Unlike many writers on such topics, Harrison and Bluestone do not simply attribute change to impersonal economic forces. They see corporate leaders making conscious decisions that have adverse consequences for their workers. They argue that there were alternatives: Instead of laying off workers, squeezing wages, and focusing on short-term profit, corporations could have saved good jobs by investing in new technology, modernizing their plants, and retraining their employees.

A more recent account of this period by Robert Reich (2007) describes the same developments. Reich differs in one important respect. He argues that major corporations were constrained by shifting market forces. When they fired workers, reduced wages, and sent production abroad, corporate leaders were doing what they needed to do in an increasingly competitive global economy. But, as they lost market power, Reich concludes, corporations gained political power. They were, for example, generally able to thwart legislation designed to protect the interests of workers in an era of rapid change.

Frank and Cook: Winner Take All

What do Placido Domingo, Miguel Cabrera, Leslie Moonves, Brad Pitt, and Danielle Steel have in common? They all compete successfully in what Frank and Cook (1995) call **winner-take-all markets**—fields in which rewards are heavily concentrated in the hands of a few top performers. The key to their extraordinary success is relative rather than absolute ability: They are a little better than the competition. For example, the Tigers' first baseman Cabrera is a little better than the guys who almost hit .300, but they are not going to be awarded contracts worth over $100 million. Many tenors are almost as talented as opera star Placido Domingo, but they will never sing starring roles in major opera houses, get lucrative recording contracts, or appear in televised concerts. Like the hundreds of actors who are almost as talented as Brad Pitt, most of these tenors will be lucky if they can even support themselves as performers.

In their book, *The Winner-Take-All Society* (1995), Frank and Cook assert that this phenomenon, well established in the entertainment industry and in professional sports, is rapidly spreading to other fields, such as business, law, journalism, medicine, and academia. They point to top executives like Leslie Moonves, CEO of CBS, whose annual pay is in the tens of millions. For reasons we do not have space to describe here, the authors are convinced that the extreme outcomes in winner-take-all competition have negative consequences for individuals and the economy as a whole.

The key question for Frank and Cook is why are winner-take-all markets proliferating? Some writers on executive compensation point to the cozy relationships between CEOs and the corporate boards that set their pay. Others emphasize the emergence, beginning in the 1980s, of "a culture of greed," tolerant of excessive rewards for those at the top. Frank and Cook stress technological and economic factors. They note that mass production, large-scale organization, modern communications, and vast markets favor large relative rewards at the top. For example, few authors can claim the millions Danielle Steel gets for one of her (less than profound) novels. But a publisher who commits large sums to producing and promoting mass-market fiction might be ill-advised to sign a writer who is not quite as popular as Steel. The largest corporations now operate on a scale that a few decades ago would have seemed extraordinary. With so much money riding on every decision, boards of directors, like CBS's, are not inclined to hire someone they think is *almost* as able as Moonves for a lot less. (Of course, anyone who reads the sports page or the business page of the newspaper knows that those who pay millions for top talent are often disappointed.)

Improvements in communications and transportation, along with growing international trade, expand the arena in which winner-take-all markets can flourish. Yet they are by no means universal. Frank and Cook cite evidence that the large relative rewards flowing to CEOs in the United States are exceptional. The pay gap between European and Japanese chief executives and their workers is modest by American standards. The authors suggest that what makes the United States different is the open competition for top slots in American corporations. In Europe and Japan—as in the United States until recently—executives typically spend their entire careers with a single firm and are promoted from within. Their corporate employers are not compelled to bid against one another for CEOs.

Much of Frank and Cook's argument rests on the idea that barriers to market competition have been falling. Corporations, sports teams, TV networks, universities, and other well-financed organizations are much more willing to raid one another's talent than they have been in the past. Federal deregulation of commercial aviation, trucking, banking, communications, the securities industry, and other sectors increases competition between firms and raises the bidding for top managers and professionals. Falling barriers to international trade and investment probably have the same effect.

Frank and Cook illuminate the market forces that are polarizing earnings, but their central concept of winner-take-all remains problematic. The notion works well enough for opera singers, ball players, and CEOs, but how much does it tell us about the more general phenomenon of rising inequality? The authors attempt to extend the idea to people they call "minor-league superstars"—successful doctors, dentists, lawyers, stockbrokers, accountants, and others who earn hundreds of thousands of dollars a year. They show that inequality of earnings among people in these occupations has been growing. But winner-take-all assumes that a few top players suck up a large share of the available rewards, leaving little for the less talented. It is difficult to imagine that this is the case among people in large, varied professions like law and accounting. On the other hand, the singers, CEOs, and doctors do have this much in common: Growing competition has raised the stakes and widened the range of compensation in their fields.

Another problem is this: Frank and Cook focus entirely on occupational earnings, as we have generally done in this chapter. But as we will learn in the next chapter, where we broaden our perspective on inequality, many of those with the highest incomes depend more on their investments than on jobs or professions.

Conclusion

This chapter emphasized the evolution of the occupational structure and its implications for the class system. We have seen the United States transformed from an agricultural society to an industrial society, built around the urban, goods-producing sectors of the economy, and finally to a postindustrial society, dominated by service-producing sectors from fast food to health care. (These shifts are summarized in Figure 3.1.) In the transition to an industrial society, the farm population dropped precipitously, while in the cities, a proletariat of industrial workers grew and a stratum of white-collar office workers appeared. During these years, a national capitalist class emerged.

As industrial society gave way to postindustrial society, farm employment was reduced to a tiny proportion of the labor force, the industrial proletariat contracted, white-collar employment swelled and diversified, and a growing stratum of service-oriented menial workers emerged. Both industrial and postindustrial society saw the displacement of independent entrepreneurs by salaried managers and professionals.

Postindustrial society drew what we described as sunny- and dark-side predictions. The sunny interpretations highlighted opportunities for well-trained professionals, technicians, and managers in the postindustrial economy. The dark interpretations emphasized the loss of good-paying blue-collar jobs associated with the decline of manufacturing. For the sunny-siders, the emerging service-producing sectors mean new jobs for hospital administrators, medical technicians, accountants, financial analysts, hotel managers, and computer specialists. For the dark-siders, the service-producing sectors mean employment in lowly service occupations for fast-food workers, janitors, and hospital orderlies. Both, as it turned out were right, because the occupational structure was polarizing. Across the economy, there were ample opportunities for well-trained professionals, managers, and technicians. But good blue-collar jobs were hard to find, especially in manufacturing, where production levels climbed as employment sank. For the unskilled and undereducated, service jobs were the likely alternative.

Recent trends in the distribution of earnings support the idea we introduced in Chapter 1 of a shift from an Age of Shared Prosperity (1946–1973) to the current Age of Growing Inequality (1973–?). Although this transition almost coincides with the transition from industrial to postindustrial society, we do not mean to identify one with the other. The developments we associate with postindustrial society have contributed to rising inequality, but we cannot say that inequality will inevitably continue to grow under postindustrial circumstances. After all, the years of industrial society (1900–1970) were not always years of shared prosperity.

The distribution of job earnings gives us a fairly precise way to measure the growing inequalities associated with economic change. The data reveal increased wage polarization, especially among men since the 1970s. At the top of the distribution, earnings have climbed rapidly—in the case of corporate CEOs, spectacularly. At the bottom, earnings have stagnated or even fallen.

The last sections of this chapter explored the possible reasons for the rising wage inequality, including economic restructuring; expanding trade;

changing technology; weakened wage-setting institutions, such as union and minimum wage protections; and deregulation. From Harrison and Bluestone (*The Great U-Turn*), we learned how business strategies designed to cut a corporation's total wage bill have contributed to the declining fortunes of many workers. Frank and Cook (*The Winner-Take-All Society*) showed how bigger, more competitive markets have reinforced the concentration of earnings at the very top.

In this chapter, we have focused on earnings, the part of income that comes from jobs, independent professional practices, and other self-employment. That misses some important sources of income. In the next chapter, we look at all sources of income, and instead of focusing on individual workers, we consider entire households. From this broadened perspective, we will reexamine the question of growing inequality.

KEY TERMS DEFINED IN THE GLOSSARY

agricultural society (see postindustrial society)
chief executive officer (CEO)
downsizing
earnings
industrial society (see postindustrial society)

minimum wage
new middle class/old middle class
occupational structure
outsourcing
pink-collar occupations
postindustrial society
productivity

service sectors
service workers
two-tier wage systems
wage-setting institutions
winner-take-all markets

SUGGESTED READINGS

Autor, David. 2014. "Skills, Education and the Rise of Earnings Inequality Among the 'Other 99 Percent.'" *Science*. 344:843–851.

MIT economist Autor and his colleagues have produced some of the most incisive research on the forces producing inequality in the labor market (see Bibliography).

Bell, Daniel. 1976. *The Coming of Post-Industrial Society*. New York: Basic Books.

Broad and optimistic interpretation of postindustrial society, emphasizing changes in technology, economic organization, and occupational structure.

Braverman, Harry. 1974. *Labor and Monopoly Capital*. New York: Monthly Review Press.

Classic work on the division of labor and the transformation of work in capitalist industrial societies. Challenge to Bell.

Clifford, Steven. 2017. *The CEO Pay Machine*. New York: Blue Rider.

A former CEO's examination of the factors behind the spiralling compensation of chief executives.

Ehrenreich, Barbara. 2001. *Nickel and Dimed: On (Not) Getting by in America*. New York: Henry Holt.

Ehrenreich took a series of low-wage jobs and tried to live on what she earned. An engaging, revealing account of her experience.

Frieden, Jeffry A. 2006. *Global Capitalism: Its Fall and Rise in the Twentieth Century*. New York: Norton.

The second half of this well-informed, gracefully written book covers the global trends that shaped the Age of Shared Prosperity and Age of Growing Inequality in the United States.

Mishel, Lawrence et al. 2012. *The State of Working America.* 12th ed. Ithaca, NY: Cornell University Press.

A wealth of information on trends in jobs, wages, and related topics. Updated editions published regularly. The material in this book is regularly updated at the Economic Policy Institute website (http://www.stateofworkingamerica .org/). The site also provides access to essential data series in downloadable format.

Reich, Robert. 2007. *Supercapitalism: The Transformation of Business, Democracy, and Everyday Life.* New York: Random House.

A lively account of the forces that have transformed the U.S. economy since the 1970s, contributing to social inequality and undemocratic politics.

Rodrik, Dani. 2011. *The Globalization Paradox: Democracy and the Future of the World Economy.* New York: Norton.

A well written, insightful assessment of globalization by a Harvard economist.

Wealth and Income

Money can't buy happiness, but it can make you awfully comfortable while you're being miserable.

Clare Boothe Luce

Procrustes, a giant of Greek mythology, had the bizarre habit of altering the stature of his houseguests to fit the length of the available bed by either stretching them or chopping inches off their legs. In the next few pages, we apply Procrustes' approach to the study of income. We have put together an imaginary parade in which the heights of the marchers are made proportional to their incomes. The parade is a convenient way of gaining an overview of the distribution of income, our first concern in this chapter. Later in this chapter we will consider the distribution of wealth and the growing inequality in the distribution of wealth and income.[1]

Income can be defined as monetary gain over a specified period of time—for example, $50,000 per year or $3,000 per month. (It should be distinguished from wealth, which is recorded at a *point in time,* such as $500,000 on January 1, 2019.) Job earnings, which we examined in the last chapter, are one source of income, but as we will see, there are other important sources of household income.

The Income Parade

The procession is organized as follows: All the 126 million households counted by the Census Bureau will be represented in the parade. In good Procrustean fashion, the marchers will be stretched or trimmed in proportion to their household's total income. Those representing households with the average annual income ($79,000) will be of average height. By this standard, a marcher representing a $140,000 household would be about 10 feet tall. A marcher from a $40,000 household would be close to 3 feet tall.

Because we want a quick impression of the distribution of income, we make the entire procession pass by our reviewing stand at a uniform pace, in exactly 1 hour. This will be rough on the marchers, but it has a particular advantage for us. At any moment, we are able to tell how much of the parade has gone by and how much is to come just by looking at our watches. Let's begin the parade with the shortest marchers, the income pygmies, and work up to the towering goliaths. (For an overview of the parade, see Figure 4.1.)

The procession opens on an odd note. In the first few seconds, we see nothing except a few wisps of hair moving across the horizon. It seems that the leaders of the parade are marching in a deep ditch. They do not appear above ground because they are business owners or investors who have suffered net income losses. Given the customary high failure rate of small businesses and periodic downturns in the stock and real estate markets, we should not be surprised at this sight, however peculiar.

Five Minutes: Poor. Next, we see people the size of a match or a cigarette. Five minutes into the parade, the marchers are Tiny people, a little over 1 foot tall; they survive on $15,000 a year. All who have gone by so far (and

---

[1] The income parade is based on pretax money income and draws on household income statistics from the Census Bureau's Current Population Survey for 2015; the Census Bureau's measures of household "well-being" at www.census.gov/hhes/well-being/; Internal Revenue Service income tax return statistics at www.irs.gov/uac/SOI-Tax-Stats-Individual-Income-Tax-Return-Form-1040-Statistics; the Labor Department's Consumer Expenditures survey at www.bls.gov/cex/tables.htm. We have also used Rose 2014.

Figure 4.1 The Income Parade

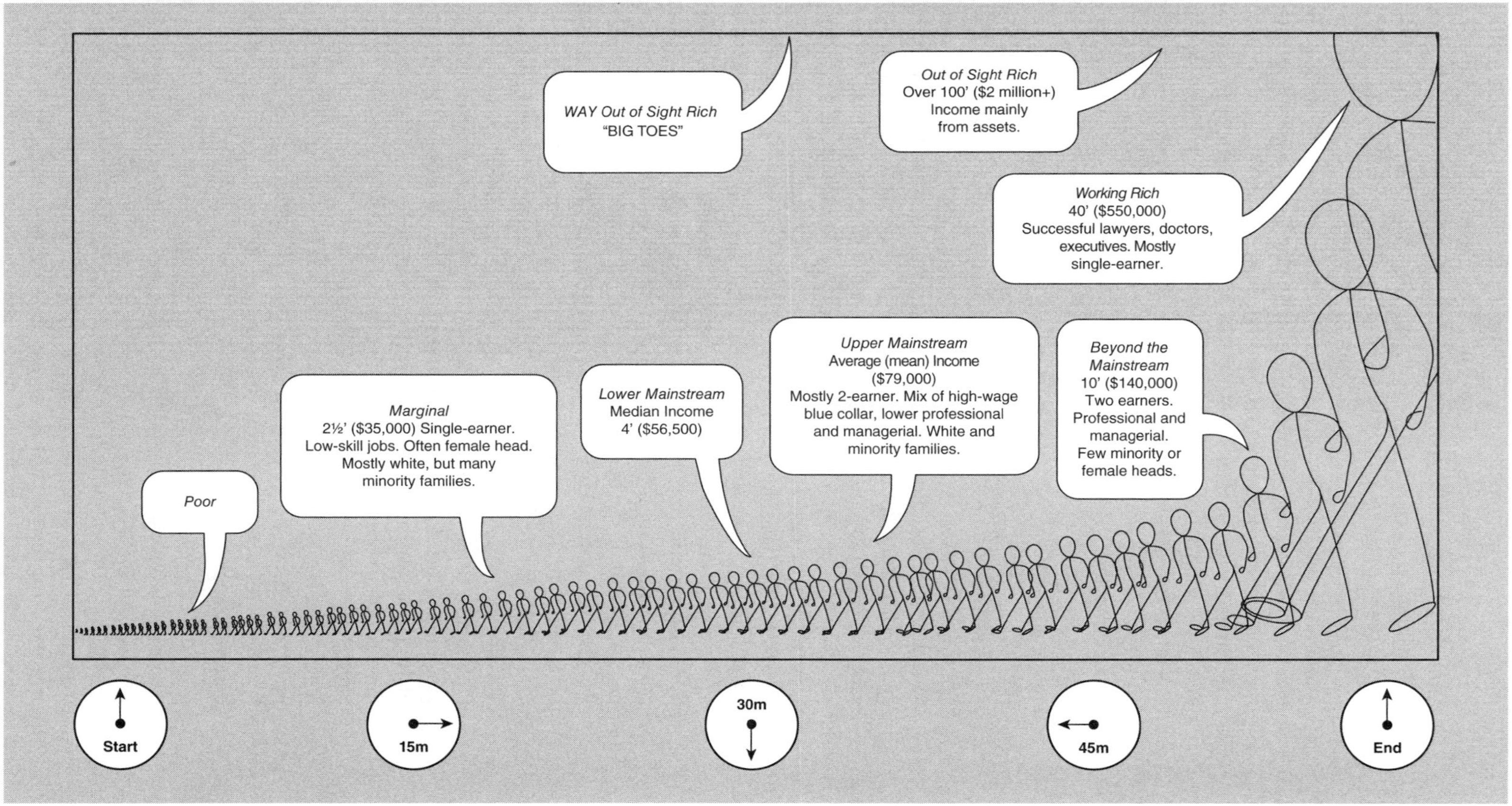

many who are to come) are "poor" by the federal government's official poverty standard. Daily life at this level can be precarious, especially for younger families. Many households report difficulty meeting their basic needs. They fall behind on bills, are unable to see a doctor or dentist when needed, and can't always put enough food on the table. They may live in fear of eviction.

There is a notable overrepresentation of women among the Tiny People. Many are female heads of families. Others are women living alone, often elderly. Many of the marchers at this early point in the parade receive part of their income from **government transfer** programs, such as Social Security, the **Earned Income Tax Credit** (EITC), disability payments, veterans benefits, or public assistance. (The EITC is a generous feature of the tax code designed to bolster the incomes of the working poor, especially those with children. We'll have more to say about it in Chapter 10.)

Blacks and Hispanics show up in disproportionate numbers in the first part of the parade. Nevertheless, the majority of the Tiny People are white and non-Hispanic. Actually, their single most common characteristic is that they are not employed because they are old or disabled, unable to find a job, studying, home with children, or not interested in working. But a substantial minority do work, and among them are many people who work full time without exceeding Tiny height; they simply are not paid much for their labor. A worker making $8 an hour (above the national minimum wage in 2017) and employed full time, all year, earned just $16,000.

Twenty Minutes: On the Margin of the Mainstream. As the procession moves on, the marchers get taller, but only very gradually, despite the breakneck pace we have imposed. After 20 minutes, one third of the parade has passed, and we are still seeing 2½ foot Little People who live on $35,000 a year. As their less than normal height suggests, these marchers are on the lower margin of the broad mainstream—above the official poverty line (about $24,000 for a family of four) but well below the average household income. We still see many female heads of households and retired people. But the typical household has one wage earner, who works at a low-skilled blue-collar, clerical, or service job.

What sort of lifestyle do these Little People buy with their money? The answer depends on factors including household size and stage of life. Families of three or four lead austere lives. Smaller households can enjoy greater comfort and security. Retirees may benefit from owning homes, free of both rent and mortgage obligations. Some households have problems meeting their basic housing, nutrition, and health needs on a consistent basis. They are significantly less likely to be homeowners than people at higher income levels. The Little People own cars, most often older models, purchased used. Because these households have little or no savings, even a few weeks of unemployment or an unexpected bill can threaten their standard of living.

Thirty to Forty Minutes: In the Mainstream. At exactly half past the hour, we catch sight of the 4-foot tall Midgets, who receive the median income of $56,500. (The **median**, by definition, is the midpoint in a distribution or, in this case, the exact middle of the parade.) A few minutes later, we notice marchers whom we can look in the eyes, assuming, of course, that we ourselves receive the mathematical average (**mean**) income of $79,000 and are therefore of average height. Though their numbers are falling off, minorities are still well represented in this part of the parade, but we do not often see female-headed households.

Many of these average-sized marchers have lower level managerial or professional positions. Others are technicians or skilled blue-collar workers. But most of the households represented here depend on the earnings of two workers. This is especially true of the black and Hispanic families marching in this part of the parade.

These average marchers live substantially better than the Little People we saw not so long ago. They are more likely to own substantial homes and drive late-model cars. The basics of food, housing costs, and transportation absorb only 60 percent of their budgets, so there is room for other necessities and some luxuries, such as family vacations. Nonetheless, they often feel financially pressed and are not much more likely than the Little People to have money left over at the end of the year.

Fifty to Fifty-Five Minutes: Beyond the Mainstream. Nearing the end of the parade now, we see marchers who would fascinate an NBA scout: They are lanky 10 to 12 footers. The "Lankies" are beyond the mainstream but not quite rich. Their $150,000 to $175,000 incomes allow them to live more gracefully and comfortably than the smaller people who went before. There is money for fashionable clothing, new cars, quality furniture, and perhaps some domestic help at home.

The Lankies typically hold professional and managerial jobs. Occasionally we see a high-earning blue-collar worker. But few households attain Lanky status with one good job. They are even more likely than the average-sized people to depend on the earnings of two working spouses. Female-headed families are rarely found here. Minority marchers have not vanished from the parade, but their ranks have thinned out since the middle of the parade.

The Final Minutes: The Rich. Now the procession has less than 2 minutes to run. Yet some of the most extraordinary moments lie ahead. If we look down the line at the people who have yet to pass, it appears as if a steep mountain peak is advancing on our reviewing stand. In the final seconds of the parade, we will see, in quick succession, 100-foot Giants; 400-foot Leviathans; and, finally, the Big Toes, who flit by in the last fraction of a second. Who are the Big Toes? People like Wall Street titans John Paulson and George Soros; tech executives Melissa Mayer and Mark Hurd; and, of course, President-sometime real estate developer Donald Trump. They have annual incomes in the tens of millions, hundreds of millions, or even billions of dollars. In 2014, 17,000 households reported incomes over $10 million to the IRS; 400 people reported incomes above $127 million. Their big toes, proportional to their towering incomes, are the size of office buildings.

The character of the marchers is changing rapidly. The Giants are typically members of the group we identified in Chapter 1 as "the working rich," whose incomes would drop sharply if they stopped working. They are generally highly successful professionals (most often lawyers and doctors or finance professionals), mid-ranking corporate executives, and the owners of prosperous small enterprises.

Next come the Leviathans and the Big Toes, all with incomes over $3 million. Two earner families are rarer here. Many of these people hold important jobs; among them, for example, are the ranking officers of large corporations. However, the greater part of income at this point in the parade does not come from jobs. These marchers own substantial business enterprises, commercial real estate, and valuable portfolios of stocks and bonds. Such income-producing assets, rather than salaries, account for their colossal incomes and overpowering stature. Their incomes do not necessarily depend on reporting to work every morning.

How do these lofty marchers spend their money? A typical urban-based family with a $1 million income owns two homes—a $2 million to $4 million apartment in the city and a substantial weekend house in the country. In addition to housing expenses, the family's annual budget includes $100,000 for domestics (including a nanny, if needed); $40,000 for private schools; and $100,000 for daily expenses, including food. This budget might sound modest to the wealthy family (net worth: $50 million) described in a recent book on the rich (Frank 2007:149). Among the family's expenses were the following:

Mortgages on two homes: $400,000

Domestics and personal assistants: $500,000

Gardening and pool maintenance: $140,000

Cars: $300,000

Air charters: $350,000

Club memberships: $225,000

Charities: $500,000

Political contributions: $61,000

Lessons From the Parade

This chapter elaborates on some of the themes introduced by the procession. But before going on, we should pause to review what we have just seen and list the general lessons that can be drawn from the parade.

1. *Many Little People, Few Giants.* Our most general impression, confirmed by Figure 4.1, is an extremely gradual increase in income levels until a break point late in the procession. At half past the hour, we were still looking at people who are 4 feet tall. The slow climb continued until the final minutes of the parade, when heights rose abruptly as the small numbers of Americans with very high incomes, and finally colossal incomes, strode by. Just 12 percent of households have incomes over $150,000. A tiny fraction of a percent exceed $1 million.

2. *Living Standards.* The parade tells us something about the relative welfare of different segments of the population. It took about 20 minutes before we caught sight of the $35,000 Little People and 50 minutes before the $150,000 Lankies appeared. The parade was in its last seconds when we saw $500,000 Giants. We saw that many families at the $35,000 level, especially younger families,

could not afford to own a home, while families at the $120,000 level were quite comfortably housed, and families earning $2,000,000 might own two luxury residences.

3. *Job(s)*. The number of workers in each household was a critical determinant of its place in the parade. At the beginning of the parade, we noted that many households had no job income. The Little People households that followed typically had one wage earner. Mainstream households usually depended on two workers. At the very end of the parade, households with just one income earner were becoming more frequent.

4. *Sources of Income*. Jobs are the main source of income for most households. However, during the parade, we noted shifts in the relative importance of different income sources. For many of the early marchers, government transfer payments, such as Social Security, and veterans benefits were crucial. In the broad middle of the parade, households depended on wage or salary income from jobs or, less commonly, on entrepreneurial income from small businesses and professional practices. In the final moments of the procession, we saw marchers who are largely supported by their wealth in the form of income-producing assets such as stocks, bonds, and rental property.

5. *Occupation*, the marchers showed us, is a key determinant of household income, but not the overpowering factor we might have anticipated. From the reviewing stand, we saw low-skilled blue-collar, clerical, and service workers gradually give way to more skilled workers and then to managers and professionals. But there was considerable overlapping of occupational categories. We saw managers relatively early in the parade, and a few blue-collar workers toward the end. One reason for this is that a two-income, blue-collar household can often outearn a manager or professional who does not have a working spouse. Another is that occupational pay scales overlap, even for very different occupations. For example, the top 25 percent of electricians earn more than the bottom 25 percent of aerospace engineers.

6. *Women's Shifting Role* was one of the defining features of the parade. At the beginning of the parade, we saw many older women and female heads of families. Among married-couple families some 20 minutes into the parade, wives without jobs were typical. But among the more prosperous households toward the end of the parade, working wives were the rule. Only in the final moments of the parade did women's employment rates decline.

7. *Minorities*. Blacks and Hispanics were at a disadvantage in the parade. They were overrepresented among the early marchers, often by female heads of households. On the other hand, given their traditional position in American society, their strong representation in the middle of the parade was probably surprising to many observers.

8. *Income and the Class Structure.* The parade suggests that the relationship between the distribution of income and the class structure is clear at the extremes but somewhat blurred in the middle. We can think about the problem in terms of the class model we introduced in Chapter 1. The people at the very beginning of the parade, who have no employment income or work at very low-wage jobs, correspond to our underclass and working poor. The towering marchers we saw in the last 2 minutes of the parade represent the top of the upper-middle class (our working rich) and the capitalist class. But in the middle of the procession, we found a surprising mix of upper-middle class, middle-class, and working-class marchers.

The Distribution of Income

Table 4.1, based on the annual Census Bureau survey, confirms our broad impression of the income parade. About one third of all households can be described as low income (under $35,000), 42 percent fall into a broad middle-income range (from $35,000 to $100,000), and the remaining 26 percent have higher incomes (over $100,000). When we look separately at family households (which quite often have two earners), the pattern is not radically different, as the second column indicates. One in four families survive on less than $35,000; about 43 percent are in the middle range; 33 percent have incomes over $100,000. For both family and non-family households, incomes over $200,000 are rare.

Table 4.1 Household Income, 2015		
Income	All Households (%)	Family Households (%)
Under $25,000	22	15
$25,000–$35,000	10	9
$35,000–$50,000	13	12
$50,000–$75,000	17	17
$75,000–$100,000	12	14
$100,000–$200,000	20	25
$200,000 and over	6	8
Total	100	100
Median Income *Number (in millions)*	*$56,500* *125.8*	*$72,200* *82.2*

Note: Households include family households, individuals living alone, and unrelated persons sharing housing.

Ethnicity and family structure create variants on this basic pattern. About one third of minority families have incomes below $35,000, one third fall between $35,000 and $75,000, and one third are above $75,000. The key to this distribution is the large income gap between families headed by females and those headed by married couples, as can be seen in Figure 4.2. Of course, female-headed families are more prevalent among minority households—reflecting in part the economic strains to which they are subjected: 44 percent of black families, 25 percent of Hispanic families, and 16 percent of white families are female-headed. Nonetheless, most female-headed families are non-Hispanic white.

In this section and in the income parade, we have singled out female-headed families. What about male-headed families—that is, families headed by single men? They are less significant for our analysis because they are uncommon, less than 5 percent of all families, and their median income ($53,700) is close to that of one-income married-couple families without working wives.

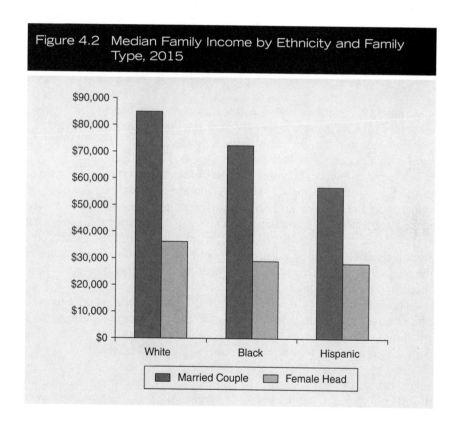

Figure 4.2 Median Family Income by Ethnicity and Family Type, 2015

Sources of Income

In the income parade, we noted shifts in the predominant sources of income. Table 4.2 traces this tendency. The story this table tells is simple but important. Wages and salaries provide most income for most people. But for the bottom 40 percent of households, a big chunk of income comes from

Table 4.2 Sources of Income

In percent

Average Income	Income Group	Wage and Salary	Small Business	Capitalist	Government	Other	Total
$25,000	Bottom fifth	53	6	1	38	2	100
$47,400	Second fifth	57	3	1	34	5	100
$69,700	Middle fifth	63	2	2	24	9	100
$103,700	Fourth fifth	69	2	3	14	11	100
$265,000	Top fifth	60	11	16	5	8	100
$1,571,600	Top 1%	35	23	38	1	3	100

Source: Congressional Budget Office 2016.

Note: Based on pretax income. Small Business = self-employment income, including business, profession, farm, partnerships, etc.; Capitalist = interest, dividends, capital gains, rent, estate, and trust; Government = government transfers including Social Security, public assistance, veterans benefits, in kind benefits such as food stamps, etc.; Other= mainly, pensions and other retirement income.

government transfers such as Social Security, veterans benefits, and public assistance. At successively higher levels, capitalist income (stock dividends, interest rents, and the like) and business profits provide increasing proportions of total income, until they exceed wage and salary income.

Aside from parades, the distribution of income is typically analyzed in one of two standard formats: (1) the distribution of households (or families) across ranges of income, and (2) the distribution of income shares among ranked segments of the population. Table 4.1 is a clear example of the first approach, which was the basic source for the income parade. The income shares approach could be called a slices-of-pie distribution. It conceives of the total income of all households as a national income pie, which has been sliced into pieces ranging from stingy to generous.

Figure 4.3 depicts the share of the total income pie that goes to each fifth or **quintile** of households. The poorest quintile, for example, receives 3 percent of aggregate income. (Obviously, if the distribution of income were perfectly equal, each quintile would receive exactly 20 percent.)

Our pie reveals a remarkable concentration of income.[2] The income share claimed by the richest fifth of households is slightly more than that of the other 80 percent of households. The concentration of income at the very top is even greater than our pie distribution suggests. The top 1 percent of households alone absorbs 20 percent of all personal income, as we will show later in this chapter.

[2] The data used for Figure 4.3 was adjusted by the Census Bureau for family size and composition, assuming, for example, that $30,000 represents a higher standard of living for a two-person family than a four-person family. This adjustment had only minimal effect on the distribution (U.S. Census 2016:9).

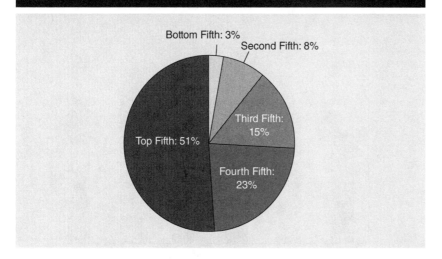

Figure 4.3 Shares of Aggregate Income Received by Fifths of Households, 2015

Bottom Fifth: 3%

Second Fifth: 8%

Third Fifth: 15%

Top Fifth: 51%

Fourth Fifth: 23%

Taxes and Transfers: The Government as Robin Hood?

To what extent does the government play a Robin Hood role, evening out inequalities? The household income statistics we have been looking at to this point don't reflect taxes, nor do they, on other side of the ledger, account for certain government programs that bolster the spending capacity of low-income families. Would the distribution of income look very different if we took into consideration everything the government does?

We do have a federal personal income tax that is **progressive** in its effect—that is, people with higher incomes pay a greater proportion of their total income to the Internal Revenue Service than do those with lower incomes. The progressive tendency of the federal income tax is reinforced by the Earned Income Tax Credit (EITC), a notable provision of the tax code designed to help the working poor, who may receive substantial payments from the IRS in excess of any taxes owed. Also progressive is the federal estate tax, levied on the assets of wealthy decedents.

However, other taxes operate in the opposite direction—that is, they impose a greater burden on the poor than the rich. Chief among these **regressive taxes** are the sales taxes that are collected by states and localities. A sales tax applies the same tax rate to a pair of children's shoes whether the purchasing parent is a low-wage worker or a millionaire. Because the low-wage worker spends a much higher proportion of her family's income on consumer items than does the millionaire (who is likely to reserve some income for savings and investment), she loses a higher percentage of her income to the sales tax than the millionaire. Formally, sales taxes are flat, but, in effect, regressive. The Social Security payroll tax, which accounts for most of the federal taxes paid by low-income people, is also quite regressive

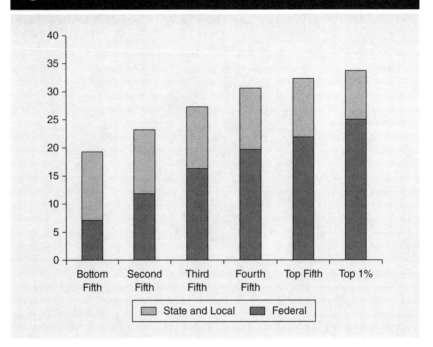

Figure 4.4 Effective Federal, State, and Local Tax Rates

Percent of household income

Note: Includes all federal, state, and local taxes on personal and corporate income, payroll taxes, sales taxes, estate taxes, and excise taxes.

Source: Citizens for Tax Justice 2016.

because it is not levied on earnings beyond an annually adjusted limit (about $127,200 in 2017). As a result, the proportion of pretax income paid in Social Security taxes would be about 6 percent on earnings of $60,000 but only 1.3 percent on earnings of $600,000.[3]

The combined effect of federal taxes is progressive, while the impact of state and local taxes is regressive. The net effect of all taxation is modestly progressive, as can be seen in Figure 4.4. The dark segments of the bars, representing federal taxation, show a steady progressive rise with income, though the difference between the upper quintiles and the top 1 percent is not great. The light segments, representing state and local taxation, actually shrink with rising income. Note that the poorest fifth pays a significantly higher proportion to states and localities than does the top 1 percent. The chart is based on **effective tax rates**, the proportion of income people actually pay in taxes, after various deductions, exemptions, and credits.

---

[3] There is some justification for this disparity, in that, when they retire, lower income workers can expect to get higher Social Security benefits relative to their earnings than higher income workers. However, the federal government has been using Social Security revenues for meeting its general expenses and not saving to meet the looming retirement needs of the baby-boom generation. At some point, federal policy makers will be compelled to make some painful adjustments in taxes or benefits.

Aside from the redistributive effect of taxes, the government can play Robin Hood through transfer payments and noncash benefits. Because transfer payments, such as Social Security and public assistance, are counted as part of cash income, they are, unlike taxes, already reflected in the income data we saw in the last section. But the value of noncash benefits, such as food stamps and Medicare (the federal health care program for the elderly), is not included in the income data.

The influence of transfer payments is generally progressive for the obvious reason that they often are specifically designed to help the poor and for the less obvious reason that a large share of transfer income goes to the elderly, who tend to be at the lower end of the pretransfer income distribution. The same can be said of noncash benefits. In general, transfer payments and noncash benefits raise the living standard of poorer households but do not dramatically alter the overall structure of economic inequality.

So how effective is the government as Robin Hood overall? Figure 4.5 estimates the combined effects of taxes, transfers, and benefits on the income shares. The "before" shares are based on pretax incomes stripped of government transfer payments, such as Social Security. The "after" shares were produced by adding in the value of cash transfers and noncash benefits and deducting all federal and state income taxes. In other words, we are looking at income inequality before and after the government Robin Hood has completed his work. The differences in income shares, as defined here, are modest in the broad middle, but notable for the top and bottom fifths. In particular, the share of the poorest fifth, though it remains tiny, is significantly higher than it would be without taxes and government programs. Despite its reduced share, the richest fifth still claims a little short of half of all personal income.

How Many Poor?

Our discussion of income distribution and redistribution has skirted an important issue: How many people have such low incomes that they can be considered poor? The easiest answer is based on official government statistics, which recorded 43.1 million poor Americans in 2015, about 15 percent of the population. However, any count of the poor depends on the standard or definition of poverty used by the counters. Many researchers would adjust these figures upward or downward because they are skeptical of the official standard, which was adopted in the 1960s and is widely regarded as inadequate. We take up the problem of defining poverty in Chapter 10, so that readers will be able to draw their own conclusions.

Women and the Distribution of Household Income

One lesson we drew from the income parade concerned the way women's situations changed with rising income. The elderly women we saw early in the parade were typically widows older than 75. Because women traditionally have had lower earnings and shorter, less continuous work histories,

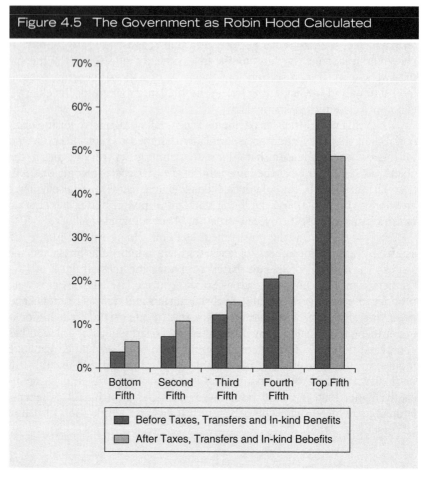

Figure 4.5   The Government as Robin Hood Calculated

| | Before Taxes, Transfers and In-kind Benefits |
| | After Taxes, Transfers and In-kind Bebefits |

Source: Congressional Budget Office 2016.

they have weaker personal claims on retirement income. Older women often depend on a husband's pension or Social Security check and can lose all or part of that income in the event of their divorce or his death. Since women tend to outlive men, they are more likely to survive long enough to use up their savings.

Although the more generous Social Security benefits of recent years have sharply reduced poverty among the elderly, older women living alone continue to have high poverty rates. Among women over 65, just 4 percent of those living with husbands are poor, compared to 15 percent of women not currently married.

Largely as a result of elevated divorce rates and the growing proportion of children born to single mothers, nearly 20 percent of all family households are now female headed—that is, not dual or male headed—compared with 10 percent in 1970. Among families with children, 26 percent are female-headed. The women who head these households face multiple disadvantages. Child care responsibilities make it difficult to work full time. Most single, divorced, or separated women who are raising children receive only limited child support. Generally, the economic situation of men improves after a marital separation, whereas that of women typically deteriorates (Hoffman 1977; U.S. Census Bureau 1994:33; U.S. Census 2011).

According to a U.S. Census report on custodial parents in 2009, (1) over 80 percent of custodial parents are women; (2) most custodial mothers did not receive child support that year; (3) among those who did, the average annual amount was only $3,700 or a little over $300 per month; (4) the great majority of custodial mothers worked—many full time, year round; (5) nonetheless, 30 percent of custodial mothers and their children were surviving on incomes below the official poverty line (U.S. Census 2011).

Women who go to work to support their families often find themselves in the generally lower paying pink-collar jobs described in Chapter 3. Although, as we noted there, women's earnings have advanced relative to men's, even women employed full time still lag well behind similarly employed men. Of course, responsibilities at home, especially for single mothers of young children, prevent many women from working full time, year round. (Single mothers and their families do better in countries where the state provides free or low-cost child care.)

Working wives face similar problems in the labor market and a similar clash between nurturer and breadwinner roles. Nonetheless, the percentage of married women in the labor force has been rising since the 1920s. From 1960 to 2000, the labor force participation rate of wives doubled.

Most married women still earn less than their partners do, though the gap has been closing. More important, in an era when men's earnings are declining at the lower end of the labor market and stagnating in the middle, women's earnings have become crucial for family incomes. Just how crucial is shown in Table 4.3, which examines wives' rising contribution to the incomes of married couples with children. Without the growth in wives' earnings, often as a result of simply working longer hours, the inflation adjusted **real incomes** of such families would have declined 15.6 percent for the bottom fifth and more or less stagnated for the second and middle fifths over a quarter century period. For higher income families, wives' rising earnings added to already significant gains. Thus, the incomes of families in the top fifth rose 70 percent over this period but would only have increased 53 percent had wives' contribution remained fixed.

How have the changing roles of women and men affected the broad trend toward increasing inequality? The increased earnings of wives have bolstered the strained incomes of many two-earner families toward the lower end of the income distribution, and thus tends to equalize household earnings. But their equalizing influence is offset by the "assortative mating" that increasingly matches well-educated, high-earning men and women with each other, producing bigger and bigger family incomes toward the high end of the distribution. This tendency is evident in the prevalence of dual-earner couples in the last minutes of the income parade and in the extraordinary increase, illustrated above, in the contribution of wives to the growth of incomes in the top fifth. Finally, the precarious finances of female-headed families, especially those with children, have depressed incomes in the lower fifths. The increase in female-headed families contributed powerfully to growing income inequality. Thus, from opposite ends of the income distribution, the rising numbers of female heads and those we might call power couples contribute to inequality. Our general answer to the question posed at the beginning of this paragraph is that changing gender roles have helped to create an Age of Growing Inequality (Esping-Andersen 2007; Karoly and Burtless 1995; Neckerman and Torche 2007).

The Distribution of Wealth

We now turn from the distribution of income to the distribution of wealth. We have already distinguished these two concepts: *Income* is *the inflow of money over a period of time*. **Wealth** is *the value of assets held at a point in time*. One year's wages, interest, and **dividends**, such as might be reported on a federal income tax return, are examples of income. The value of real estate, bank accounts, and stock shares someone owns on, say, December 31, 2019, are examples of wealth.

Wealth, in a sense, is nothing more than accumulated income (assuming, of course, that income is not spent, but saved). True, but this underestimates the significance of wealth as a distinct dimension of class inequality. Income allows us to meet our daily necessities. Wealth enhances what Max Weber called "life chances" in more basic ways. It provides safety net protection against a sudden drop in living standard in the event of job loss or other emergency. Most families do not hold significant wealth and would be in difficult straits if they missed 1 or 2 months' paychecks. Wealth can be converted into home ownership, business ownership, or a college education. As we saw earlier in this chapter, people with very high incomes typically derive most of their income from wealth in the form of stock dividends, bond interest, commercial real estate rents, and other capitalist sources.

Wealth provides a critical mechanism for the intergenerational transmission of inequality. As we will see in Chapter 8, a significant proportion of the wealthiest people in America inherited family fortunes. On a more modest level, the high school student who knows that there is money in the bank to pay for her college education and the young couple who purchase a house with help from their parents are the beneficiaries of the wealth accumulated by previous generations. Most Americans can expect, at best, a modest inheritance. From this perspective, it is hardly surprising that upwardly

Table 4.3 Wives' Contribution to Change in Family Income, 1979 to 2006

Increase in Family Income	Percent Change				
	Bottom Fifth	Second Fifth	Middle Fifth	Fourth Fifth	Top Fifth
Actual increase	4.2	12.5	23.4	34.4	70.2
Increase without wives' additional contribution	−15.6	2.8	2.6	15.0	53.2

Source: Modified from Mishel et al. 2009:Table 1.22.

Note: Refers to married couple families with children and head of household ages 25 to 54.

Table 4.4   Average Net Worth of Households, 2013

Households	Average Net Worth
Bottom 40%	–$10,800
Middle Fifth	$68,100
Fourth Fifth	$236,400
Top Fifth	$2,260,300
Top 1%	$18.6 million

Source: Wolff 2014.

mobile African Americans with comfortable incomes lag far behind white peers in wealth and are therefore less able to help their children and more vulnerable in economic downturns (Oliver and Shapiro 1995).

Wealth is measured in two ways: **gross assets** and **net worth**. The first refers to the total value of the assets someone owns. Net worth, a more realistic concept, is the value of assets owned minus the amount of debt owed. The net worth of most households, according to a Federal Reserve survey summarized in Table 4.4, is modest. The average net worth of the middle fifth of households is only $68,100. The average of the bottom 40 percent of households is actually negative—that is, their debts exceed the value of whatever they own. Most households own little in the way of investment assets, such as stocks, bonds, or commercial real estate. These assets boost the net worth of the top 1 percent to $18.6 million. But most families derive the greater part of their net worth from three asset types: home equity, car equity,[4] and bank deposits.

We can distinguish three broad classes of wealth holders[5]:

1. *The Nearly Propertyless Class.* About 40 percent of households, with net worths under $50,000 in 2010 dollars. The majority have a negative net worth, and few are worth more than $10,000. Most have automobiles and many own their homes. But the **nearly propertyless class** is a debt-ridden class: What they owe is quite high relative to the value of their assets. Younger families and most African American and Hispanic households fall into this **wealth class**. This class was especially hard hit by the Great Recession of 2008–2009.

2. *The Nest-Egg Class.* About 50 percent of households, with net worths ranging from $50,000 to $1 million. The families in the **nest-egg class** might be described as savers rather than

---

[4] Home and car equity refer to the value of the assets less the amount owed on them.

[5] This discussion draws on Bricker et al. 2014; Wolff 2014 and 2016; U.S. Census 2016; and Mishel et al. 2012.

investors. Their debt is modest. They accumulate retirement savings in IRAs and 401k accounts. Some hold other financial assets, such as CDs and stocks. But this class's largest single asset is likely to be the home they live in. Since net worth tends to rise with age, families in this class are, on average, older than those in the first class.

3. *The Investor Class.* Just 10 percent of households, worth more than $1 million. The households in the **investor class** own most of the privately held investment assets and typically control portfolios of stocks, mutual funds, and bonds. Many members of this class have interests in small businesses, professional practices, and commercial real estate. Many own second homes. On the other hand, equity in homes contributes a modest proportion of their net worth. This class is relatively free of debt. Although this class controls most of the total of gross assets owned by households, it is responsible for a small proportion of total liabilities.

As the privileged finances of our top class suggest, wealth is highly concentrated—much more concentrated than income. For example, in 2013, the highest income 1 percent received about 21 percent of aggregate income, while the wealthiest 1 percent of households owned about 37 percent of net worth. The concentration of wealth at the top is so great that the top 1 percent now holds more net worth than the bottom 90 percent (Table 4.5).

Another important conclusion that can be drawn from studies of wealth is that investment assets are much more concentrated than consumption-oriented assets such as automobiles[6] and owner-occupied homes. As Table 4.6 indicates, ownership of corporate stock and mutual fund shares, investment real estate, and small-business equity is almost entirely concentrated in the hands of the top 10 percent of wealth holders.

Table 4.5 Concentration of Wealth, 2013

In percent

Wealth Group	Share of Aggregate Net Worth
Top 1%	36.7
Next 9%	40.4
Bottom 90%	22.9
Total	100.0

Source: Wolff 2014.

---

[6] The vehicle share of the top 1 percent was unavailable for 2013, but has varied little over time. The figure given here is based on previous surveys. The 10 percent and 90 percent shares are from 2013.

Table 4.6 Concentration of Key Assets, 2013

In percent

	Share Held by		
	Top 1%	Top 10%	Bottom 90%
Widely Held Assets			
Principal Residence	9.8	40.8	59.2
Bank Deposits, CDs, Money Mkt. Funds	24.8	67.2	32.8
Retirement Accounts	17.8	34.8	65.2
Vehicles	6.5	24.0	76.0
Concentrated Assets			
Stocks and Mutual Funds	49.8	90.9	9.1
Trusts	49.5	83.5	16.5
Business equity	62.8	93.8	6.2
Investment Real Estate	33.7	77.8	22.2

Source: Wolff 2014; www.federalreserve.gov/econres/files/BulletinCharts.pdf.

The Changing Distribution of Wealth

Sometime in the early 1970s, a great shift began in the distributions of wealth and income, paralleling the growing disparities in job earnings we examined in the last chapter. We recognized this transformation in the distinction we made earlier between the post–World War II Age of Shared Prosperity and the current Age of Growing Inequality. The trend toward increasing inequality in the distribution of wealth was especially notable in the 1980s and 1990s.

By 2010, in the wake of the Great Recession, the average net worth of families in the bottom four fifths of the population was 3 percent less in real terms than it had been in 1983.[7] Over the same period, the average net worth of families in the top fifth climbed 80 percent. At the top of the wealth pyramid, the combined net worth of the 400 richest Americans more than doubled in the 1980s and doubled again in the 1990s. By 2007, the neediest of the 400 was worth more than a billion dollars and their combined net worth was a figure comparable in magnitude to the entire federal budget. Although many of the 400 fortunes were squeezed by the stock-market decline that accompanied the recession, by 2012, their combined net worth had bounced back to about what it was in 2007. Incredibly, the 400 were,

---

[7] All comparisons over time in the section are based on real, inflation-adjusted dollar values.

by then, collectively worth as much as 9 million average Americans (*Forbes* 1996, 2001a, 2006, 2012; Kennickell 2009:Table A1; Saez and Zucman 2014:3).

Figure 4.6, which we previewed in Chapter 1, traces the proportion of aggregate net worth held by the top 1 percent. The curve assumes a familiar U-shape trajectory, bottoming out in the 1970s and then climbing steeply in the 1980s. By the 1990s, the top 1 percent held one third or more of aggregate net worth—more, as we have seen, than the bottom 90 percent of households, and probably more than at any time since the 1930s.

The increasing concentration of wealth in the Age of Growing Inequality was accompanied by a leap in the number of wealthy people. In other words, at the same time that the distribution of wealth was becoming more and more unequal, the expansion in total wealth in the economy left room for the creation of new fortunes. In just 1 decade, from 1995 to 2004, the number of families worth over $25 million doubled. By 2016, there were 156,000 households in this category.[8]

What accounts for these remarkable increases in the concentration of wealth and the number of wealthy families in recent decades? Many new fortunes were rooted in information technology, the Internet, finance, and other high growth sectors of the economy. Globalization generated new wealth and new opportunities. What has been described as "a river of money coursing around the world . . . looking for outlets" fed the growth of finance (Frank 2007:41). Since the 1980s, a generally rising stock market had swelled the fortunes of those who were able to invest in it. (Although the 2008–2009 stock market crash erased half the market value of the largest corporations, the market gradually rebounded to pre-crash levels. By late 2013, the inflation adjusted value of the 500 stocks in the S&P 500 Index was 5 times what it had been in early 1980—a potential bonanza for anyone who had held stocks over that period.)[9] Over this same period, declining tax rates on high incomes allowed affluent households to retain (and reinvest) more of what they made.

Finally, many readers of this text will be aware of another trend that is contributing to growing inequality of wealth: student loan debt. In 2013, 38 percent of young families (head under age 40) had educational debt. From 2001 to 2013, the average amount owed by such families rose 70 percent to $29,800. Educational debt is rising as a proportion of all debt. But not all households are affected. Student loan debt is common among households in the lower 50 percent of households but rare among the wealthiest 10 percent (Bricker et al. 2014; Mishel et al. 2012:403–404).

The Changing Distribution of Income

The distribution of income has followed a path similar to the distribution of wealth. During the Age of Shared Prosperity, family incomes at all levels were

---

[8] Frank 2007:2, and the CNBC, Millionaire Survey (cnbc.com/millionaire-survey/). The 1995–2004 figure is based on 2004 dollars.

[9] Calculated from data assembled by Robert Schiller at www.econ.yale.edu/~shiller/data.htm

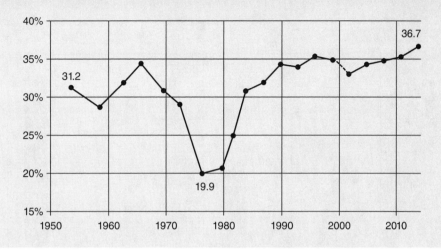

Figure 4.6   Share of Net Worth Held by Top 1% of Households

Source: Wolff 2002 and Wolff 2014. Data points before and after 2000 not compatible.

growing at a brisk pace and gradually becoming more equal. After the early 1970s, income growth tapered off, and the fortunes of American families began to diverge.

The transition from the Age of Shared Prosperity to the contemporary Age of Growing Inequality can be seen most clearly in Figure 4.7. The bars in this figure represent the percentage increase in real incomes at each level during the 25-year periods before and after 1975. Comparing the side-by-side panels for these two periods, we can see a stark reversal of the image. Two conclusions are obvious: (1) Income growth was broadly shared in the first period but steeply stratified in the second, and (2) growth was fastest at the bottom in the first period and fastest at the top in the second period. The lines that cut across the two panels represent the growth of the national economy relative to the population (Gross Domestic Product/Capita) in each 25-year period. Remarkably, the per capita expansion was nearly the same, close to 75 percent, in both periods, but the benefits of growth were being distributed very differently after 1975.

Imagine the shifting fortunes of three families under the conditions described by Figure 4.7. The first family, in the poorest fifth, sees its income more than double (120 percent growth) in the first period but practically stagnate in the second. The next family, in the middle fifth, undergoes a similar but less dramatic shift from high growth to slow growth. The third family, in the privileged top 5 percent, finds moderate gains in the first period and a doubling of income in the second.

John F. Kennedy liked to say, "A rising tide lifts all boats." The phrase describes family incomes in the Age of Shared Prosperity, but not in the Age of Growing Inequality.

Figure 4.8 focuses more narrowly on the income share of the top 1 percent, which absorbed about 13 percent of all household income in 1950. This

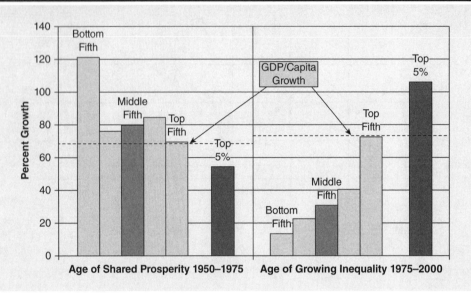

Sources: Census Bureau and Commerce Dept. Bureau of Economic Analysis data at http://research.stlouis fed.org/fred2/data/GDPC1.txt.

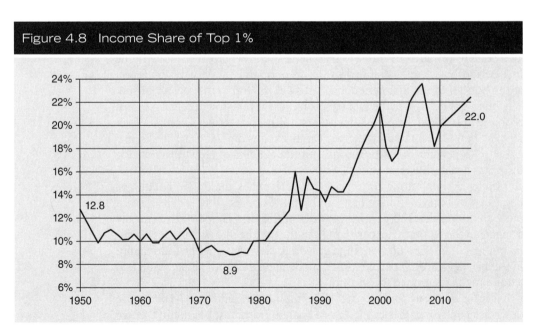

Source: Piketty and Saez 2003, data updated at http://elsa.berkeley.edu/~saez/.

Note: Includes capital gains.

figure had been falling more or less continuously since the late-1930s and continued to do so until (as we might guess) the 1970s, when it started to climb again, reaching 24 percent in 2007. The 2008–2009 market crash took a big bite out of incomes at this level, but the 1 percent bounced back. In 2015, they were claiming a little more than 1 of every 5 dollars of household income.

Although the growth of family incomes in recent years has been slower and more concentrated, a rising proportion of families have been able to attain relative affluence. As Figure 4.9 shows, the percentage of households with incomes greater than $150,000 (in inflation adjusted dollars) has climbed fairly steadily since the 1960s. The top 1 percent has not wholly monopolized the material benefits of a rising GDP. A broader range of relatively privileged households, roughly corresponding to the upper-middle class, has also benefited.

Income Dynamics

The three hypothetical families whose fortunes we traced above had one thing in common: Their relative positions in the income distribution were stable, even when their incomes were changing. We assumed, for example, that the family that started in the bottom quintile was still there several decades later. We almost automatically make this kind of assumption when we talk about shifts in the distribution of income. But the government income surveys we have been analyzing in this chapter do not follow families over time. They are, in effect, periodic snapshots of the income distribution, which tell us nothing about the degree to which families are moving up or down relative to one another.

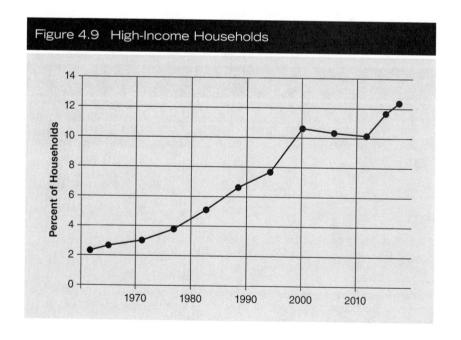

Figure 4.9   High-Income Households

Following the incomes of individual families over time is difficult and expensive. The few studies that have done so reveal a surprising amount of movement. From one year to the next, a family's income may change abruptly because someone lost a job or a spouse rejoined the labor force. Over longer periods, earnings tend to expand with experience and successive promotions. For example, during an academic career, the salary of a college professor might double in real-dollar terms. Even the earnings of low-skilled workers tend to rise over time, though more slowly than those of professionals.

Table 4.7, based on a study that has followed several thousand families over 3 decades, shows considerable movement ("income mobility") in the distribution of family income. In the 1990s, for example, approximately 30 percent of families moved to a higher income quintile and about the same proportion moved down. But the table also reveals a gradual slowing of income mobility since the 1970s: Fewer families are moving up or down; an increasing proportion end the decade where they began. Closer examination of the data from all 3 decades shows that most movement, in either direction, was short range, from one quintile to an adjacent quintile. Only rarely do families rocket from the bottom quintile to the top or plunge from the top to the bottom in the course of a decade.

Changing Tax Rates

The trend toward greater income inequality since the 1970s was magnified by regressive changes in the federal tax system. (Census Bureau income figures are, as noted earlier, pretax.) In general, rates have come down for households at all levels, but the reductions have been most dramatic for the wealthiest. The top tax rate on personal income (the top bracket or marginal rate)[10] plunged from 77 percent to as little as 28 percent. Corporate and inheritance taxes, whose main effects are felt by the wealthy, were also reduced. At the same time, payroll taxes, paid largely by lower- and middle-income workers, were jacked up. The one change that ran against

Table 4.7 Family Income Mobility				
	Change in Income Quintile (in Percent)			
Years	Up	Stable	Down	Total
1970s	33.0	35.7	31.3	100.0
1980s	32.4	37.0	30.6	100.0
1990s	30.1	40.4	29.4	100.0

Source: Author's analysis of Table 2.3, Mishel et al. 2007:106.

---

[10] Increasing marginal rates on personal income are imposed over specified ranges of income. A high-income household might, for example, pay 20 percent or so on the first $50,000 of income, but 40 percent on income beyond the first $400,000.

the generally regressive tide was the Earned Income Tax Credit, described earlier, which was designed to help the working poor.[11]

Tax rates on the rich have fluctuated as conservative Republican and liberal Democratic administrations have shifted the tax code back and forth. Under legislation signed by President Obama in 2012, rates for the highest income households were raised from those left in place by his immediate predecessor, George W. Bush, to a level closer to those approved by Bill Clinton in the 1990s. The top marginal rate, imposed on personal income above $400,000, went up a few percent to almost 40 percent. The estate or inheritance tax, which had been trending downward under Bush-era law, was increased slightly but to a level well below historical precedents. Under the new law, an individual estate worth under $5 million is entirely exempt from the inheritance tax. The exemption for the combined estate of a married couple is, in effect, $10 million. The value of an estate beyond the exemption is subject to a 40 percent tax. Only 1 or 2 percent of estates are large enough to pay anything (Nunn and Rohaly 2013).

Of course, the "official" income and estate tax rates (comparable to the sticker rates on a new auto) may not reflect what the wealthy end up paying, due to generous provisions of the tax code and artfully calculated tax strategies. For example, Congress requires the IRS to keep track of the income taxes paid by the households with the 400 highest incomes. In 2008, each of the 400 earned over $110 million (a slow year, it seems, since they earned over $270 million in 2007) and paid an average of $19.8 million in personal income taxes—18 percent of gross income (Wessel 2012:121).

While federal taxes have tended downward for taxpayers at all income levels, state and local taxes have been rising. An analysis by the *New York Times*, with the help of tax experts, estimated the combined effect of changing federal, state, and local taxes since 1980 (Applebaum and Gebeloff 2012). The most important federal taxes (except the estate tax) were included in the analysis, along with state and local income, sales, and property taxes. For households at three different income levels, the changes in combined effective taxation levels from 1980 to 2010 were as follows:

> *Top 1 Percent.* The total taxes paid by a family with a $350,000 income (in 2010 dollars) dropped from 49 percent to 42 percent of income, a savings of roughly $24,000.
>
> *Middle Income.* The total paid by a family making $52,000 fell from approximately 31 percent to 28 percent, a savings of $1,500.
>
> *Low Income.* The total paid by a family with income at the poverty line of $22,000 declined from about 20 percent to 19 percent, a savings of $200.

The general conclusion from the analysis is that the overall tax system remained progressive—people at the top pay more. But the biggest tax cuts have gone to the wealthy, so that over the 30-year period, the system became less progressive.

---

[11] Applebaum and Gebeloff 2012; Congressional Budget Office 2016; U.S. House of Representatives 1991a. .

Conclusion

In this chapter, we added evidence of growing inequality in the distribution of income and wealth to the evidence of growing inequality in earnings that we explored in the last chapter. The polarization of incomes is all the more remarkable because it reverses a well-documented trend toward greater income equality from the 1930s into the 1970s (Miller 1971; U.S. Census Bureau 1996). How can we account for the shift? This question is an enlarged version of the one we asked at the end of Chapter 3. There, we were interested in the increasing disparity in earnings. Here, we were concerned with all sources of income and with whole households rather than individual workers. In this section, we review what we have learned in this chapter, giving particular attention to developments that can help explain change.

We began the chapter with an imaginary income parade, a device to visualize the income distribution and the factors that shape it. The parade began with a long line of small people—not just the poor but also millions of families living marginally on the earnings of low-wage workers. At the end of the parade, we were struck by the abrupt increase in the size of the marchers, who grew in a matter of minutes to astronomical proportions, reflective of astronomical incomes.

The changing mix of occupations during the course of the parade was about what we expected. More surprising were the other factors that powerfully influenced where people marched in the ranks—in particular, the sources of household income and the number of workers in a family. Most households, of course, depend on job earnings. We noticed that single-worker families were common in the first half of the parade. Much later in the procession, among people with incomes around $100,000, we found very few families without two employed adults. But we discovered that jobs were less significant for those at the beginning and the very end of the procession. The first marchers were often dependent on government transfers, from Social Security to public assistance. The very last marchers—especially those with incomes above $1 million—depended less on jobs than on investments for their incomes.

If those at the end of the parade draw the greater part of their incomes from financial wealth, the rising concentration of wealth is certainly strengthening income inequality. Of course, the accumulation of wealth is also a *result* of income inequality—as well as the changes in effective tax rates that enabled those with the highest incomes to retain a higher proportion of their incomes.

The parade focused attention on the social factors leading to increased income inequality. We noted, for example, that families headed by females were crowded into the early part of the parade. The prevalence of such families is growing as a result of increased divorce and births to single mothers, contributing inevitably to the growth in income inequality. These social trends are strengthening the economic pressures toward polarization that we discussed in Chapter 3. The result is what we have called an Age of Growing Inequality.

KEY TERMS DEFINED IN THE GLOSSARY ——————

dividend
Earned Income Tax
   Credit (EITC)
effective tax rates
government transfers
gross assets
income
investor class
   (see wealth classes)

mean
median
nearly propertyless class
   (see wealth classes)
nest-egg class
   (see wealth classes)
net worth (see wealth)
progressive tax
quintile

real income
regressive tax
wealth
wealth classes

SUGGESTED READINGS ——————————————

Atkinson, Anthony. 2015. *Inequality. What Can be Done?* Cambridge: Harvard University Press.

A clear, thoughtful introduction to economic inequality by a man who has devoted his career to the topic.

Burman, Leonard and Joel Slemrod. 2013. *Taxes in America: What Everyone Needs to Know.* New York: Oxford University Press.

Useful primer on taxes.

Gornick, Janet and Markus Jantti, eds. 2013. *Income Inequality: Economic Disparities and the Middle Class in Affluent Countries.* Stanford, CA: Stanford University Press.

Income and wealth inequalities in comparative perspective, with special attention to the middle class, women's work, politics, and public policy.

Mishel, Lawrence, Jared Bernstein, and Heidi Shierholtz. 2012. *The State of Working America.* 12th ed. Ithaca, NY: Cornell University Press.

Long-term trends in the distribution of income and wealth, wages, and other topics. Updated editions published

regularly. The material in this book is regularly updated at the Economic Policy Institute website (http://www .stateofworkingamerica.org/). The site also provides access to essential data series in downloadable format.

Rose, Stephen. 2014. *Social Stratification in the United States: The American Profile Poster.* New Edition. New York: New Press.

Ingenious poster with companion booklet, illustrating the distribution of income, education, occupation, and household types.

Shapiro, Thomas. 2004. *The Hidden Cost of Being African American: How Wealth Perpetuates Inequality.* New York: Oxford University Press.

The role of wealth and inheritance in perpetuating racial inequality.

Wessel, David 2012. *Red Ink: Inside the High-Stakes Politics of the Federal Budget.* New York: Crown Business.

A clear, concise introduction to the class issues surrounding federal taxing and spending.

Socialization, Association, Lifestyles, and Values

Let me tell you about the rich. They are different from you and me.

F. Scott Fitzgerald

The title of this chapter might have been "So Does Class Matter?" We have examined the distribution of income and wealth, the occupational structure, and conceptions of the class structure. But, aside from a hint here or there, we have not shown that class really matters in our everyday lives. In this chapter, we demonstrate that class shapes our experience, through the life cycle, from early childhood to mature adulthood. We will find that class position affects some of the most intimate aspects of our lives.

We will follow up on our earlier discussions of Max Weber's ideas about status communities, Lloyd Warner's description of social life in Yankee City, and the Lynds' account of the emergence of the wealthy X clan in Middletown. These authors noted that people with similar class positions tend to draw together. They live in the same neighborhoods, develop friendships, spend leisure time together, and join the same clubs and churches. Their children go to the same schools, form social cliques, become teammates, develop romantic attachments, and grow up to marry one another. Gradually, shared experiences become the basis for a distinctive lifestyle and common set of values, which parents pass on to their young. They develop, in other words, a self-perpetuating class subculture.

Our discussion emphasizes two of the basic variables we mentioned in Chapter 1: *socialization*, the learning process that prepares new members of society for social life; and *association*, social patterning of human relationships. We will, for example, be looking at class differences in child rearing and the influence of class position on the selection of friends and mates.

Bourdieu: The Varieties of Capital

The work of French sociologist Pierre Bourdieu (1986) on class reproduction and the varieties of capital will help us understand the larger significance of the material covered in this chapter. Capital may be defined as value accumulated over time and capable of yielding future benefits. We are accustomed to thinking of capital as another name for financial wealth. But Bourdieu extends the concept. He distinguishes three forms of capital: **economic capital**, the basic monetary form, institutionalized as property rights; **cultural capital**, knowledge in its broadest sense, institutionalized as educational credentials, but encompassing such matters as table manners and how to swing a tennis racket; and **social capital**, mutual obligations embodied in social networks such as kinship, friendship, and group membership.

Bourdieu emphasizes that the value of each of these forms of capital is enhanced by its capacity for transformation into one of the others. For example, before he entered politics, George W. Bush took advantage of his social capital—the extensive social connections he had developed growing up in a prominent upper-class family—to gather economic capital for a series of business ventures (Kelly 2004). Generations of novelists have won readers with characters who strive to develop cultural and social capital to further their personal ambitions.

From Bourdieu's perspective, the sum of the various forms of capital they hold is the cumulative advantage of the privileged classes. It is a key to the reproduction of the class system by transmission from generation to generation. As several of the authors we examine in this chapter confirm, the class advantages or disadvantages that a child inherits are not just economic, but also, as Bourdieu would have it, cultural and social.

Children's Conception of Social Class

As they grow up, children absorb from their elders increasingly sophisticated notions about social class. An early study of primary school students in a New England town of 15,000 showed that by the sixth grade, children understood the class significance of items such as an English riding habit, an elegantly furnished room, tattered clothing, and different occupational activities, all presented to them in pictures. And when they were asked to place their classmates in one of three classes, the sixth graders agreed 70 percent of the time with adults who rated parents from the same households (Stendler 1949).

Simmons and Rosenberg (1971) demonstrated that young children have a clear conception of occupational prestige differences. Even the third graders in their sample from the Baltimore city schools ordered 15 occupations from the National Opinion Research Center (NORC) list in a way that correlated almost perfectly with the rankings in a national survey of adults.

Subsequent studies have concentrated on the development of conceptions of class distinctions as children grow up. Tutor (1991) showed first, fourth, and sixth graders photographs of upper-, middle-, and lower-class people. She asked the children to group the adults and children depicted into families and match them with the corresponding pictures of cars and houses. The first graders did substantially better than chance at this task, the sixth graders produced near-perfect scores, and the fourth graders were not far behind.

Leahy (1981, 1983) probed the developing conceptions of "poor people" and "rich people" held by children ages 7 to 17. He found that young children conceive of the rich and the poor in overt, physical terms, while older children think in terms of psychological characteristics of individuals and their positions in the society. Here are some of their observations.

Joe, age 6:

[Poor people have] no food. They won't have no Thanksgiving. They don't have nothing. . . . [R]ich people have crazy outfits and poor people have no outfits.

Mary, age 6:

[People can become rich by going] to the store and they give you money. . . . [Or] if your husband gives you money, and your grandmother or your grandfather.

Pete, age 10:

[People are rich] because they save their money and they earn it. They work as hard as they can and don't just go around and buy whatever they want.

Dean, age 12:

> I think that [rich and poor people] should all be the same, each have the same amount of money because then the rich people won't think they are so big.

In general, these studies show that even preschool children are aware of class differences. They suggest that as children grow older, their ideas about stratification become more consistent, abstract, and "accurate." By the time they reach 12 years of age, children are not very different from adults in their thinking about class.

Kohn: Class and Socialization

While studies such as those just reviewed approach socialization through the child's developing conception of the social world, a separate research tradition focuses on the child-rearing practices of parents. For decades, studies of the latter type have recorded class differences in the way people raise their children (Bronfenbrenner 1966; Gecas 1979). Annette Lareau, whose research we examine in the next section, and Melvin Kohn have made intriguing contributions to this literature.

Kohn studied class differences in the values parents impart to their children. He wanted to understand exactly why such differences exist and how they contribute to the perpetuation of the class system. In a series of surveys in the United States and abroad, Kohn and his associates asked parents to select from a list of characteristics those they considered most desirable for a child of the same age and sex as their own child (Kohn 1969, 1976, 1977; Kohn and Schooler 1983).

> Here are a few examples:
>
> That he is a good student.
>
> That he is popular with other children.
>
> That he has good manners.
>
> That he is curious about things.
>
> That he is happy (Kohn 1969:218).

Although the studies found consensus across class levels about the importance of some values (parents of all classes wanted their children to be happy), there was less agreement about others. For example, parents at higher class levels were more likely to choose "curiosity," and those at lower-class levels were more likely to select "obedience." The top panel (A) of Table 5.1 compares the values characteristically cited by parents in the upper or the lower halves of the class structure (for convenience, labeled middle class and working class). Parental views were varied at every class level, but the values we are calling working class become increasingly common at lower-class levels and those we have labeled middle class become more common at successively higher class levels.

Families were assigned to classes on the basis of the father's occupation. The researchers found that mothers' value preferences for children reflected

Table 5.1 Typical Class Patterns in Parental Values and Occupational Experience

Middle-Class Pattern	Working-Class Pattern
A. Parents' Values for Children	
Self-control	Obedience
Consideration of others	Manners
Curiosity	"Good student"
Happiness	Neatness, cleanliness
B. Parents' Own Value Orientations	
Tolerance of nonconformity	Strong punishment of deviant behavior
Open to innovation	Stuck to old ways
People basically good	People not trustworthy
Value self-direction	Believe in strict leadership
C. Job Characteristics	
Work independently	Close supervision
Varied tasks	Repetitive work
Work with people or data	Work with things

their husbands' occupations. But they also observed that the class patterning of parental values could be strengthened or diluted according to the occupations of employed mothers. For example, among women married to working-class men, mothers with manual jobs were much more likely to conform to the working-class value pattern than were mothers with white-collar jobs.

Kohn interpreted the class patterns of parental values for children as follows: The middle-class parents who stress the values of self-control, curiosity, and consideration are cultivating capacities for self-direction and empathetic understanding of others in their children. The working-class parents who focus on obedience, neatness, and good manners are instilling behavioral conformity. The middle-class pattern—particularly in the emphasis laid on happiness, curiosity, and consideration—is oriented toward the *internal* dynamics of the person, both the child and others. The working-class pattern, on the other hand, assumes fixed *external* standards of behavior. This general difference is neatly illustrated in the top panel (A) of Table 5.1 by four pairs of contrasting values, beginning with "self-control" and "obedience." In each case, the first (middle class) choice favors internal development, and the second (working class) emphasizes conformity to external rules or authority.

An additional finding substantiates this interpretation. Parents were asked about the specific sorts of misbehavior for which they would discipline their children. Their responses revealed that middle-class parents were more likely to punish a child for the *intent* of his or her behavior, in contrast with working-class mothers, who were more likely to discipline for the *consequences* of behavior. For example, a middle-class mother might penalize her child for throwing a temper tantrum, while a working-class mother penalizes for boisterous play. The first suggests a loss of internal control, the second a violation of external standards.

Kohn labeled the two underlying patterns *self-direction* and *conformity*. At successively higher class levels, he concluded, parents value self-direction more and conformity to external standards less. But what are the roots of these class differences? Kohn hypothesized that they reflect generalized value orientations that develop out of a specific aspect of social class: occupational experience. He reasoned, for example, that people who hold professional and managerial jobs, which are relatively unsupervised and require considerable exercise of individual judgment and initiative, are more likely to value self-direction than those who work at highly routinized, blue-collar jobs. In brief, self-direction at work should produce self-direction in values.

Evidence from the surveys supported these ideas. They showed, for example, that parents' general judgments about authority, deviance, and the goodness of human nature are related to social class (Table 5.1, Panel B). In particular, Kohn noted that "authoritarian attitudes" stressing "conformance to the dictates of authority and intolerance of nonconformity" become more frequent at lower-class levels (Kohn 1969:79).

Finally, the surveys demonstrated that these general attitudes are systematically related to the character of respondents' occupational experience. Men whose work is (1) closely supervised, (2) repetitive, and (3) oriented toward things rather than people or data are the most likely to subscribe to authoritarian values and to judge jobs on their extrinsic qualities. Of course, what are ordinarily considered working-class jobs are most likely to fit this occupational pattern—though some (plumber) do not fit it as well as certain menial office jobs (data entry operator). Kohn also notes that the wives of men who share this occupational experience tend to hold similar values.

The results and interpretative logic of Kohn's research are summarized in Table 5.1. Remember that the middle-class side of this chart represents patterns that are increasingly frequent at higher class levels, and the working-class side describes patterns that become more frequent at lower-class levels. (We are dealing with statistical tendencies here, not absolute contrasts between classes.) Reading the table from the bottom up on the middle-class side, we find that parents at higher class levels are more likely to work at jobs requiring intellectual flexibility and independent judgment (Panel C), more open to innovation and tolerant of nonconformity (Panel B), and more likely to encourage self-direction in their children (Panel A). The parallel finding on the working-class side is that parents at lower-class levels are more subject to authority and routinization at work, more authoritarian in their judgments, and more likely to favor conformity in their children. These two contrasting patterns fit the causal chain that Kohn had anticipated to explain the relationship between social class and socialization patterns: Occupational experience gives rise to general value orientations, which in turn shape parental value preferences for children.

Further scrutiny of the data revealed that a second aspect of social class, level of education, exercises an independent influence on parental value orientations and value preferences for children and thus reinforces the class patterning of socialization. Kohn observed that education appears to "provide the intellectual flexibility and breadth of perspective that are essential for self-directed values" (1969:186). Kohn found that education and occupational conditions have independent impacts on parental values, although the effect of occupational conditions is substantially stronger.

Kohn's research on class differences in the socialization of children has important implications for our understanding of the class system as a whole. Since Marx, sociologists have been aware that life experience, especially occupational experience, shapes social values. Kohn (1969) observed that "the essence of higher class position is the expectation that one's decisions and actions can be consequential; the essence of lower-class position is the belief that one is at the mercy of forces and people beyond one's control, often, beyond one's understanding" (p. 189). If this is true, we should expect people in top positions to learn to value self-direction and those at the bottom to learn to value conformity to authority. We might also anticipate that they will teach these values to their children.

At this point, the larger significance of Kohn's work becomes clear. When parents inculcate values that reflect their experience of the class system, they are preparing their children to assume a class position similar to their own and, by so doing, are contributing to the long-term maintenance of the class system. Kohn explicitly rejects the notion that these outcomes reflect the conscious intentions of parents. Annette Lareau's research, which we turn to next, reaches a different conclusion. She shows that upper-middle-class parents are quite conscious of the career-enhancing objective of their child-rearing practices.

Lareau: Child Rearing Observed

Like Kohn, Lareau (2003) was interested in class differences in socialization. But Lareau went one step beyond Kohn. In addition to interviewing parents, she and a team of research assistants spent hundreds of hours observing parents and their 9- or 10-year-old children—usually at home, but also during routine activities outside the home. Such "naturalistic observation" is rare because it is expensive and time-consuming. It has the methodological disadvantage of generalization from an inevitably small sample (the team interviewed 88 families and observed 12). But observation can also be enormously rewarding, as it was for Lareau, because it yields information unfiltered by respondents and exposes researchers to important aspects of social life they may not have thought to ask about. Lareau's team asked families they observed not to treat them as guests, but to carry on their normal daily lives. They hoped to be as inconspicuous and taken for granted "as the family dog," and they seem, by and large, to have succeeded.

The study focused on families at three class levels, which Lareau labels middle class, working class, and poor. Her sample includes both black and white families at all three class levels. Judging from the high incomes and managerial or professional jobs she reports for the first group of families, Lareau's middle class could better be described as *upper*-middle class. Her working-class families seem to be a mix of what we would call working class and working poor. There is, then, a considerable economic gap separating

Lareau's top class and the other two classes in this study. Perhaps it is not surprising that Lareau finds a corresponding gap in child-rearing practices.

Generalizing from rich observational data, Lareau describes two basic approaches to child rearing, which we can label *cultivated growth* and *natural growth*.[1] Parents who take the first approach hover over their children, scheduling their activities, fostering their talents, reasoning with them, and intervening on their behalf. Parents who take the second want to provide a safe and stable environment within which they expect the child to develop naturally; they guide their children with clear directives but allow them considerable autonomy in their everyday activities. Lareau reports that the upper-middle-class families she observed practice cultivated growth, while both the working class and poor families practice the natural growth pattern of child rearing.

Lareau's observations cluster around three facets of children's lives: the organization of daily activities, the use of language, and relations with institutions such as schools.

Daily Activities. The upper-middle class 9- and 10-year-olds Lareau studied spend much of their time with adults or in activities organized by adults. The monthly calendar on the refrigerator door records a hectically scheduled life, with times for soccer practice, piano lessons, swim team, church choir, school play rehearsal, Girl Scouts, gymnastics, and violin lessons. There are scheduled play dates. One boy complains, "My mother signs me up for everything!" but says his activities make him feel "special" and admits he would be "bored" without them. On their own, these upper-middle-class children are not sure how to use the limited free time they have.

Working-class and poor children, Lareau finds, lead slower, less structured lives. Much of their time is their own, and unlike their upper-middle-class peers, they have no trouble entertaining themselves—generally in informal play with neighborhood children and cousins. Their parents do not, by and large, involve them in organized activities. Often, parents lack the prerequisite resources of time, money, and transportation. But many do not see the value of such activities, which upper-middle-class parents regard as character building. Lareau finds that working-class and poor parents regard the child's world and the adult world as distinct realms. Other than providing for their children's safety, they take only limited interest in the former.

Language. Lareau's interest in language extends more generally to the way that parents interact with children. Upper-middle-class parents, she finds, engage in almost continual conversation with their children when they are together. They are intent on cultivating their child's facility with language. They teach children to express their own views and to believe that their opinions matter. They encourage them to ask questions of other adults and people in authority like teachers and doctors. In upper-middle-class families, language is the main mechanism of discipline. Parents reason with children. Even when issuing directives,

---

[1] We have substituted these simplified labels for Lareau's more cumbersome "concerted cultivation" and "accomplishment of natural growth."

they attach reasons to them. And children learn to negotiate with their parents for what they want. When negotiation is, from the children's viewpoint, unsuccessful, they often resort to whining, a tendency that the researchers did not observe with children at lower class levels.

Conversation between parents and children in the working-class and poor homes was much less extensive. These parents and children were often silent in each other's company. Working-class and poor parents regard it as their responsibility to shelter, feed, and clothe their children; teach them right from wrong; and comfort them. In these matters, Lareau reports, "language plays an important, practical role" (2003:139). But the parents did not focus on developing their children's language skills. They did not draw out their opinions or expect to be challenged by them. They disciplined their children with short, clear directives— sometimes coupled with physical punishment—which children generally accepted without complaint.

Institutions. Upper-middle-class parents, Lareau finds, confidently engage institutions, and they teach their children to do the same. They are at ease with teachers, doctors, and others in authority, feeling free to ask questions and make demands, and they expect institutions to respond to their child's individual needs. In preparation for a wellness exam, an upper-middle-class mother encourages her child to think of questions he wants to ask the doctor. "Don't be shy," she urges him, and he is not (p. 124). When another mother learned that her daughter had narrowly missed out on her school's gifted program, she sought advice from a network of well-informed friends, arranged to have her daughter retested, and prevailed on the school to assign her to the program. (Lareau found that high percentages of upper-middle-class respondents, but few working-class or poor respondents, know people who are doctors, lawyers, and psychologists [pp. 171, 285].)

Working-class and poor parents are, according to Lareau, intimidated by institutions and the professionals who represent them. Mothers who have no difficulty making loud demands on the cable company are subdued in the presence of their child's teacher or doctor. They may not understand the words professionals use and do not feel competent to challenge their expertise. One mother whose fourth grader cannot read gets contradictory explanations from her child's teachers. But she makes no demands, leaving her daughter's education to the school's presumed experts. At the same time, passivity often masks an underlying resentment and distrust of middle-class institutions, which working-class parents openly share with their children. They feel that such institutions operate according to an alien set of values. The parents of a fourth grader involved in playground conflicts encourage him to hit back, in defiance of the school's rules; the child is suspended. Working-class and poor parents, who use physical punishment, fear having their children removed from the home if the school reports them to welfare authorities for child abuse.

Summarizing, Lareau suggests that the cultivated growth pattern encourages a sense of *entitlement* in upper-middle-class children. Having been encouraged to participate in challenging organized activities, to speak freely with adults, to express their own opinions, to ask questions, to negotiate for what they want, and to expect institutions to respond to their needs, these children grow up with an enhanced sense of self-worth. They can be expected to deal confidently with institutions, which they see as sharing their own values.

In contrast, the natural growth pattern leads toward what Lareau characterizes as a sense of *constraint* in working-class and poor children. They have not been encouraged to cultivate formal language skills, to express their own opinions, or to question, challenge, or negotiate with adults. They have less experience than more privileged children with institutions, which they have been taught to regard with distrust.

Lareau sees her research as demonstrating the power of class to shape young lives. On the other hand, she concludes that race matters little, for children at this age, on the key dimensions of daily life, language, and relations with institutions. While the black parents in the study were inevitably concerned with the effects of racism on their young children, they differed little from white parents of the same class in their approach to child rearing.

To Lareau's surprise, the only class distinction that mattered was the one separating the child-rearing practices of the upper-middle class from those of the two lower classes. Although she detected some differences between working-class and poor families, she found that they raised their children according to the same natural growth pattern. Perhaps a larger sample and the inclusion of families from the intermediate lower-middle class would have yielded a more complicated picture.

Bourdieu, whom Lareau cites as an inspiration for her work, would say that the upper-middle-class children she studied were developing valuable cultural capital, which will serve them well as they move through the education system and into professional and managerial careers beyond. Kohn might add that the very character of upper-middle-class occupations supports the cultivated growth pattern of child rearing, with its self-confident values. Both would agree that class differences in socialization support the reproduction of the class system.

Patterns of Association in Early Life

The class differences in patterns of socialization are reinforced by the tendency of children and adolescents to associate with others of like class background as they are growing up. Because neighborhoods tend to group people of similar economic means, the kids on the block are likely to be of the same social class. Local schools reproduce the class patterns of the neighborhoods they serve. Many upper-class and upper-middle-class families make sure that their children's classmates will be from similar households by buying homes in "better" school districts or sending their children to private schools. As Lareau's research shows, the upper-middle-class pattern of scheduled activities outside of school reinforces class segregation.

Large public high schools in some communities bring together students of diverse backgrounds, but they do not necessarily mix freely. Often class differentiation within the school is institutionalized through curricula that separate students on the basis of their academic ability or postgraduation aspirations, which tend to be correlated with social class (Colclough and Beck 1986; Oakes 1985).

Students' own preferences contribute to the class patterning of association. A series of somewhat dated studies of adolescent cliques and friendships shows that students are inclined, though by no means certain, to choose friends who share their own class backgrounds (Cohen 1979; Duncan, Haller, and Portes 1968; Hollingshead 1949).

From 1988 to 2007, we surveyed groups of students at a selective college regarding their associations in high school. Approximately 180 students were asked the occupations of the parents of their three best friends and most significant romantic interest in high school. Students also provided information on the occupations and incomes of their own parents. Families were stratified according to the Gilbert-Kahl model introduced in Chapter 1. The results are summarized in Table 5.2, which shows that the high school associations of this relatively privileged group of students were largely restricted to people with class backgrounds similar to their own but quite different from the class distribution of Americans generally. The first column shows the class distribution of all American households: Most (55 percent) are working class or below in our schema; relatively few (15 percent) are upper-middle class or higher. As the second column indicates, the class distribution of students bound for an elite college is almost the reverse, with the large majority (71 percent) concentrated in the top classes. The third and fourth columns reveal that the students have usually formed friendships and romantic relationships with people who fit their own privileged class profiles. The strong pattern of class segregation among these generally affluent teenagers is, as we will see later in the chapter, consistent with the highly restricted association patterns of upper-middle-class adults.

Like friendship, mate selection is influenced by social class. Sociologist Martin K. Whyte (1990) confirmed this conclusion from earlier studies in a survey of women in the Detroit metropolitan area. Whyte asked the respondents about the class positions of their parents and in-laws, at the time the women and their husbands were in high school. Given a choice of five classes, 58 percent of the respondents placed their parents and in-laws in the same class.

Table 5.2 Association Patterns of High School Students Bound for a Selective College

	Class Distribution (percent)			
	U.S. National	Students Surveyed	Students' Best Friends	Students' Best Dates
Capitalist/Upper-Middle	15	71	62	57
Middle	30	22	26	30
Working and Below	55	7	12	13
Total	100	100	100	100

Source: Cumulative surveys of approximately 180 college students enrolled in social stratification course, 1989 to 2007.

Research on educational homogamy (marriage between educational equals) also suggests the influence of class on marital choices. Education is a useful class indicator, which is correlated with both family background and earning potential. In 2000, 65 percent of young wives with college degrees and 50 percent of young wives with high school diplomas were married to similarly educated men. Both figures are well beyond what would be expected if cupid were indifferent to relative education. Moreover, educational homogamy has been increasing. In 1960, the odds of having a spouse with the same level of education were 3 times greater than pure chance. By 2003, the odds of educational equality were 4 times greater than chance (Schwartz and Mare 2005).[2] In practice, this meant that the executive who might have married his secretary or the doctor who might have married the nurse, are now more likely to marry high earning professionals like themselves.

Social class not only influences whom we marry, but also the character of marital relationships and, as we will see later in this chapter, whether we marry and stay married.

Marriage Styles

Sociological studies of husbands and wives have long found clearer sex-role distinctions at lower class levels and greater intimacy, equality, and companionship at higher class levels. A classic study conducted by Lee Rainwater (1965) supports this view.

Rainwater analyzed the marital role relationships of several hundred couples and distinguished three types of relationships, on a continuum: joint, intermediate, and segregated. **Joint marital relationships** focus on companionship and deemphasize the sexual division of labor. Husbands and wives with joint role relationships share the planning of family affairs, carry out many household duties interchangeably, and value common leisure activities. Even when responsibilities are parceled out by gender (wife–homemaker, husband–breadwinner), each partner is expected to take a sympathetic interest in the concerns of the other. In **segregated marital relationships**, there is clear differentiation of concerns and responsibilities, which minimizes the husband's involvement with household matters and the wife's with the world of (the husband's) work. Husband and wife are likely to have distinct leisure pursuits and separate sets of friends. Intermediate marital relationships fall between these two poles.

Based on answers to questions about family decision-making, duties of husbands and wives, interests and activities of the partners, and the general character of the relationship, Rainwater placed each couple in one of the three categories. Of course, all couples were in some sense "intermediate." So the ratings were based on relative differences. When Rainwater compared the distributions of these three types of role relationships at four class levels, unmistakable differences emerged (Table 5.3). Joint relationships predominate in the upper-middle class (88 percent) and segregated relationships in

---

[2] All figures refer to couples with wives age 18 to 40. Odds are net of changes in the distribution of husbands' and wives' education.

Table 5.3 Social Class and Conjugal Role Relationships

Class	Role Relationships (percent)				
	Number	Joint	Intermediate	Segregated	Total
Upper-middle class	(32)	88	12	–	100
Lower-middle class	(31)	42	58	–	100
Upper-lower class	(26)	19	58	23	100
Lower-lower class	(25)	4	24	72	100

Source: Family Design: Marital Sexuality, Family Size, and Contraception, by Lee Rainwater. Chicago, IL: Aldine. Reprinted by permission of Lee Rainwater.

the lower-lower class (72 percent), while the classes between them exhibit a neat gradient.

The relationship between social class and marital role types is more than a matter of academic curiosity. Reported marital happiness increases with class level, especially for women (Bradburn 1969:156), and this phenomenon is tied to the character of the organization of marital roles. In Rainwater's study, middle-class couples reported greater sexual satisfaction than lower-class couples, but the difference was largely a function of the level of role segregation. For example, most lower-class wives in segregated relationships evaluated their sexual experience in marriage negatively, but the minority of lower-class wives in intermediate relationships were generally positive in their evaluation (Rainwater 1965:28). In national surveys, companionship in marriage (which would appear to be similar to joint organization) is positively correlated with social class and with marital happiness (Bradburn 1969:163).

Let's take a closer look at conjugal role types by examining how they function in upper-middle class and working-class families (L. Rubin 1976; Sussman and Steinmetz 1987:226–231). In important ways, the very character of upper-middle-class life lends itself to the joint role relationship. College life, generally a prologue to upper-middle-class careers, delays marriage and encourages informal, relatively egalitarian association between men and women. High rates of social and geographic mobility are typical of this class. Husbands and wives are isolated from kin and removed from successive sets of friends as they move from community to community and up the career ladder. They must look to each other for support and companionship. Together, they are drawn into the career-oriented social life, such as entertaining clients or associates at home, that is one of the keys to success for ambitious executives and professionals.

Upper-middle-class wives are expected to be "gracious, charming hostesses and social creatures, supporting their husbands' careers and motivating their achievements" (Kanter 1977:108). The traditional result has been the "two-person career" that links a husband's advancement to his wife's unpaid efforts. A more recent phenomenon, typical of younger couples, is the dual-career family, in which both spouses pursue demanding professional or managerial careers. A survey of 1,000 working-age women in Chicago (Lopata et al. 1980) found that dual-career couples are as likely as single-career couples to mix social and professional life. About 60 percent of wives employed as managers or professionals reported that their husbands helped them with career-related entertaining at home. Husbands with professional or managerial jobs were somewhat more likely to receive such help from their wives. (It made little difference whether the wife was employed.) On the other hand, women employed in blue-collar jobs or married to blue-collar men reported little job-related entertaining.

As the Chicago study suggests, the career-oriented social life that becomes a shared endeavor for upper-middle-class couples has no working-class equivalent. Working-class men and women do develop social ties on the job, but these tend to segregate rather than join husbands and wives. For example, many of the workers in a New Jersey chemical plant studied by David Halle (1984) drank together after work and joined coworkers on fishing trips and at sports events. Working-class occupations are less likely to require geographic mobility. Remarkably, most of Halle's chemical workers were born within two miles of the plant where they worked (p. 303). Under such circumstances, it is easier for spouses to maintain ties with kin and friends from adolescence and early adult years. Dependency on the couple's parents is intensified by the economic insecurity that is especially typical of young working-class families. These social ties tend to draw husband and wife to separate sources of support and companionship outside the marriage.

Bott's (1964) work in England showed that couples who come to a marriage with separate, tight-knit networks of friends and kin and maintain these ties are the most likely to develop segregated marital relationships. Her data suggest that social networks of that sort are least typical of professionals and most typical of manual workers.

We have dealt with the origins of joint and segregated role relationships in experiences typical of the top and bottom of the class order. What can we say about the mix of marriage types Rainwater found in the middle of the class structure (Table 5.3)? Two social factors seem relevant. One is social mobility: People moving up or down in the class structure may carry with them lifestyles acquired in their class of origin. Thus, the upper-middle-class origins of many lower-middle-class couples (especially younger couples) can help explain the predominance of joint relationships among them. An analogous argument can be made for the spread of segregated relationships upward. The second factor is cultural: the tendency of upper-middle-class lifestyles to become generally fashionable models and filter downward. Through these processes, couples are exposed to conflicting influences, which may be reflected in intermediate role relationships.

Sex-role socialization is another source of class differences in marital role organization. Kohn's research (1969), which we touched on earlier in this chapter, found that working-class parents are more likely than middle-class parents to hold separate sets of expectations for boys and girls. A study of college-age women (Vanfossen 1977) found that college-age daughters of working-class fathers are more likely than their middle-class peers to subscribe to traditional sex-role values as expressed in questionnaire items such as, "A woman should not expect to go to exactly the same places or have the same freedom as a man." Such women are the most likely to find the segregated marital role acceptable.

Boys of all classes have traditionally been taught to be more controlled, more instrumental, less emotional, and less empathetic than their sisters, but the distinction is made much more emphatically in blue-collar families. Lillian Rubin (1976), a sociologist and psychotherapist who conducted lengthy interviews with working-class and upper-middle-class couples, noted big differences in the behavior of their sons:

> Not once in a professional middle-class home did I see a young boy shake his father's hand in a well-taught "manly" gesture as he bid him good night. Not once did I hear a middle-class parent scornfully—or even sympathetically—call a crying boy a sissy or in any way reprimand him for his tears. Yet, these were not uncommon observations in the working-class homes I visited. Indeed, I was impressed with the fact that, even as young as six or seven, the working-class boys seemed more emotionally controlled—more like miniature men—than those in the middle-class families. (p. 126)

Boys who are taught to be "manly" in this way are less likely as adults to feel comfortable with joint role relationships in marriage.

Blue-Collar Marriages and Middle-Class Models

Two studies of intimate working-class life, Rubin's book and another by E. E. LeMasters (1975), published about the same time, cast further light on the differences between working- and middle-class marriages. Rubin, who interviewed young parents in their Northern California homes, and LeMasters, who spent 5 years getting to know the somewhat older patrons of the Oasis, a "family-type" working-class tavern in Wisconsin, reached surprisingly similar conclusions. Both found that marital norms filtering down from the upper-middle class were creating enormous strains in blue-collar marriages.

One of LeMasters' (1975) informants, a woman married for 30 years, bitterly described the traditional pattern of segregated blue-collar marriages:

> The men go to work while the wife stays home with the kids— it's a long day with no other adult to talk to. That's what drives mothers to the soap operas—stupid as they are.
>
> Then the husband stops at some tavern to have a few with his buddies from the job—not having seen them since they left to drive home 10 minutes ago. The poor guy is lonely and thirsty and needs to relax before the rigors of another evening before the television set. Meanwhile the little woman has supper ready and is trying to hold the kids off "until Daddy gets home so we can all eat together." After a while, she gives up this little dream and eats with the kids while the food is still eatable. About 7 o'clock, Daddy rolls in, feeling no pain, eats a few bites of the overcooked food, sits down in front of the TV set, and falls asleep.

This little drama is repeated several thousand times until they have their twenty-fifth wedding anniversary and then everybody tells them how happy they have been. And you know what? By now they are both so damn punch drunk neither one of them knows whether their marriage has been a success or not. (p. 42)

Such dissatisfaction was probably nothing new, but as the tone of her comment suggests, expectations were changing. By the 1970s, the traditional pattern was being challenged by notions of intimacy, companionship, sharing, and equality received from above. The problem was and still is that these ideals do not appeal equally to wives and husbands. Women were prepared for them by their socialization and in many cases by contact with a middle-class world through white-collar employment and exposure to popular media. Men, LeMasters found, were satisfied with established role relationships, which they had long regarded as part of the natural order of things. The traditional women's role was, according to one of LeMasters' informants, "natural for them so they don't mind it" (p. 105). Men sensed, of course, that many women did "mind it," but they were inclined to think that women's complaints are groundless. At the Oasis, a construction worker asks LeMasters,

What the hell are they complaining about? My wife has an automatic washer in the kitchen, a dryer, a dishwasher, a garbage disposal, a car of her own—hell, I even bought her a portable TV so she can watch the goddamn soap operas right in the kitchen. What more can she want? (p. 85)

But behind the bluff, there is fear. From the less "macho" setting of his living room, one of Rubin's (1976) informants phrased the problem differently:

I swear I don't know what she wants. She keeps saying that we have to talk, and when we do, it always turns out I'm saying the wrong thing. I get scared sometimes. I always thought I had to think things to myself; you know, not tell her about it. Now she says that's not good. But it's hard. You know, I think it comes down to that I like things the way they are, and I'm afraid I'll say or do something that'll really shake things up. So I get worried about it, and I don't say anything. (p. 121)

For their part, working-class women in these studies were very dissatisfied but also frightened and confused and occasionally given to wondering whether asking a man to be more than a conscientious provider is indeed asking too much.

I'm not sure what I want. I keep talking to him about communication, and he says, "Okay, so we're talking, now what do you want?" And I don't know what to say then, but I know it's not what I mean. I sometimes get worried because I think maybe I want too much. He's a good husband; he works hard; he takes care of me and the kids. He could go out and find another woman who would be very happy to have a man like that and who wouldn't be all the time complaining at him because he doesn't feel things and get close. (Rubin 1976:120)

A second aspect of blue-collar marriage was under strain in the 1970s: sexual adjustment. Problems in this area were not new. For instance, husbands and wives had long clashed over the desirable frequency of sexual intercourse. LeMasters (1975) heard this complaint among patrons of the Oasis (p. 101). However, difficulties of more recent origin, deriving from the sexual revolution of the 1960s and 1970s, were evident in the comments of the younger couples interviewed by Rubin. In the 1970s, working-class sexual behavior was moving closer to middle-class norms. For example, working-class couples had nearly caught up with middle-class couples in their willingness to engage in once-exotic sexual variants such as cunnilingus and fellatio; working-class men had become similar to middle-class men in their concern for their wives' sexual satisfaction (Rubin 1976:134–135, 137–148). But change had psychological costs. Again, differential receptivity to new standards was creating stress for working-class marriages. In this case, men were more open to change. The blue-collar workers Rubin interviewed wanted freer, more expressive, more mutually satisfying sexual relationships with their wives, as their remarks show:

I think sex should be that you enjoy each other's bodies. Judy doesn't care for touching and feeling each other, though. She thinks there's just one right position and one right way—in the dark with her eyes closed tight. Anything that varies from that makes her upset. It's just not enjoyable if she doesn't have a climax, too. She says she doesn't mind, but I do. (p. 136)

Rubin and LeMasters portrayed the powerful, contradictory impact of upper-middle-class models on working-class marriages in the 1970s. Two subsequent studies of working-class life, Halle's (1984) book on chemical plant workers referred to earlier and a later book by Rubin (1994), traced the influence of these new conceptions of marriage into the 1980s and 1990s. They describe a changing world in which notions of gender equality, companionship in marriage, and mutually fulfilling sexuality were becoming more current among working-class husbands and wives—though there was generally a wide gap between professed ideals and everyday behavior. But still missing in the lives of these working-class couples were influences that encourage companionate marriage for the upper-middle class—in particular the gender-egalitarian college experience, the less authoritarian character of the upper-middle-class jobs, and the mixing of social and professional life that requires spouses to be partners.

The most obvious change for working-class couples in the 1980s and 1990s was economic. Wives were much more likely to work and to do so full time. The idea that working men could and should support their families by themselves and that women's wages were merely supplementary had become untenable. Rubin found that the teenage daughters of the working-class women she had originally interviewed in the 1970s were in no rush to marry. Their mothers had typically wed right out of high school. The daughters told Rubin that they expected to marry "someday," but first they wanted to work, to live on their own, to travel, and experience the world. As we will see later on in this chapter, the domestic lives of their generation of working-class women would be very different from the experiences of their mothers and their own, upper-middle-class contemporaries.

Social Class and Domestic Violence

In *The Unknown City: The Lives of Poor and Working-Class Young Adults*, sociologists Michelle Fine and Lois Weis (1998) deal at length with a topic that is often slighted in the literature on class and family life: domestic violence. Fine and Weiss conducted in-depth interviews in the early 1990s with an ethnically diverse group of young men and women (ages 25 to 35) in Buffalo, New York, and Jersey City, New Jersey. Most of their respondents would seem to fit into our "working poor" and "underclass" categories. Living in two deindustrialized cities in a period of high unemployment and low wages for less-educated workers, they are very much the victims of the Age of Growing Inequality.

Domestic violence is a persistent theme in the researchers' interviews with the young women—white, black, and Hispanic—in their sample. One respondent recalls her childhood as follows:

> [T]here was blood in our house just about every day. Somebody was always wacked with something. And dinner, to this day, I don't sit and eat dinner with my kids. We eat in the parlor in front of the TV, or whatever. Because every time we sat and ate. . . . a fight broke out, and you couldn't leave the kitchen. So you had to sit there and listen to it. (Fine and Weis 1998:143)

Another young woman describes a brutal, chaotic relationship with a boyfriend who would beat her regularly and then claim,

> It was my fault. I made him do it because I yelled at him and he couldn't handle it. . . . I'd block the door and he'd kick the door right in. . . . And this went on for a year. I told him the next time you hit me, don't sleep here, 'cause I will chop you up. I sat in a chair with an ax in my hand and said I was gonna chop him up that night. (p. 151)

In such lives, "not getting beat up" is one mark of a good relationship. A 21-year-old mother offers this assessment of her current relationship with her fiancé, the father of her son:

> It's good; I mean, he's there for me. It's good. I don't know what to say (laughs). . . . He listens to me. He's a friend. I don't know, I guess I got all the conveniences of a nice relationship. . . . I don't get beat up; I don't get put down. (pp. 153–154)

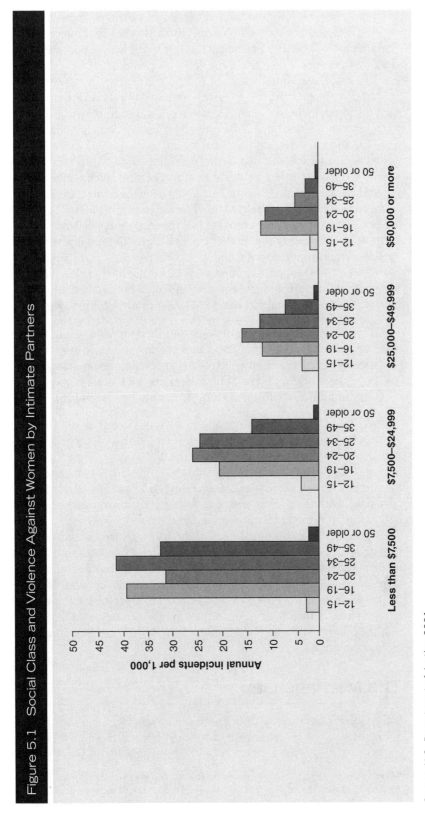

Figure 5.1 Social Class and Violence Against Women by Intimate Partners

Source: U.S. Department of Justice 2001.

Fine and Weis (1998) observed that domestic violence can be found in all social classes, but they emphasized the high rates and intergenerational character of family violence at lower-class levels. The lives of poor and working-class women, they write, "are saturated with domestic terror" (p. 134). It is possible that these young adults in Buffalo and Jersey City, drawn from the poor and, it appears, the lower fringe of the working class, during a period of high unemployment, represent an extreme. Young adults are the most prone to violence in relationships and especially so in difficult economic times.

Rubin did the research for her second book (1994) during the same period, with a sample that was, on average, probably a little better off than the Buffalo and Jersey City respondents. Fourteen percent of her families acknowledged domestic violence, but the true figure could be higher, she writes, since "this is one of the most closely guarded secrets in family life" (p. 116). A teenage boy Rubin interviewed refused to join the conspiracy of silence: "I bet they didn't tell you he beats my mother up, did they? Nobody is allowed to talk about it; we're supposed to pretend like it doesn't exist" (p. 116).

Rubin (1994) found that men were especially likely to become abusive in periods of unemployment. One respondent, who said he had not abused his wife but feared he might, shared his feelings with Rubin:

> It's hard enough being out of work, but then my wife gets on my case, yakking all the time about how we're going to be out on the street if I don't get off my butt, like it's my fault or something that there's no work out there. When she starts out like that I swear I want to hit her, anything to shut her mouth. (pp. 115–116)

We can gain a more systematic picture of class patterns in domestic violence by looking at statistics on violence against women by "intimate partners" drawn from the Justice Department's National Crime Victimization Survey (U.S. Department of Justice 2001). "Intimate partners" as defined by the survey includes current and former husbands and boyfriends.[3] The great advantage of this survey is that it collects data anonymously and includes both crimes reported and not reported to the police.

Figure 5.1 reports annual rates of intimate partner violence by age and income level. Two facts stand out in sharp relief. First, victimization is most frequent between the ages of 16 and 49, especially between 16 and 34. Second, there are enormous differences by income level. Women between 16 and 35 at the lowest income level are 3 to 5 times more likely to be victims of intimate partner violence than their peers in the top income category. These data support the claims of Fine and Weis, among others, that domestic abuse is much more common at lower-class levels.

The Marriage Gap

Today, social class not only influences whom we marry and the character of our marriages, but, more generally, what might be called our romantic careers.

---

[3] Violent "intimate partners" may also be females, but it is unlikely that there are enough offenders in this category to affect the statistics. The crimes covered include simple and aggravated assault, sexual assault, rape, robbery, and murder (U.S. Department of Justice 2001).

People at mid-to-lower class levels are now more likely to cohabit, divorce, and have children out of wedlock than are their higher class peers. Most people of all classes get married sooner or later, but upper-middle-class couples have more enduring marriages, especially if they have children. Studies using education as a class indicator find that a widening "marriage gap" is developing between the well-educated upper-middle class and the rest of the population. The college educated are much more likely than other Americans to live in "a traditional, 1950s style family" with husband, wife, and one or more children. In 1960, there was little class difference on these dimensions (Lundberg et al. 2016; Pew Research Center 2010:12; Wilcox 2010).

The large class differences today are evident in Table 5.4, which compares the marital status of women at the likely "mothering" ages of 25 to 44. The right-hand column refers to women who are raising children. The table shows that college-educated women are more likely to be married and, most notably, that college-educated *mothers* are at least 20 percent more likely to be married than mothers at lower levels of education. There is remarkably little difference among women with "less than high school," "high school," "some college." The college degree obviously marks a critical boundary.

The class marriage gap reflects rising rates of out-of-wedlock births, cohabitation, and divorce that have disproportionately affected people without college degrees. Births to unwed mothers were rare in 1960. They accounted for over 40 percent of all births by 2010, but the proportion of such births among college graduates remained in the single digits. The divorce rate climbed in the 1960s and 1970s and then declined somewhat, especially for the college educated. A 2010 study of middle-age adults found that 58 percent of people with less than high school, 48 percent of high school graduates, but only 30 percent of college graduates were divorced. Cohabitation has become increasingly common, most notably among high school graduates. College grads are less likely to cohabit, more likely to transition from cohabitation to marriage, and much less likely to have children

Table 5.4 Marital Status by Education for Women, Ages 25–44

Education	Percent Married	
	All	With Children
Less than high school	54	60
High school	56	64
Some college	57	66
College +	66	86
(N)	(41,175)	(27,054)

Source: Calculated from Current Population Survey data for years 2007–2009, using Census Bureau Table Calculator (http://www.census.gov/hhes/www/cpstc/cps_table_creator.html).

Note: Married = "married with spouse present." Children = "related children" under 18.

within cohabiting unions (Cherlin 2014:140; Lundberg et al. 2016:84–85; Solomon-Fears 2014).

Cherlin: The Disappearing Working-Class Family

As a result of the trends just described, the working-class family is threatened with extinction. That, at least, is the conclusion of a recent book by sociologist Andrew Cherlin (2014). Cherlin first focuses on the traditional working-class family that Rubin and LeMasters described in the 1970s: a married couple and children, with the husband employed as a skilled or semi-skilled worker in manufacturing, construction, or some related sector, and the wife wholly or largely devoted to home and family. This kind of breadwinner-homemaker family was the predominant domestic form among working-class people during the postwar years we have called the Age of Shared Prosperity. It had not been, Cherlin shows, in earlier periods, and it would not be in subsequent decades, when a widening gulf separated the domestic arrangements of working-class and upper-middle-class households.

Cherlin attributes the decline of the working-class family to a combination of economic and cultural factors. The key economic element is the shrinking number of blue-collar jobs, especially in manufacturing, that would allow a high school graduate with limited skills to support a family. Jobs in the service sector where many unskilled young men find employment today, are typically low paid, subject to frequent layoffs, provide few benefits, and offer limited opportunities for advancement. Cherlin finds that men in such positions are unlikely to be married. Among white men 25 to 49, approximately 30 percent of service workers were married in 2010, compared to 45 percent of blue-collar workers, and 60 percent of professionals and managers. The numbers for African American men were lower, but the pattern of occupational disparities in marriage was the same (p. 17).

The obvious cultural factor is the broad shift in attitudes surrounding gender roles, extra-marital childbirth, and cohabitation, which Cherlin confirms with opinion surveys going back to the 1970s. Most Americans no longer think, as they once did, that the breadwinner-homemaker model is ideal. They no longer believe that out-of-wedlock childbirth or cohabitation are shameful. Ironically, the one thing that has not changed is the high value young adults at all class levels place on marriage. For working-class men and women, especially, marriage is a capstone event, an ultimate life accomplishment. It requires, they believe, a strong emotional bond and a secure economic base. But they also want children and are unwilling to delay childbearing until marriage as they envision it is possible. And they do not see pregnancy as a sufficient reason for getting married. So-called "shotgun" weddings were once common. Nearly half of the working-class women Rubin interviewed in the 1970s were pregnant at the time of their weddings (Rubin 1976:60). Today, as a working-class man insists, "You need to have a way better reason than having a kid to get married." A working-class woman, similarly skeptical of shotgun unions, explains, "I want this to be because you are marrying me, not because you're marrying because I'm pregnant" (Cherlin 2014:139; Strassler and Miller 2011).

"Neither cultural change nor economic change," Cherlin concludes, "is sufficient by itself to produce a group of non-college educated young adults who now have the majority of their children outside of marriage" (p. 147). Their college educated peers have, of course, been exposed to the same cultural shift and have absorbed similar attitudes, but they only rarely have children outside of marriage. The difference, obviously, is privileged position of the college educated minority within the postindustrial economy, which allows them to contemplate both marriage and childbearing from a more secure perspective. (Currently about 30 percent of adults hold college degrees.)

Cherlin is not making a moral argument about sex and marriage. And he denies any feeling of nostalgia for the often conflict-ridden working-class family of the postwar decades. His concern is with the fragile domestic arrangements which have replaced the traditional family for a large part of the population without college degrees. The proportion of children who are living with an unmarried mother has risen steeply since 1980, except among the children of college educated women (p. 136). In many cases, unmarried mothers without college degrees are in cohabiting relationships, but these unions often began with pregnancy and prove to be short-lived. These relationships may be followed by new consensual unions, so that children growing up may see a succession of "parents, parents' partners, and stepparents enter and exit their homes" (p. 22). Cherlin points to an extensive literature showing that children living with this kind of domestic instability are prone to problem behaviors and cognitive deficiencies (p. 167). In contrast, children of the college-educated upper-middle class are usually growing up in a more stable domestic environment, which has changed little since 1980. Here again the Age of Growing Inequality favors the upper-middle class over those at lower-class levels.

Informal Association Among Adults

Warner, whose classic Yankee City study we examined in Chapter 2, considered patterns of association so critical to understanding the class system that he sometimes appeared to define class in terms of association. A social class, he suggested, is a group of people who belong to the same social cliques, intermarry, dine in each other's homes, and belong to the same organizations.

Warner defined a **social clique** as "an intimate nonkin group," with no more than 30 members. Warner's research team collected elaborate data on the clique membership of families in Yankee City. They found that most cliques brought together people of the same or adjacent classes (Warner and Lunt 1941:110–111, 350–355).

The notion that social class is about "who you hang out with" is widely shared. Asked to discuss the basis of social class differences, almost half of the skilled blue-collar workers and two thirds of the white-collar workers in a Providence, Rhode Island, study referred to patterns of association. Their comments suggest that people belong to the same class if they "run around together"; intermarry; "belong to the same churches, clubs, organizations"; "live in the same neighborhoods"; or send their kids to the same schools (Mackenzie 1973:148).

Numerous studies suggest that patterns of association are shaped by social class—though association is also influenced by factors that cut across class lines, including gender, race, age, religion, and shared interests. Earlier in this chapter, we saw that adolescent friendships and mate selection reflect class backgrounds. Adult friendships are also patterned by class, according to surveys done in Providence, the Boston area, and metropolitan Detroit (Allan 1989; Argyle 1994:66–92; Laumann 1966, 1973; Mackenzie 1973; Smith and Macaulay 1980).

Social class, then, channels friendship choices. Research shows that it also influences the extent and character of informal association. The literature suggests that people at higher class levels (1) have more friends and more active social lives; (2) are less likely to preserve friendships from their youth; (3) spend proportionately less time with relatives; (4) are more likely to entertain friends at home and, in particular, to host dinner parties; (5) are more inclined toward couple-oriented social activities; (6) are more likely to develop (nonromantic) cross-sex friendships; and (7) are more likely to mix career and social life.[4] From Bourdieu's perspective, these generalizations, taken together, suggest that people at higher class levels accumulate greater social capital.

How can we explain the class patterning of informal association? Why do people tend to marry and maintain friendships with class peers? What accounts for the class differences in the character of social life? Two obvious but powerful factors are money and propinquity (physical or social proximity). Dinner parties can be costly affairs, and guests are expected to reciprocate in kind. Skiing and sailing are more expensive than bowling. These price-of-admission differences segregate leisure activities and the people who engage in them by ability to pay. In everyday life, people tend to encounter others who are close to them in status. They live in neighborhoods and send their children to neighborhood schools that are relatively homogeneous in household income. Their coworkers have similar jobs—except for their bosses, whose authority places them at a social distance. In short, daily life is structured in ways that limit the opportunities to develop social ties across class boundaries.

Beyond money and propinquity are a series of more subtle factors—matters of prestige, style, interests, values, and comfort level, which Bourdieu would place under the broader heading of cultural capital. Their influence on patterns of informal association is suggested by some of the comments of respondents to an early Boston-area study of the friendships of adult men. One man indicates that he has "nothing in common" with people in lower occupations, another characterizes factory workers as "rough," and a third complains about the "uppity" attitudes of a relative who is a successful executive (Laumann 1966:28–29). These men seem uncomfortable with disparities in social prestige. But their attitudes also reflect objective differences in areas including education and occupational experience. Education produces contrasts in language usage, attitudes, and personal interests. Adults with limited education are likely to be uneasy in

---

[4] Allan 1989; Argyle 1994:66–92; Curtis and Jackson 1977:169; Dotson 1950; Kahl 1957:138; Kanter 1977; Rubin 1976, 1994; Shostak and Gomberg 1964; Whyte 1952.

the presence of the well-educated. Different experiences at work, as Kohn's studies of socialization demonstrate, contribute to class differences in values. Halle (1984) emphasizes that working-class people typically have dull "jobs," while upper-middle-class people have engaging "careers." The former are inevitably less interested in conversations that revolve around work and generally less inclined to mix work and leisure.

Formal Associations

Like informal ties, participation in formal associations is patterned by social class.[5] Formal associations are large groups or organizations with explicit purposes and rules of membership, including the YMCA, the neighborhood swim club, the Teamsters union, the Burning Tree Country Club, and the Boy Scouts. From its beginnings, the United States has been characterized by observers as a nation of joiners. Today, this generalization is somewhat less than half true. Most working- and lower-class Americans have little or no participation in formal associations. Even the participation of the lower-middle class is modest. The true joiners are members of the upper-middle and upper classes, who are especially likely to participate in civic and charity organizations.

Members of these top classes are not just the most likely joiners. They are also the most active participants in organizations and, even when organizational membership cuts across classes, the most likely to serve in leadership positions. The reasons for this phenomenon are not hard to imagine. These managers and professionals enjoy the prestige attached to high-class position. They have more education. At work, they develop organizational skills and confidence as leaders. Finally, many see active participation in community organizations as a way to bolster their careers.

Associations often draw their membership from a limited range in the class structure. Country clubs and exclusive social clubs such as New York's Links or Boston's Sommerset draw from the upper and upper-middle classes. Service organizations such as Rotary or Lions, fraternal orders like the Elks Club, and patriotic organizations like the Veterans of Foreign Wars recruit members from successively lower class levels.

Even churches—institutions supposedly rejoicing in our common humanity—are class typed. People of higher status are likely to attend churches of the Protestant denominations that feature services of quiet dignity and restrained emotion, such as the Episcopal or Unitarian groups. Middle-status people are more often seen at the Methodist, Mormon, and Lutheran churches. Lower status individuals are most likely to join revivalist and fundamentalist churches, such as the Pentecostals. The class level of Catholic congregations seems to vary with the ethnicity of the congregation, reflecting the timing of their immigration to the United States.[6]

---

[5] Hodges 1964:105–115; Mackenzie 1973:81–84; Smith and Macaulay 1980; Warner et al. 1949a.

[6] Demerath 1965; Kosman and Lachman 1993:257–269; Laumann 1966:55; Smith and Macaulay 1980:514.

Separate Lives

Americans are increasingly segregated by social class. No one has made this point more vividly than Tom Wolfe in his novel *Bonfire of the Vanities* (1987). The novel's protagonist, Sherman McCoy, is a smug, young Wall Street trader with a $3 million Park Avenue apartment and few redeeming qualities.

Driving into the city in his Mercedes one evening, accompanied by his mistress, Sherman blunders into an impoverished ghetto neighborhood, where he is involved in a fatal hit-and-run accident. Subsequently, McCoy finds himself locked up in a courthouse holding cell in the unwanted company of dozens of tough young men—poor and dark-skinned like the victim of his Mercedes. These events initiate a downward spiral in McCoy's life. By the end of the novel, a year after the accident, McCoy is separated from his wife, his mistress, his money, and his lawyer, who has resigned from the case because McCoy is broke.

The action of *Bonfire of the Vanities* is driven by its satisfying but improbable premise: Sherman McCoy has smashed through the wall that normally separates privileged people like the McCoys from people like the accident victim and Sherman's cellmates—or for that matter, from the $36,000-a-year assistant D.A. who prosecutes the case. "If you want to live in New York," a friend once advised McCoy, "you've got to insulate, insulate, insulate" (Wolfe 1987:55). Before the accident, McCoy used his money to do just that. His world was as insulated from the grimy reality of the city as the posh cabin of his Mercedes from the asphalt below.

Wolfe's novel reflects the growing disparities of the current era. It portrays a society whose members, divided by class and race, live in increasing isolation from one another; they no longer share (despite McCoy's strange fate) a common destiny. Journalist Mickey Kaus develops this theme in *The End of Equality* (1992), arguing that rising economic inequality has been accompanied by rising social inequality. Money, fear of the poor, and an inflated sense of their own superiority are motivating prosperous Americans to develop separate lives. "An especially precious type of equality—equality not of money but in the way we treat each other and live our lives—seems to be disappearing" (p. 5).

Kaus (1992) looks back at the post-World War II era as (with the "evil" exception of race) "a golden age of social equality." The war, perhaps more than any event in our history, provided Americans with a common experience and a sense of shared destiny. Wealthy 26-year-old John F. Kennedy served on a small PT boat in the South Pacific with men who had been machinists, factory workers, truck drivers, and night school students. Seventy percent of able-bodied young men, most of them drafted, served in the military (Kaus 1992:50). Some, like Kennedy's brother Joe, did not survive. Those who returned brought with them a network of friendships, forged under the threat of death, with little regard for class differences.

After the war, the GI Bill, passed by Congress and signed by President Roosevelt, offered all veterans scholarships, low-cost home mortgages, and other benefits. In the midst of the shared prosperity of the 1950s, there was a sense that the social distance between Americans of different classes was shrinking. Today, it appears to Kaus that just the opposite is happening. Against a backdrop of growing economic inequality, Americans worry about the emergence of what they take to be a permanent underclass. The opulent lives and social pretenses of the rich—objects of ridicule in a more egalitarian age—inspire fawning articles in glossy magazines aimed at upper-middle-class readers in search of role models. Professionals with merely comfortable incomes see themselves as "not just richer, but more civilized, better educated, wittier, smarter, cleaner, prettier" than the average American (Kaus 1992:27).

"Who killed social equality?" asks Kaus. Oddly, he rejects the most obvious suspect, rising economic inequality, and insists that the guilty party is "the decline of the public sphere." What he has in mind is the reduction of the social realm where Americans of different classes meet on more or less equal terms. He points to the end of the draft and the replacement of a broad-based citizen military with a volunteer force, which recruits few soldiers from the upper end of the class structure. But most of his examples revolve around residential segregation by class. As the rich and relatively rich retreat to exclusive suburbs (sometimes even to "gated private communities"), they separate themselves from the less privileged. Here, public spaces—the mall, the supermarket, the drugstore, the coffee shop—are largely inhabited by other members of the privileged classes. There is no place like the bar portrayed in the 1980s TV sitcom *Cheers*, a democratic setting where the postman and the psychiatrist meet informally. Above all, children attend school with others of the same class, even if they do not enroll in private academies. And, not surprisingly, upper-middle-class parents, who may support budget-slashing politicians, do not hesitate to vote for local school taxes. They know their own kids will benefit.

Residential Segregation

There is good recent evidence of the class-segregating trend that novelist Wolfe and journalist Kaus describe. Since the 1970s, according to analyses of U.S. census data, the proportion of families living in distinctively lower income or higher income neighborhoods has increased, as the proportion in middle-income neighborhoods has sunk. The general pattern is evident in Figure 5.2, based on a study by Reardon and Bischoff (2011) of the 117 metropolitan areas in the United States with populations over 500,000. They range from New York City to Chattanooga, Tennessee. As the bar chart indicates, in 1970, about two thirds of families lived in middle-income neighborhoods. By the 2000s, the proportion living in such neighborhoods had sunk to a little over 40 percent, as the proportions in higher and lower income neighborhoods expanded.

Using a sophisticated income-segregation measure, Reardon and Bischoff determined the extent to which population groups are isolated in neighborhoods that are homogeneous and distinct from the general population.[7] They found that isolation by income level grew most rapidly in the

---

[7] This measure, with the cumbersome name "rank-order information theory index," is designed to get around a significant methodological problem. Income segregation as indicated in Figure 5.2 may increase simply because income inequality is increasing, even if the distribution of people among neighborhoods is constant. The index measures change in segregation beyond that caused by the increased income inequality.

1980s and 2000s, and that the top 10 percent and bottom 10 percent of income-earning families were notably and increasingly isolated from others. The isolation of the top 10 percent was especially high. It appears that even Americans of relatively modest affluence are heeding the advice of Sherman McCoy's friend in *Bonfire of the Vanities*: "Insulate, insulate."

The authors also looked separately at isolation *among* blacks and *among* Hispanics. Given the increasing occupational differentiation among African Americans noted in Chapter 3, we should not be surprised to learn that residential separation by income has also increased. A similar pattern holds for Hispanics. Both of these groups are much more income-segregated among themselves than are whites.

Does sorting people into neighborhoods by income matter? Yes, it does. Higher income neighborhoods are likely to have better schools, safer streets, stronger civic organizations, and superior amenities from parks to well-stocked supermarkets. Reardon and Bischoff refer to research demonstrating that living in higher or lower income neighborhoods affects people in ways that go beyond simply being richer or poorer. It matters who your neighbors are. They influence important life outcomes in areas such as health, education, and career prospects. Thus, increasing income segregation is likely to reinforce the growing inequality in American society.

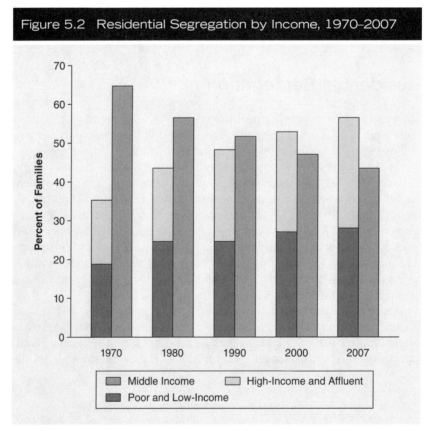

Figure 5.2 Residential Segregation by Income, 1970–2007

Source: Derived from Table A1 in Reardon & Bischoff, 2011:28.

Note: 2007 is average for 2007 to 2009.

Conclusion

This chapter has explored the social implications of class structure, emphasizing socialization and association. The life cycle has served as a guiding thread. We learned that children are precociously aware of class distinctions and that they are socialized according to patterns that reflect the class position of their parents. Adolescents tend to form friendships and romantic ties with others who share their class background. Young adults typically marry class equals or near equals. Adult friendships, romantic relationships, marital styles, residential distribution, organizational activities, and even church membership are all patterned by social class.

These observations bring us back to Max Weber's idea that prestige classes (or "status groups," as he called them) are social "communities," characterized by distinctive lifestyles and values. To a remarkable extent, our social lives and outlooks are molded by class position. Consider the typical differences we have found between the upper-middle and working classes. Members of the upper-middle class generally share the life-shaping experiences of college, geographic mobility, and a career-oriented social life. More likely to have stable marriages and to raise children within a marriage, they are drawn to a joint model of marriage and to values of self-direction and tolerance, which they stress for their children. Their child-rearing practices inculcate formal language skills, confidence in dealing with institutions, and a general sense of entitlement. Their exclusive choices of friends and mates suggest that this class is relatively isolated from the rest of the population. In contrast, members of the working class are more likely to cohabit and to have children out of wedlock. In marriage, they develop segregated relationships and separate social and work life. They have higher divorce rates. Their child-rearing practices convey a sense of constraint to their sons and daughters.

These differences reinforce Bourdieu's conclusion that the advantages of the privileged classes extend beyond economic capital to cultural and social capital. The upper-middle-class child who grows up with superior command of the English language and has learned to deal confidently with people in authority has accumulated valuable cultural capital. Upper-middle-class parents, whose friends and relatives typically include doctors, psychologists, lawyers, and other professionals, possess valuable social capital they can tap when they need advice or a new job.

We should expect these social differences to widen as economic differences grow. We know, in particular, that marriage differences and residential segregation by class are increasing. (In many other important areas, unfortunately, we do not have recent studies that permit us to talk about trends.) But the American class system is still far from becoming an archipelago of discrete class cultures. The differences we have described in this chapter are statistical tendencies, not absolute contrasts. College-educated mothers are *more likely* to be married, but some are not; and over half of mothers with high school diplomas are married. Americans of all classes are influenced by a national culture and share many key values. They are exposed to many of the same ideas and lifestyles in pervasive mass media. At the same time, the diversity of American society and continuing social mobility (as we see in the next chapter) guarantee that the membership of any social class will be quite varied.

KEY TERMS DEFINED IN THE GLOSSARY

association

cultural capital
  (see capital)

economic capital
  (see capital)

joint marital
  relationships

segregated marital
  relationships

social capital
  (see capital)

social clique

socialization

SUGGESTED READINGS

Bourdieu, Pierre. 1984. *Distinction: A Social Critique of the Judgement of Taste.* Cambridge, MA: Harvard University Press.

Class cultures and their function in defining and reproducing class differences.

Bourdieu, Pierre. 1986. "The Forms of Capital." In *Handbook of Theory and Research for the Sociology of Education,* edited by John Richardson. New York: Greenwood Press.

A compact discussion of the economic, cultural, and social forms of capital.

Brooks, David. 2000. *Bobos in Paradise: The New Upper Class and How They Got There.* New York: Simon & Schuster.

The origins, lifestyles, and values of the emerging, knowledge-based privileged class. Witty and insightful.

Cherlin, Andrew 2014. *Labor's Love Lost: The Rise and Fall of the Working-Class in America.* New York: Russell Sage Foundation.

Important book tracing shifts in working-class family life since the nineteenth century and their relation to economic and cultural change.

DiTomaso, Nancy. 2013. *The American Non-Dilemma: Racial Inequality Without Racism.* New York: Russell Sage Foundation.

How racial economic inequality is unintentionally sustained by whites' preferential treatment of individuals in their own social networks.

Fine, Michelle and Lois Weis. 1998. *The Unknown City: The Lives of Poor and Working-Class Young Adults.* Boston, MA: Beacon.

Family and economic lives of white, black, and Hispanic young adults in the context of two economically troubled cities in the Northeast. Most are working poor or underclass.

Lamont, Michele. 1992. *Money, Morals, and Manners: The Culture of the French and the American Upper-Middle Class.* Chicago, IL: University of Chicago Press.

_____. 2000. *The Dignity of Working Men: Morality and the Boundaries of Race, Class, and Immigration.* Boston, MA: Harvard University Press.

The moral boundaries that working-class and upper-middle-class men draw between themselves and others. Both based on in-depth interviews conducted in the United States and France.

Lareau, Annette. 2003. *Unequal Childhoods: Class, Race, and Family Life.* Berkeley, CA: University of California Press.

An original and influential study of class differences in child rearing.

Murray, Charles. 2012. *Coming Apart: The State of White America, 1960–2010.* New York: Crown Forum.

Growing economic and cultural distance between working-class and upper-middle-class white Americans. Covers some of the same ground as Cherlin from a conservative perspective.

Rubin, Lillian Breslow. 1976. *Worlds of Pain: Life in the Working-Class Family.* New York: Basic Books.

_____1994. *Families on the Faultline: America's Working Class Speaks About the Family, the Economy, Race, and Ethnicity.* New York: HarperCollins.

Sensitive portrayals of working-class life. First volume makes revealing comparisons with upper-middle class. Though dated, still valuable.

Social Mobility
The Societal Context

Some people's money is merited. And other people's is inherited.

Ogden Nash, *The Terrible People*

A rising tide lifts all boats.

John F. Kennedy

Social mobility, our topic in this chapter and the next, may be defined as the extent to which people move up or down in the class system, especially from one generation to the next. The study of social mobility is motivated by curiosity about a seemingly simple question: Is our place in the class system, in Ogden Nash's words, merited or inherited?

We will look at mobility from two perspectives, societal and individual. The first, the focus of this chapter, considers the system as a whole, emphasizing the general pattern of social mobility. We ask these questions: How much mobility is there in America? How does the United States compare with other countries? Are the opportunities for mobility increasing or decreasing? What factors determine mobility rates? In Chapter 7, we look at individuals. We ask why, given the available opportunities, some move ahead, some fall behind, and others just stay in place. In particular, we want to know how much importance to attach to family background factors, like parental occupation and race, and how much to an individual's educational attainment.

The keys to the societal perspective are the shape of the class structure and its relative openness. Consider, for example, a hypothetical feudal society made up of a mass of impoverished peasants—let's call them "the poor bastards"—who are dominated by a handful of large landowners and their overseers. Its structure is that of a very steep pyramid: broad at the base, narrow in the middle, and needle-pointed at the top. Even if this society were perfectly open or "fair" and gave everyone an equal opportunity in the competition for the higher positions (extremely unlikely in a real feudal society), the chances of getting ahead would be slim. With rare exceptions, the children of poor bastards would grow up to be poor bastards, but so would the children of landed aristocrats.

Now suppose this society begins to industrialize. A new class of urban capitalists emerges. Its activities promote the growth of an industrial working class. The middle sectors expand because an industrial society requires rising numbers of engineers, accountants, managers, teachers, electricians, and other specialists to function efficiently. The social pyramid is becoming fatter in the middle and somewhat wider at the top. Even if this society does not treat everyone equally, the chances of moving up are now much greater. The children of peasants might become factory workers (an improvement over tilling the lord's land), and their grandchildren could aspire to even higher positions. In short, there is a quickening of upward social mobility due to structural change.

How Much Mobility?

A common way to measure **intergenerational mobility** is to compare the occupations of fathers and sons, as we have done in Tables 6.1 and 6.2. (We will look at the mobility of women in the next section.) These tables are based on national surveys that ask respondents their occupations and the occupations of their fathers when they were growing up. Using this information, we can answer questions like these: What chance does the son of an unskilled worker have of attaining a professional or managerial position? What are the social origins of people in high-status occupations?

Table 6.1 Outflow From Father's Occupation to Son's Occupation

Father's Occupation	Son's Occupation (in percent)					
	Upper White Collar	Lower White Collar	Upper Manual	Lower Manual	Farm	Total
Upper White Collar	42	31	12	15	1	100
Lower White Collar	34	33	13	19	1	100
Upper Manual	20	20	29	29	1	100
Lower Manual	20	22	20	36	2	100
Farm	16	18	19	35	12	100
Total (N = 3,398)	27	25	19	27	3	

Summary			
Up	Stable	Down	Total
41	33	26	100

Source: Author's analysis of General Social Survey data, 1995 to 2004.

Note: Occupational categories: *upper white collar*—higher professionals and managers; *lower white collar*—semiprofessionals, technicians, sales, clerical; *upper manual*—skilled blue collar; *lower manual*—operatives, service workers, laborers; *farm*—farmers and farm workers.

Table 6.1 is an **outflow mobility table** that starts with fathers and asks about the mobility of their sons. For example, reading across the row that begins with "lower manual" on the far left, you can trace the sons of fathers who held unskilled "lower manual jobs." Some of these sons (20 percent) rose to "upper white-collar" (professional or managerial) positions, but the largest group (36 percent) followed their fathers into unskilled manual jobs. The top row shows that the sons of upper white-collar fathers were much more successful or fortunate. Over 40 percent had jobs at the same high level as their fathers; only a few (15 percent) sank to lower manual jobs. (See the notes at the bottom of the table for a fuller description of the five occupational categories.)

Several general conclusions can be drawn from this table:

1. There is a high level of occupational inheritance—sons following fathers into jobs at the same occupational level.

2. The higher the father's occupation level, the better the son's chances for occupational achievement.

3. Nonetheless, there is also considerable movement up and down the occupational ladder from one generation to the next, as the summary statistics at the bottom of the table suggest.

4. By a considerable margin, sons are more likely to move up than down.

Table 6.2 presents the same data in an altered form that allows us to answer a different set of questions. It is an **inflow mobility table**. Unlike the previous outflow table that started with fathers and traced the fortunes of their sons, this table starts with sons and asks about their fathers. Here we want to know where people at different levels in the occupational structure come from. To answer this question, the table is percentaged down the columns, rather than across the rows, like the outflow table.

Reading down the Farm and Lower Manual columns on the right side of Table 6.2, you will not be surprised to learn that farmers are typically sons of farmers and lower manual workers are most often sons of lower manual workers. But you may be surprised to learn from the statistics in the upper white-collar column that the people in these higher status occupations are of very diverse social origins. Only a third are sons of men with higher white-collar occupations (people we might call upper-middle class). Approximately the same proportion are from manual occupations. We get this result, despite the high level of father-to-son succession at the top revealed in the previous table, because the relative number of professional and managerial jobs has been growing, creating opportunities for advancement from below. Many men in privileged occupational positions apparently grew up in relatively modest circumstances, and their lifestyles, values, and political outlook may, in some degree, differ from those who began life at the top of the pyramid.

The mixed social origins of people at all levels are relevant to a question we raise at various points in this book: the degree of consistency or clarity in the class system. Intergenerational mobility undermines the tendency of the class structure to crystallize into a hierarchy of distinct, stable, internally homogeneous classes.

Table 6.2   Inflow From Father's Occupation to Son's Occupation

Father's Occupation	Son's Occupation (in percent)					
	Upper White Collar	Lower White Collar	Upper Manual	Lower Manual	Farm	Total
Upper White Collar	34	27	14	13	11	23
Lower White Collar	23	24	13	14	11	19
Upper Manual	17	18	36	25	11	23
Lower Manual	19	23	28	36	19	26
Farm	6	7	10	13	49	10
Total (N = 3,398)	100	100	100	100	100	

Source: Author's analysis of General Social Survey data, 1995 to 2004.

Note: See Table 6.1 for category definitions.

Table 6.3 Outflow From Father's Occupation to Daughter's Occupation

Father's Occupation	Daughter's Occupation (in percent)					
	Professional and Managerial	Sales and Clerical	Service	Blue Collar	Farm	Total
Upper White Collar	54	33	9	3	1	100
Lower White Collar	49	34	11	6	.05	100
Upper Manual	35	37	18	8	1	100
Lower Manual	32	39	19	9	1	100
Farm	34	28	22	14	2	100
Total (N = 3,398)	40	35	16	8	1	

Source: Author's analysis of General Social Survey data, 1995 to 2004.

Notes: See Table 6.1 for father's category definitions. Daughter's professional/managerial is a broader category including many semiprofessional jobs. Sales/clerical includes technicians, most notably those in health fields. Blue collar includes a small proportion of skilled manual workers.

Social Mobility of Women

Studies of intergenerational social mobility have largely focused on men. Until recently, this emphasis seemed justified by the traditionally limited labor force participation of women. But as we have seen, in the Age of Growing Inequality, families have grown increasingly dependent on women's paid labor.

Studying women's mobility presents special problems. For one, with whom do we want to compare the women workers—their mothers or their fathers? Many mothers in previous generations did not work or worked only part time or intermittently. They were not the economic mainstay or foundation of social status for their households. If the comparison is with fathers, we face the problem that women workers are distributed across occupations in a very different fashion than men, making father–daughter comparisons tricky. Women are, for example, more likely to be nurses, secretaries, sales clerks, and maids. If we see that many daughters of lower manual workers have moved "up" to white-collar work, are we looking at a difference between generations or between genders?

Table 6.3, which compares the occupations of fathers and daughters, does not resolve these problems (a task beyond the scope of this book), but it does give us a preliminary picture of women's mobility. We have drawn on the same data we used to measure men's mobility but applied a different set of occupational categories to daughters, to capture the typical pattern of female employment. The one conclusion that we can confidently draw from this table is that women's occupational attainment, like men's, is powerfully influenced by class origins. For example, 54 percent of the daughters of upper white-collar men hold a broad range of managerial and professional jobs, including doctors and lawyers but also teachers and nurses.[1] In contrast, daughters of lower manual workers are more likely to hold clerical, sales, technical, and service jobs, and a significant minority hold unskilled blue-collar jobs, most typically as factory workers. But there is also ample evidence of social mobility in the table. For example, a third of the daughters of lower manual men have managerial or professional occupations.

Circulation and Structural Mobility

We have been looking at the pattern of intergenerational movement up and down the occupational hierarchy. But what are the underlying causes of this mobility? To simplify the problem, imagine a completely closed society of workers in which sons and daughters inevitably replicate the positions of their parents. Now consider the factors that could open it up. There are two basic ones.

1. **Circulation mobility**. Some privileged members of the second generation might slip down the scale and thereby make room for others to climb up. In this instance, mobility is a "zero sum game" based on intergenerational turnover at or near the top.

2. **Structural mobility**. If technological and organizational changes occur in a way that creates jobs at a faster rate in the middle and upper levels of the occupational structure than in the lower levels, then some lower ranking sons and daughters will have the chance to climb into the new positions without displacing others—not a "zero sum game" this time, but a "win-win" situation. (Of course, change could also reduce opportunities to move up and force some people down.)

In fact, both of these processes are at work in any modern society, though we have no practical way of determining precisely how much mobility to attribute to each. And we certainly cannot determine which is responsible for any individual's mobility (or lack of mobility). The world is more complex than our simple model suggests. For example, total mobility is inflated by what we might call the multiplier effect: If new jobs are created toward the top of the hierarchy, they are likely to be filled by people moving up from the middle, creating, in turn, new opportunities for people at lower levels to move up. Thus, each new opening can create two or more moves in a step-by-step progression.

We can, however, get a sense of the influence of occupational change by reexamining the occupational trend data we saw in Chapter 3. We saw that some occupational categories grew rapidly, while others expanded slowly or shrank. For example, from 1940 to 2000, the white-collar categories grew at several times the 84 percent expansion of the labor force as a whole, while the numbers of low-skilled operatives and farm workers and laborers actually

---

[1] The inclusion of these semiprofessionals makes the professional/managerial category used for daughters much broader than the upper white-collar category applied to fathers.

shrank (Table 6.4). The effect of these dual trends was to create what might be described as a mobility updraft, drawing people into higher positions. (The updraft was somewhat offset by the growth of service employments.)

During these decades, the categories of professional and technical, managers and proprietors, and clerical and sales taken together grew from about 10.5 million to 35 million positions—a 330 percent expansion. If these occupations had grown at the same rate as the average for the whole labor force, there would have been only 19 million men in white-collar jobs in 2000. The difference of the actual over this "expected" average growth was about 15 million positions: That number of men had the chance to move up in the system to fill the newly created jobs. They constituted 21 percent of the male labor force in 2000—and this estimate is the absolute minimum of structural mobility because we have no way of adding those men who moved up because of the multiplier effect described earlier.

Declining Social Mobility

In earlier chapters, we examined trends in income, wealth, and occupational structure. What can we say about trends in social mobility? Is there more or less upward mobility than there was in the past? How has the pattern of mobility changed? To answer these questions, we compare the mobility of two groups of workers, the first interviewed in the 1970s and the second around 2000, and we single out younger workers, ages 25 to 44, whose

Table 6.4 Male Occupational Distributions, 1940 and 2000

	In Millions		
	1940	2000	Percent Change
Total	39.2	72.3	+84
Professional/technical	2.3	11.8	+413
Managers/proprietors	3.4	10.8	+218
Sales/clerical	4.8	12.1	+152
Craftsmen/foremen	6.1	13.5	+121
Operatives	7.1	2.6	−35
Service workers	2.4	7.2	+200
Laborers, except farm	4.7	4.4	−17
Farm occupations	8.5	2.7	−70

Sources: U.S. Census Bureau 1975; U.S. Department of Labor 2001a.

Note: Because of modifications in Census Bureau occupational categories and the shift from 14 to 16 as the minimum age for which occupational data are typically tabulated, these 1940 and 2000 distributions are not strictly compatible (see Table 3.2, especially 1972 tabulation). But they are an appropriate basis for the rough comparisons made here.

experience most clearly reflects recent change. Note that the younger workers interviewed in the 1970s entered the labor force during the postwar Age of Shared Prosperity and those interviewed around 2000 began their careers in the current Age of Growing Inequality.

We find that upward mobility has, in fact, declined and downward mobility has increased. Among younger workers, upward mobility dropped from 45 percent to 37 percent (Table 6.5). The basic reason is that the mobility updraft created by the swelling of the higher occupational categories and the shrinkage of some of the lower categories had largely played itself out by 2000. There was, in other words, less structural mobility in later years. We confirm this with an Index of Structural Mobility, based on the difference between the occupational distributions of fathers and sons. The index shows a decline in structural mobility, especially for younger workers.[2]

Further scrutiny of the same data reveals that the sons of upper and lower white-collar workers are a little less likely to inherit their father's position. Their privileged background counts for less, though it still counts. This tendency indicates that the decline in structural mobility is being offset, albeit modestly, by an increase in circulation mobility.

Table 6.5 Trends in Social Mobility (Percentages)

Mobility	All Men		Men 25 to 44	
	1970s	2000	1970s	2000
Up	48	41	45	37
Stable	34	33	34	34
Down	19	27	21	30
Index of Structural Mobility	18	11	16	8

Source: Author's analysis of General Social Survey data, 1972–1979 and 1995–2004.

Note: Refers to occupational categories and sample as defined in earlier tables.

American Mobility in Comparative Perspective[3]

For Americans, the topic of social mobility is inevitably intertwined with the promise of the American Dream. We like to believe that the United States is uniquely a place where anyone who is able and hard working can prosper. The idea is not new. It was a commonplace in the nineteenth century. But it was named and re-popularized by James Truslow Adams, in *The Epic of*

---

[2] The index is the minimum percentage of sons who have moved because of changes in the occupational structure between generations. It is calculated by subtracting the percentage of fathers from the percentage of sons for each occupational category in which the latter exceeds the former. The sum of these differences is the index number.

[3] This section draws on Corak 2013, Corak 2013a, Isaacs 2008, and Beller and Hout 2006.

America (1931), an optimistic national history published at the onset of the Great Depression. For Adams, the American dream was not "a dream of motor cars and high wages merely, [but also] a dream of a social order in which each man and each woman shall be able to attain the fullest stature of which they are innately capable, and be recognized by others for what they are, regardless of the fortuitous circumstances of birth or positions" (Noah 2012:14).

But is the United States a uniquely open society? Figure 6.1 gives us one way of answering that question, and it suggests that the answer is no. The bars in the chart compare countries on what economists call "inter-generational earnings elasticity" or, more informally, the "stickiness of earn-ings." They measure the degree to which the relative economic position of sons reproduces or "sticks to" the earlier position of fathers. Higher elasticity means less mobility. As might be expected, sons' earnings are far stickier in Peru or Brazil than in Denmark or Norway. By this measure, the United States is closer to Peru than Denmark. Its elasticity of 47 tells us that the advantage the son of a high earning American father carries to adulthood is almost twice that enjoyed by a Canadian peer.[4]

The American handicap in this international income mobility contest seems to derive from differences at the extremes of the class structure. Mobility prospects for boys born to families in the middle of the income distribution are similar to those for middle-income boys in other wealthy countries. But the formidable advantages of the sons of high-income families and disadvantages of sons of low-income families set the United States apart from other wealthy societies. These outcomes reflect class differences in child-rearing patterns we

Figure 6.1 "Stickiness" of Earnings From Father to Son

Intergenerational Elasticity of Earnings in Percent

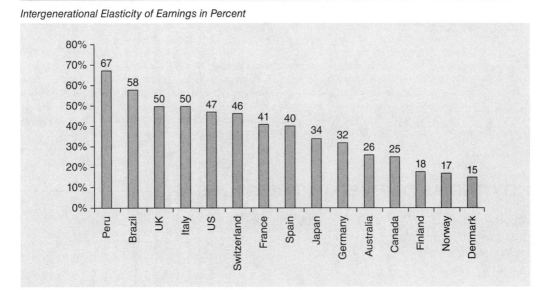

Source: Corak 2013:111.

---

[4]More precisely, it tells us that that a 100% difference in fathers' earnings will, on average, produce a 47% difference in sons' earnings.

discussed in Chapter 5 and the large income gap between college-educated and high-school educated workers we noted in Chapter 3.

This is not to say that the American Dream is dead. As we have seen in this chapter, the mobility machine has slowed, but upward mobility, measured by occupational advancement, is still common and more frequent than downward mobility. International comparisons of mobility based on occupation, rather than income show that the United States is not exceptional, but about average among high-income countries (Beller and Hout 2006).[5]

Conclusion

Our most consistent and predictable conclusion in this chapter is simple: In the race to the top, it helps to start there. This is confirmed by mobility tables, based on recent data that reveal a strong association between the occupations of fathers and sons or daughters. Nonetheless, there is a great deal of intergenerational social mobility. Two thirds of sons, for example, have moved up or down from their fathers' occupational level, and upward mobility is still more common than downward mobility.

But when we sharpen our focus and compare the experience of younger men in recent years with an earlier cohort at the same age, we see evidence of stagnating opportunities. The structural change that has fueled mobility in the past is waning. In international comparisons, the U.S. is, at best, average among affluent countries.

These trends could have powerful political implications. Many workers feel that they do not have the same opportunities for advancement that their parents enjoyed, and younger people fear that they might never attain the living standard that they grew up with. Especially in periods of economic stagnation, such feelings can turn them against politicians they identify with the status quo.

---

[5] The two measures differ, in part, because earnings elasticity is a relative measure of inherited advantage or disadvantage. It doesn't tell us the extent to which people are moving up or down in an absolute sense. We can get that from father-to-son occupational mobility, an absolute measure. In a thriving economy people are generally moving up in occupation from one generation to the next because new opportunities are being created. It is logically possible for everyone to move up without changing the relative occupational or income ranking of fathers and sons.

KEY TERMS DEFINED IN THE GLOSSARY

circulation mobility
intergenerational mobility
   (see social mobility)

outflow mobility table/inflow   social mobility
   mobility table
structural mobility

SUGGESTED READINGS

For social mobility readings, see suggested readings list at the end of Chapter 7.

Family, Education, and Career

The transmission of property from generation to generation, in the same name, raised up a distinct set of families, who, being privileged by law in the perpetuation of their wealth, were thus formed into a Patrician order, distinguishable by the splendor and luxury of their establishments. From this order, too, the king habitually selected his counselors of State. . . . To annul this privilege, and instead of an aristocracy of wealth, of more harm and danger than benefit to society, to make an opening for the aristocracy of virtue and talent, which nature has wisely provided for the direction of the interests of society, and scattered with equal hand through all its conditions, was deemed essential to a well-ordered republic.

Thomas Jefferson (1821)

In the quotation that begins this chapter, Thomas Jefferson, himself the wealthy son of a planter family, urges the replacement of the corrupt old "aristocracy of wealth" with a new "aristocracy of virtue and talent." The aristocracy of wealth, Jefferson thought, could be eliminated by changing the laws of inheritance so that men would divide their landed estates equally among all their children and thus eventually arrive at small holdings. The aristocracy of virtue and talent—characteristics Jefferson assumed were "scattered with equal hand" among all classes—could be cultivated by creating a public school system that would provide primary education for all citizens and then select the best students for further training in high schools and universities. In his later years, Jefferson founded the University of Virginia as the capstone to this system and was so proud of it that he ordered that his tombstone should record his two greatest accomplishments: the writing of the Declaration of Independence and the founding of the University of Virginia.

From Thomas Jefferson forward, American political leaders have endorsed high rates of social mobility. In doing so, they have reflected the general values held by most Americans, which accept some inequality in society, believing that people should get different rewards for different kinds of work, but also believing that each generation should start fresh and compete in a "fair" way for those rewards. In other words, Americans believe that young people ought to have careers based on their own talents and effort (Jefferson's "aristocracy of virtue and talent"), rather than have their lives determined by the class positions of their parents; they should have "equality of opportunity" but not necessarily "equality of result." Accepting the fact that some aspects of the talent and drive of the children are inherited from or shaped by the parents, Americans have believed, or at least hoped, that equality of opportunity can be achieved through the school system. If all children have access to good schools at all levels, regardless of the financial resources of their families, then the graduates should be able to compete on a reasonably fair basis.

The connections among family background, education, and career success, often the focus of heated debate, will be our main concern in this chapter. Here we shift away from the systemic or structural perspective of the last chapter to highlight the experience of individuals. Instead of asking how much mobility exists in the system as a whole, we ask why some individuals are more successful than others. Obviously, these are closely related topics. An individual's chances for success will depend on both the available opportunities and his or her personal characteristics, including family background and educational achievement.

In what follows, we are often interested in establishing the strength of the connections between variables—for example, the influence of father's occupation on son's occupation. We use two yardsticks for this purpose: **simple correlation** and **variance explained**. Both tell us how accurately we can predict the value of one variable by knowing the values of preceding variables. Correlation is measured by a coefficient that ranges from 0.0 (there is no relationship between two variables) to 1.00 (we can, with perfect accuracy, predict the second variable by knowing the first). In the social sciences, most correlation coefficients are intermediate. For example, the correlation between father's education and son's education is around 0.45.

Variance explained, which is closely related to correlation, is typically invoked when we are trying to measure the influence of a series of prior variables on a single dependent variable. Variance explained is expressed as a percentage of total variance in the dependent variable, with higher percentages expressing stronger relationships. We might, for example, determine that father's occupation and education together "explain" 45 percent of the variance in son's occupational success—meaning that the differences in occupation and education among fathers statistically account for 45 percent of the differences in occupational level among sons. Other factors, both known and unknown, account for the remaining 55 percent.

Blau and Duncan: Analyzing Mobility Models

What makes the study of the social mobility of individuals complicated and debatable is this: Everything is related to everything else. We know, for example, that a son's "occupational attainment" (that is, the occupational level he reaches) is correlated with both his father's occupational status and his own education (both approximately 0.50). These relationships are depicted in Diagram A in Figure 7.1. But, as Diagram B indicates, the father's occupational status is also correlated with the son's education. This introduces a complication. How are we to interpret the relationships among the three variables? One possibility, portrayed in Diagram C, is a simple causal chain. Concretely, sons with high-status fathers have the opportunity to get a good education and, as a result, to get good jobs; sons with low-status fathers cannot get a good education and end up with crummy jobs. The effect of the father's socioeconomic status on the son's career is mediated through education.

But things might be more complicated than that. Imagine that a son with a high-status father completes his education and then gets an additional career boost: The old man hires his son or finds him a good job through a family connection. Diagram D adds another arrow to represent this possibility, but the additional arrow opens a new mystery. Which is more important, education or easy access to the job? Perhaps education did not really count for much and was just the inevitable result of a privileged background like, say, driving an expensive car; in the end, what really mattered was the job opportunity. Of course, the opposite is also possible or some unequal combination of the two influences.

Things would get even more complicated if we considered additional factors—for example, race and parents' education. A black child might get less encouragement in school than white schoolmates and end up quitting school early, only to face discrimination in the job market. This outcome would be less likely if the child's parents were well educated themselves. Of course, well-educated parents would be likely to have high-status jobs, an additional career advantage for the son or daughter. If we added new arrows to the diagram to represent these and other interrelated influences, we would soon have a tangle of causal pathways resembling a New York City subway map—a complicated image for the complex realities of social mobility.

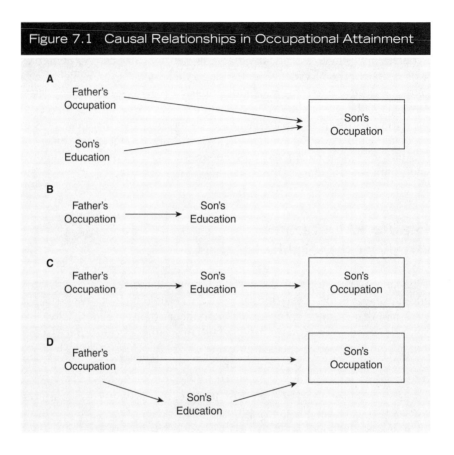

Figure 7.1   Causal Relationships in Occupational Attainment

In 1967, Peter Blau and Otis Dudley Duncan introduced an innovative methodology for analyzing the complexities of career success and failure. Their book, *The American Occupational Structure,* which analyzed the results of a large-scale national mobility survey, inspired much of the subsequent research in the field. Blau and Duncan depicted career development in formal "path diagrams"—more elaborate versions of our drawings—that became the basis for their statistical analysis of the survey data. Their goal was to sort out the influence of each variable, independent of the others. **Path analysis**, as this method is called, helped Blau and Duncan conceptualize two key aspects of the problem: **chains of causation** (father's occupation influences son's education, which in turn, influences son's career prospects) and **multiple causal pathways** (father's occupation influences son's education and later directly influences his job search).[1] Note that path analysis emphasizes the temporal element in social mobility. Blau and Duncan's analysis dealt sequentially with family background, education, son's first job, and job at the time of the survey, examining the influences operating at each stage.

Figure 7.2 summarizes a later national mobility study that used the methods pioneered by Blau and Duncan (Featherman 1979; Featherman and Hauser 1978). The study is based on a representative sample of adult

---

[1] Our examples are sons because the literature we are discussing here was initially limited to fathers and sons.

men who answered questions about their family background, education, and career experience. Each respondent's occupation at the time of the survey was rated on a scale of **socioeconomic status (SES)** developed by Duncan and akin to the occupational rankings we discussed in Chapter 2. The family background variables examined in the study include father's SES, father's education, parents' marital status, and race. The analysis sorts out the determinants of occupational attainment as measured by respondent's SES.

Our very simplified path diagram and the related pie graph in Figure 7.2 emphasize the study's main conclusions. The diagram indicates that both family background and education, as expected, contribute to son's socioeconomic status. It shows direct and indirect (through education) connections between family background and son's SES. The pie graph parcels out responsibility for the result (son's SES) between the background variables and educational achievement in terms of variance explained.

What do we learn from Figure 7.2?

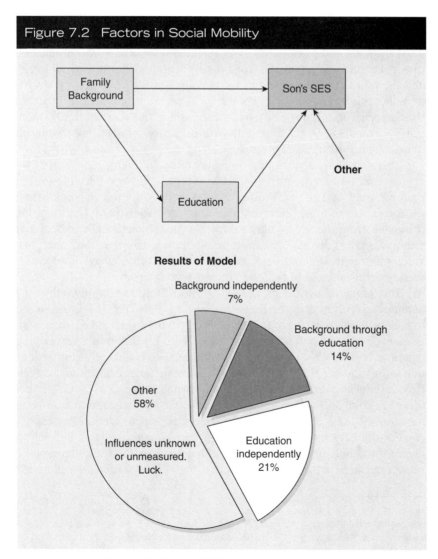

Figure 7.2 Factors in Social Mobility

Family Background → Son's SES

Education

Other

Results of Model

Background independently
7%

Background through
education
14%

Other
58%

Influences unknown
or unmeasured.
Luck.

Education
independently
21%

Source: Based on data from Featherman 1979.

1. *Family background through education.* The main effect of family background (that is, the background variables taken together) is its influence on education, which, in turn, contributes to career success (14 percent of total variance). In other words, rich kids generally get good educations; poor kids normally do not.

2. *Family background independently.* Family background also has a smaller, independent effect on son's SES (7 percent). This refers, for example, to the father who uses his connections to help his child find a job or get him into the electricians union, but also to the negative effects of racial discrimination on blacks.

3. *Education independently.* Education has a substantial independent effect (21 percent). This tells us that educational achievement does more than just reflect the privileges or disadvantages of family background. Some rich kids flunk out and lose the career-enhancing benefits of education. Some not-so-rich kids graduate from college and get a big career boost.

Figure 7.2 indicates that the total influence of family background on career success (1+2) is equal to the independent influence of education (3). Together, background and education account for 42 percent of total variance. But this leaves 58 percent of the variance, corresponding to "other" in the diagram, "unexplained." As we will see later in this chapter, recent, more elaborate models reduce the amount of unexplained variance, but significant unexplained variance always remains.

There are two basic reasons for unexplained variance. One is that we cannot always measure our variables as precisely as we would like to. For example, the father's or son's job may be better or worse than it sounds from the rough occupational titles recorded in surveys. The other is that there are many influences that we do not, and often cannot, include in the model. For example, some individuals are more ambitious and able than their academic accomplishments suggest. Personal charm or good looks may also contribute to career success, but they are not easy to measure.[2]

The family influences on mobility (1 and 2) do not simply reflect the financial advantage of some households over others. Yes, it is easier to go to college if you don't have to worry about paying for it. But as we saw in Chapter 5, cultural and social capital are also powerful influences. Having parents who know about getting into college or having family connections to a social network that can provide job leads are potent career advantages. Parental education and occupation, as we saw in Chapter 5, are good predictors of cultural and social capital. But sometimes, the background variables we use don't quite capture essential aspects of a person's circumstances.

Consider the experience of young Barack Obama, a black kid with a divorced mother, growing up in a household with modest resources. Not a very promising start in life. But Obama's mother had started college by the

---

[2] Unfortunately, many of the variables we might add turn out to be largely "redundant" because they overlap with variables already included. For example, this model does not include mother's education, but mother's education is highly correlated with father's education and occupation, which are included. Therefore, this additional variable would not contribute much to explained variance.

time he was born and was determined that he should go to college. Equally important, Obama's grandfather was an outgoing guy with lots of useful, casual connections, who helped Barack get a scholarship to Punahou, an elite prep school in Honolulu. Barack, by his own telling, was an indifferent student at this stage of his life, but he got a good intellectual foundation at Punahou, which likely contributed to his success in college and beyond (Obama 2004).

Some of the unexplained variance in mobility models is certainly the result of dumb luck. Someone starts a career at just the right moment (the economy is booming, her field is hot) and gets ahead fast. Someone else experiences a traumatic event early in life and never quite gets over it. This is all very frustrating for sociology, but from a more romantic viewpoint, it's nice to know that life is not entirely predictable.

Jencks on Equality

Blau and Duncan inspired a large new literature on status attainment, including two important books by Christopher Jencks and a research team at Harvard University titled *Inequality: A Reassessment of the Effect of Family and Schooling in America* (1972) and *Who Gets Ahead?* (1979). Jencks and his coresearchers integrated new variables, such as son's IQ at age 11, into the analysis to build a grander version of Blau and Duncan's model. They compared the life experience of brothers to get a better sense of the total influence of social origins on life chances.

The Harvard team was able to reduce the unexplained variance in the prediction of son's occupation (SES) but further complicated matters by adding an outcome variable that went one step beyond SES: son's earnings. They found that the resemblance between brothers, or total family background, explained almost half the variance in occupational status of men, but less than a third of the variance in their earnings.

Despite the heroic efforts of the research team to assimilate all relevant information, there was no escaping the randomness in the causal chain that extended from background factors to cognitive ability to education to occupation to earnings. Early factors in the chain didn't do a very good job of predicting later ones. Jencks annoyed some critics by calling this randomness "luck." But what is luck? The accidents of life we referred to in the last section? A thousand small things whose total influence is beyond calculation? The acts of gods or demons? Some of the randomness surely does reflect imperfect measurement of variables. But Jencks seemed to be saying that the course of our lives is just more arbitrary than we care to admit.

Some of the most interesting conclusions from these studies concern the role of education. The research demonstrated that the relationship between education and earnings is not smoothly linear but chunky. A year of college is worth more in additional income than a year of high school, and the incremental value of the final year of college leading to a degree is even bigger. The high school years bring a 40 percent increase in dollar earnings over the earning of elementary school graduates, and a college degree brings an increase of almost 50 percent over the earnings of high school graduates. Even when the results are controlled for family background and IQ, the high school diploma yields a 20 percent gain in lifetime income over elementary school completion, and the college degree generates an additional 35 percent over the high school diploma (Jencks et al. 1979:Chapter 6 by Michael Olneck).

The researchers detected a gradual reduction in the impact of background variables as one gets older. The payoff of higher education (especially for those who stay long enough to get the degree) is almost as great for those from poorer families as for those from more privileged backgrounds. Of course, the latter are much more likely to start life with the resources, especially economic and cultural capital, that will get them into and through college. In the earlier years, then, education is both a reflector of family background and an equalizer that offsets family background, but in the later years, education has more independent influence.

In the first book, Jencks made a point with radical political implications about the relationship between education and career. Economic inequality in the United States is very large, he observed, and simply improving the quality of bad schools and reducing the differences among individuals in the number of years they attend school will not go very far in eliminating the economic differences. The reason is that education is only a modest determinant of individual incomes. In fact, Jencks estimated that barely a quarter of the variance in the incomes of adult men could be predicted by combining all the usual predictors: family background, IQ score, years of education, and even job title. Jencks wrote,

> Economic success seems to depend on varieties of luck and on-the-job competence that are only moderately related to family background, schooling, or scores on standardized tests. . . . The fact that we cannot equalize luck or competence does not mean that economic inequality is inevitable. Still less does it imply that we cannot eliminate what has traditionally been defined as poverty. It only implies that we must tackle these problems in a different way. Instead of trying to reduce people's capacity to gain a competitive advantage on one another, we would have to change the rules of the game so as to reduce the rewards of competitive success and the costs of failure. (Jencks et al. 1972:8)

In short, we need not accept the colossal inequalities in American society, but we cannot fix them with education. If we want to reduce economic inequality, we must interfere with capitalist markets, so that CEOs earn less and ordinary blue- and white-collar workers earn more. Ironically, economic inequalities have only grown since the Jencks studies were published.[3]

The Fortunes of Sons and Daughters

The last status attainment study we want to look at is more recent and more narrowly focused. Jencks and three colleagues (Harding et al. 2005) examined the influence of family background on the household incomes of

---

[3] Jencks general point is well taken here. But education has a bigger effect on earnings today than it did when Jencks was writing in the 1970s, and this has contributed to growing inequality.

adult sons and daughters. They didn't explicitly consider the son or daughter's education or occupation. Instead they studied the joint effect of the seven background factors. Their focus on household income (rather than individual earnings) reminds us that income is a product of both the job market and the marriage market. People with advantaged childhoods are more likely to get advanced education and better jobs. They are also more likely to be married and more likely to have a spouse with above average earning potential. For the disadvantaged, obviously, these tendencies are reversed

The family background factors they considered include familiar items, like parents' occupation and race, along with two novel ones, Southern origins and the number of siblings. For whatever reasons, growing up in the South and having more siblings negatively affect adult incomes. The other factors are parents' education, Hispanic origin, and intact family.

One of the tables in their report presents their main findings in a way that is intuitively easy to grasp. It compares the outcomes for the most advantaged and least advantaged groups in the sample. The first group is the top 25 percent in terms of the combined weight of the family background advantages. The second group is the bottom 25 percent by these same factors. They compared the household income distributions of the two groups, presenting results for sons and daughters separately. (The researchers didn't include separate results for the middle 50 percent.)

Table 7.1 is based on this analysis. It is no surprise that the most advantaged are most likely to end up in the top income group and the least advantaged in the bottom income group. But in each case, about 60 percent were spread out across the other income levels. So family background influences but doesn't rule our fortunes. (There is, in other words, still lots of unexplained variance.) We might expect men's household incomes to more

Table 7.1 Household Income of Adult Sons and Daughters by Family Background

Sons _____ Household Income Quartile _____

Background	Bottom	Second	Third	Top	TOTAL
Most Advantaged	11.6	21.4	29.0	38.0	100
Least Advantaged	40.6	25.8	21.1	12.6	100

Daughters _____ Household Income Quartile _____

Background	Bottom	Second	Third	Top	TOTAL
Most Advantaged	11.7	23.5	27.1	37.7	100
Least Advantaged	43.7	25.9	18.8	11.6	100

Source: Harding et al. 2005:123.

Note: Household incomes and background characteristics of respondents, age 30 to 59, as reported in 1990s GSS national surveys.

closely reflect inherited advantage or disadvantage, since men are traditionally more career oriented than women. But there is no significant difference
between the distributions for sons and daughters.

The researchers wanted to see if the impact of family background had
changed over time. They compared the results for the 1990s, shown in
our table, with parallel results for the 1970s (not shown here), and found
surprisingly little difference. The most notable change concerns daughters
born into the advantaged families: They were 5 percent less likely in the
1990s to land in the top income group than they had been in the 1970s.
The analysis tells us that the Age of Growing Inequality has not significantly
altered the influence of family background on our life chances (Harding
et al. 2005:123).

Who Goes to College?

Not all people with college degrees have outstanding careers, but few people now achieve important positions without them. And the income gap
between the high school and college educated is growing. So we need to
ask: Who goes to college? And, more important, who comes out with a
degree? As Figures 7.3 and 7.4 indicate, students from families in the top
income quartile are more likely to attend and much more likely to complete
a college degree. College attendance rates have increased substantially at all
income levels in recent decades. Currently, about half of high school graduates from the lowest income quartile enroll in college. But only 26 percent
of these low-income college students will finish a degree by age 24—that is,
about 12 percent of the original cohort of low-income high school graduates.
The completion rate for their high-income high school classmates is about
5 times higher.[4]

The most obvious reason for the big class differences in college attendance and completion is that college is expensive and getting more so.
Another is the home advantage available to upper-middle-class students.
Their parents have likely been to college and, as we saw in Chapter 5, know
how to help them prepare for successful college careers. Of course, lower-
class students have, on average, lower test scores. But, even among students
with excellent scores, those from privileged families are much more likely to
attend and complete college. For example, among students with top math
scores who attended high school in the early 1990s, 74 percent of those from
high-SES families completed college. Among their top-scoring classmates
from low-SES families, 15 percent got no further than high school; just 29
percent completed college (U.S. Department of Education 2005).[5]

---

[4] These are approximate figures, since the enrollment and completion statistics are not strictly compatible.

[5] Top scores = highest 25 percent. High SES = highest 25 percent based on parental occupation and
education. Earlier studies produced similar results (Sewell and Hauser 1975; Sewell and Shah 1977).
Our own analysis of data from the "High School and Beyond" study, presented in earlier editions of
this book, showed that, in the 1980s, students with mediocre cognitive abilities from high income
families were more likely to attend college than students with high cognitive abilities from low
income families.

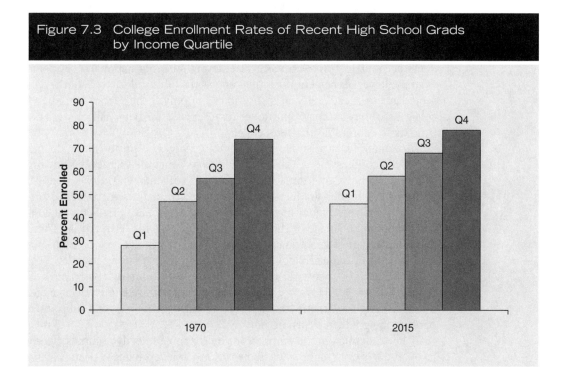

Figure 7.3 College Enrollment Rates of Recent High School Grads by Income Quartile

The Stratification of Higher Education

Class not only influences the chance of continuing education after high school, it also influences the type of school selected. Students from lower status families are more likely to enroll at 2-year community colleges. These schools' curricula permit students to transfer later to 4-year colleges. But many community college students will drop out of school before they complete 2 years, while others concentrate on 2-year technical courses that lead to careers as computer programmers, dental assistants, automobile mechanics, and the like.

The American system of higher education is stratified according to the quality of the education provided and the particular career preparation emphasized, and this academic hierarchy is paralleled by the stratification of students' families. Working-class and lower-middle-class students are only thinly represented at the most selective institutions. It is hardly coincidental that the majority of students at the "Big Three" (Harvard, Yale, and Princeton) are able to cover, without financial aid, college costs that exceed the annual incomes of most American families (Karabel 2005:537).

The connection between class and selective college admissions was clearly demonstrated in a national study conducted by Carnevale and Rose (2004). The researchers divided first-year college students into four socioeconomic quartiles, based on family income, education, and occupation. They found that students from the top 25 percent of families make up three quarters of the freshman classes at the most selective institutions, while students from the bottom 50 percent of families account for only 10 percent

(Table 7.2). The 146 institutions in this highest tier of selectivity include top research universities such as Harvard and UC-Berkeley, along with prestigious liberal arts colleges such as Vassar, Pamona, and Hamilton; their students account for just 9 percent of entering students nationally. Students from the lower 50 percent of families are, as the table indicates, better represented at less selective 4-year institutions, but only at the 2-year community colleges do they reach proportional representation. About half of students from these families don't attend college.

Acceptance by a selective college or university is no empty honor, devoid of real-life consequences. Carnevale and Rose conclude that, even allowing for their generally superior academic abilities, students who attend selective schools have higher graduation rates, better access to postgraduate studies, and somewhat higher lifetime earnings. Google CEO Eric Schmidt suggests another advantage of elite education: "Colleges like Harvard, MIT and Stanford are part of a social network. You can be a brilliant entrepreneur, but if you go to a no-name school, you don't have access to these networks. Take my word for it, the networks count for a lot in this industry" (Bernstein and Swan 2007:38–39). However, as we noted earlier in this chapter, on average, a college degree, even one from a less competitive school, gives a substantial boost to the graduate's earning power.

The academic criteria emphasized by the most selective schools clearly favor students from high-status homes over their less privileged peers. Nearly two thirds of students from the top SES quartile of families, but only 7 percent of students from the bottom 50 percent, score above the equivalent of 1,200 points on the SAT exam (Carnevale and Rose 2004:110, 129–130). But even these disparate statistics suggest the existence of a substantial pool of qualified potential applicants from lower status families.

Selective institutions, even the most competitive among them, do not recruit students solely on the basis of academic merit. Most give special consideration to so-called legacies (children of alumni), athletes, and minority applicants. At Princeton, for example, students from these categories recently filled about 40 percent of the freshman class (Karabel 2005:544). These preferences tend to reinforce the privileges of the privileged. By and large, sons and daughters of selective-college alumni grow up in affluent homes with ample opportunities to develop cultural capital. Potential varsity athletes are likely to attend well-financed high schools with strong athletic programs, to participate in the competitive nonschool leagues typical of prosperous communities, and to benefit from expensive summer training camps. Affirmative action at selective schools has mainly benefited middle- to upper-middle-class black students, who were once systematically excluded from these institutions (Bowen and Bok 1998:49).

At selective institutions, the admissions deck seems stacked against white students from lower status families. Carnevale and Rose (2004:135) find that such students would actually do better under an admissions regime based strictly on grades and test scores—which, they estimate, would boost their presence at top-tier institutions from 9 percent to 12 percent. Carnevale and Rose do not, however, favor such a system, since it would still favor the privileged. Like some others who have studied competitive admissions, they urge selective institutions to adopt some form of economic affirmative action, analogous to racial affirmative action, that would take into

Table 7.2 Socioeconomic Status and College Selectivity

Percent of Incoming Students	Student Family SES			
	Selectivity	Top 25%	Second 25%	Bottom 50%	Total
	4-Year Colleges				
9	High	74	16	10	100
32	Middle	39	34	27	100
13	Low	33	30	37	100
46	*Community Colleges*	22	28	50	100
Total: 100					

Source: Carnevale and Rose 2004; additional data provided by Stephen J. Rose.

Figure 7.4 Bachelor's Degree Completion Rates for Those Who Entered College by Family Income Quartile

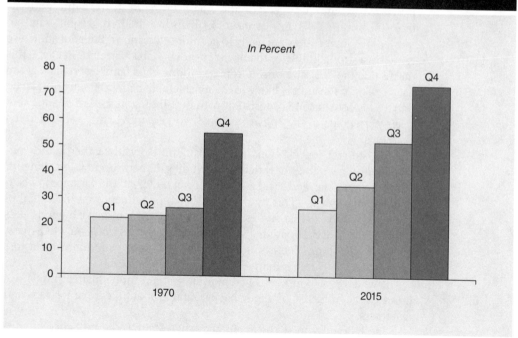

Source: Pell Institute 2017

account the difficulties economically disadvantaged students must overcome (Carnevale and Rose 2004; Kahlenberg 2004; Karabel 2005).

Though selective college admissions are tilted in favor of the sons and daughters of the upper-middle class, the great majority of them will not win admission to a top-tier institution. The social legitimacy of such institutions depends, after all, on their being selective. About 37 percent of students from families in the top SES quartile will attend a mid-selectivity school, and

43 percent will attend a low-selectivity school or community college. Only 20 percent will attend a highly selective institution.[6] For such families, this hard fact of life is a source of anxiety surrounding the pre-college education of their children. It has given rise to a college prep industry offering expensive SAT courses and advice from independent counselors, who commonly charge $15,000 or more for their services.

Conclusion

The previous chapter looked at intergenerational social mobility from a macro or structural point of view. We focused on the gross pattern of mobility—how many people move up, down, or not at all. We considered the extent to which this movement reflected equality of mobility chances among individuals or simply opportunities generated by a changing occupational structure. In this chapter, we shifted perspective and concentrated on the determinants of individual success within the framework of gross mobility.

Research shows that two factors, family background and education, are notably correlated with career success. But measuring their separate influence is complicated because the two are intertwined. In general, people from privileged backgrounds get a double boost for their careers: a direct advantage (for example, father's connections help his children get jobs) and an indirect advantage (they are likely to get more education). But education also exercises a strong influence that is independent of background. In effect, this means that the daughter or son from a working-class family who manages to get a college education is likely to do considerably better than his peers who don't. This conclusion is consistent with our finding in the last chapter that a fair percentage of the sons of manual workers move into upper-middle-class jobs.

Christopher Jencks, building on Blau and Duncan's earlier work, concluded that background variables (including father's occupation, parents' education, income, and race) account for not quite half the variance in occupational attainment. (This figure includes family influence on the extent of a son's education.) If Jencks' estimate is correct, we can make a good guess at a boy's odds of occupational success on the day he is born—a good guess, but not a sure thing: There is another 50 percent to be determined by factors ranging from personal initiative and charm to pure luck.

If we look at household income (rather than individual earnings), we find that the influence of family background is about the same for sons and daughters.

The literature on status attainment suggests that the influence of education on occupational success is of similar magnitude to the influence of family background. Earnings rise—this is hardly surprising—with years of education. Jencks' research revealed something less obvious at the time: The final year of college, if it results in a degree, is worth much more than any of the preceding years. The power of the degree is such that, among those who manage to graduate, the influence of family background is greatly reduced.

---

[6] According to our calculations based on data assembled by Carnevale and Rose.

But if college graduates are equalized in this sense, access to college remains very unequal. There is, for example, an enormous gap in the college participation rates of young adults from high- and low-income families, and lower status youth are nearly shut out of selective institutions.

In sum, the research supports two seemingly contradictory views of higher education in this country: (1) The American system of higher education is so big and varied that it provides broad opportunities for youths from lower- and middle-class families to prepare themselves for careers that raise them above the level of their parents, and (2) the American system of higher education is so steeply stratified that it stifles social mobility under the politically palatable banner of academic merit. Of course, both are true. The system is relatively open to the ambitious and talented, but it is also remarkably successful at reproducing the privilege of the privileged.

KEY TERMS DEFINED IN THE GLOSSARY ───────────

chain of causation
correlation, simple

multiple causal pathways
path analysis

socioeconomic status (SES)
variance explained

SUGGESTED READINGS ───────────────────

Beller, Emily and Michael Hout. 2006. "Intergenerational Mobility: The United States in Comparative Perspective, *The Future of Children*. 16:19–35.

Useful overview. Examines long-term trends in occupational and income mobility, with comparisons to other countries.

Bowen, William, Matthew Chingos, and Michael McPherson. 2009. *Crossing the Finish Line: Completing College at America's Public Universities*. Princeton, NJ: Princeton University Press.

Why 40 percent of the students who enter high prestige public universities are slow to graduate or fail to graduate at all. The contribution of family income, parental education, race, gender, and other variables to student outcomes at 21 flagship public institutions.

Bowles, Samuel, Herbert Gintis, and Melissa Osborne Groves, eds. 2005. *Unequal Chances: Family Background and Economic Success*. New York: Russell Sage Foundation.

Important collection of research papers on the influence of family background on earnings and income.

Elmelech, Yuval. 2008. *Transmitting Inequality: Wealth and the American Family*. New York: Rowman & Littlefield.

An original and revealing conception of the class structure emphasizing inequalities in wealth and their transmission through marriage and intergenerational transfers.

Golden, Daniel. 2007. *The Price of Admission: How America's Ruling Class Buys Its Way Into Elite Colleges and Who Gets Left Outside the Gates*. New York: Three Rivers Press.

A Wall Street Journal reporter explores what happens when meritocracy meets money.

Karabel, Jerome. 2005. *The Chosen: The Hidden History of Admission and Exclusion at Harvard, Yale, and Princeton*. New York: Houghton Mifflin.

The history of class, ethnicity, and the changing meaning of merit at three elite institutions.

Khan, Shamus. 2011. *Privilege: The Making of An Adolescent Elite at St. Paul's School*. Princeton: Princeton University Press.

This book, discussed in the next chapter, shows how the privileged have preserved their privilege by redefining privilege as merit.

Lemann, Nicholas. 2000. *The Big Test: The Secret History of the American Meritocracy.* New York: Farrar, Straus & Giroux.

The history of the SAT. Created to break the grip of a social elite on the Ivies, the test provided the basis for a new elite, as privileged and exclusive as the old.

McLeod, Jay. 2008. *Ain't No Makin' It: Leveled Aspirations in a Low-Income Neighborhood.* Third ed. Boulder, CO: Westview.

Engaging portrait of black and white teens in a public housing project. Shows how their occupational aspirations are shaped by peer group, family, and school.

Stevens, Mitchell. 2007. *Creating a Class: College Admissions and the Education of Elites.* Cambridge, MA: Harvard University Press.

How selective institutions reproduce class privilege: Firsthand study of the admissions process at an elite liberal arts college.

Elites, the Capitalist Class, and Political Power

Those who hold and those who are without property have ever formed distinct interests in society.

James Madison (1787)

[Campaign finance has become] an elaborate influence peddling scheme by which both parties conspire to stay in office by selling the country to the highest bidder.

Senator John McCain (2000)

James Madison and Alexander Hamilton were political opponents in the early years of the republic. But they agreed on this much: Politics and social class are unavoidably linked. Why? Because there is an inevitable conflict between those whom Madison, quoted above, calls "the propertied and the propertyless" and Hamilton, in the epigram at the start of Chapter 1, described as "the few and the many."

Chapters 8 and 9 examine the connection between politics and social class. We see these chapters as complementary. In Chapter 8, we deal with power, focusing on "the few," those at the top of the class structure and the apex of the political order. In Chapter 9, we take up class consciousness, concentrating on "the many, the mass of the people."

Our emphasis on the few in this chapter is typical in studies of power and might appear to be guided by the inherent logic of the subject. After all, those at the top have the best opportunity to exercise power. But "the many" are far from powerless, especially—and here is where class consciousness comes in—when they are united by a sense of common identity and shared interests.

Three Perspectives on Power

We may define **power** as the potential of individuals or groups to carry out their will even over the opposition of others. Here we focus on issues of national power, beginning with an examination of three competing theoretical perspectives: elite, class, and pluralist. The **elite perspective** makes a sharp distinction between an organized minority (the elite) that rules and an unorganized majority that is ruled. Elite theories often focus on specific institutional bases of power. The **class perspective**, which has its origins in Marxist theory, also focuses on a ruling minority, but class theory is more specific about the identity of the rulers and the structure that creates them: They are the owners of productive wealth, the capitalist class. The **pluralist perspective** denies that power is concentrated in one group. It maintains that, in democratic societies, there are multiple bases of power representing the interests of competing groups, so that no minority can easily impose its will. Obviously, the first two approaches have much more in common with one another than with the third.

A final prefatory note: To avoid questionable usage and conceptual confusion, we consistently use the term **elite** as a collective noun like class or jury. Such terms refer to groups rather than individuals. In this chapter, elite (singular) alludes to some notable group (business executives) and elites (plural) connotes two or more such groups (executives, military officers, and public officials). Collective nouns should not be used to refer to individuals, as in, "three elites walked into a bar."

Mills: The National Power Elite

We begin our discussion with C. Wright Mills' classic work *The Power Elite* (1956). Critical of American institutions at a time of growing domestic prosperity and (like our own) of perceived international threat, *The Power Elite* inevitably evoked controversy when it was published in the 1950s. Mills characterized this self-satisfied era in our national life as "a material boom, a nationalist celebration, a political vacuum" (p. 326). His description of national political arrangements suggested that the growing power of a few was undermining American democracy. Although *The Power Elite* is over 50 years old, it is worth examining in detail because the issues it raises are still relevant for contemporary students of national power.

Mills' conception of the national power structure centered on the growing significance of three major interlocking institutions: the modern corporation, the executive branch of the federal government, and the military establishment. He saw each of these institutions enlarging and centralizing power at the national level. A few hundred major corporations were taking the place of thousands of smaller competing firms that had once typified the economy. The federal executive had gathered enormous powers and resources previously nonexistent or scattered among other units of government. The military, once small and decentralized, had developed into a colossal bureaucracy, commanding a war machine of unprecedented scale and destructive power. As the corporations, the federal government, and the military grew, they eclipsed and subordinated other institutions:

> No family is as directly powerful in national affairs as any major corporation; no church is as directly powerful in the external biographies of young men in America today as the military establishments; no college is as powerful in the shaping of momentous events as the National Security Council. Religious, educational, and family institutions are not autonomous centers of national power; on the contrary, these decentralized areas are increasingly shaped by the big three in which developments of decisive and immediate consequence now occur. (Mills 1956:6)

The implication Mills drew from these trends was that the basis of national power had been reduced to control over these three crucial institutions. Those who sit at the "commanding heights" of the corporate, political, and military hierarchies make the critical national decisions. Who are they? In the corporations, an amalgam of very rich families with corporate-based fortunes and the ranking executives of the top national corporations (together, Mills calls them "the corporate rich"); in the federal government, the president, vice president, cabinet, heads of major agencies, and members of the White House staff; among the military, the generals and admirals. These three institutional elites together constitute Mills's power elite.

Mills argued that the emergence of a national elite undercut important traditional bases of power. Community elites decline in importance as the power of national institutions grows. Investment decisions that are crucial for a community may be made in a distant corporate boardroom. Even the significance of personal wealth as a power resource is reduced. Very sizable individual fortunes seem lightweight relative to the massive assets of any major national corporation. However, large personal fortunes, like those of the Waltons (Wal-Mart), Mars (candy) or Fords (auto) may be invested in national corporations, and in this form, personal wealth can retain its significance as a basis of power.

Mills conceived the national structure of power as consisting of three tiers (see Figure 8.1). The top tier is, of course, the power elite. The bottom tier, which Mills labels "mass society," encompasses the great majority of the population. Subject to large-scale national institutions beyond their control or comprehension and misinformed by media that are dominated by national elites, the members of mass society are passive participants in the political system. Between mass society and the power elite are "the middle levels of power," comprising a multitude of competing interest groups from labor unions to the gun lobby, whose typical arena of conflict is the Congress. The middle levels of power are the source of most political news, but they are not, according to Mills, the locus of the most important political decisions. In the welter of competing interests, none can impose itself. This "semiorganized stalemate," as Mills characterized it, only reinforces the dominance of the power elite. The key decisions are, of course, reserved for the power elite. But which are the key decisions? Mills is unambiguous on this point. Two issue areas are of sweeping importance: economic policy and national security. These matters unmistakably, often brutally, intrude into the lives of ordinary men and women as boom or bust in the economy and peace or war abroad.

In Mills' schema of national power, his conception of the military as a separate, more or less autonomous, elite evoked the most skepticism, even among those generally sympathetic to his argument. Mills seems to have mistaken the militaristic direction of foreign policy in the Cold War era for the power of the military over policy decisions. But since George Washington led the revolutionary army, the American military has been subject to civilian elites, who are responsible for the major war/peace decisions that concerned Mills. This was demonstrated in 2003 by the Bush administration's fatal decision to go to war in Iraq. While some officers doubted the wisdom of this move, the impetus to war came from civilian officials in the White House and Department of Defense.

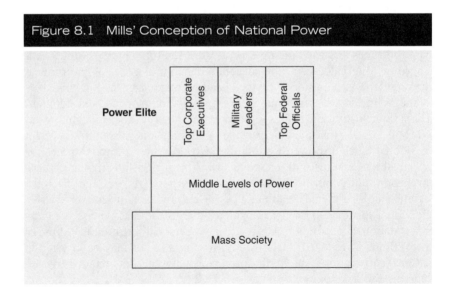

Figure 8.1 Mills' Conception of National Power

Mills, His Critics, and the Problem of Elite Cohesion

Mills' pluralist critics accused him of assuming what needs to be proven. If his elite was as powerful as Mills claimed, it should be able to impose its policy preferences in national decision-making. But, pluralists noted, Mills had not tested the power of the elite by examining actual decisions. In this section, we focus on a related issue that has provoked extensive debate among Mills' readers: the problem of **elite cohesion**—that is, the extent to which the members of a hypothesized elite hang together in pursuit of common objectives and in opposition to other groups.[1] Not just Mills, but any elite theorist must somehow address this problem.

The cohesion issue was effectively posed in an influential essay by Robert Dahl, directed at Mills and other elite theorists, whom Dahl (1967) accused of "confusing a ruling elite with a group that has a high potential for control" (p. 28). To be politically effective, potential for control must be coupled with "potential for unity." The American military has the potential to impose a dictatorship on the nation, but that potential means nothing unless military leaders agree on that objective. Mills defined an elite in terms of the top positions in organizations that possess vast resources (potential for control). But he failed, according to Dahl, to demonstrate a political consensus among the members of his elite (potential for unity).

Mills' pluralist critics are clearly predisposed to the belief that unity among power contenders is difficult to achieve. This view found early expression in David Riesman's *The Lonely Crowd* (1953), a pessimistic but influential book on American society and culture. Riesman asked two questions about power in America: "Is there a ruling class left?" and "Who has the power?" His answers were, respectively, no and no one. As the first question implies, Riesman believed that the country had a ruling class in the past. Early in the history of the republic, the ruling class consisted of the landed gentry and mercantile interests that constituted the Federalist leadership and, later, of captains of industry. But by the 1950s, the ruling class had been supplanted by an amorphous constellation of "veto groups"—organized representatives of specialized interests that included "business groups, large and small, the movie-censoring groups, the farm groups and the labor and professional groups, the major ethnic and major regional groups" (p. 246). The veto groups are distinguished from the powerful of previous eras by their inability to impose their own will. Feeling themselves powerless, chary of offending other groups, their function is largely defensive, "to neutralize those who might attack them" (p. 247).

How can any decision be made in such a political context? Is anyone in charge? Riesman's reply was that leadership may be needed to initiate something new or halt something in progress, but little leadership is needed to maintain the status quo. To the extent that anyone exercises power, it is over very specific and narrow issues. Bigger, broader national power is smothered by the action of veto groups.

---

[1] For other lines of criticism, see Dahl 1961, 1967; Domhoff and Ballard 1968; Polsby 1970.

Mills (1956) characterized Riesman's amorphous power structure as "a recognizable although a confused statement of the middle levels of power, especially as revealed in congressional districts and in Congress itself" (p. 244). Power at that level is indeed a semiorganized stalemate. In Mills' view, Riesman was guilty of a mindless empiricism that equated all interest groups and all issues. Banks and organizations representing motorcycle riders are both concerned with national legislation. But to describe them as two veto groups misses the point. Some groups are more important than others because they have powerful resources at their command and because they deal with issues that are more vital to the nation. As we have seen, Mills was only interested in the big economic and national security questions and regarded as trivial most of the other issues that consume the attention of the middle levels of power.

But elite cohesion presented a special problem for Mills. He had to demonstrate both that the three distinct elites are internally cohesive and that they are drawn together into a single power elite. Mills did present a series of mechanisms through which elite unity might be achieved. They fall into two categories: social-psychological and structural. The social-psychological mechanisms include similarities in origins, education, career, and lifestyles, which produce "a similar social type" and contribute to ease in informal association (Mills 1956:19). Mills presented evidence on these topics for each elite. He noted that elite men tend to be drawn from upper-class or upper-middle-class, urban, white, Protestant families and that they are likely to be educated in the same Ivy League schools. He found a significant overlap between the world of the power elite and upper-class "society," with its intertwined families, select prep schools, distinctive class values, and conservative notions of style. (These commonalities, as Mills conceded, apply more to the civilian elites than to the military.)

In addition, members of the three elites have similar career experiences, even if they do not move through the same institutions. The corporate rich, the "political directorate," and the chiefs of the Pentagon share the experience of managing large organizations. The character of modern bureaucratic life has tended to blur the distinction between leadership in a large corporation, a civilian department of government, and an army. Mills contended that these shared elements of background and career along with the privileges attached to elite position make members of the power elite conscious of the differences between themselves and the rest of the population. They are drawn together and develop a common perspective on the world.

The structural mechanisms of cohesion examined by Mills concern the more or less formal connections between institutions. One critical link is the interchange of personnel among the three institutions, especially the movement of representatives of the corporate world into and out of top political positions. Another tie between these two is the dependence of political candidates on financing from the corporate rich. The military is closely allied with the corporations, who are its suppliers, while the militaristic foreign policy pursued by the political directorate strengthens its ties to the generals and admirals. All three elites are, of course, compelled to consider each other by virtue of the inevitable interdependence of institutions operating on such a scale.

In sum, the pluralists are persuasive when they argue that Mills must prove that his power elite is cohesive. Otherwise, it is little more than a list of important people. In reply, Mills points to a series of factors that tend to unify the individual members of the power elite and draw the three major institutional sectors together: common social background, shared lifestyle and values, similar job experience, interchange of personnel, campaign financing, and institutional interdependence. In this chapter, we examine contemporary evidence on most of these topics.

Power Elite or Ruling Class?

If pluralists believe that Mills fails in his efforts to prove that his tripartite elite is cohesive, one Marxist critic contends that Mills is all too successful. In a perceptive essay on *The Power Elite,* Paul Sweezy contends that there is an unresolved tension in the book between two views of the power elite. The first is based on social class: Mills provided evidence that "those who occupy the command posts do so as representatives or agents of a national ruling class which trains them, shapes their thought patterns, and selects them for their positions of high responsibility" (Sweezy 1968:123). Much of the evidence Mills presented for elite unity seems to point in this direction—for example, his emphasis on the higher class origins of members of the power elite and the recruitment of capitalist-class leaders to powerful cabinet positions. (Ironically, Sweezy's own origins were distinctly upper class [Karabel 2005:542].)

The second view Sweezy finds in *The Power Elite* focuses on the bureaucratic elites at the top of three "major institutional orders"; here Mills treated the corporate, military, and political realms as distinctly separate domains with autonomous leadership, which come together to form the power elite. Sweezy is highly skeptical of the second view, particularly given the evidence that Mills presented for the first. The American military, Sweezy contended, is firmly under civilian control, and the political elite is dependent on the class that rules the corporations; thus, the justification for thinking in terms of three discrete institutional elites collapses.

Sweezy's criticism supports an alternative to both the Millsian and the pluralist views of national power: the identification of power with the class that controls income-producing wealth, which he calls the ruling class. This approach—the last of the three theoretical conceptions of power we mentioned at the beginning of the chapter—proposes that Mills' "corporate rich" have largely subordinated competing elites to their will.

A ruling class theory of national power has one big advantage. It has a credible answer to the question of internal cohesion: The ruling class is united because its members have well-defined economic interests in opposition to other classes.

Mills (1968) never dealt at length with this Marxist line of criticism, although in a breezy reply to critics on the left, he commented, "They want to believe that the corporation and the state are identical. . . . I don't believe it's quite that simple" (p. 224). It probably is not "quite that simple." But Mills appears to underestimate the power of wealth because he wants to fit it into a broader conception of elite power.

Who Rules?

The issues raised by *The Power Elite* have been reexamined in more recent works by Dye (2016); Lerner, Nagai, and Rothman (1996); and Domhoff (2006), which we describe in this section. Dye's and Domhoff's contributions, it should be noted, are revised versions of books originally published around 1970.

According to Thomas Dye (1976, 2002, 2016), America is an "elitist" society. Citing writers from Alexander Hamilton to the Italian political theorist Gaetano Mosca, Dye asserts at the very beginning of his book that elite rule is inevitable in *all* societies, from the simplest to the most advanced. In particular, he stresses that a society such as the United States, which is dependent on large institutions, is ruled by those who hold the top institutional positions—the elite. Here he sounds like Mills, though his conception of the elite is much broader.

Much of Dye's book *Who's Running America?* (2016) is devoted to defining the top institutional positions and describing the people who hold them. His elite consists of those who hold some 4,102 leadership positions in 12 critical sectors of American society.

> These top positions, taken collectively, control over half of the nation's industrial assets, over half of all U.S. banking assets and over three-quarters of all insurance assets. They control the television networks, the investment firms, the influential newspapers and the media conglomerates. They control over half of the assets of all private foundations and two-thirds of all private university endowments. They direct the nation's largest and best known law firms in New York and Washington, as well as the nation's major civic and cultural organizations. They make the largest political campaign contributions. They occupy key federal government positions in the executive, legislative and judicial branches. (p. 10)

For Dye, the control over these key sectors by a small elite—its members would fit in a typical high school auditorium—is evidence of the concentration of power in American society.

Dye focuses on the phenomenon of "interlocking directorates"—the implicit ties created between organizations when executives or directors of one hold positions in another. An example would be the bank executive who serves on the board of an industrial firm or a foundation. Corporations seem especially likely to be connected in this fashion, both with other corporations and nonbusiness institutions. Most members of the elite are "specialists," who hold just one position. A minority are "interlockers," people who hold two or more positions. They constitute the core of the elite, men and women who are able to take a broader view of common problems and contribute to elite consensus. Dye suggests that the proportion of interlockers is shrinking, from 20 percent in the 1970s to 15 percent in the 1980s and, he estimates, 10 percent today (Dye 2016:177). Does this mean that the elite is less integrated than it once was? Dye does not venture an opinion.

With an elite sprawling across a dozen institutional sectors, Dye is compelled to address the problem of cohesion. He points to interlocking directorates and other bonding mechanisms, which, by and large, will be familiar to readers of Mills. Members of the elite share broadly similar backgrounds, with origins in the **privileged classes** (upper-middle and upper classes) and education in elite institutions. Thirty percent, he says, came from distinctly upper-class families, but the relevance of this figure is questionable, since it seems to date from the early 1970s (Dye 2016:194; Dye 1976:152–153). Dye places particular emphasis on the foundations, "think tanks," and policy-planning groups, which are discussed later in this chapter, as venues where the elite can explore problems and develop shared solutions. Although he describes internal factions within the elite, he seems to regard it as relatively cohesive.

Though he does not explicitly say so, the business sectors seem to be first among equals in his broader elite. They are the most likely source of interlockers. They support political campaigns. They finance and sit on the boards of major civic and cultural institutions. Dye proposes an "oligarchic" model of the policy making process, in which corporations and wealthy individuals are the sources of the most important policy initiatives, which are refined in the foundations, universities, think tanks, and policy-planning organizations subject to their influence. Only after ideas have passed through this process are they turned into law.

In *American Elites* (1996), Lerner, Nagai, and Rothman are skeptical of claims for elite cohesion. They argue for a pluralist conception of national power based on differentiated elites. Note that the authors, unlike Mills or Dye, refer to elites in the plural. They see a division of national power among 12 "strategic elites" with distinct functional responsibilities. The leaders of business, the media, and the military are examples. This brand of pluralism does not deny that power is concentrated in the hands of a few, but denies that elites exercise much influence outside their own sectors. There is, in other words, no core elite like Mills' power elite or Dye's interlockers.

Probably because it is difficult to obtain interviews with CEOs, four-star generals, and the like, the *American Elites* researchers adopted a broad conception of elite status. The corporate respondents, for example, were from "upper and middle management." The government officials were "high-ranking bureaucrats" not appointed by the president (which is to say, not very powerful). The interviews, conducted in the 1980s, focused on the social backgrounds and opinions of the members of the 12 elites, two topics which are directly relevant to the question of elite cohesion. Rothman and Black (1999) later conducted a smaller-scale follow-up survey and reported broadly similar results.

By showing that strategic elites differ in their origins and viewpoints, the authors of *American Elites* expected to undermine the notion of a unified central elite. A chapter titled "Room at the Top" describes a pattern of recruitment to elite positions that favors the children of privileged backgrounds, but not exclusively. The great majority of respondents report that their families had average (33 percent) or above-average (38 percent) incomes when they were children. A little more than half had fathers who were professionals or managers, well above the national proportion of men in these categories during the years these leaders were growing up. (The researchers do not differentiate respondents of upper-class origin.) But many had fathers with less impressive jobs and below-average incomes. Almost all their elite respondents completed college, but surprisingly few (31 percent) graduated from highly selective institutions.[2] Most members of the strategic elites appear to be from upper-middle-class backgrounds, but there is enough diversity among them to doubt that shared background could be a dependable basis of elite cohesion.

The authors claim to have found a high-level ideological division among American strategic elites. But the evidence they present is not decisive. Asked to classify themselves as conservative, moderate, or liberal, respondents differed in predictable ways: Corporate executives and military officers generally took the conservative label; majorities of labor leaders, movie makers, journalists, bureaucrats, and religious leaders described themselves as liberals. But answers to specific opinion questions reveal a more complicated picture. For example, responses to a series of questions about the desirability of liberal social and environmental policies show the bureaucrats quite close to the conservative thinking of business and the military. More liberal responses to these items came, as expected, from labor officials and public interest group leaders. Some questions revealed an unexpected degree of inter-elite consensus—agreement, for example, that the legal system favors the wealthy. Virtually no one thought that corporations should be owned by the government, and strong majorities in the various elites (except labor and public interest) agreed that business is "fair to workers." The right to abortion was strongly supported by all but the religious elite. In short, *American Elites* does not document a clear pattern of diverging opinion among the strategic elites.

G. William Domhoff (2006) in *Who Rules America?* presents an interpretation of power in America that he describes as "a class theory." But he begins by examining a specific economic elite, the directors of major corporations. (A corporation's board of directors, as he explains, is its legal governing body, typically composed of officers of the company and so-called outside directors.) Domhoff analyzed the interlocks among the directors of almost 2,000 large corporations and concluded that they link firms in a network he labels the corporate community. The average firm had 6.1 interlocks with others.

Domhoff's analysis revealed an elite within the elite—15 percent to 20 percent of directors who sit on multiple corporate boards. These individuals tend to be associated with the largest corporations. They are also likely to be on the boards of nonprofit organizations, to participate in business leadership organizations, and to assume government positions. They are, concludes Domhoff, the "inner circle" of the corporate community.

The next step in Domhoff's argument is his claim that the corporate community is "closely intertwined with the upper class" (2006:49). He is referring to the upper class in a social rather than economic sense. Here his evidence is stale. In a 1960s version of this book, Domhoff (1967) had concluded that 53 percent of corporate directors could be considered upper

---

[2] Detailed tabulations in the book show that these generalizations hold up fairly well for the 12 elites taken individually. The biggest exceptions were labor leaders, who are, as might be expected, largely from blue-collar backgrounds, and corporate lawyers and public interest group leaders, who come disproportionately from higher class backgrounds.

class, based on social indicators (p. 51). Now he cites Dye's finding that 30 percent of the corporate elite is of upper-class origins, but this number is from Dye's 1970s research. Domhoff notes that corporate directors are likely to belong to elite social clubs like the Links Club in New York and the Pacific Union Club in San Francisco. Here again, the evidence is from the 1970s. That aside, it is not clear whether membership in such clubs is an indication that one is part of an upper-class status community or, more narrowly, just recognition of the prestige of corporate position.

(Domhoff's recent research shows that the corporate community has been diversifying to include more minorities and women. But he writes that their presence in the boardroom does not change the atmosphere, since they tend to come from the same class and educational background as their white, male counterparts.)

The third piece in Domhoff's theory is corporate participation, through funding and membership on relevant boards, in the same foundations and policy organizations that also interest Dye. Although the information he presents is dated, it is likely that these ties continue to be significant since such organizations need corporate financing and their work is of continuing interest to the corporate elite. Domhoff illustrates the relationship among the corporate community, the social upper class, and the policy-formation organizations with a diagram consisting of three, modestly overlapping circles. Within this universe of partially overlapping groups, he defines what he calls "the power elite" as those who sit on the boards of corporations, the boards of corporate-controlled policy organizations, or both. Members of the upper class are only part of this power elite if they also fall into one of these categories. The power elite, suggests Domhoff, "provides a leadership basis for the exercise of power on behalf of the owners of all large income-producing properties . . . those who have a stake in maintaining the current wealth and income distributions" (Domhoff 2006:103).

Although they define the structure of power differently, Dye, Domhoff, and the authors of *American Elites* all accept Mills' premise that power in this country is concentrated in the elites at the head of large organizations in critical sectors of American society. All find that the members of their elites are from relatively privileged backgrounds, though they differ on the details. All deal, in one way or another, with the problem of elite cohesion. Dye finds a more or less unified elite of 4,000 leaders (a remarkably small number) of the dominant organizations in 12 key sectors. The authors of *The American Elites* describe multiple elites whose power is limited to their own sectors and whose divergent views limit collaboration. Domhoff finds one dominant elite, the leaders of an interconnected corporate community, linked to a social upper class and the network of policy organizations. Dye, less explicitly, reaches a similar conclusion.

Winters' Oligarchy

Jeffrey Winters, author of *Oligarchy* (2011), has a different way of looking at the problem of national power. The literal sense of "oligarchy" is rule by the few. For Winters, it is the power differential inherent in extreme concentration of wealth in a society and it may or may not involve actual "rule." Winters emphasizes the power of money, a potent resource distinguished from other sources of power by its reach and versatility. It extends the power of those who possess it beyond the limits of their own talents and energy. Historically, across societies from ancient Rome to the contemporary United States, it has been used to buy armed defenders; to gain the cooperation of politicians, soldiers, and judges; to pay for the services of lawyers, lobbyists, accountants, and other trained professionals; to purchase legislative action, buy elections, and call mobs into the street to destabilize governments. The overriding objective of oligarchic power is the defense of property and income.

Winters describes four types of oligarchic regimes and places the United States in the category of civil oligarchy. In a civil oligarchy, the oligarchs are not armed (as they were in medieval Europe) and they do not rule (as they did in Rome); they depend on political institutions, guided by law, to defend their property rights. Their concern shifts from defense of property to defense of income. They remain powerful. The measure of their power proposed by Winters is a Material Power Index (MPI), the average wealth or income of the oligarchs divided by the average of the bottom 90 percent of households. Moving up the income scale, the MPI, reflecting the extreme concentration of income in the United States, rises steeply. Winters draws a somewhat arbitrary line separating the top one tenth of 1 percent from the other 99.90 percent of the population. These are the oligarchs, about 135,000 people, with incomes in the millions and a three digit MPI. The political significance of this threshold, he says, is that those above can afford the supremely expensive, individually tailored services of what he calls the "Income Defense Industry." This is what separates the oligarchs from the "merely rich"—the rest of the top 1 percent, with whom its interests sometimes clash.

Winters strives to cast his oligarchy as a collection of Lone Rangers. They may, he suggests, sometimes work together for some political purposes, but they can usually achieve their objectives, such as lowing their tax burden, on their own. He is reluctant to think of the oligarchs as a class, either in the Marxian or Weberian sense: They are fewer than the national capitalist class and not bound by social ties. He also resists describing them as an elite, a term that would raise the problem of internal cohesion (Winters 2011:220–221; Winters and Page 2009:738).

Civil oligarchy, Winters contends, is not inconsistent with democracy. The two may coexist because only a small range of issues is of interest to the oligarchs. As oligarchs, they have no concern with abortion, the environment, or U.S. relations with Russia. Instead, they are focused on economic issues related to the defense of income, which, by and large, they can pursue quietly, away from public view. This is where the Income Defense Industry (IDI) comes in. It consists of elite law firms, accounting firms, banks, lobbyists, and investment advisors, whose purpose is the preservation of oligarchic fortunes. The IDI enables the oligarchs to minimize taxation by, for example, artfully structuring their transactions, investments, and estates. Well paid IDI professionals invent novel (sometimes marginally legal) interpretations of tax law, challenge Internal Revenue Service regulations, defend the oligarchs in court, and lobby Congress over the tax code. The best measure of their success is the low effective tax rates of the very rich.

As we explained in Chapter 4, the effective tax rate is the proportion of their income households actually pay after various deductions, exceptions, and credits. Americans got glimpses of the gap between the "sticker price" marginal tax rates and effective tax rates of the very rich during the last two presidential campaigns. Republican candidate Mitt Romney's 2011 income tax return, released during the 2012 campaign, revealed an effective tax rate of 14 percent on income of $13.7 million—a rate below that paid by many middle-income households. During the 2016 campaign, Donald Trump resisted releasing his returns, but an expert analysis of a partial return from 1995 obtained by the *New York Times* concluded that Trump was probably able to legally avoid paying any taxes on millions of dollars in income for nearly 2 decades.[3] Winters shows that, in recent years, the effective tax rate of the top tenth of 1 percent have fallen below that paid by the "Mass Affluent," the majority of the top 1 percent of households with incomes below the oligarchic level (Winters 2011:246).

Winters takes a careful look at the legislative battles over the estate tax that began under President Bush in 2001 and extended into the Obama years. His focus is on the conflict between two well-represented groups: the oligarchs and the merely rich. Simplifying somewhat, it can be said that the oligarchy wanted abolition of the estate tax, while the merely rich were willing to settle for a high dollar exemption from the tax, which would fully shield their large but not enormous estates. Winters notes that much of the Income Defense Industry was opposed to abolition, which would eliminate the need for its expensive services. The 2001 legislation that emerged was a qualified victory for the oligarchs. We will return to this issue later in the chapter.

A political contest between the rich and the very rich over the estate tax is not exactly what the pluralists had in mind when they wrote about contending veto groups. But the fight shows that the oligarchs do not necessarily get what they want, even on an issue so critical for them. And, far from being a bunch of Lone Rangers, the oligarchy is a sector of the capitalist class that needs to work collectively against competing interests to get what it wants. Moreover, the range of economic issues of importance to the oligarchy, including, besides taxation, trade, monetary policy, and even the general redistributive effect of the federal spending (Winters and Page 2009:738), is far too broad to escape the interest of other parties both within and outside of the capitalist class.

The National Capitalist Class: Economic Basis

The capitalist class figures, one way or another, in all the accounts of national power we have reviewed so far. We devote the remainder of this chapter to a closer examination of this class in its economic, social, and political aspects. The discussion touches on many of the issues that came up as we discussed elite theories and their critics.

We defined the capitalist class as consisting of people who receive most of their income from invested wealth. Although such people exist at virtually all income levels, only at very high levels does dependence on income derived from wealth become the predominant pattern. A traditional division within the capitalist class is that between local and national capitalists. The national capitalists are those who own or manage major national corporations; Mills

---

[3] http://money.cnn.com/2012/09/21/pf/taxes/romney-tax-return/; *New York Times*, Oct. 1, 2016.

collectively dubbed them "the corporate rich." The locals are affluent but community-oriented businesspeople, such as local media owners, real estate investors, car dealers, and other large retailers. In recent decades, this distinction has become less meaningful. Heirs to large local fortunes have tended to convert them into diversified national wealth. The community banks, newspapers, and other enterprises owned by their families are often sold to national corporations.

In Chapter 4, we found that households with the highest incomes derive most of their income from accumulated wealth, in such capitalist forms as interest, dividends, and rents or from lucrative family-owned businesses (see Table 4.2). We discovered that wealth—especially corporate wealth—is highly concentrated in the United States. The richest 10 percent of households own 90 percent of corporate stock and mutual fund shares. Within this stratum of wealth holders, the top 1 percent of all households hold about half of stock and fund shares, 63 percent of bond investments, and 63 percent of equity in private businesses (see Table 4.6).

In the Age of Growing Inequality, large new fortunes have emerged on a scale that recalls the burst of new wealth in the so-called Gilded Age of the late nineteenth century. While the Gilded Age fortunes often came from manufacturing and related sectors of the economy, the fortunes of this new Gilded Age most typically derive from the vastly expanded financial sector and enterprises related to information technology and the Internet.

By the beginning of the twenty-first century, there were a few hundred individuals worth more than a billion dollars, thousands of households with net worths in excess of $100 million, and more than 2 million with net worths over $10 million (Bernstein and Swan 2007:331–360; Frank 2007:8). Some of these fortunes were rooted in earlier periods, but most probably originated in the 1980s and especially the 1990s, extraordinary years of private wealth accumulation. Surprisingly few—only 10 percent of those with fortunes over $10 million—inherited their money, according to one survey (Frank 2007:45).

Many people with net worths of a few million dollars are not members of the capitalist class. Rather, they can be counted among the working rich, as described in Chapter 1—highly successful professionals, salespeople, executives, and small-business owners, whose incomes depend more on their jobs than their assets. But among those worth over $25 million, both working rich and inheritors are rare. Instead, many of these very rich are typically entrepreneurs, founders of large enterprises, who have built up their private fortunes by offering stock in their firms to the public or selling them to larger companies. Two famous examples are Larry Ellison, founder and still CEO of Oracle, the business software giant, and Ted Turner, creator of CNN and related cable enterprises, who sold his interests to Time-Warner. Others made their fortunes as early employees of successful "start-ups," who accepted stock in lieu of large salaries and profited as the value of their shares soared. Seattle and the San Francisco Bay Area are reportedly home to hundreds of Microsoft and Google millionaires. Still others have been able to accumulate very large fortunes managing other people's money or as CEOs of major corporations, whose annual compensation, often in the form of stock options, may run into tens or hundreds of millions.

One way to keep track of the wealthiest members of the capitalist class is through *Forbes* magazine's annual list of the 400 wealthiest Americans. Table 8.1

contains a sampling of the 2016 *Forbes* 400, with information on the size and source of their fortunes. Like the full list, it contains many familiar names, including Donald Trump (156th on the list when it was published a few months before his election to the presidency), Bill Gates (Microsoft), Oprah Winfrey, Mark Zuckerberg (Facebook), and Jeff Bezos (Amazon). Two sectors are strongly represented: finance and technology. But the list also includes people no one heard of before they landed on the *Forbes* list (Tom and Judy Love, Allan Goldman) and billionaires with fortunes rooted in unglamorous sectors of the economy (gas stations, chewing gum, canned soup).

When the *Forbes* 400 list was first published in 1982, it seemed timeless, since it included many heirs to the great fortunes of the late nineteenth and early twentieth centuries. But over time, the character of the list has shifted as old fortunes were displaced by new wealth. The newcomers fall into one of three categories:

1. *Inherited Significant Wealth but Not at Forbes 400 Level*— President Trump, whose father had accumulated a notable real estate empire is apparently in this category. Trump began his ascent with the help of a $50 million stake from his father (Dye 2016:192).

2. *Inherited Modest Wealth or Other Advantage*—Bill Gates fits here. His father was a successful lawyer. Gates attended a private school.

3. *Without Inherited Advantage*— Ralph Lauren and Michael Bloomberg are examples. Fashion designer Lauren is the son of East European immigrants, whose father was a house painter. Bloomberg is founder of a financial media company and recently mayor of New York City. His father was a bookkeeper for a dairy.

A study of the *Forbes* lists from 1982 to 2006 found that the proportion of heirs had slipped from nearly half in 1982 to 30 percent in 2006 (Bernstein and Swan 2007:65). In 1982, there were, for example, 24 heirs to the DuPont chemical fortune; by 1999, there were none. In 1986, there were 10 descendants of John D. Rockefeller; David Rockefeller, the last of his family on the 2016 list, died in early 2017. Much of the change seems to have taken place in the 1990s.

Why the decline in old-money listings? In part, because of the normal dynamics of family fortunes. The founder (a John D. Rockefeller or a Jeffrey Bezos) accumulates enormous wealth, often in a breakthrough period of national economic dynamism. The money is divided among the heirs, who may not be as talented and, having inherited great wealth, have no need to be as ambitious. Even if it is well managed, after two or three generations the family fortune is sufficiently dispersed that no individual has sufficient net worth to claim a place among the *Forbes* 400— $1.7 billion in 2016. But the abruptness of the drop-off in old-money listings in recent years suggests something more: A renewal of the capitalist class toward the end of the twentieth century, when the stability of the class, which lasted through the middle decades of the century, was upset by the sudden influx of new fortunes based on new sources of wealth.

Though edged off the *Forbes* list by new wealth, many of the older fortunes persist. A clan's money may be preserved by family trusts. Several

Table 8.1 Sample of the "Forbes 400" Fortunes

Personal Fortunes	Estimated Net Worth (Billions)	Primary Source of Wealth
Bill Gates	81.0	Microsoft
Jeffrey Bezos	67.0	Amazon
Warren Buffett	65.5	Berkshire Hathaway. Investments
Mark Zuckerberg	55.5	Facebook
Larry Ellison	49.3	Oracle
Michael Bloomberg	45.0	Bloomberg Financial Services & Media Company
David Koch	42.0	Diversified, Industrial, Inheritance
Larry Page	38.5	Google
Jim Walton	35.6	Wal-Mart, Inheritance
Sheldon Adelson	31.8	Casinos
Jacqueline Mars	27.0	Candy, Inheritance
George Soros	24.9	Hedge Funds
Laurene Jobs & Family	17.7	Apple, Disney. Widow of Steve Jobs
Abigail Johnson	14.7	Fidelity Investments. Inheritance
Steven Cohen	13.0	Hedge Funds
Rupert Murdoch	11.0	Newspapers, Fox Networks
Donald Newhouse	10.5	Publishing
Micky Arison	7.2	Carnival Cruises
Ralph Lauren	5.9	Fashion
Richard DeVos	5.4	Amway
Scott Duncan	5.2	Pipelines
Tom & Judy Love	5.1	Retail & Gas Stations
George Lucas	4.6	Star Wars
Henry Kravis	4.5	Leverage Buyouts
Donald Trump	3.7	Real Estate, Television
S. Curtis Johnson	3.7	SC Johnson Cleaning Products, Inheritance
Fredrick Smith	3.7	FedEx
Tom Gores	3.3	Private Equity

Personal Fortunes	Estimated Net Worth (Billions)	Primary Source of Wealth
David Rockefeller	3.1	Banking, Inheritance (Oil)
Allan Goldman	3.0	Real Estate
Bennett Dorrance	3.0	Campbell Soup, Inheritance
Wilbur Ross, Jr.	2.9	Investments
Oprah Winfrey	2.9	Television
William Wrigley, Jr.	2.6	Chewing Gum
Julio Mario Santo Domingo	2.4	Beer
Meg Whitman	2.3	eBay
Judy Faulkner	2.2	Gap
Gordon Getty	2.1	Inheritance (Getty Oil)
Lee Bass	1.8	Oil, Investments

Source: www.forbes.com/forbes-400/list/#version:static.

thousand wealthy families maintain "family offices" to manage their common financial affairs (Bernstein and Swan 2007:250). In 2016, *Forbes* published a list of the 25 largest family fortunes, all worth $10.7 billion or more. Ten of them were not represented on the 400 list because of the way ownership was parceled out among family members. At lower levels still are many important families with lesser but still substantial collective fortunes— among them, the DuPonts; the Coors brewery family; the Sulzbergers, who control the *New York Times;* and the Grahams, recently owners of the *Washington Post.*[4]

The rapidly rising wealth of the *Forbes* 400 was one more indication of the rising concentration of wealth in the Age of Growing Inequality. From the early 1980s to 2013, the net worth of the average *Forbes* listee leapt from 1,700 times to nearly 10,000 times that of the average household.[5] More generally, there has been, as we saw in Chapter 4, a steep increase in the concentration of the wealth in the top 1 percent of households. This growing concentration of personal wealth is paralleled by the concentration of wealth in the corporations themselves. The dominant position of the largest corporations has advanced considerably since Mills wrote. In 1950, shortly before the publication of *The Power Elite*, the 100 largest U.S. industrial corporations (among nearly 200,000) already controlled approximately 40 percent of all industrial assets; by the 1990s, their share had grown to 75 percent (Dye 1995:15, 19).

---

[4] www.forbes.com/sites/kerryadolan/2016/06/29/billion-dollar-clans-americas-25-richest-families-2016/#ece3fc232f59; *Forbes* 1998.

[5] Calculated from Kennickell 2009:17 and Wolff 2016.

Mills observed that even the largest personal fortunes were small, relative to the assets concentrated in large corporations. Economic power, he contended, belonged to those who controlled the corporations. But who controls the corporations? Mills' answer, as we have seen, was "the corporate rich": top corporate executives and extremely wealthy families like the Fords with substantial stakes in major corporations.

But as major corporations have grown larger, their stock has become more dispersed, and their relationship to even the largest stockholders has grown more distant. The biggest corporations have hundreds of thousands of stockholders; individual holdings of even 5 percent (enough to give the owner significant influence over management) are uncommon. At the same time, many wealthy families have sought to reduce the risks to their fortunes by spreading investments across different corporations and sectors of the economy. Today, owners are rarely seen at helms of major corporations.

Small- and medium-sized corporations are more likely to be controlled by their owners—typically families or small groups of stockholders, including many of the Forbes 400 listees.[6] But by 1980, only 22 of the 100 largest industrial corporations were controlled by owners. Most were run by professional managers, relatively free of owner influence (Herman 1981:61). The current exceptions to this rule tend to be relatively young corporations, like Jeffrey Bezos' Amazon or Ellison's Oracle, that have experienced spectacular growth in new sectors of the economy.

The displacement of owners at the top of major corporations set the stage for the spectacular rise in executive compensation of recent years. In 2016, the average compensation for the CEOs of 200 major corporations surveyed for the New York Times was $19.7 million. At the same time that executive compensation has reached unprecedented heights, it has become more dependent on the financial performance of the corporation. Incentives, including yearly bonuses and long-term stock purchase plans (called stock options), are added to base pay to reward executives who enrich their stockholders. For senior corporate officers just below the rank of CEO, the pattern is similar: high and rapidly climbing rewards, with total compensation more dependent on return to investors.[7]

Although top executives seldom hold more than small shares of the billions of dollars of outstanding stock in their companies, they can easily accumulate sizable personal fortunes. For this reason, we did not hesitate to include them in our capitalist class, along with founders like Ellison and Bezos and the owner-managers of smaller corporations. For example, General Electric CEO Jeffrey Immelt earned a modest (by CEO standards) $5.7 million in 2008, but he already held $52 million in GE stock, $27 million in his company pension fund, and a $4 million balance in deferred compensation.

---

[6] Forbes also publishes an annual list of the largest privately owned (not publicly traded) companies. Most have few stockholders. Included are some large corporations such as the Mars candy company and Fidelity Investments. In 2009, all had revenues in excess of $2 billion. Many are owned by individuals included in the Forbes 400 list (see forbes.com/private).

[7] New York Times May 28, 2017; DeCarlo 2007; Useem 1996:243–250.

The National Capitalist Class: Social Basis

Parallel to the economic basis of a national capitalist class in the corporate economy, there is an upper-class social world built on prestige and exclusive patterns of association. Among the institutions identified with this world are select prep schools, the *Social Register,* and the elite metropolitan social clubs. These three have been widely used by researchers as formal indicators of membership in a socially defined upper class.

We have already described the appearance of the *Social Register* in early industrial America, when the new rich were being socially merged with the established upper classes. Although occasionally capricious in its inclusions and exclusions, a century after its creation, the *Social Register* remains, as Mills (1956) once described it, "the only list of registered families . . . the nearest thing to an official status center that this country, with no aristocratic past, no court society, no truly capital city, possesses" (p. 57).

A small circle of prestigious prep schools, such as St. Paul's (New Hampshire), Hotchkiss (Connecticut), Foxcroft (Virginia), and Chapin (New York), traditionally draw most of their students from upper-class families. These day schools and boarding schools tend to be concentrated in the Northeast, but they draw many students from throughout the country. They are secular or nominally Episcopalian (the religious affiliation most common in the upper class) and traditionally single-sex institutions, although most have become coeducational. A few are older than the republic, but most were founded or experienced their major expansion around the time the *Social Register* appeared. They have, moreover, traditionally served a similar function: the integration of old prestige and new money (Baltzell 1958:292–319; Domhoff 1970:9–32).

Prep school graduates are informally referred to as "preppies," a term with mixed undertones of admiration and derision, which is used more loosely to refer to various aspects of an upper-class lifestyle (Birnbach 1980). The extension of the term is not inappropriate. The style and values the prep schools inculcate in their students equip them for participation in an upper-class social community. The network of personal ties that develops among prep school students and their families will serve them well in their subsequent careers and social lives. Prep schools contribute to a pattern of upper-class endogamy by bringing students and their siblings into contact with potential marriage partners, both directly and through upper-class social functions to which prep school students are likely to be invited. Among the latter are the debutante balls, the traditional events at which young women of the upper class are presented to society.

Most major metropolitan areas have one or two elite social clubs, such as New York's Knickerbocker, San Francisco's Pacific Union, or Philadelphia's Philadelphia Club, with generally upper-class memberships. The clubs provide an informal setting where upper-class associations can be developed and maintained and, on occasion, important business or political matters can be discussed free from outside scrutiny (Baltzell 1958:336–354; Domhoff 1970, 1974).

The prep schools and elite metropolitan clubs draw not only from their own regions but from a broader upper-class population. In this sense, they perform a national integrating function. It is not surprising that George W. Bush's upper-class family sent him from Texas, where he grew up, to study at Andover in Massachusetts, or that years later his father, former President George H. W. Bush, used San Francisco's exclusive Bohemian Club to introduce him to a group of friends who might be useful to the son's own presidential ambitions (Domhoff 2006:58).

As we saw in earlier chapters, social scientists have long emphasized the affinity between the worlds of wealth and prestige. Weber noted that the rich tend to draw together into upper-class "status communities," with common lifestyles, values, and patterns of association. Just such a social upper class developed around the wealthy "X family" in newly industrialized Middletown, as described by the Lynds (see Chapter 3). On a national level, industrialization brought a social merger of the traditional upper class and the owners of new industrial fortunes. By 1940, virtually all the founders of great fortunes in the late nineteenth or early twentieth centuries had traceable descendants listed in the *Social Register.* Studies in the 1960s and 1970s pointed to the continuing link between national wealth and prestige. Domhoff (1967) and Dye (1976), in research reviewed earlier in this chapter, traced the upper-class connections of corporate leaders.

For the student of national power arrangements, the significance of a link between upper-class society and corporate wealth is related to the problem of cohesion raised earlier. The achievement of consensus on specific policy issues and, more generally, the maintenance of class solidarity are made easier when those who own and control the major concentrations of national wealth encounter each other in a private sphere of informal relations. The schools and clubs are merely the outer manifestations of this realm whose deeper meaning resides in shared experience, intimacy, and the bonds of friendship and kinship that produce a consciousness of common identity and common values.

Domhoff (1974) points to group dynamics research in social psychology, which has established that physical proximity among the members of a group, frequent contact, a group reputation of high prestige, and an informal atmosphere all contribute to group solidarity. These are characteristic features of the upper-class world we have been describing and prepare us for another basic conclusion of the same research: "Members of socially cohesive groups are more open to the opinions of other members and more likely to change their views to those of other members" (pp. 89–90, 96). E. Digby Baltzell (1958), in his earlier study of upper-class Philadelphia, made a related point, which he phrased in terms of social control: An upper-class community inculcates and sustains "a mutually understood code of conduct" in its members. Upper-class people are especially subject to the "norms and sanctions of their peers. A man caught in an act of dishonesty or disloyalty fears, above all, the criticism of his class of lifelong friends" (p. 61).

In the 1950s, when Mills and Baltzell were writing, and as late as 1970s, it was still possible to speak of the Protestant (or WASP)[8] **Establishment**: an informal network of wealthy, powerful men who (1) were drawn from the upper-class social world described here; (2) held many of the top positions

---

[8] WASP, denoting White Anglo-Saxon Protestant but connoting something like adult "preppie."

in industry, finance, and law; and (3) often served in high government office and, in or out of office, influenced national policy, especially economic and foreign policy. Never a formal organization, much less an elite conspiracy, the Establishment was more a set of personal relationships among people bound by social background, common values, and shared experiences.

The social world that produced the Establishment has not disappeared. The traditional prep schools are thriving, young women are still presented at debutante balls, the exclusive social clubs still function in major cities, and the *Social Register* is still published. The people who grow up in this privileged world certainly have much better than average chances for successful careers. But there is no longer an Establishment, in the sense we have described.

The Establishment faded away in part because recruitment to positions of power in business and government has become more open and meritocratic. In the past, graduates of exclusive prep schools could expect more or less automatic admission to Ivy League colleges, leading to top positions in business, finance, or law. But in the 1960s, the Ivies and other selective colleges broke this key link between social position and career success when they began to depend on the new SAT exam and give more emphasis to academic potential than family background in admissions. The change worked to the advantage of ambitious upper-middle-class students with good public school educations.[9]

At the same time, both colleges and businesses came under pressure to eliminate discriminatory practices that had severely restricted the access of those who did not fit the Establishment's WASP-male profile to top positions. Today, women, Jews, Catholics, and blacks, though still underrepresented, are much more likely to serve on corporate boards, in the president's cabinet, and in other elite positions than they were in the 1960s, but the class base for recruitment is still upper-middle to upper class.[10]

Economic change also contributed to the demise of the Establishment. There are fewer family-dominated companies, like the former Chase Manhattan Bank, long led by David Rockefeller, a quintessential Establishment figure. As we have noted, the postindustrial economy has given rise to large new fortunes in areas such as finance, information technology, and the Internet, much as the new industrial economy did a century ago. These developments raise interesting, unanswered questions. Will the new money merge socially with old money, as it has in the past, to produce a renewed upper class? Will the social upper class become more diverse in religious and ethnic terms, reflecting the diversification of national elites?[11] We cannot even begin to answer such questions with the existing, dated literature on upper-class society. Perhaps future research will satisfy our curiosity.

---

[9] It remained possible for very wealthy families to buy places for their sons and daughters at selective institutions through donations to university endowments. But this mechanism did not require upper-class credentials, just money (Golden 2007).

[10] See D. Brooks 2000; Davidson, Pyle, and Reyes 1995; Judis 1991; Lemann 2000; Zweigenhaft and Domhoff 1998.

[11] Graham (1999:51, 59–61) notes that some members of the black upper class now participate in traditionally white debutante balls and attend traditional WASP boarding schools.

For now, we can say that there is significant overlap—though probably a good deal less than in the past—between the upper-class social world and the national capitalist class, and that the social institutions of the upper class provide some of the glue that binds the members of the capitalist class together.

A New Elite?

Sociologist Shamus Khan recently spent a year at an elite New England boarding school, teaching and gathering material for a book. What makes Khan's study intriguing is that he had graduated from the school, St. Paul's in New Hampshire, a decade earlier and was sensitive to the ways it had changed. One of the first things he noticed was that students of color and those who overtly identified with the old money elite had literally switched places. As a student at St. Paul's, Khan, the son of a Pakistani immigrant, lived with other minority students in a separate dorm. This arrangement was not imposed by the institution but preferred by these students, who felt most comfortable with others "like themselves." When Khan returned, the minority students were no longer self-segregated, but some members of the old elite were. They lived in a dorm with others "like themselves"— kids from wealthy families, many with long standing ties to the school, who spent summers on the same islands and knew each other or knew of each other through social networks before they ever got to St Paul's. Many of their classmates, including others from similar backgrounds, regarded them with contempt. As Khan makes clear, St. Paul's "is still a place for the already elite" (p. 13). Two thirds of St. Paul's families can afford the $40,000 annual cost for high school. Parents arrive in Mercedes, BMWs, if not a chauffeured Rolls Royce. But the tone of the place has changed, and it certainly looks more diverse than it did in the past.

St. Paul's, whose student body was once entirely white male, likes to think of itself as open to everyone and everything. Students are encouraged to be cultural omnivores, who are at ease with both opera and rap and can find connections between the medieval epic poem *Beowulf* and a contemporary horror movie. Diversity and cultural openness have allowed St. Paul's to transform its self-image: "Paulies" once knew themselves as members of a social elite, "with particular histories and tastes"; today they see themselves as "a collection of the most talented and hardest working of our nation" (p. 194). Khan makes two points about this new self-image. One is that it is not entirely accurate. As he gradually discovers, most students are not especially hard working. They don't do much during the evening study period. And they don't actually read *Beowulf*, but depend on Google, Wikipedia, and *SparkNotes* as sources for their papers. They are superior students, but not so uniquely talented as they often imagine. St. Paul's is a selective institution (though it helps to be from a legacy family), and most of its graduates will go to Ivy League or other top-ranked colleges. But Khan, a faculty member at Columbia University, is stunned when an earnest student tells him that he expects his planned 10-page research paper to be a "contribution to the literature" on the topic. Students apparently believe that a classmate who is an accomplished violinist could, if he wanted, quit school and become an international star and that another who excels at math will one day win the equivalent of the Nobel Prize for mathematics. These illusions can be attributed to adolescent innocence, but they also reflect the way the school encourages students to think of their place in the world.

Khan's second point has to do with the ideological function of St. Paul's new vision of itself. It justifies the existence of a "New Elite," that claims to be based on merit rather than lineage. In the midst of growing inequality, it provides a seemingly "democratic" basis for the privilege of the privileged. Perhaps the New Elite is not all that new, and St. Paul's is doing what such schools have done in the past, integrating new wealth and old money.

The National Capitalist Class: Participation in Government

In December 1960, at a time when the Establishment was still very much alive, President-elect John F. Kennedy was selecting his cabinet. One of the people he turned to was a quintessential Establishment figure, Robert Lovett, a Wall Street investment banker with impeccable social credentials and extensive corporate connections (Halberstam 1972:16). In a perceptive book on the Kennedy-Johnson years, journalist David Halberstam relates their conversation, in which Kennedy artfully flattered Lovett, a Republican who had voted against him, and offered him a major cabinet post.

> Lovett declined regretfully . . . explaining that he had been
> ill. . . . Again Kennedy complained about his lack of knowledge
> of the right people, but Lovett told him not to worry, he and his
> friends would supply him with lists. Take Treasury, for instance—
> there Kennedy would want a man of national reputation, a skilled
> professional, well known and respected by the banking houses.
> There were Henry Alexander at Morgan, and Jack McCloy at Chase
> [Manhattan Bank], and Gene Black at the World Bank. Doug
> Dillon too. Lovett said he didn't know their politics . . . (their
> real politics of course being business). At State, Kennedy wanted
> someone who would reassure European governments: They
> discussed names, and Lovett pushed . . . young fellow Dean Rusk
> over at [the] Rockefeller [Foundation]. He handled himself very
> well, said Lovett. The atmosphere was not unlike a college faculty,
> but Rusk had stayed above it, handled the various cliques very
> well. A very sound man. (pp. 16–17)

The three top cabinet appointments made by Kennedy, a liberal Democrat, reflected the advice of Lovett and other Establishment conservatives like him. For secretary of the treasury, he chose C. Douglas Dillon, an investment banker connected with Dillon, Read, and Company, a major Wall Street firm started by Dillon's father; for secretary of defense, Robert McNamara, who had just been made president of Ford Motor Company; and for secretary of state, Dean Rusk, then president of the Rockefeller Foundation, a man with many admirers in corporate circles (Burch 1980:175–177).

Cabinet recruitment studies show that Kennedy's appointments followed a pattern inherited from his predecessors and maintained by his successors. Although the Establishment and men like Lovett are phenomena of the past, presidents continue to appoint the kind of sound, reassuring figures he recommended to Kennedy. Contemporary cabinets are more ethnically diverse and more likely to include women, but the most important cabinet positions are still overwhelmingly drawn from the top of the class structure, most notably from the national capitalist class and the national prestige class we have been describing.

Two thirds of people who served in the cabinet from 1897 to 1980 were, prior to their appointments, corporate officers, investment bankers, or corporate lawyers, many with clear upper-class social connections, according to studies by Mintz (1975) and Burch (1980). The prominence of investment bankers and corporate lawyers among cabinet officers is notable; these two groups have long played a crucial mediating role between business and government, akin to the coordinating roles they play within the corporate world. Our own survey of the people who have held the top cabinet posts (state, defense, and treasury), from Kennedy's inaugural cabinet in 1961 through Donald Trump's in 2017, produced similar results: 63 percent of these cabinet officers were drawn from major corporations, financial institutions, or corporate law firms.[12]

Trump presented himself as a populist in the 2016 campaign, who would break the elite's hold on Washington. But when he had to organize his own administration he looked to wealthy businesspeople and generals. His choices for the top three cabinet positions were (1) for Secretary of State, Rex Tillerson, CEO of ExxonMobil; (2) for Treasury Secretary, Steve Mnuchin, a banker and hedge fund manager; and (3) for Secretary of Defense, Jim Mattis, a recently retired four-star general. His administration was probably the wealthiest in the country's history. Commerce Secretary Wilbur Ross was on the 2016 *Forbes* 400, with a fortune estimated at $2.9 billion. Education Secretary Betsy De Vos is a member of one of Michigan's wealthiest families, known for the millions of dollars contributed to political campaigns and philanthropic endeavors. Tillerson, Mnuchin, and Gary Cohn, the president's chief economic advisor, all have fortunes estimated to be in the hundreds of millions. If the concentration of wealth in the new government was unprecedented, the tilt toward business was consistent with a long history.

Ironically, modern presidents have generally come from lower levels in the class structure than their top cabinet secretaries. Harry Truman, Dwight Eisenhower, Lyndon Johnson, Richard Nixon, Bill Clinton, and Barack Obama, all grew up in modest circumstances and had pre-presidential careers in politics (or in Eisenhower's case, the military), rather than business. Recent exceptions, aside from Trump, are the two Bushes, descended from an affluent, socially prominent Connecticut family. Both made considerable fortunes on their own before entering politics.

What can be said of the class background of Congress? Evidence going back to 1906 indicates that most members of Congress come from business

---

[12] For this purpose, we have drawn on Brunner 2001; Dye 1995 and 2016; *Who's Who in America*; and *Who's Who in American Politics*.

or the professions. They have typically been lawyers, executives, or small-business owners (LTV Corporation 1990; Nagle 1977). In 2012, the median net worth of members of the House of Representatives was $969,000, a figure that does not include the value of the family home, the major source of wealth for most Americans. The equivalent figure for the Senate was $2.7 million.[13] In contrast, the median net worth of U.S. households, exclusive of housing, verges on zero. The late Senator Daniel Patrick Moynihan was close to the truth when he observed, "We've become a plutocracy. . . . The Senate was meant to represent the states; instead it represents the interests of a class" (*New York Times*, Nov. 25, 1984).

Congress, then, is recruited from the upper levels of the class structure, although often from a notch or two below that of the top cabinet officers. Members of the House and Senate are also more likely to be career politicians rather than top executives or corporate lawyers on temporary assignment, like many cabinet officers. The law and business backgrounds of many members of Congress suggest a smaller-scale, more localized version of the corporate world so amply represented in the cabinet. If the cabinet is recruited from the national capitalist class, the Congress draws on local upper-middle and capitalist classes.

What do cabinet and congressional recruitment patterns tell us about national politics? It certainly cannot be argued that class position allows us to predict the political behavior of individual decision makers. For example, Dianne Feinstein, a liberal Democrat, and Mitch McConnell, a conservative Republican, who seldom vote together, are among the wealthiest members of the Senate, with fortunes in the tens of millions. But we have already seen that the behavior and opinions of people, in the aggregate, are shaped in important ways by class. And we have noted how informal association shapes receptivity to opinions. The senator or representative whose personal associations are largely capitalist class or upper-middle class is likely to be more open to viewpoints common at the top of the class structure than to those prevalent toward the bottom.

There are issues that are obviously of much greater concern to working-class people than to people of higher class rank, like the great majority of members of Congress. For example, there is considerable resistance in Congress to raising the minimum wage, on which many low-income households depend. Despite occasional increases (the last one was in 2009), the purchasing power of the minimum wage is allowed to lag well behind inflation. On the other hand, wealthy members of Congress, like Senators Feinstein and McConnell, who have voted to lower the estate tax, were doing their heirs a big favor. Votes on these issues are influenced, not only by partisan and ideological considerations, but also by the milieus in which senators and representatives move. Most of them know few people who work at low-wage jobs, but many who regard the inheritance tax as unduly burdensome.

---

[13] Estimates based on data from 2012 financial disclosure filings submitted by members of Congress and provided by the Center for Responsive Politics (CRP). The filings specify a range (e.g., $15,000 to $50,000) for each asset or liability. Summing the item-by-item range limits, CRP calculated a minimum and maximum net worth and provided an average of the two for each member of Congress.

So does class matter? Yes, according to political scientist Nicholas Carnes (2013) who took a systematic look at the relationship between the class background of members of Congress and the legislation they support. He compared the records of those who served from 1999 to 2008 with their occupations before they were elected. He found that the minority of lawmakers who had held working-class jobs before coming to Congress were the most likely to take progressive positions on economic issues like the minimum wage, tax cuts, and the federal response to the 2008 recession. Members who were former businesspeople or farm owners were the most conservative on the same issues. These differences held even after Carnes controlled for other obvious influences, like the lawmaker's party or the political character of a member's district. As a Washington lobbyist explained, several decades ago, "'A man doesn't change a whole lot just because he has been elected to the Senate. If he's been a small-town lawyer, or a banker, or a businessman, he is going to think and act like one when he gets to the Senate'" (Matthews 1960 quoted in Carnes 2013:83). We can assume that the same holds for the women and men who serve today.

Money and Politics

- Included in a bill that passed the Senate in late 1996 was a provision of particular interest to Frederick Smith, founder and chairman of Federal Express Corporation. Smith, whose fortune would soon earn him a place on the *Forbes* 400 list, personally lobbied senators for the provision, which has made it nearly impossible for FedEx workers to form unions and gave the company a distinct advantage over its unionized competitor, UPS. Federal Express has long been generous to lawmakers and their campaign treasuries. It keeps a fleet of airplanes on standby for the use of lawmakers. In 2012, campaign donations from company-affiliated sources totaled $2.5 million. It also spent $12 million to employ 71 Washington lobbyists who cover a wide range of issues important to the company.[14]

- Legislation signed by President Bush in 2001 placed the federal estate tax on a 10-year path to extinction. A January 2012 law, signed by President Obama, reestablished the tax, but with a generous exemption for smaller family fortunes. The campaign to repeal the inheritance tax was promoted by the Policy and Taxation Group, a low-profile organization amply funded by several dozen national capitalist-class families, including heirs to the Mars (candy), Gallo (wine), and Campbell (soup) fortunes. They hired some of Washington's best lobbyists, pollsters, and public relations people and financed sympathetic policy research. Among their backers were some of the most generous contributors to political campaigns (Graetz and Shapiro 2005).

---

[14] All figures on campaign donations and lobbying cited in this section, unless otherwise noted, are from the Center for Responsive Politics website (www.opensecrets.org).

- In July 2007, the federal minimum wage, much eroded by inflation, was raised for the first time in over a decade. The increase was resisted by business interests, among them some generous campaign contributors. Like the 1996 law mandating the last increase, the 2007 legislation was sweetened for opponents with several billion dollars in business tax relief. It provided for a phased increase of the minimum to $7.25.

These three cases illustrate the power and limits of political money in the hands of wealthy individuals and organized business interests. They do not consistently get all they want, but they are well funded and persistent. Over time, they are remarkably successful.

Labor unions lobbied hard against the Federal Express provision but were overwhelmed by the company's well-financed efforts. With meager resources, supporters of the estate tax could barely respond to the repeal group with its virtually limitless funding. As we saw earlier in this chapter, resistance to total repeal came from the "merely rich," especially well-organized small business owners, who feared that the 2001 legislation risked the return of heavy estate taxes.[15] The Obama-era 2012 measure, was passed under the pressure of a budget crisis. It exempted couples with estates under $10 million—which is to say, all but the wealthiest 1 or 2 percent of the population (see Chapter 4 for details). The Policy and Taxation Group has not surrendered and continues to lobby for full repeal (Graetz and Shapiro 2005; Winters 2011:249–254). They have the support of President Trump—whose own family has an obvious interest in the issue—according to a tax plan released in the early days of his administration.

Business groups were unable to block the efforts to increase the national minimum wage, when Congress returned to Democratic control in 2007. But they retained sufficient influence to extract compensatory tax relief for themselves and resist, for at least a decade, further increases. In mid-2017, the federal minimum wage remained at $7.25, its buying power much eroded by inflation. By delaying increases for long periods, representatives of the capitalist class have made the national minimum wage largely irrelevant most of the time. (Recently some states and cities have increased the minimum for their own people.)

The Fate of Campaign Finance Reform

Political money was at the heart of the Watergate scandals that drove President Nixon from office and sent some of his top advisors to jail. In the wake of these events, a series of reform laws were enacted that imposed strict limits on individual campaign donations to federal candidates and parties; limited the amounts federal candidates could spend; regulated group donations, which had to be made through registered **political action committees (PACs)**; provided for federal financing of presidential campaigns on a

---

[15] Adopted under complicated budget rules, the 2001 measure would have led to reinstatement of the original estate tax regime the year after a decade phase-out period. The mistaken assumption of supporters of the measure was that Congress would not have permitted the return of estate taxes.

matching basis for candidates who accept limits on campaign expenditures; required public disclosure of campaign donations, including the identity of anyone contributing more than $200; and mandated detailed disclosure of campaign expenditures. The legislation prohibited corporations and labor unions from contributing money from their treasuries to political candidates. But they were allowed to use their resources to run PACs that solicit donations from union members, corporate executives, or stockholders.

Perhaps the most significant benefit of the new campaign finance laws was transparency: The Watergate reforms allowed the public to see who was contributing to campaigns, how much they were giving, and how the money was being spent.

Over time, the efficacy of the Watergate laws has been undermined by a combination of court decisions, artful interpretations by campaign lawyers, and weak enforcement (Garrett 2016). Soon after the laws were enacted, the Supreme Court ruled that the imposition of spending limits on federal candidates was unconstitutional and that candidates could make unlimited donations to their own campaigns. (Such self-financing does not guarantee success, but does help explain the large number of millionaires in Congress.) More recently, in the 2010 *Citizens United* decision, the court lifted the century-old ban on contributions made directly from corporate or union treasuries; such contributions could not be constitutionally limited if they were for activities independent of a candidate's campaign organization. That same year, a federal appeals court ruled that contributions to so-called super-PACs, which make independent expenditures on behalf of candidates could not be limited, and in 2014 the Supreme Court ruled that no limit could be placed on the aggregate amount an individual could make to multiple federal candidates.

Beginning with the 2012 campaign, political operatives began to take advantage of a provision of the tax code, denominated 501(c)(4), which, very loosely interpreted, provided a mechanism for stealth campaign contributions—so called "dark money." Nonprofit "social welfare organizations" created under 501(c)(4) could accept limitless donations from unnamed individuals, corporations, and other organizations and use it to pay for campaign ads on behalf of candidates.

These developments undercut the post-Watergate effort to reduce the influence of money in national politics through contribution limits and transparency. Nonetheless, the individual limits on *direct* contributions to individual candidates and to most PACs are still in place, as are the requirements that campaigns report donations and expenditures.

Who Gives?

Who makes campaign contributions? Studies going back to the 1920s indicate that contributors are, not surprisingly, better educated, higher in occupational status, and richer than the average American. A 1997 study of donors to congressional campaigns revealed that 81 percent had incomes over $100,000 and almost half had incomes in excess of $250,000, which would place them in the top 1 percent of households at the time. Even as candidates learned that they could raise large sums

Table 8.2 Campaign Contributions, 2015–2016

	Amount	Democrats	Republicans
Business	$3,282,959,637	49%	51%
Labor	$194,009,852	87%	13%
Ideological	$459,758,369	66%	43%
Other	$699,308,461	58%	42%

Source: Center for Responsive Politics website, www.opensecrets.org.

Note: Includes individual and PAC contributions. Ideological covers proponents of gun control, right-to-life, and other political causes.

in small contributions ($10, $50, $250) via the Internet, their campaigns remained heavily dependent on the larger donations raised by more traditional methods.

Most campaign money comes from business sources, such as individual corporate executives and corporate PACs. As Table 8.2 indicates, business contributions far exceed labor contributions.[16] Corporate money has generally favored the Republicans, but never neglected the Democrats. In 2016, probably because Donald Trump was widely expected to lose to Hillary Clinton and Democrats seemed likely to regain control of the Senate, business contributions were evenly divided between the parties. In fact, the dollar amount the Democrats received from business was almost 10 times more than what they got from labor, whose resources were limited. Thus, both parties are wary of offending business interests.

The campaign finance landscape shifts from election to election with changing fund-raising strategies, jurisprudence, regulations, and legislation. What has remained constant is the predominance of the affluent and business interests in campaign giving.

What Do Rich People Want?

Are the rich, as novelist F. Scott Fitzgerald claimed, "different from you and me"?[17] If Fitzgerald was wrong and the rich are pretty much like everyone else, their disproportionate representation in government positions and among campaign contributors is of little consequence. For better or worse,

---

[16] These figures should be taken as useful approximations. They only account for reported contributions, thus excluding amounts under $200 and 501(c)(4) donations. They assume that big donations from corporate executives can be considered business donations.

[17] The quotation is from a widely reprinted story, "The Rich Boy," which Fitzgerald wrote just after he completed *The Great Gatsby*. It begins, "Let me tell you about the very rich. They are different from you and me. They possess and enjoy early, and it does something to them, makes them soft where we are hard, and cynical where we are trustful, in a way that, unless you were born rich, it is very difficult to understand. They think, deep in their hearts, that they are better than we are because we had to discover the compensations and refuges of life for ourselves. Even when they enter deep into our world or sink below us, they still think that they are better than we are. They are different."

most of what we know about the rich comes from novels. A small and generally inaccessible minority, they do not show up in big surveys and are difficult to recruit for more focused studies. An important exception is a national study of the politics of the rich being conducted by Benjamin Page, Larry Bartels, and others. Their objective is to learn what "wealthy Americans seek from politics and how their policy preferences compare to those of other citizens." Initial results of their study, based on interviews with high net-worth individuals (mean net worth, $14 million) recruited in the Chicago area suggested that the rich are, in fact, different (Page et al. 2013).

The Chicago interviews were conducted in the aftermath of the 2008–2009 recession, when unemployment rates lingered near the highest levels recorded since the Great Depression of the 1930s. But the problem of unemployment seemed less urgent to these high net-worth respondents than it did to most Americans, according to contemporary polling. They agreed that unemployment was an important issue, but gave greater weight to federal budget deficits, an issue of limited significance for the general public. Asked what the "most important" issue facing the country was, only 10 percent of the study respondents compared with 53 percent of the public named unemployment. They were also much less supportive of government efforts to deal with the problem. About 20 percent of the wealthy compared with 70 percent of the public agreed that the government should "see to it that everyone who wants to work can find a job."

On a series of other national issues with obvious class implications, there were large opinion gaps. The public was much more likely than the wealthy to favor raising the minimum wage above the poverty level, increasing the EITC (Earned Income Tax Credit) to help the working poor, and "[making] sure that everyone who wants to go to college can do so." By a large margin, the public favored spending more on health care, food stamps, and Social Security. The wealthy favored spending less on these items.

There were some matters on which the wealthy and the general public concurred. Strong majorities of both agreed that income differences between the rich and poor were higher than they had been 20 years ago and that these differences were "too large." But only 17 percent of respondents compared with 52 percent of the public thought the government should "redistribute wealth by heavy taxes on the rich."

One reason to think that these differences in opinion are consequential is that the rich are much more politically engaged than most Americans. The researchers found that their respondents were far more likely to talk politics, to vote, and to attend political events, from rallies to private dinners. The majority had made campaign contributions and had contacts with members of Congress or executive branch officials.

Business Lobbies

We have examined the political influence of the capitalist class exercised through direct participation in government and through campaign finance. We now turn to a third channel of influence: organized efforts to convince public officials to adopt (or abandon) particular policies. Especially since the emergence of the modern corporate economy, business representatives have actively lobbied Congress, the federal departments, and regulatory agencies that carry legislation into practice. In the late nineteenth and early twentieth centuries, corporate lobbies—backed by abundant flows of cash—moved Congress with dependable ease. For example, a lobbyist for the National Association of Manufacturers (NAM) publicly acknowledged that he had bought legislative favors with bribes and influenced House leaders to appoint congressmen favorable to NAM to important House committees and subcommittees (*Congressional Quarterly* 1976:654, 662). In recent decades, major business lobbies have generally employed more subtle methods. But money still counts.

Currently, the principal business lobby organizations in Washington are the U.S. Chamber of Commerce and the Business Roundtable. Also important are the National Association of Manufacturers, which speaks for smaller industrial corporations, and the increasingly influential National Federation of Independent Business, which represented small business in the fight over the estate tax. "Small business" is a broad term which refers to independent enterprises that may have hundreds of employees and do millions of dollars in business annually.

The Chamber's strength has traditionally come from its ability to mobilize pressure on individual members of Congress through local affiliates. The local businesses, which control the affiliates, are likely to include important elements of the power structure in a legislator's home district, including people who belong to the same social networks as the legislator. When the Washington office wants to pressure senators or representatives on a vote, it can systematically mobilize letters, e-mails, phone calls, and personal visits from local business owners, a legislator's former law partner, or a fellow member of the local country club. In recent years, the Chamber has become a more formidable presence in Washington. It employs 500 lobbyists, researchers, lawyers, and communications experts dedicated to promoting pro-business government policy. It spent $35 million in 2012, supporting friendly Congressional candidates and $136 million on lobbying—far more than any other organization (Stolberg 2013).

The Business Roundtable consists of the CEOs of approximately 200 of the largest corporations. Its power is based on the formidable resources controlled by these corporations and the prestige of those who lead them. The Roundtable typically operates more quietly than the Chamber does. Its stock-in-trade is the personal visit from a CEO and the carefully crafted economic study or legal brief supporting its position. The leaders of the Roundtable have access to members of the House and Senate and even to the President—entree that no ordinary lobbyist could hope to duplicate. A congressional aide commented, "A visit from a CEO has an unbelievable impact, as perhaps it should. It shows a commitment" (Green 1979:29).

The class element in U.S. politics becomes clearest when issues arise, like health care, the minimum wage, or taxation, that pit a liberal lobby alliance, often led by labor unions, against a conservative alliance led by business groups and representing capitalist-class interests. Since the late 1970s, the business alliance has more often than not won such confrontations. It has, for example, blocked legislation that would strengthen labor unions, slowed the rise of the minimum wage, and promoted lower taxes on high incomes and multimillion-dollar estates. But the business alliance doesn't always win.

In the wake of the 2008–2009 recession, facing a liberal Democrat in the White House, it lost two, hard-fought legislative battles, one over expanding access to health care ("Obamacare") and the other over finance sector reform (the Dodd-Frank Act). When the business alliance fails to stop legislation it doesn't like, it often manages to water it down as it passes through two houses of Congress and undercut its implementation with legal appeals or by lobbying the agencies responsible for carrying it out. In 2017, President Trump and the Republican-controlled Congress, with strong business backing, were working to repeal or undermine Obamacare and the Dodd-Frank Act.

Policy-Planning Groups

A step removed from the conflictual world of political campaigns and legislative battles is a quieter and less visible realm of organizations dedicated to formulating and disseminating broad proposals for national policy. Groups such as the Council on Foreign Relations, the Council for Economic Development, and the Business Council are created and financed by the corporate elite, which plays a prominent role in their activities.

Similar to the policy groups, both in their functions and their links to the capitalist class, are the major charitable foundations and the policy research "think tanks." Foundations such as Rockefeller, Ford, Lilly, and Kellogg (all named for the wealthy families that endowed them) fund research and pilot projects to test policy ideas. Many of the best-known think tanks are clustered in Washington, where they can feed their research findings and policy recommendations to sympathetic politicians, lobbyists, and journalists. Among them are the Brookings Institution, which has particularly influenced Democratic policy makers, and the American Enterprise Institute (AEI), which is influential among Republicans. One crucial function of the policy groups, foundations, and think tanks is to back the careers of public policy intellectuals, many of whom are channeled into government positions. Recent years have seen the rise of a group of more explicitly political, public policy organizations like the Heritage Foundation, the Cato Institute, and the Center for American Progress.

Indirect Mechanisms of Capitalist-Class Influence

Capitalist-class influence over government is not limited to the direct means we have been describing (recruitment to decision-making positions, campaign financing, lobbying, and domination of policy-planning institutions). The capitalist class can also affect government policy indirectly, through its control of the economy and the mass media. A defining characteristic of a capitalist society is the existence of a relatively small class that controls most productive wealth and therefore independently makes investment decisions that can decisively affect the welfare of other classes. Although governments in capitalist societies have limited control over what business leaders do, their political fortunes are closely linked to business decisions. The connection is often described in terms of a "business confidence." If business leaders lack confidence in a government or its policies, they will be reluctant to risk their capital in new investments. The resulting decline in the aggregate level of investment may be reflected in a rising level of unemployment, which, in turn, will subject the government to pressure from an electorate dissatisfied with the state of the economy. What sorts of government policies are likely to alienate business confidence? Basically, any that threaten profits, including those concerning taxation, environmental protection, worker compensation, workplace safety, and corporate financial affairs. The precise factors that lead to a loss of confidence are less important than the essential fact that this mechanism gives the capitalist class an indirect veto over government policy.

Two implications of the business-confidence veto are particularly worth noting. One is that it can influence a government without actually curtailing investment. The mere risk of such action is enough to persuade decision makers to reconsider a proposed policy or the appointment of a cabinet officer whose opinions might sound threatening to business. The possible effect of government action on investor behavior is frequently raised as an issue in public policy debates. The other implication is that the veto mechanism does not require conscious, concerted action by members of the capitalist class to be effective. Individual investment decisions, based on objective assessment of potential risk and profitability, can collectively produce a downturn in business activity and subject a government to popular pressure (Bloch 1977).

Governments are also subject to the limits imposed by private control of the mass media, through which people receive information about public affairs. They remain influential, despite the growing use of social media as a news source. In the United States, most media organizations are owned by the local and national capitalist classes—though they could conceivably be organized as cooperatives, like the respected French paper Le Monde; as semiautonomous public bodies, like the British Broadcasting Company; or as organs of political parties, like a number of European papers. Control of the media has become highly concentrated, and the principal media organizations are themselves typically major corporations or are owned by major corporations. The notable exceptions to this rule are the Public Broadcasting Service (PBS), which does not have an audience on the scale of the major TV networks, and National Public Radio (NPR), which has a large audience in some markets.

In a world of multiplying information channels, most Americans who pay any attention to national and international affairs are still likely to receive their news from one of five TV networks: ABC, CBS, NBC, CNN, and Fox. All are owned by large media conglomerates. The three most important daily newspapers, the New York Times, the Washington Post, and the Wall Street Journal, like Time, the most widely read newsmagazine, are owned by large corporations or wealthy individuals. A dozen or so newspaper chains account for more than half of the country's daily newspaper circulation. They get much of their national and international news from a single source, the Associated Press (AP), a cooperative owned by the media it serves. These media do not speak with one voice, but the predominant ownership structure may limit the range of political perspectives represented.

Capitalist-class influence over the media is not limited to the power of ownership. Because the media are operated for private profit and most of their income comes from corporate advertising, media managers cannot be indifferent to the sensitivities of advertisers. The networks are also subject to the influence of the affiliated stations that broadcast their programs to local audiences. Early in the history of television broadcasting, Edward R. Murrow's brilliant and controversial current affairs program *See It Now*, carried by CBS, was forced off the air after its corporate sponsor withdrew and no regular replacement could be found. In the 1950s, programs that dealt with the issue of racial discrimination or employed black actors could not appear on network television because corporate sponsors refused to be associated with them, and some affiliates (particularly in the South) refused to carry them. Today, confrontations between advertisers and networks are uncommon. These early confrontations established unwritten standards that continue to guide commercial television. As an executive of a major advertising agency explained, direct interference by the advertiser is rare "because the producers involved and the writers involved are normally pretty well aware of what might not be acceptable" (Barnouw 1978:54).

Of course, to sell advertising, commercial media must attract an audience, and they would only lose that audience with content that merely reflected the self-serving views of their owners. But as the ad man's comment suggests, the main power that the capitalist class exercises over the media is the power of setting implicit limits on what is "acceptable." The media, in turn, operate on their audiences not by imposing specific ideas but by defining the subjects that are appropriate for consideration and delineating the range of reasonable opinion. In other words, they help define the public agenda. Their ability to do so is increased by the concentration of media control. Thus, until the late 1950s, racial inequity was not a national issue, though it was most certainly a serious national problem. For decades the issue of national health care was invisible, though it certainly was a problem for many Americans. Until quite recently, the question of the fundamental fairness of the criminal justice system for minorities and low-income people did not have a place on the public agenda though it affected the lives of millions. Without media attention, these concerns were largely invisible.

The Capitalist-Class Resurgence

Who has the power? This is the question that pluralists, elitists, and class theorists were trying to answer in the debate we examined at the beginning of this chapter. The question more or less assumes that the distribution of power is stable—it does not vary over time. But this is a bad assumption. It seems clear, in particular, that the capitalist-class and business interests in the United States have gained at the expense of other competitors for power during the Age of Growing Inequality.[18]

In the early 1970s, there was a growing sense of vulnerability and declining power in capitalist circles. The economic system was changing in ways that seemed threatening and unpredictable. Wages had been rising, profits had been stagnating, and productivity had been declining. The international

---

[18] See Blumenthal 1986, Blumenthal and Edsall 1988, Edsall 1984, Ginsberg and Shefter 1990, Smith 2012.

economy, dominated by the United States since the end of World War II, was becoming much more competitive. The U.S. economy was twice shaken in the 1970s by abrupt leaps in the world price of oil. Increasing government regulation in areas from environmental practices to consumer protection and workplace safety seemed to be raising the cost of doing business. Many business leaders felt politically isolated.

In a "Confidential Memorandum" prepared in August 1971 for the U.S. Chamber of Commerce, corporate lawyer Lewis Powell, Jr. warned that the "American free enterprise system" was "under attack" in the universities, the media, and the political arena; its very "survival" was at risk. For Powell, the wide-spread notion that the country was "controlled by big business" was exactly wrong: "Few elements of American society today have as little influence in government as the American businessman, the corporation or . . . stockholders." Business, he contended, needed to learn what labor understood all too well: "that political power is necessary . . . must be assiduously cultivated . . . used aggressively . . . and with determination." Powell urged a broad capitalist counteroffensive—long-term, effectively organized and well financed. His vision encompassed a much expanded role for the national Chamber of Commerce.[19]

Since the early 1970s, in response to Powell and others who issued similar warnings, corporate leaders and wealthy members of the capitalist class have taken a more direct and "aggressive" role in national politics. Within a few years of his memo, the Chamber of Commerce had doubled its company membership, tripled its budget, and fielded dozen of full-time lobbyists to defend business interests. By the late 1970s, national business organizations and trade associations had mobilized 9,000 lobbyists and 8,000 public relations professionals—a force that outnumbered the membership of Congress by 32 to 1. Corporations seized the opportunity presented by the post-Watergate campaign finance reforms and related court decisions. Business political strategists perfected the upscale "grassroots" campaign—mobilizing local business leaders, stockholders, depositors, suppliers, or dealer networks to influence Congress.

In 1972, the chief executives of DuPont, General Electric, General Motors, and Citibank joined with other top corporate leaders to found the Business Roundtable. About the same time, the Heritage Foundation was started, with the help of a $250,000 donation from Colorado brewer Joseph Coors, and the American Enterprise Institute began its transformation from an inconsequential research center into a key player in public policy. Both received financial backing from major corporations and foundations endowed by wealthy families such as the Mellons, the Pews, the Olins, and the Kochs (Blumenthal 1986; Edsall 1984:Chapter 3).

These efforts to reassert the power of the privileged have paid off. In the late 1970s, the capitalist class and corporate interests won a series of key legislative battles—for example, defeating labor reform legislation that would have made it easier for unions to organize workers. They achieved deep reductions in income, corporate, and inheritance taxes and the distribution

---

[19] Powell was appointed to the Supreme Court that same year. His memo titled "Attack on American Free Enterprise System" (August 23, 1971) is available at http://law.wlu.edu/deptimages/Powell%20 Archives/PowellMemorandumTypescript.pdf

of income has become more concentrated. In the next chapter, we will see that the power of organized labor declined as the power of business grew.

The power shift contributed to Republican victories in 6 out of 10 presidential elections since 1980 and broke the near monopoly the Democrats had held over both houses of Congress since the 1930s.

Conclusion

We began this chapter by defining elite, pluralist, and Marxist perspectives on power. We then took a close look at C. Wright Mills' *Power Elite*, his pluralist and Marxist critics, and some recent elitist conceptions of the structure of power in America. Mills emphasized the growing scale of corporate, government, and military organization and the corresponding concentration of national power in the "corporate rich," top government officials, and the leaders of the military. Much of the criticism of Mills centered on the question of elite cohesion. Do the members of a putative elite act together in pursuit of common objectives and in opposition to other groups? Mills did point to mechanisms that tended to unify the members of his power elite, including similar social backgrounds, shared elite education, association through upper-class society, movement of personnel between elites, and the common experience of managing large organizations. But the pluralists were unconvinced. Where Mills saw one cohesive elite, the pluralists saw many competing veto groups.

On the other hand, Marxist critics of *The Power Elite* thought Mills had been altogether too successful in demonstrating cohesion, and the unifying force in the power structure was the dominant corporate sector. America was not ruled by a power elite but by a corporate-based capitalist class. The contemporary writers on elites we reviewed agreed with Mills on one thing: Power is concentrated in large organizations and the elites that control them. But their accounts of the system diverge, especially on the issues surrounding cohesion.

Our extended examination of the national capitalist class established the following: A small class controls most corporate stock, and although major corporations are typically run by their top executives, the interests of corporate stockholders and top managers are aligned. We therefore consider these executives part of the capitalist class. There is apparently—our information on this is somewhat dated—a degree of overlap between the national capitalist class and the national upper class represented by such institutions as the *Social Register* and exclusive social clubs and prep schools; the upper class provides at least some of the social glue that binds the members of the capitalist class together. Finally, the national capitalist class has powerful means to shape national politics; these include placement of its members in top decision-making positions, campaign financing, lobbying, creation of policy-planning organizations, exercise of the business-confidence veto, and influence over the public agenda through the mass media. Looking back over the last 3 decades, we concluded that the power of the capitalist class has grown.

A pluralist would be quick to point out that neither the formidable array of political resources available to the capitalist class nor recent indications of growing capitalist-class power are definitive proof of domination by that class. We make no such claim. But we are committed to examining how social classes participate in the political system and how the balance of power between them has shifted in the Age of Growing Inequality. With those goals in mind, we amplify the picture we have painted here in the next chapter, which deals with class consciousness and conflict between classes in electoral and industrial contexts.

KEY TERMS DEFINED IN THE GLOSSARY

class perspective
elite
elite cohesion

elite perspective (see
  pluralist perspective)
Establishment, the pluralist
  perspective

political action
  committee (PAC)
power
privileged classes

SUGGESTED READINGS

Bottomore, Tom. 1966. *Elites in Modern Society.* New York: Pantheon.

Short, lucid survey of elite theory.

Domhoff, G. William and Hoyt B. Ballard, eds. 1968. *C. Wright Mills and the Power Elite.* Boston, MA: Beacon.

Excellent set of critical essays on Mills' power elite thesis.

Dye, Thomas R. 2016. *Who's Running America? The Obama Reign.* 8th ed. Boulder, CO: Paradigm Publishers.

The national elite, sector by sector. Watch for likely new edition with Trump people in political sector.

Frank, Robert. 2007. *Richistan: A Journey Through the American Wealth Boom and the Lives of the New Rich.* New York: Crown.

A well-informed examination of the fortunes, lives, and politics of the new rich by a reporter who has covered them for the Wall Street Journal.

Graetz, Michael J. and Ian Shapiro. 2005. *Death by a Thousand Cuts: The Fight Over Taxing Inherited Wealth.* Princeton, NJ: Princeton University Press.

How a small, well-financed group turned the estate tax into the "death tax" and promoted legislation to abolish it.

Hacker, Jacob and Paul Pierson. 2010. *Winner-Take-All Politics: How Washington Made the Rich Richer and Turned Its Back on the Middle Class.* New York: Simon & Schuster.

Argues that changes in American politics, reflected in public policy, are responsible for the growing concentration of income at the top.

Judis, John B. 1991. "Twilight of the Gods." *Wilson Quarterly* 5 (Autumn):43–57.

Intriguing account of the rise and fall of the "American establishment" of bankers, corporate lawyers, and scholars who once made U.S. foreign policy. Helpful annotated bibliography.

Khan, Shamus 2011. *Privilege: The Making of an Adolescent Elite at St. Paul's School.* Princeton, NJ: Princeton University Press.

Columbia University professor returns to his elite prep school and finds it changed.

Kendall, Diana. 2008. *Members Only: Elite Clubs and the Process of Exclusion.* Lanham, MD: Rowman & Littlefield.

The functions of highly exclusive city, country, and golf clubs.

Mayer, Jane 2016. *Dark Money: The Hidden History of the Billionaires Behind the Rise of the Radical Right.* New York: Doubleday.

The role of a pair of billionaire brothers and their network of wealthy allies in the rise of the right.

Phillips, Kevin. 2002. *Wealth and Democracy: A Political History of the American Rich.* New York: Broadway Books.

Concentrated wealth, democracy, and the tensions between them in American history since colonial times.

Compares current era of concentrated wealth and power with previous gilded ages.

Smith, Hedrick. 2012. *Who Stole the American Dream?* New York: Random House.

A well-regarded reporter's narrative of the shifting balance of power in American politics since the 1970s and its effects on average Americans.

Class Consciousness and Class Conflict

I believe that leaders of the business community, with few exceptions, have chosen to wage a one-sided class war today in this country.

Douglas Fraser, president of the
United Auto Workers (1978)

The forgotten men and women of our country will be forgotten no longer.

Donald J. Trump,
inaugural address (2017)

Class consciousness, a concept central to our concerns in this chapter, plays a pivotal role in Karl Marx's theory: It transforms individual resentment of the capitalist present into shared struggle for the socialist future. Class consciousness implies (1) an awareness of membership in a group defined by economic position, (2) a sense that this shared identity creates common interests and a common fate, and, finally, (3) a disposition to take collective action in pursuit of class interests. At some points in his work, Marx implied that only a group whose members experience such a consciousness can be defined as a class. Elsewhere, he carefully distinguished between a *class-in-itself* and a *class-for-itself*. The first is a class in a formal, definitional sense: Its members have the same **objective class position**, defined by their place in the economy, but are not conscious of their common situation. The second is a class in an active, historical sense: Its members share a subjective class consciousness; they engage in militant action to defend interests that they conceive as being in direct opposition to those of other classes. Thus, embodied in Marx's conception of class consciousness—especially in the notion of a class-for-itself—is the expectation of class conflict.

In its fullest sense, class consciousness is not just an aspect of public opinion ("What percentage of working-class voters supported the candidate?"), but an intense, collective involvement in the events of a critical historical juncture. It develops out of a long series of strikes against bosses who exploit workers and riots against authority that brutalizes the masses. It culminates in urban mobs roaming the streets and burning the buildings that symbolize upper-class domination and in peasants seizing the land they work, and it ends with a revolutionary seizure of power in the name of the oppressed: Paris in 1871, Mexico in 1910, Moscow in 1917, Peking in 1949, Havana in 1959.

Revolution is rare, but simmering class struggle is historically common. Slave revolts, violent strikes, local mobs on a rampage—these have occurred in many societies. More institutionalized and controlled forms of class struggle, such as union-organizing campaigns and political movements that seek legislative power to help the underprivileged, are considered a normal and healthy part of a democratic society. In this chapter, we examine the extent to which people are aware of sharing a class identity and class interests, the social factors that advance or retard the development of this consciousness, and its relationship to political opinion and behavior. We will also focus on class conflict as reflected in two arenas: electoral politics and labor relations.

Class Identification

Our interest in the concept of class consciousness is based on the idea that it connects objective class position (measured by occupation, income, or wealth) and political behavior. That is, we can assume, as Marx did, that people who recognize and articulate their class position are more likely to promote their class interests. We have seen that the United States is a very unequal society and becoming more so. But we often hear that the United States is a classless society, since, it is claimed, the great majority of Americans consider themselves "middle class." But is this true? Not quite. It depends on how you ask the question.

A famous poll conducted by *Fortune* magazine in 1940 concluded that about 70 percent of Americans call themselves middle class (*Fortune* 1940:27). Some popular writers seized these figures to proclaim that America was a middle-class country—that if Americans had any class consciousness at all, it simply meant that they mostly thought of themselves as belonging to the same big group. But sociologist Richard Centers (1949) was skeptical. He noticed that this figure quoted came from responses to the following survey item, which offers three alternatives:

What social class do you consider that you belong to?

1. Upper class

2. Middle class

3. Lower class

Centers also noticed that when respondents were asked the question in open-ended form (without a specific list of answers from which to choose), many called themselves working class. Centers made a reputation for himself by adding "working class" to the reply alternatives offered by the *Fortune* survey. When he asked a national sample which of the four classes they belonged to, the results were radically different. Now the majority of respondents chose the label working class. Most of those who didn't, picked middle class. In retrospect, it seems that Americans in that lower half of the class structure just didn't like the label "lower class," with its negative suggestion of "low class." So they answered middle class, until Centers offered them a better option.

Variants on Centers' question have been used in hundreds of surveys over the years and gotten roughly similar results. Since the 1970s, it has been asked regularly in the General Social Survey (GSS), a periodic national poll, covering a broad range of social and political matters. Table 9.1 shows the responses from the 2016 GSS. What is being measured here? It's not class consciousness in the fullest sense, but an aspect of class consciousness, Centers called **class identification**, the sense of belonging to a particular social class.

Table 9.1   Class Identity, 2016

In percent

Upper Class	2.6
Middle Class	41.0
Working Class	46.7
Lower Class	9.1
Don't know/Other/None	0.5
TOTAL N=2,867	100.0

Source: Author's tabulation of General Social Survey 2016.

In 2016, as in previous years, less than 1 percent of respondents to Centers' class identification question said they didn't know, belonged to some other class, or rejected the idea of class altogether. This suggests that question taps something real to respondents. Identifying with one of the four classes is not a stretch for them. In 2016, working class was the most frequent answer, followed by middle class, but almost 1 in 10 respondents identified themselves as lower class. In fact, since the 1990s, both the working-class and lower-class categories have grown at the expense of middle class in the GSS surveys. This suggests that many Americans have a sense of declining status in the Age of Growing Inequality.

Centers' question has proven useful and durable. It challenges the notion of the United States as a middle-class society and provides a sense of our evolving class identities. But it is worth recalling that it is, like most items on surveys, a forced-choice question. Open-ended questions on this topic that do not provide a list of potential answers produce less orderly results. People invent all kinds of class labels for themselves. Middle class is a common answer, but many respondents to an open-ended query deny the existence of classes until they are presented with specific alternatives. We cannot, then, use the answers to Centers' question as a literal description of the way people freely conceive of their own class position. But we can assume that it tells us something about the relationship between class and political consciousness because, as we will see, the answers we get are related to both objective class position and political attitudes.

Correlates of Class Identification

Occupation and income are good predictors of the choices people make when presented with the class identification question. In the 2016 GSS survey, about 80 percent of people in blue-collar jobs with family incomes under $50,000 identified themselves as working or lower class. Ninety percent of managers and professionals with family incomes over $100,000 identified as middle class or upper class. But at middling levels of occupation and income, the responses were more mixed. Office and retail settings seem to be ambiguous places for class identification. For example, the majority of people in low-level office and sales jobs identify as working class, but about 40 percent consider themselves middle class. The old distinction between blue-collar and white-collar workers is still relevant here. Manual workers, as might be expected, are much more likely to think of themselves as working or lower class than office and retail workers at similar levels of income.

Centers and subsequent researchers concluded that occupation is the best predictor of class identification, followed by income. One other factor had a significant, independent effect on class identification: *association*. The class positions of friends, neighbors, and kin were strong influences on the formation of class identification. People with largely high-status associations, whatever their own position, were more likely to identify as middle class. Likewise, those with predominantly low-status associations were more likely to think of themselves as working class. Put differently, your class identification depends partly on your objective class position and partly on whom you know (Centers 1949; Hamilton 1975; Hodge and Treiman 1968; Schreiber and Nygreen 1970).

Class Identification, Political Opinion, and Voting

Our interest in subjective class identification, like our concern with class consciousness generally, stems from the idea that consciousness is a link between objective class position and political attitudes or behavior. If there is anything to the notion of class identification, we would, for example, expect people at lower-class levels who identify themselves as working class to take more liberal positions on economic and social spending issues than others at the same class level who think of themselves as middle class. We would expect a similar pattern in candidate preferences in elections. Centers and some subsequent research showed that political opinion and voter preferences were, in fact, affected by class identification (Campbell 1954, 1960; Centers 1949). Our own analysis of data from two surveys, the GSS 2016 and American National Election Study 2016, provided some support for these ideas. We found that working-class and lower-class identifiers were somewhat more likely to take liberal positions on social spending items such as child care, health, and aid to the poor than were middle-class and upper-class identifiers at the same income level. In the 2012 presidential election, low income voters (below $50,000) were 10 percent more likely to vote for Democrat Barack Obama if they identified as working class or lower class. (The same did not hold at higher income levels.) But the relationship between class identification and voters' choice in the 2016 presidential elections was weak. Donald Trump's unexpected victory that year may have been a unique case or evidence of the declining significance of class for American politics. We will return to that question later in the chapter.

Elections and the Democratic Class Struggle

Although no advanced industrial country has experienced the convulsive class revolution envisioned in Marx's *Communist Manifesto*, most have passed through periods of bitter class confrontation and continue to experience less dramatic, institutionalized struggles over conflicting class interests. Class conflict has been evident in two realms: electoral politics and labor relations. Most of the remainder of this chapter will be devoted to these topics.

Elections in modern democracies have been characterized as manifestations of "democratic class struggle" in recognition of the representative role of political parties. Synthesizing the available evidence in 1960, Seymour Martin Lipset wrote,

> Even though many parties renounce the principle of class conflict or loyalty, an analysis of their appeals and their support suggests that they do represent the interests of different classes. On a world scale, the principal generalization which can be made is that parties are primarily based on either lower classes or the middle and upper classes. (p. 230)

In most parliamentary systems, parties can be arrayed on a spectrum from right to left, with the former upholding the interests of the privileged classes, and the latter attacking them on behalf of the less fortunate. In Great Britain, for example, the Labor Party has traditionally drawn working-class support, while the Conservatives have run strong among managers and professionals. In France, manual workers lean toward the Socialists (and, in the past, the Communists); business owners, executives, professionals, and farmers tend toward the right-wing parties. The relationship between classes and parties has traditionally been looser in the United States than in most Western democracies, which typically have at least one major party that identifies itself as socialist and presents itself as a partisan of the working class. The Democratic Party in the United States has traditionally been regarded as the party of the "common man," but it has never called itself socialist, and has gradually became reticent about appealing directly to working-class interests. Nevertheless, the Democrats have long done better among working-class voters than among those at higher class levels.

The modern Democratic Party, which emerged from Franklin Roosevelt's New Deal in the 1930s, developed a strong working-class base without becoming a working-class party. Roosevelt and his party won over workers and their families with special programs that helped them get through the economic crisis of the Great Depression and popular, pro-worker measures like the minimum wage and Social Security. The party could mobilize working-class voters with the help of the labor movement, which grew rapidly under the New Deal, and the party's big-city political machines. As historian William Leuchtenburg later observed, the New Deal "drew a class line across the face of American politics" (2015:201). But the Democrats also attracted significant middle-class support.

Regional differences, ethnicity, and religion blurred the class boundaries between the two major parties. The Democratic Party was the party of white Southerners, a legacy of the Civil War and Reconstruction eras. Working-class Southerners, but also middle- to upper-class Southerners who might otherwise have backed the conservative, business-oriented Republicans, faithfully supported the Democrats. Nationally, most white, working-class Protestants voted for the Democrats, but, outside the South, a significant minority of them voted Republican. Catholics and Jews of all classes, especially the sons and daughters of Italian and east European immigrants, were typically drawn to the Democratic Party. Among them were the "ethnic rich"—men such as John F. Kennedy's multimillionaire father, Joseph, an Irish Catholic, or Jewish financier Bernard Baruch—who helped bankroll the party.

The New Deal coalition of blue-collar workers, Southerners, and "white ethnics" gave the Democratic Party a lock on national politics. Democrats held the presidency and controlled both houses of Congress almost continuously for nearly 4 decades. But beginning with Richard Nixon's 1968 victory, the Republican Party aggressively challenged the political status quo. The Republicans won 8 of 13 presidential elections from 1968 to 2016. After 1994, they often controlled both houses of Congress.

In part, this shift reflected some peculiarities of American political institutions, which sometimes permitted the Republicans to win control of the presidency and the Congress when the majority of voters had, by a modest margin, supported the Democrats. But the remaking of national politics was largely the result of important changes in American society. In the prosperous years after World War II, many of the children and grandchildren of immigrants moved into the middle and upper-middle classes. Even if they retained their Democratic affiliation, these people tended to become more open to the political message of the Republicans. They were increasingly likely, for example, to see themselves as beleaguered taxpayers rather than as beneficiaries of government programs. The class differentiation of the descendants of immigrants convinced Democratic leaders that the party needed to broaden its appeal, deemphasizing working-class issues. As second- and third-generation Americans moved to the suburbs, the urban Democratic political machines they had supported went into decline, undercutting the party's ability to turn out voters.

Over time, Democratic positions on a shifting constellation of issues including the Vietnam War, the Iraq War, affirmative action, welfare, abortion, gay rights, gun control, and environmental policy have strained the loyalty of working-class supporters. These so-called "wedge issues," which were ably exploited by the Republicans, divided a large sector of blue-collar Democrats from the party's many upper-middle-class activists. Affirmative action issues in the workplace split black and white working-class Democrats, at a time when both were feeling the financial strains that came with the Age of Growing Inequality.

Two developments were of critical importance: the decline of the labor movement and the political realignment of the white South. The first, discussed later in this chapter, cut into a key source of working-class support and reduced the weight of specifically working-class issues in the concerns of Democratic politicians. The second grew out of the party's identification with the Civil Rights Movement and the legislation of the mid-1960s that ended legal segregation in the South and guaranteed the voting rights of African Americans in the region. Nationally, the Democratic Party won the near unanimous support of blacks but lost its hold on the white South. As Bartels (2008:76–78) has shown, the change was most notable among middle- and upper-income Southern voters, but slower and smaller among low-income whites.

The End of the Democratic Class Struggle?

The critical role of region and race in American politics, the prominence of "wedge issues" unrelated to class concerns, and Republican victories since the 1980s have led some to conclude that social class is a declining influence in American elections. Many argue that racial and ethnic identity have become more important than class. To address this issue, Brewer and Stonecash (2007) looked at class differences among voters for the U.S. House using income as an indicator. They calculated the difference between voters in the bottom third and the top third of the income distribution since the 1950s and found that low-income voters were consistently and significantly more likely to support Democratic candidates (see Table 9.2). Moreover, class differences were not declining. As the table indicates, they were *lower*

Table 9.2 Party Preference by Household Income Difference, 1952–2004

Percent Voting for Democratic Candidates to U.S. House

Year	Bottom Third All voters	Top Third All Voters	Top/Bottom Difference All Voters	Top/Bottom Difference, Whites Separately
1952–1958	57	49	9	8
1960s	60	53	7	4
1970s	66	52	14	12
1980s	68	51	17	14
1990s	66	44	22	11
2000–2004	60	44	16	12

Note: Income thirds refer to relative position in the income distribution of voters.

in the 1950s and 1960s than in recent decades. Among white voters considered separately, the class differential was smaller but still substantial (see the right-most column in the table). Brewer and Stonecash (2007) got similar results when they looked at voters in presidential elections, as did Wood (2017) who carried the analysis to 2016. Wood found that in every presidential election from 1948 to 2012, low-income white voters were more likely, often much more likely, to vote for the Democratic presidential candidate than higher income white voters.

Now let's look at income differences in the last two presidential elections, as shown in Table 9.3. For both years we see an income gradient.

Table 9.3 Party Preference in Presidential Elections by Income

Household Income	2016			2012		
	Clinton (D)	Trump (R)	Total	Obama (D)	Romney (R)	Total
Under $30,000	56	44	100	64	36	100
$30,000–$50,000	55	45	100	58	42	100
$50,000–$100,000	48	52	100	47	53	100
$100,000–$200,000	49	51	100	45	55	100
$200,000 and above	49	51	100	44	56	100

Source: National Election Pool exit poll, as reported on the web by NBC and CNN.

Note: Percentages are of voters who expressed preference for major party candidates.

Fifty thousand dollars seems to be an inflection point. Below this level, the voters favored the Democrat (Clinton or Obama), above, they favored the Republican (Romney or Trump). But the differences were smaller in 2016 than 2012. And race had become more important. As Table 9.4 reveals, Obama lost the white vote in 2012, though he did better (by 7 points) among low-income whites than among higher income whites.

By 2016, the income differential in the presidential vote had vanished altogether among whites.[1] That year low-income white voters were no more likely to vote for Democrat Clinton than were those with higher incomes. The income gradient apparent in the previous table is driven by minority voters, who are, of course, disproportionately represented among lower income households. (Two thirds of Hispanics and 90 percent of African Americans voted for Clinton, according to the exit poll.) In the 2016 U.S. House races, the Democrats retained a small advantage among low-income white voters, albeit narrowed from 2012.

Why Trump?

Do these results represent the demise of the democratic class struggle in American elections? Against the long history of class voting in American elections, that conclusion would be premature, especially based on the extraordinary candidacy of Donald Trump. No Republican candidate in recent history has been so successful in drawing the support of white working-class voters.

Some attribute Trump's victory to his willingness to appeal to racial and ethnic resentments among working-class Americans. He connected

---

[1] Or largely vanished. Wood's analysis (2017) shows minimal variation among white voters, but indicates that white voters in the top few percent of the income distribution were less likely to vote for Trump than those at the very bottom of the distribution.

Table 9.4 White Vote for President and U.S. House in 2012 and 2016.				
	2016		2012	
President	Clinton	Trump	Obama	Romney
Under $50,000	39%	61%	45%	55%
Over $50,000	39%	61%	38%	62%
U.S. House	Democrat	Republican	Democrat	Republican
Under $50,000	42%	58%	46%	54%
Over $50,000	37%	63%	37%	63%

Source: National Election Pool exit poll.

Note: Percentages are of voters who expressed preference for major party candidates. White refers to non-Hispanic whites.

with these sentiments by means both indirect and blatant.[2] Well before he launched his campaign, he attracted attention by perpetuating the falsehood that Barack Obama, a black man, was not a native born American and therefore not a legitimate president. Trump introduced his candidacy with remarks that characterized Mexican immigrants as "drug dealers" and "rapists." During the campaign, he asserted that a Mexican-American federal judge, born in Indiana, could not be objective in a civil case involving his defunct "Trump University" because he is "a Mexican." Candidate Trump proposed a ban on Muslims entering the country. He was notably reluctant to repudiate the support he was attracting from white racists and neo-Nazis and tolerated racist behavior at campaign rallies. Whatever his intention, racism contributed to Trump's victory. According to two early statistical analyses, the strongest predictor of support for Trump was, in fact, the strength of a voter's racist attitudes (Klinkner 2017; Wood 2017).

Racism is nothing new in American society or politics. It is repellant to many, if not most Americans. But the appeal to racist sentiment worked for Trump because it connected with something larger: the declining fortunes of less educated workers in the globalized, postindustrial society that we described in Chapter 3. (In Chapter 5, we saw how economic change was undermining working-class family life.) An economist might explain the new economy with abstract talk of comparative advantage, industrial robotics, and "skill biased technological change." Trump put a human face— usually a brown face—on the trends that were troubling many Americans. The Mexicans, the Chinese, the illegal immigrants, he repeatedly asserted, are stealing American jobs. It is no coincidence that Trump did especially well in counties where local industries had lost jobs to Chinese and Mexican imports (Cerrato et al. 2016).

Trump's rhetoric also tapped into anxieties about the changing demographics of American society. In 1970, according to the Census Bureau, less than 5 percent of the U.S. population was foreign born and the country was overwhelmingly white and non-Hispanic. By 2014, 13 percent of the population was foreign born. The white, non-Hispanic proportion was 62 percent and shrinking steadily. The political assertiveness of minority groups and the sympathetic reception they received from Democratic politicians further unnerved many working-class whites who felt they were at a disadvantage in a society they no longer recognized.

In an insightful book titled *Strangers in Their Own Land*, sociologist Arlie Hochschild (2016) uses an apt metaphor to capture the way many alienated whites now view the world. She imagines people stuck in a long line leading up a hill to the American dream, which lies just over the crest. According to the dream, those who are willing to work hard can move up the hill and live better than their parents, just as successive generations before them have done. But something has gone wrong, according to the people Hochschild studied in conservative southern Louisiana. The line has stalled. For many, especially those without college degrees, it is moving backward. The problem is that some people are cutting in line. Often they are black people, favored

---

[2] See for examples, www.huffingtonpost.com/entry/president-donald-trump-racist-examples_us_584f2ccae4b0bd9c3dfe5566

by affirmative action in hiring and college admissions. Some are immigrants or refugees. Some are women. The narrative of the unjust line is not simply about economic advantage and disadvantage, but, at least as much, about the emotions of those who feel themselves marginalized, "strangers in their own land." In Hochschild's conception, the line is the "deep story" underlying the political views of many who were drawn to Trump. By appealing to racial resentment and vowing to cancel unfair trade pacts, Trump was telling them he could restore the dream. That was the promise of his slogan, "Make America Great Again."

The notion of a fading American dream is not an illusion. A study comparing the incomes of parents and their adult children found that fewer Americans are earning more than their parents did. For example, 90 percent of people born in 1940 had higher incomes than their parents. But only 50 percent of those born in the 1980s, had higher incomes. In part, this dramatic fall reflects slowing economic growth. But a bigger influence is the increasing inequality in the distribution of income that channels the benefits of growth to fewer households (Chetty et al. 2017).

In an Age of Growing Inequality, the dream remains a class issue, since those at the head of the line are not, by and large, minorities or refugees, as many Trump voters apparently believe, but men and women equipped by some combination of skills, capital, and political power to prosper in the new economy.

Finally, the analysis offered here should not lead us to stereotype Trump voters. His supporters—close to half the electorate—had varied reasons for their decision at the ballot box. Some, whatever their class, didn't like or trust Trump's opponent, or thought her too liberal. But racial resentment and its connection to the economic dislocations of the Age of Growing Inequality, apparently tipped the political balance among white working-class voters to the advantage of Donald Trump.

Policy Preference and Government Response

Many surveys have found that support for social programs and for liberal positions on economic issues varies in predictable ways with social class. For example, the majority of Americans support periodic increases in the minimum wage, but people at lower income levels are much more likely to do so. In a 2014 poll, 60 percent of respondents with incomes below $50,000, but only 40 percent of those with higher incomes, said they would be more likely to support a candidate who favored an increase in the minimum wage. In the wake of 2008–2009 recession, a majority of affluent Americans surveyed agreed with the idea that "private enterprise" would "solve" the country's problems, a proposition generally rejected by the less well off.[3]

---

[3] See www.gallup.com/poll/20710/Public-Solidly-Supports-Increase-Minimum-Wage.aspx., www.gallup.com/poll/160913/back-raising-minimum-wage.aspx; www.washingtonpost.com/page/2010-2019/WashingtonPost/2014/03/04/National Politics/Polling/question _13274.xml?uuid=XNJodqNaEeO4ZTiyVNkgYw; www.huffingtonpost.com/entry/minimum-wage-poll_us_570ead92e4b08a2d32b8e671. Private enterprise item based on authors' analysis of the 2010 General Social Survey.

Results from the 2016 GSS show that strong majorities of lower income Americans, but fewer high-income respondents, think the government is spending too little on child care, Social Security, and aid to the poor (Table 9.5). There seems to be no class difference in support for education and minimal difference with regard to treatment of drug addiction. (In the 2010 GSS, the income differentials on the latter item were quite large. The change by 2016 suggests that the problem of drug addiction had spread upward.) Public enthusiasm for spending on poverty drops precipitously at all income levels when the question is about "welfare programs" rather than aid to poor people. This phenomenon is a demonstration of how easily language can skew survey results (Smith 1987), but it may also indicate a particular distaste for public assistance, in contrast to other poverty programs.[4] However the question is phrased, support is strongest at lower income levels. There is, in contrast, one issue on which those at lower incomes take a more conservative position: abortion. Although public opinion on abortion has varied over time, a consistent and substantial gap has separated the bottom third from the top third of the distribution (Bartels 2008:76–78).

The class differences over these and other policy matters pose a challenge for democracy. Whose preferences count when an affluent minority disagrees with the less privileged majority? Martin Gilens has answered this question in a book titled *Affluence and Influence: Economic Inequality and Political Power in America* (2012). Gilens is not concerned with the power exerted by the plutocrats and CEOs we met in the last chapter, but with the collective influence of people we would categorize as upper-middle class, people who are not rich but, with incomes on the order of $100,000 or $200,000, are certainly "comfortable." He wanted to know how likely the opinions of this affluent minority are to prevail over those of people at lower-class levels. Gilens collected data from some 2,000 questions posed in national surveys over a 20-year period, asking whether respondents favor or oppose a specific policy proposal. He then compared the opinions of people in the affluent top fifth with those in the low-income bottom fifth and asked how did government respond when there was significant disagreement between them? Specifically, over the next several years, whose preference prevailed on issues such as Social Security, Medicare, progressive taxation, abortion, and gay rights? The answer, more often than not, was the affluent fifth. When the difference between the two groups over a policy matter was as little as 10 percent, the low-income group virtually never got what it wanted. (Of course, rich and poor sometimes agreed, in which case, there was a fair chance that policy will reflect their common conviction.)

Gilens' central finding is not surprising. In a real-world democracy, we might not expect the poor to regularly triumph over the rich. But what about the people in the broad middle? Do they fare any better than the poor? No. Gilens finds that middle-income Americans are as powerless as the bottom fifth when they disagree with the top fifth. The affluent, he notes,

---

[4] See the relevant discussion in Chapter 10.

Table 9.5 Support for Spending on Social Programs by Income Class

	In Percent		
	Low Income	Middle Income	High Income
"Assistance to poor"	80	72	62
Social Security	62	63	52
Child care	60	58	55
"Dealing with drug addiction"	66	68	62
Education	74	76	74
"Welfare"	29	18	21

Source: Author's tabulation of data from 2016 General Social Survey.

Note: Respondents were asked if spending on a program is too little, about right, or too much. Percentages are those who answered "too little." Income levels correspond roughly to the bottom 25% of households, the middle 50% ($30,000 to $110,000), and the top 25%.

don't always get what they want, but the contrary preferences of people at lower-class levels have little effect on their chances.[5]

Gilens did find some exceptions to this general pattern. People at lower income levels were more likely to prevail over the privileged when their preferences were supported by strong interest groups. A prime example was the 2005 defeat of the Bush administration's plan for partial privatization of Social Security, accomplished with the help of the powerful American Association of Retired People (AARP), which vigorously opposed the measure. From this perspective, it can be assumed that the decline of labor unions is contributing to the powerlessness of the poor and more generally the working class. He also found that governments are somewhat more evenhanded in periods of intense partisan competition, when they feel the need to broaden their electoral appeal. If Gilens is right, American democracy is often, but not quite always, weak in the face of steep economic inequality.

An earlier study by Bartels produced similarly discouraging conclusions. Bartels (2008:Chapter 9) compared the votes of U.S. senators in the 1980s and 1990s with the preferences of their own constituents in the top, middle, and bottom thirds of the income distribution. He concluded that senators gave the opinions of the upper third "50 percent more weight than those in the middle third," while those in the bottom third "received no weight at all"

---

[5] We have simplified Gilens' language here. His references to the affluent, the poor, and the middle are based on multivariate analysis of the survey data estimating policy preferences at the 90th, the 10th, and the 50th percentiles. Exploring the broad middle, he also looks at the 30th and 70th percentiles.

(Bartels 2008:234). Bartels did find a difference between political parties. Republican senators were twice as responsive to the top third. Republicans and Democrats were about equally responsive to the middle third and equally indifferent to the bottom third.

Class and Political Participation

Why is government most attentive to those who least need its help? In part because people toward the top of the class structure are more politically engaged, better informed, more likely to share their opinions with their representatives, and more likely to participate in political activities. They are, as we have seen, much more likely to contribute money to political campaigns. Surveys consistently show that voter participation is higher at higher income levels and suggest that the class bias inherent in unequal representation at the polls is increasing. In the November 2014 national elections, according to Table 9.6, people with incomes above $100,000 were almost twice as likely to vote as those with incomes below $30,000. The figures in the table may overestimate participation, since many survey respondents are reluctant to admit they have not performed the minimum duty of citizens, but there is little doubt that high-income households are disproportionally represented in the electorate and its class disparity seems to be increasing.

Does it make a difference that 40 percent or more of eligible adults don't vote in national elections? Political scientists Leighley and Nagler (2014)

Table 9.6 Voting in 2014 Elections by Family Income

Family Income	Percent Voting
Under $10,000	24.5
$10,000 to $15,000	30.1
$15,000 to $20,000	30.8
$20,000 to $30,000	35.2
$30,000 to $40,000	40.7
$40,000 to $50,000	42.4
$50,000 to $75,000	48.0
$75,000 to $100,000	52.9
$100,000 to $150,000	55.4
$150,000 and above	56.6
All adult citizens	43.9

Source: Census Bureau.

Note: Proportion of U.S. citizens above 18 years old who reported voting in the November 2014 elections.

answered this question with a study of nonvoters in elections from 1972 through 2008. They found that nonvoters have, on average, lower incomes and less education than voters and that they are less informed about differences between candidates. They also discovered systematic differences of opinion. Compared to voters, nonvoters are generally more liberal on redistributive issues, like health insurance, job guarantees, and federal assistance to schools and more conservative on social issues like abortion and gun control. Based on this class and opinion profile, the authors' answer is yes, it does make a difference.

Of course, astute politicians are as attentive as political scientists to these matters, and they tend to craft their message for people who vote, who are, as it happens, the same people who write them and donate to their campaigns.

Class Conflict and the Labor Movement

The preceding sections focused on government as an arena of "democratic class struggle." Here, we shift our attention to the conflict between capitalists and workers in the workplace. American labor history has been distinguished by an ironic combination of violent struggle and limited class consciousness that sets the American experience apart from the labor history of other Western nations. Violence has grown out of tenacious capitalist resistance—not so much to specific economic demands as to the very right of workers to organize labor unions. At the same time, the class consciousness of American workers has been limited in the sense that they and their leaders have typically sought circumscribed goals—basically union recognition, economic security, and decent working conditions, rather than more fundamental changes in the social system, the original goal of many European labor organizations.

For years, employers successfully exploited differences of race, ethnicity, and skill level among workers—for example, by hiring blacks to replace striking workers—and used violence to suppress strikes. Anti-union violence was common because local and national authorities generally sided with the owners. In effect, civil liberties were routinely suspended in strike situations. Without the normal protection of the laws, workers could be physically intimidated (often by thugs hired for this purpose), union organizers harassed, and leaders jailed. Much of this activity was coordinated by special firms that sold "union-busting" services (Litwack 1962:95–115).

In Chapter 3, we sketched the history of the labor movement to World War I. A brief review of the decades that followed will provide a framework for understanding recent developments. Unions expanded during the war, but the anti-union postwar "red scare" and determined employer resistance reduced membership from 20 percent to 10 percent of the labor force in the 1920s (Brooks 1971:148). Change came with the Great Depression and the concomitant shift in national politics, particularly during the years 1933 to 1937. A labor historian has described this period as "the highwater mark of class struggle in modern American history" (Davis 1980:47). When the United Textile Workers announced an industrywide strike in 1934, *Fibre and Fabric,* the New England trade journal, declared, "A few hundred funerals will have a quieting influence" (*Fortune* 1937:122). Before this bitter, violent strike had completed its 3-week run, thousands of National Guard troops had been mobilized in seven states, and 12 strikers and one deputy had been killed. The union lost.

In this period, however, there were more labor victories than defeats. Some of the most significant were gained through a new tactic—the sit-down strike: Workers forced concessions from employers by taking physical control of the workplace. First used in the rubber industry in 1936, the innovation, which appealed to the militant mood of workers at the time, spread rapidly. One labor official remembers 1937 as the year he received calls daily like this one from a drugstore food-counter worker: "My name is Mary Jones; I'm a soda jerk at Liggett's; we've thrown the manager out, and we've got the keys. What do we do now?" (Brooks 1971:180).

By 1938, the right to union representation had been written into law through the National Labor Relations Act, known as the Wagner Act, and unions had successfully established themselves in the key mass-production industries, such as steel, automobiles, rubber, and electrical goods. A conjunction of social and political developments made these developments possible. Of critical importance was overcoming the division within the working class and the labor movement that had plagued earlier unionization drives. The significance of ethnic differences declined as the sons and daughters of immigrants joined the labor force. No longer cut off from one another by language barriers, more confident of their place in American society than their parents had been, and more demanding of their rights, these second-generation Americans helped recast labor relations just as they contributed to the revamping of national electoral politics.

Differences between skilled and unskilled or semiskilled workers in manufacturing did not disappear, but a barrier to unionization was removed when the Committee for Industrial Organization (CIO) was formed within the old American Federation of Labor (AFL) in 1935, with the explicit purpose of organizing workers on an industry-by-industry basis rather than on the craft basis that was typical of the AFL unions. The following year, the more militant CIO broke with the tradition-bound AFL, retitling itself the Congress of Industrial Organizations. The CIO strove to remove another source of weakness by organizing both black and white workers.

CIO organizers in this period found American workers receptive. The story of Mary the drugstore striker may be apocryphal, but it suggests the atmosphere of the times. The rank and file frequently ran ahead of union organizers, who found themselves forced to restrain premature action they were not in a position to support. Working-class solidarity grew to the extent that big strikes attracted workers from other industries and localities, who came to offer moral and even physical support (Greenstone 1977:44).

A key to the worker militancy of the 1930s was the experience of the Depression. Since Marx, social scientists have recognized that economic insecurity feeds class consciousness. The insecurity that workers experienced during this period was connected to the breakdown of the entire economic system. The confidence that workers had in their employers was shattered by the recognition that even such powerful companies as U.S. Steel and General Motors were subject to the vagaries of the marketplace and apparently indifferent to the fate of their workers. When capitalists responded to the Depression by laying off workers, reducing benefits, and speeding up work, they lost the loyalty of many workers.

The transformation of industrial relations of the 1930s also reflected the changed political context of the New Deal and the legal protections of the Wagner Act, which guaranteed the right of workers to form labor unions, prohibited employers from interfering with the exercise of that right, and set up a National Labor Relations Board (NLRB) to ensure compliance. As the experience of the 1920s made clear, if government is hostile to labor, or at least so indifferent as to ignore patently illegal forms of employer resistance, unionization is stifled.

The Postwar Armistice:
Unions in the Age of Shared Prosperity

If the 1930s represented a period of open class conflict in the workplace, the decade after World War II was the time when an armistice in labor relations was negotiated. The end of the war in 1945 brought a renewal of labor conflict. The economy was disrupted by frequent strikes. President Harry Truman convened a conference of key labor and business leaders at the suggestion of conservative Republican Senator Arthur Vandenberg, who assured the president, "Responsible management knows that free collective bargaining is here to stay . . . and that it must be wholeheartedly accepted" (Brody 1980:175).

Although many business leaders were willing to accept the existence of unions, they were determined to preserve for the capitalist class what they termed the "right to manage." At stake was participation in decisions regarding such matters as investment (including plant openings and closings), product design and production methods, and the pricing of final products. Had labor gained a share in these decisions, as did some contemporary European unionists, the labor movement could have had meaningful influence on employment and other basic economic questions. The issue was resolved in a labor contract signed between General Motors and the United Auto Workers in 1950. Later known as the "Treaty of Detroit," the contract became a model for many subsequent agreements. It limited workers' right to strike and preserved management's exclusive control of business decisions in exchange for generous wage and benefit concessions, including health care and pension guarantees.

By the late 1950s, the shape of the industrial peace was unmistakable. Labor unions represented over a third of American workers. Unions were firmly established among blue-collar workers at the core of the economy in heavy industry. Here they could gain substantial benefits for their members as long as they did not interfere with management prerogatives—benefits that would allow a large segment of the working class a life of relative affluence. "The labor movement," concluded auto union leader Walter Reuther, "is developing a whole new middle class" (Brody 1980:192). Serious industrial conflict was banished to the periphery of the economy—to the smaller firms, weaker economic sectors, and backward regions (especially the South). If such conflict was relatively infrequent, that was mostly because the labor movement had grown satisfied and unaggressive. The giant AFL-CIO (the two had re-merged in 1955) was behaving, in the words of labor economist Richard Lester, like a "sleepy monopoly" (Dubofsky 1980:8).

Ironically, labor came to play a more dynamic role in national politics than it did in the workplace. Long reluctant to involve itself directly in politics, the labor movement become a major supporter of the Democratic Party and a broad array of liberal social and economic programs. Labor now spoke not just for union members but also for the working classes generally. Unions were politically active in two broad arenas: electoral and legislative. In the former, the labor movement promoted liberal candidates, both within and on behalf of the party; raised a substantial part of the party's campaign money; and fielded thousands of campaign workers. Where unions were especially strong, the party and the union's political organization became virtually indistinguishable (Greenstone 1977).

In Washington, labor maintained a formidable lobbying apparatus. During the 1960s and early 1970s, the labor representatives played a major role in obtaining passage of liberal legislation in such areas as civil rights, health care, minimum-wage protection, public employment programs, nutrition programs for the poor, and occupational health and safety. Union lobbyists were frequently the leaders of broad liberal coalitions that confronted business lobbies and other conservative groups over critical pieces of legislation. In effect, a class cleavage ran through the center of national legislative politics, and the unions were critical players on one side. Although that cleavage was irrelevant to many issues (such as the Vietnam War, abortion, and gun control), it was still significant during the 1990s and early 2000s in the struggles over budget and tax policies and issues such as the minimum wage, parental leave, and health care.

Labor in Decline

The Age of Growing Inequality has been a period of devastating decline for the American labor movement. Private sector union membership, which exceeded 35 percent of workers in the mid-1950s, has almost continuously declined since the late 1970s. By 2016, according to the Bureau of Labor Statistics, only 10 percent of all wage and salary workers and just 6.4 percent of private sector workers belonged to labor unions. Persistent high unemployment in the wake of the 2008–2009 recession has reinforced longer term trends of union decline. American unions have not been so weak since the 1920s (Bennett and Kaufman 2007; Chaison 2006).

Labor's problems stemmed in part from the basic shifts in the economy and occupational structure, which we discussed in Chapter 3. Manufacturing employment, the bastion of union strength since the 1930s, had been in decline since the 1970s. New technologies reduced the labor requirements. American manufacturers had closed many older U.S. plants and moved operations to low-wage havens abroad or to the anti-union states of the Sunbelt. Employment growth in the Age of Growing Inequality has been strongest among those categories of workers who are the most difficult to organize: private sector white-collar employees, service workers, employees of small establishments, and female workers. The only area in which the unions have made significant gains in recent decades is in one corner of the labor force, the public sector. In short, labor's natural base has eroded over time.

But these changes cannot fully explain the decline of American labor. The United States and Canada had about the same levels of unionization in 1960 and have operated under similarly challenging economies, but Canadian unions have retained a larger share of the labor force.[6] This contrast suggests the importance of other factors, especially the political environment and the attitudes of American employers toward unions.

Erosion of labor's political strength became evident in the battle over the 1978 Labor Reform Bill, which gave an early warning of what was to come. Both labor and business regarded the measure, which sought to restore the effectiveness of the 1935 Wagner Act in protecting workers' right to union representation, as a crucial test of strength. The legislation was critical to union hopes of regaining lost ground. Over the years, employers had discovered that they could stave off union organizing efforts by legal maneuvering and other tactics designed to discourage union activists and postpone representation elections. The longer the delays stretched out, the greater the probability that a union drive would collapse. The basic provisions of the bill were designed to guarantee speedy elections to determine whether workers wanted union representation and to stiffen penalties for violation of existing labor laws.

The AFL-CIO spent $3 million on a hard-fought campaign in support of the bill. A coalition of business groups, including the Business Roundtable, National Association of Manufacturers (NAM), U.S. Chamber of Commerce, and National Federation of Independent Business (NFIB), spent approximately $5 million to oppose it (Cameron 1978:80). Though backed by majorities in both houses of Congress, the bill was stopped by a filibuster in the Senate.

Unionists were stunned by the defeat and the composition of the coalition that had opposed them. They were used to the idea that the lesser capitalists represented by the NFIB, the U.S. Chamber of Commerce, and the NAM harbored strong anti-union sentiments. But the Business Roundtable represented the largest American corporations, the firms that had made their peace with the unions in the 1950s. The Roundtable's role in thwarting the bill came as a bitter revelation. Shortly after the defeat in the Senate, Douglas Fraser (1978), president of the United Auto Workers, resigned from the semiofficial Labor-Management Group in Washington, with an angry letter to his Business Roundtable colleagues in the group:

> I believe leaders of the business community, with few exceptions,
> have chosen to wage a one-sided class war today in this
> country. . . . The leaders of industry, commerce, and finance in the
> United States have broken and discarded the fragile, unwritten
> compact previously existing during a past period of growth and
> progress.[7]

Clearly the postwar armistice in labor-management relations, one of the key features of the Age of Shared Prosperity, was over. A new

---

[6] www.statcan.gc.ca/pub/11-630-x/11-630-x2015005-eng.htm

[7] https://en.wikiquote.org/wiki/Douglas_Fraser

atmosphere prevailed in Washington, especially under the Republican's administrations. Pro-management appointments to the National Labor Relations Board (NLRB) diluted the protections of the labor laws. Pro-labor appointments to the board by Democratic presidents were often held up by Senate Republicans. Many Republican officials, on both state and national levels, and businesspeople have come to regard unions as a social problem, like alcoholism or juvenile delinquency, that ought to be treated. Where possible, they have erected new legal barriers to union organizing.

The reduced political weight of the unions became obvious in Washington, . Corporate PACs began to outspend labor PACs. On Capitol Hill, the ability of labor lobbyists to move (or block) legislation receded with the decline in union membership. One indicator of labor's political weakness was the erosion, almost continuous since the 1970s, of the purchasing power of the minimum wage, which is periodically reset by federal legislation. A stronger labor movement would have successfully promoted legislation to automatically "index" the minimum wage to the rate of inflation. Another was the defeat in 2010 of labor's too-familiar legislative priority: a reform law to lower barriers to union organizing.

On the state level, Republican controlled governments have undermined unions with so-called "right-to-work" laws. When the majority of a company's workers vote for union representation, the union becomes their exclusive representative in contract negotiations. Workers cannot be forced to join the union as a condition of employment, but the labor contact may require nonmembers to pay a fee (less than the cost of full union dues) to cover the costs of representation. Right-to-work laws free nonmembers of this requirement. And by refusing to join or leaving the union, a worker can gain the advantages of union representation, like higher wages and better benefits, without paying for them. The effect, of course, is to check the power of unions by depriving them of resources, reducing their ability to organize and participate in political activities. Such laws have long been common in the South, where unions have always been weak. Today, over half the states have enacted them—one more indication of labor's weakness.

Business, encouraged by the changed atmosphere in Washington and Republican controlled states, has assumed a more demanding stance in labor relations and became more determined in its resistance to union organizing. Even large, established corporations have been taking advantage of the services of a new breed of labor consulting firms. Eschewing the violent union-busting methods of the past, the consultants are masters of manipulation. They show management how to convey to employees an artificial sense of participation in company decisions and how to use systems of subtle rewards and punishments to influence employee attitudes or create anxieties that undercut pro-union sentiment. Consultants also instruct corporations in the advantages they can glean from calculated violations of poorly enforced labor laws (Langerfeld 1981).

Corporations commonly resist union-organizing drives with methods including threats to cut wages or close plants, interrogation of individual workers about their attitudes toward unions (illegal under federal law), and dismissals of union activists (also illegal). Workers who are fired for union activity can appeal to the NLRB (a 2- or 3-year process) for reinstatement and payment of lost wages, minus whatever they have earned from interim employment. The price is modest for a company opposing unionization (Bronfrenbrenner 2009). Corporations also use legal tactics to avoid, delay, or invalidate union representation elections. They may claim that all or some of their employees are not entitled to representation because they are undocumented workers, they are really supervisors, or they are not employees at all but contractors—the status Federal Express claims for its delivery drivers.

Organized labor has contributed to its own problems. After the purges of leftist union activists in the late 1940s, the well-paid officers of many unions grew complacent, in a few cases corrupt, and distant from the problems of ordinary workers. Such leaders might have been qualified to conduct the daily business of established unions in quiet times, but they were less effective against the swirling currents of political and economic change. In 2005, some of the more militant unions broke off from the AFL-CIO to form Change to Win, an alternative labor federation focused on expanding the labor movement, especially among low-wage service workers. The organizers seem to have had the history of the CIO in mind, but they have not been able to slow labor's decline in a very different era (Aleks 2015).

Labor's defeats in the Age of Growing Inequality have real implications for the dynamics of the American class system. The unions speak for a much wider constituency than their own members. In the workplace and in national politics, however indirectly and imperfectly, organized labor has represented the interests of working-class Americans against those of the capitalist class. At work, the benefits unions obtain for their members establish standards that pressure the employers of nonunion workers. In politics, union voters, activists, and campaign contributions encourage liberal candidates and policies. When George Meany, the head of the AFL, testified in 1954 in favor of expanding Social Security, he grandly declared that his union confederation spoke for "every person in America who works for a living" (Hacker and Pierson 2010a:149). Labor's long decline, along with the rise of business power, has altered the balance of power among social classes in ways that may affect this country for years to come.

Hacker and Pierson: Winner-Take-All Politics

In this and the previous chapter, we have examined the growing inequality in American politics that favors the capitalist class and the upper-middle class over the rest of the population. Political scientists Hacker and Pierson (2010a, 2010b) go a step further in a recent book titled *Winner-Take-All Politics*. They argue that our unequal political system is the primary cause of growing class inequalities. As the title of their book suggests, their focus is on the concentration of economic gains, not simply among the rich, but among the super-rich—beyond the top 1 percent of families, the top 0.1 percent, or even the top 0.01 percent. They note that the top 0.1 percent, comprising the country's richest 150,000 families, saw their share of the economic pie expand from about 3 percent to 12 percent of pretax household income from 1974 to 2007, when these families earned an annual average of

$7 million (Hacker and Pierson 2010a:16). This extraordinary reallocation of income toward the top, they contend, is the result of (1) shifts in the organizational context of American politics that have produced and (2) changes in national policy strongly favoring the wealthy.

Hacker and Pierson claim that students of American politics have been too focused on what they describe as "the electoral spectacle"—the exciting, made-for-television, periodic competition that fits neatly with our celebrity culture—while ignoring the quieter, less colorful process that continues between elections and ultimately shapes national policy. Voters are also mesmerized by the spectacle, but suffer from a kind of attention deficit disorder. Once the cameras are off, their attention inevitably wonders. Organizations, in contrast, can sustain focus. They develop expertise, mobilize resources, build coalitions, and coordinate actions. Effective organizations are relentlessly attentive to things that are important to them. All of which matters, according to the authors, because the organizational framework of American politics has changed.

Hacker and Pierson emphasize, as we have in this and the previous chapter, the shifting balance of organizational power between business and labor since the 1970s. The unions that have long represented working-class Americans are much diminished in membership and resources, while the diverse organizations that represent business are bigger, more powerful, and better endowed with political money than they have ever been. The authors note other critical changes in the organizational landscape. Grassroots organizations like the American Legion that represented average Americans have lost membership and influence. The Legion, a veterans organization that once had millions of members in chapters across the country, was responsible for a major piece of redistributive legislation: the GI Bill, which provided extensive benefits, including college scholarships and home financing, for service members returning from World War II. Such groups are being replaced by more centralized, professionally managed organizations, like the advocacy groups that lobby in Washington on the environment, women's rights, and civil liberties. Their members, whose participation is limited to writing checks, are typically upper-middle class and their concerns are rarely with the economic matters that affect people at lower-class levels. A notable exception to this pattern are the evangelical Christian groups, which have a strong, activist, popular base, but are, ironically, tied to a business-oriented Republican Party. These changes, say the authors, have weakened organized support for the economic interests of average citizens and strengthened the representation of the privileged.

In recent decades, according to Hacker and Pierson, the wealthy have been favored by policy enactments and policy drift—both promoted by powerful organizations. Drift becomes significant when old policies are maintained even though they are proving inadequate in changed circumstances. An example would be the continuing failure, discussed earlier in this chapter, to enact reforms to labor law designed to counter growing corporate resistance to unions and new anti-union tactics. Tax policy reflects both enactment and drift. Since the 1970s, enacted reductions to the top marginal income tax rate, capital gains taxes, corporate taxes, and estate taxes have especially favored the very rich. At the same time, hedge fund managers, whose annual earnings are often in the hundreds of millions, sometimes billions, of dollars, have benefited from drift: The obsolete "carried interest" provision of the tax code has allowed them to treat most of their earnings as capital gains, taxable at a minimal rate of 15 percent. (Does this sound esoteric? Of course, and that's the point. "Carried interest" may be gibberish to the average voter, but such provisions are the daily diet of the expert, well-financed, patient organizations, from the U.S. Chamber of Commerce to the lobby group Americans for Tax Reform, that defend the interests of the wealthy.) Efforts to reform carried interest have failed. As Hacker and Pierson note, the deregulation of the financial sector that led to soaring incomes on Wall Street was achieved through specific enactments, such as the repeal of the 1933 Glass Steagall Act that had restrained banks and through regulatory drift in the face of risky financial innovations. Unfortunately, deregulation also created conditions for the near collapse of the financial sector in 2008 and the subsequent Great Recession.

Hacker and Pierson are convinced that organizationally structured political action and inaction, in these and other critical areas, is the best explanation for growing inequality. In *Winner-Take-All Politics* they discount, without entirely denying, the importance of other factors commonly cited, including globalization, technological change, and widened income disparities based on educational differences. Their explanation is most convincing with regard to those at the very high end of the income distribution, the top 0.1 percent. Winner-take-all politics has certainly helped them to make more and keep more of what they make. But it is hard to imagine the colossal new accumulations of wealth reflected in the annual *Forbes* 400 list without technological change (from the Internet to containerized shipping) and the expansion of global trade and capital markets. Like Frank and Cook's similarly titled *Winner-Take-All Society*, which we discussed in Chapter 3, Hacker and Pierson's account is less satisfactory at lower-class levels. As we have seen, the professionals and managers of the upper-middle class—especially those we labeled the working rich—have thrived in the Age of Growing Inequality. Like the very rich, albeit on a more modest scale, they have benefited from a less demanding tax code. But their relative affluence is largely based on the value of their knowledge and skills in a highly competitive labor market. In contrast, low skill workers at the bottom of the class structure are the victims of technological change and global markets. Hacker and Pierson would rightly remind us that markets are themselves influenced by politics.

Hacker and Pierson's interpretation of American politics puts the election and presidency of Donald Trump in perspective. Trump, a media celebrity before he became a candidate, raised the electoral spectacle to an unprecedented level. His presidency is young at this writing. But it is notable that Trump, who promised, in his inaugural address, to favor the "forgotten men and women" over the privileged "establishment," has appointed a cabinet full of billionaires and corporate executives and backed policies in areas such as tax reform and health care that show little concern for the forgotten people. Hacker and Pierson would emphasize that the organizational context of politics and policy making has not changed. If anything, Trump's lack of governing experience and thin knowledge of the issues, makes him more subject than his predecessors to established institutions and ways of doing things in Washington.

Conclusion

Our concerns in this chapter have been class consciousness and class conflict. Marx first raised the issue of class consciousness because he believed that subjective awareness of one's objective economic position would lead to a sense of belonging with others of similar position and promote conflict with those above or below. Marx's thinking about class consciousness focused on society-wide developments over extended historical periods. Modern social science researchers, like Richard Centers or Martin Gilens, have tended to focus on individual opinion measured at a point in time. Centers got at one aspect of class consciousness with a simple forced choice survey question about class identity. He showed, and subsequent research has confirmed, that about half of adults brand themselves working class, that people are most likely to choose class identities that reflect their objective class position, and that class identities tell us something about their political attitudes and behavior.

In the Western democratic countries, class consciousness has not expressed itself in the sort of revolutionary upheaval that Marx anticipated. Instead, class conflict has been channeled into electoral competition and labor politics. The democracies typically have a right-left spectrum of parties, with the left parties tending to draw their members from the lower half of the class structure and the right parties from among the privileged.

American politics has generally fit this pattern, but the class orientation of our major parties has always been blurred by ethnicity, religion, and regional loyalties, and the class differences in party support have never been as great as the corresponding differences in European systems. From the 1930s until the 1970s, the Democratic Party dominated national politics. 200 The party was built on a working-class base, reinforced by traditional ethnic and regional loyalties. In recent decades, the strength of this so-called New Deal (or Democratic) coalition has eroded, changing the shape of national politics.

National surveys have long shown that Americans are influenced by class position in their political opinions and electoral preferences. But class, for the first time in memory, had little or no influence on the choices of white voters in the 2016 presidential election. The policy preferences of Americans continue to reflect their class position. Yet recent research shows that the opinions of the working- and middle-class majority are generally ignored by Congress in deference to the opinions of the privileged classes. There is no simple explanation for these phenomena. Among the factors that appear important are (1) the effect of superior rates of political participation (including voting) at higher class levels; (2) the growing power of money in American politics described in Chapter 8; (3) the influence of divisive issues such as affirmative action, welfare, abortion, same-sex marriage, and gun control that cut across social classes; and (4) the waning strength of labor unions and, more generally, the changing organizational context of American politics.

American labor history has been marked by violence and management resistance to the right of workers to unionize. The labor movement consolidated its position at the same time that the New Deal coalition emerged under Roosevelt in the early 1930s. Labor became one of the pillars of the Democratic Party. The post-World War II period produced an "armistice" in labor relations, as the major corporations accepted unions as a fact of life. But the armistice came undone in the late 1970s and 1980s—a characteristic development of the Age of Growing Inequality. Business, often supported by conservative Republican administrations in Washington and the states, became much more resistant to unions and union organizing. As they had in the late nineteenth century and again in the 1930s, American capitalists sought, albeit with more subtle methods, a world without unions. Management resistance, a changing economy, and the lethargy of union leadership led to a sharp decline in the proportion of workers who belonged to unions.

These developments, along with the increased political activism of corporations and the capitalist class described in the last chapter, have produced a critical shift in the class balance in American politics in favor of the capitalist class—a shift that has contributed to the growing inequality of the current era.

KEY TERMS DEFINED IN THE GLOSSARY

class consciousness   class identification   class position, objective

SUGGESTED READINGS

Bartels, Larry. 2016. *Unequal Democracy: The Political Economy of the Gilded Age.* Second edition. Princeton, NJ: Princeton University Press.

The political causes and consequences of growing inequality.

Bennett, James and Bruce Kaufman, eds. 2007. *What Do Unions Do? A Twenty-Year Perspective.* New Brunswick, NJ: Transaction Publishers.

A superb collection of essays on the contemporary condition and influence of labor unions.

Brewer, Mark D. and Jeffrey M. Stonecash. 2007. *Split: Class and Cultural Divides in American Politics.* Washington, DC: CQ Press.

Argues that both class and culture influence voters and politicians.

Brody, David. 1993. *Workers in Industrial America: Essays on the 20th Century Struggle.* 2nd ed. New York: Oxford University Press.

A lively introduction to the history and historiographic literature of the labor movement in the twentieth century.

Hacker, Jacob and Paul Pierson. 2010. *Winner-Take-All Politics: How Washington Made the Rich Richer and Turned Its Back on the Middle Class.* New York: Simon & Schuster.

Argues that organizational changes in American politics, reflected in public policy, are responsible for the growing concentration of income at the top.

Hochschild, Arlie Russell 2016. *Strangers in Their Own Land: Anger and Mourning on the American Right.* New York: The New Press.

Insightful ethnography exploring the political culture responsible for Trump's victory in 2016.

McCarty, Nolan, Keith T. Poole, and Howard Rosenthal. 2006. *Polarized America: The Dance of Ideology and Unequal Riches.* Cambridge: MIT Press.

The relationship between growing inequality and polarization in American politics.

Page, Benjamin and Lawrence Jacobs. 2009. *Class War? What Americans Really Think About Economic Inequality*. Chicago, IL: University of Chicago Press.

A compact, readable examination of public opinion about inequality, social programs, and progressive taxation.

Thompson, E. P. 1963. *The Making of the English Working Class*. New York: Vintage.

Classic historical portrayal of the development of working-class consciousness.

10 Poverty and Public Policy

We stand at the edge of the greatest era in the life of any nation. . . . Even the greatest of all past civilizations existed on the exploitation of the misery of the many. This nation, this people, this generation, has man's first chance to create a Great Society; a society of success without squalor, beauty without barrenness, works of genius without the wretchedness of poverty.

Lyndon B. Johnson (1964)

[T]his legislation will end welfare as we know it.

Bill Clinton (1996)

During the era we have titled the Age of Growing Inequality, Americans added a new word to their political lexicon: homelessness. The term was not a recent addition to the dictionary, but beginning in the 1980s, it was being used in a new way—to name a social problem. And although homelessness had once referred to people without fixed residences, who drifted from place to place, it was now being applied to people who literally had no access to conventional housing, hundreds of thousands of people who slept in doorways, packing crates, bus stations, and shelters (Rossi 1989; Wright 1989).

The problem has not gone away. According to recent official reports, about 550,000 people sleep on the street or in a homeless shelter on a single night. One in five of these homeless are children. At least 1.5 million persons have an episode of homelessness at some point in the course of a year; this figure only covers those who entered shelters. A much larger population of 6.6 million can be considered precariously housed; they are poor renters at risk of eviction because their housing costs exceed 50 percent of their income. Another 6.9 million people are at risk because they are "doubled up" on a temporary basis in a household not their own.

Visible on city streets, the homeless population was the ominous tip of the poverty iceberg. In the 1980s and early 1990s, poverty rates spiked to levels not seen since the 1960s. The rate has fallen somewhat since then, but by the official count, from 1981 to 2015, there were never fewer than 30 million poor people in America. Another troubling indicator relates to the prevalence of hunger or what the government prefers to call "food insecurity." According to a recent survey, 12.7 percent of American households, with 42 million members, are "food insecure," including 7.7 percent of households with "low food security" and 5 percent suffering "very low food security." The first category suggests inadequate nutrition, the second, episodes of actual hunger. Almost 18 percent of children live in food insecure households, though they may be protected by adults, who compromise their own nutrition to feed their children (Coleman-Jansen et al. 2016).

Most Americans and their leaders in Washington give little thought to the problem of poverty. Neither major presidential candidate made poverty an issue in 2016. Americans were more concerned about the performance of the national economy and their own (in many cases, shrinking or stagnant) incomes. They were not as confident as they had once been in the capacity of government to tackle big social problems. Many were convinced that the poor were responsible for their own situations. As we will see, the national will to fight poverty has waxed and waned in recent American history.

In this chapter, we answer some important questions about American poverty, including these: How do we define and measure poverty? How many Americans are poor, and what are the long-term trends in poverty? What are the causes of poverty? We will give special attention to the changing ways government policy has responded to poverty, beginning in the 1930s, when poverty was first recognized as a problem requiring federal action.

Roosevelt and the Beginnings of Welfare

The Great Depression of the 1930s hit the nation with devastating effect. The unemployment rate was above 20 percent from 1932 through 1935 and did not go below 15 percent until the eve of war in 1940. Those who had jobs saw their wages fall. Frightened, angry citizens joined widespread and often violent protests. The efforts of private charities and local governments to provide assistance were overwhelmed by the magnitude of the crisis. After the election of Franklin D. Roosevelt in 1932, for the first time, the federal government assumed primary responsibility for providing assistance in an economic crisis.

The Roosevelt administration moved quickly and devised entirely new approaches to the problems of unemployment and poverty. The federal government began a massive program of "direct relief"—cash payments to families in desperate need, managed by the states. Like many Americans, national leaders were uncomfortable with the idea of direct relief, except as an emergency measure. Emphasis soon shifted to job relief. Under the federally funded Works Progress Administration, millions of workers were hired, often to work on needed public works projects, such as roads, bridges, and schools. The programs created in response to the emergency of the Depression were soon phased out, but a new federal program was created to provide workers and their families a long-term safety net.

The core of that new system was the 1935 Social Security Act, which established a national social insurance system. Enrolled individuals (not everyone was included, especially in the earlier years) would receive full coverage after 10 years of contributions made by employees and employers to the trust funds. Retired persons would get permanent pensions, as would those who were disabled to the point of not being able to work. Widows and orphans (survivors) of insured workers would get benefits. A system of unemployment insurance was also established that would give temporary payments to insured workers during periods of layoff, usually up to 26 weeks. Unemployment benefits not only protected workers' families, but also provided a safety net for the economy by maintaining consumer purchasing power during slack periods.

These programs, and others that would be added later, came to be called **entitlements**, because all who meet specified prerequisites are entitled to receive them and the government is committed to providing the necessary funding. Some entitlements, such as the Medicaid and the food stamp program, are **means-tested**: They are available only to people with incomes below a specified threshold. Others, such as old-age benefits under Social Security, are available to people at all income levels.

These features would, in the long run, have significant political consequences. Entitlement spending, because of its open-ended character, proved difficult to contain. Means-tested entitlements and their powerless beneficiaries (the poor) would become a natural target for politicians concerned with budget deficits.

Rediscovery of Poverty: Kennedy and Johnson

During the Age of Shared Prosperity after World War II, the Social Security system was beginning to pay out large sums to the elderly. Because it was viewed by the public as an insurance program that returned to them in the form of pensions money that they had earlier contributed in taxes on wages, Social Security was not stigmatized as "relief" or "welfare" and was broadly popular. (Actually, the program taxes current workers to pay retirees, who generally receive much more than they pay in, but most people do not think of it that way.) The "make-work," or special public jobs, had disappeared. But the unemployment compensation system was working smoothly and was taken for granted.

Although these programs were created by New Deal Democrats over Republican opposition, a national, bipartisan consensus developed around them. When the Republicans regained the White House in the 1950s, they did not attempt to undo what the New Deal had done. A benign mood had settled on the generally prosperous country, and neither party had much taste for innovations in social policy.

Around 1960, two influential books challenged the nation's complacency mood: John Kenneth Galbraith's ironically titled *The Affluent Society* (1958) and Michael Harrington's *The Other America: Poverty in the United States* (1962). Galbraith and Harrington reminded the country that many Americans, perhaps a fourth of the population, remained poor in the midst of general prosperity.

The new generation of Democrats who came to Washington with John Kennedy in 1961 was keenly aware of these problems. The president and his influential brother Robert had been shocked by the misery they saw in West Virginia during the campaign. They and many other members of the administration had read Harrington's book. Galbraith became an advisor to the president.

The Kennedy and Johnson (1961–1968) administrations would make important improvements in both the welfare and Social Security systems. They added three new programs: the food stamp program for low-income families, which reduced malnutrition and simultaneously helped farmers; Medicare, guaranteeing health insurance for the elderly; and Medicaid, providing health insurance for the poor, especially children on public assistance and (increasingly) seniors receiving long-term care in nursing homes.

Lyndon Johnson regarded what he called the "War on Poverty" as one of the top priorities of his administration. In a 1965 speech, Johnson proclaimed,

> We stand at the edge of the greatest era in the life of any nation. For
> the first time in human history, we have the abundance and the ability
> to free every man from hopeless want, and to free every person to
> find fulfillment in the works of his mind or the labor of his hands.

From the cold perspective of the early twenty-first century, Johnson's grandiloquent rhetoric sounds quaint, and his optimism appears misplaced. In fact, poverty declined steadily during the Age of Shared Prosperity. But after the early 1970s, progress was uneven. More serious, Americans lost the hope and commitment that Johnson and many of his contemporaries displayed.

The Official Definition of Poverty

Officials in the Kennedy-Johnson administration quickly recognized that to accurately assess the problem of poverty and develop remedial measures, they needed a reliable official definition of poverty—something the government had never before enunciated. The definition adopted by the administration was designed by Mollie Orshansky (1974), a government economist. Orshansky put two pieces of information together from government surveys: the cost of a minimum nutritious diet for a typical family of four and the proportion of income (approximately one third) that the average family then spent on food. Multiplying the price of the food budget by 3 to allow for nonfood costs, Orshansky calculated an income **poverty line** of approximately $3,000 for a family of four. If you were a member of a four-person family with an annual income below $3,000, you were poor by this standard. On the assumption that family needs vary with size, somewhat higher and lower **poverty thresholds** were computed for households that were larger or smaller than the typical four.

Orshansky's poverty line became the official federal standard. Each year, the Census Bureau uses it in conjunction with the annual survey of household income to estimate the number of poor people in the country. Any family whose total pretax income is lower than the poverty threshold for its size is counted as poor. By this new standard, 22 percent of Americans were poor in 1960.

Because prices change, the poverty line must be regularly adjusted for inflation. At first, this was done by sending government employees to grocery stores to determine the cost of feeding a family of four, the original basis of the standard. Later, poverty thresholds were simply adjusted each year in proportion to the annual increase in the Consumer Price Index, the government's general measure of inflation. By 2015, the poverty line for a family of four was about $24,000.

Although the **poverty standard** is adjusted for changes in prices ($23,000 was required in 2015 to purchase what $3,000 bought in 1960), it is not updated for changes in the general standard of living. It does not take into account the fact that, on average, Americans lived at a higher material standard in the twenty-first century than they had in the 1960s. By recycling the old standard year after year, the government is saying something about the meaning of poverty. It is telling us that what defines people as poor is their material deprivation in an absolute sense, rather than the relative gap between their standard of living and the standard typical of people in the same society. We will come back to this issue shortly.

The Orshansky standard was as reasonable a poverty measure as anyone could come up with at the time. But it was problematic from the beginning and remains a target of controversy to this day. The trouble started when the proposed measure was being considered by administration's Council of Economic Advisors. Government nutritionists had come up with not one, but two family food plans. (Both were based on the dubious assumption that the family cook was a sophisticated dietitian who never wasted a penny.) The first food plan was an emergency diet, suitable to maintain a family for a short period. The second plan, which cost 25 percent more, was designed to provide the nutrition necessary for long-term family health. It was left to the Council of Economic Advisors to decide which food plan to use as the basis for measuring poverty. Adopting a standard based on the second plan would result in a higher poverty line and, as it turned out, a much higher estimate of the number of impoverished Americans. That was apparently unacceptable to the administration. The Council of Economic Advisors chose to base the official poverty line on the emergency food plan, thus opting for a more restrictive definition of poverty. The decision had little to do with nutrition and nothing to do with economics; it was essentially political.

In principle, the poverty line was based on an objective, scientific standard: minimum nutritional need, plus a proportional allowance for rent and other essentials. In retrospect, however, it appears that there is no wholly objective way to specify minimum requirements. Even when political considerations don't get in the way, contemporary cultural values always intercede when we define poverty. The history of opinion on this topic shows clearly that when the general standard of living goes up, public and the expert notions of minimum living standards go up with it (Ornati 1966; Rainwater 1974). Conceptions of poverty are inevitably relative. They change over time and from place to place. The material standard we define as the poverty threshold would have qualified as middle-income comfort in 1900 and would still be regarded as such in Bolivia today.

This brings us back to the federal standard. If we could somehow summon the Kennedy-Johnson administration experts, erase their collective memory of the poverty line they created in the 1960s, and make them do it again in our own time, they would almost certainly come up with something that reflected current living standards. But for over a half century, the government has treated the poverty line as an **absolute poverty standard**, one that is annually adjusted for increasing prices, but not for changing lifestyles.

Most sociologists believe that the government should adopt an explicitly **relative poverty standard** that would change with the changes in the average standard of living. They reason that what makes people think of themselves as poor and causes others to regard them as poor is the gap between their lives and the mainstream lifestyle in their community. The relative standard most frequently proposed is half the median family income (that is, a family with income lower than half the median income would be considered poor). In 1960, the median family income was around $6,000, which meant that the official poverty line of $3,000 for a four-person family was, in fact, close to half the median income when it was first minted. But by 2015, the official standard, adjusted for inflation, had fallen to less than 35 percent of the median family income—or, more precisely, the real value of the median had increased, leaving the government poverty line behind.

The official poverty standard has other defects. It is based on *money income* as measured by the government's annual household survey. The survey's income figures do not reflect taxes: neither the payroll taxes deducted from the earnings of the poor, nor, in the other direction, the payments many now receive through the Earned Income Tax Credit (more about the EITC later). And money income does not include the value of noncash (so-called **in-kind**) benefits given to people in such forms as food stamps, subsidized housing, or health care. At least some of these are the equivalent of money, and including their value in family income might lower our estimates of poverty. In recent years, the government has experimented with an alternative way of measuring poverty, but the Kennedy-Johnson era measure remains the official standard.

How Many Poor?

Table 10.1 presents four different estimates of American poverty. They tell us that somewhere between 43 million and 67 million Americans were poor in 2015. All are based on poverty thresholds adjusted for family size. Note that relatively modest differences in the income thresholds associated with these standards produce big differences in the estimated poverty population.

The first and lowest estimate is the official statistic published each year by the Census Bureau. The third is also produced by the Census Bureau using the same method but based on a poverty line 25 percent higher than the official standard. It counts as poor those living under the equivalent of about $30,000 for a family of four, including most of those who belong to the class we call the working poor. By this broader measure, more than 1 in 6 Americans was poor in 2015.

The second estimate, which we've called the Census Alternative is the Bureau's recently devised **Supplemental Poverty Measure** (SPM). Formally "unofficial," the SPM represents the efforts of government experts to fix the obvious technical defects in the official measure. Among other things, it corrects for taxes, the EITC credit, the cash value of food stamps, and regional differences in living expenses. But, unfortunately, the SPM remains close to the obsolete material living standard of the early 1960s. That choice was political, like the original decision of the Council of Economic Advisers to use the lower food budget when the official standard was adopted. No administration, it seems, is willing to accept a poverty measure that magnifies the problem of poverty. The various improvements that the SPM made tended to cancel each other out, with the net result in 2015 of a poverty rate 1 percent above the official rate or an additional 3 million poor people. The SPM does a better job of measuring changes over time in the poverty rate and differences between some subgroups of the population, but it clings to a living standard that was frozen in place a half century ago.[1]

The last estimate, unlike the other three, measures poverty relative to today's mainstream living standards. It is based on the most commonly

---

[1] The SPM is basically an absolute standard, though it has an odd inflation adjustment mechanism that could bring it closer to mainstream standards over time. U.S. Census 2016a; Wimer et al. 2016; Moskowitz, Haskins, and Smeeding 2010.

Table 10.1 Four Estimates of Poverty in the United States, 2015

Poverty Standard	Income Threshold for Four	Poverty Rate	Persons in Poverty (millions)
Census Official	$24,000	13.5%	43.1
Census Alternative (SPM)	$25,000	14.3%	45.6
125% Census Official	$30,000	17.9%	56.9
Relative (1/2 Median Income)	$36,000	21.0%	67.0

Note: Relative income figure is author's estimate based on Census pretax money income statistics.

proposed relative poverty standard: half the median family income. It says you are poor if you can't afford even half of what a middle-income family has. It is designed to change as living standards change. By this relative standard, about 1 in 5 Americans is poor.

If all these poverty income thresholds seem to be on the low side, they may be. In 2007, a Gallup poll asked Americans what they thought a "family of four would need to get along in your community." The median answer was $45,000, a little more than twice the official poverty at the time (Halpern-Meekin et al. 2015: 24). If less than the-minimum-to-get-along is the standard, about 100 million Americans were poor in that year.

Who Are the Poor?

The debate about how to measure poverty is seemingly endless, and it is not difficult to imagine why. Any serious discussion of poverty in an affluent society that regards itself as democratic inevitably stirs political emotions. Just below the surface, the technical dispute about measurement is also a debate about the fairness of our political and economic institutions.

The practical take-away for consumers of poverty statistics is simple: Know the assumptions behind the measures used to produce them. Then you will understand what they are telling you. For our purposes here, we will usually depend on the official measure because most of what the government publishes on poverty is based on it. But we will use statistics based on the alternative SPM measure when they are available and capture significant differences the official measure misses.

Figure 10.1 uses the official poverty data statistics for 2015 to answer a key question: Who are the poor? It starts with the total number of poor people, 46.5 million, and breaks this figure down in various ways. Here are some of the things we learn:

* There are many more white poor than black or Hispanic poor.

*People in female-headed families are a minority of the poor. There are almost as many people in families headed by married couples as in female-headed families.

*Only a minority of the poor live in the cities at the center of metropolitan areas. The majority are spread out among suburbs, small towns, and rural areas.

There is enough information here to contradict some popular stereotypes. In particular, the typical poor person is obviously not a member of a black, female-headed family, living in a central city. As it turns out, less than 1 in 10 of the poor fit that description.

Figure 10.2 answers a different kind of question: If you belong to a particular social group, what are your *chances* of being poor? This is the **risk of poverty** (or **poverty rate**), calculated as the percentage of the people in a group that falls below the poverty line. Just a quick glance at the chart reveals that there are some very big differences in the risk of poverty. Blacks, although they are a minority of the poor, are more than twice as likely as

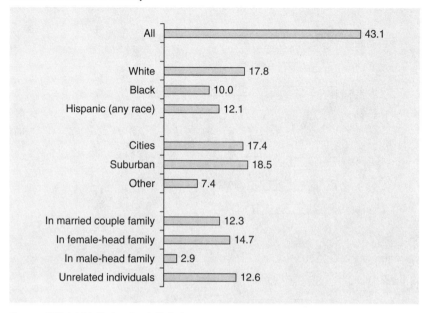

Figure 10.1   Distribution of Poverty, 2015

Millions of Persons in Poverty

All	43.1
White	17.8
Black	10.0
Hispanic (any race)	12.1
Cities	17.4
Suburban	18.5
Other	7.4
In married couple family	12.3
In female-head family	14.7
In male-head family	2.9
Unrelated individuals	12.6

Source: Official Statistics. Racial/ethnic categories mutually exclusive.

whites to be poor. The same can be said for Hispanics. And whatever their race or ethnicity, people in female-headed families are far more likely— almost 3 to 6 times as likely—to be poor than people in families headed by couples. On the other hand, the differences by age appear modest.[2]

Trends in Poverty

When Lyndon Johnson became president and promised to build a society free from poverty, ignorance, and exploitation, the poverty rate was already falling. Official poverty statistics indicate a steep decline in the early 1960s. Figure 10.3, based on the SPM measure, shows a 40 percent reduction in the rate between 1967 and 2000. Since then, the poverty rate has more or less stagnated, varying within a narrow band. Even the Great Recession that began in 2008 had remarkably little effect.

What drove the long-term decline in the poverty rate?[3] The short answer is government policy. If we remove all taxes and government transfers that are factored into income calculations for the SPM poverty rate, we are left

---

[2] We have, for this category only, used figures based on the alternate SPM poverty measure. The official measure exaggerates age differences by underestimating the disposable income of younger households.

[3] This section draws on Furman 2017 and U.S. Census 2016a.

Figure 10.2   Risk of Poverty for Selected Groups in 2015

Percent in Poverty

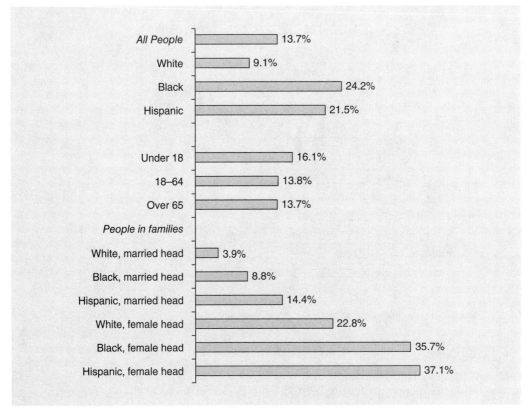

Note: Official Statistics. Racial/ethnic categories mutually exclusive.

with what economists call **market income**. Measured purely by market income, there was absolutely no reduction in poverty over the half century from 1967 to 2015. But the disposable incomes of the poor and near poor—that is, their effective spending capacity—rose during this period. Three programs were largely responsible: Social Security, the Earned Income Tax Credit (EITC), and food stamps (officially known as the Supplemental Nutrition Assistance Program or SNAP). Rising Social Security payments in the 1960s and 1970s sharply reduced the traditionally high poverty rate of the elderly.[4] Of course, Social Security is not specifically an antipoverty program, but without it half of the elderly would have been poor and the general poverty rate would have been 8 percent higher in 2015.

The EITC and a related child tax credit reduce poverty among families supported by low-wage workers. By design they incentivize work. Before the EITC was added to the tax code in the 1970s, low-income families could actually be taxed into poverty. They especially help families with children.

---

[4] As noted earlier, Social Security also helps widows and orphans and the disabled, but most of its beneficiaries are elderly.

Figure 10.3　Percent of Americans in Poverty, 1967 to 2015

By Supplemental Poverty Measure

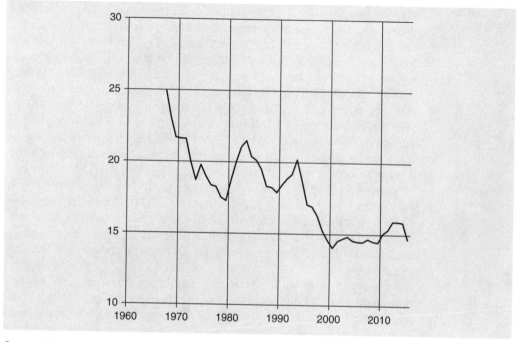

Source: Wimer et al. 2016 and extended data supplied by the authors.

The poverty rate of children would have been 6.5 percent higher and the general poverty rate 2.2 percent higher without these credits in 2015. Like the EITC, the food stamp program reduces overall poverty and, especially, the child poverty rate. Without these three programs—Social Security, EITC, and food stamps—the poverty rate would have been nearly twice what it was in 2015. Other programs, including unemployment insurance and Supplemental Security Income, have only modest effects on the general poverty rate, though they are vital to the targeted populations. Surprisingly, the effect of public assistance ("welfare") is barely measurable.

The Transitory Poor and the Underclass

Knowing how many people are poor from year to year does not tell us how sustained poverty is on an individual level. Many people fall below the poverty line during a given year as a result of temporary circumstances: loss of a job, health problems, or divorce. When they get back on their feet, they are no longer poor. Others remain poor for many years. They might be disabled, living on meager retirement incomes, or supporting a family with a low-wage job, or afflicted with substance abuse problems.

Accurately measuring the duration of individual poverty is difficult. It requires a "panel study"—finding the same individuals to ask the same questions, year after year. The Census Bureau did this for the years 2009 to 2012, a period that began during the Great Recession. They found that 42 percent of the people who were poor in 2009 were no longer poor in 2012. But the poverty population actually grew over this period, because a larger number of people who were not poor in 2009 had slid into poverty by 2012. Similar data from the 1980s and 1990s indicate that approximately 25 percent of the people who were poor one year were not poor the next.

The richest source of data on the duration of poverty is the University of Michigan's Panel Study of Income Dynamics (PSID), which has been tracking the incomes of a large national sample of families since 1968. The PSID data indicate that brief spells of poverty are quite common; longer spells are rare. For example, a PSID-based study tracking adults age 25 to 60 found that half had experienced a year or more of poverty[5] by age 40, as had 62 percent by age 60 (Rank and Hirschl 2015). But only 25 percent were poor for 5 or more years; and only 15 percent for 5 or more *consecutive* years. A more troubling study of childhood poverty found that during the first 15 years of life (1) 35 percent of children experienced a poverty spell, (2) only 10 percent were poor for 8 years or more, but (3) the chances of sustained poverty were much greater for African American children and children with unmarried mothers; the majority of these children were poor at some point, and at least one third were poor for 8 years or more (Magnuson and Votruba-Drzal 2009:154).

These and other studies point to a continuous turnover in the poverty population. Only a minority of those who experience poverty fall into a pattern of long-term poverty. Can we equate this minority, whatever its size, with what is sometimes called "the underclass"? That depends on how the term is understood. In the class model we presented at the beginning of this book, underclass was used in a purely economic sense to refer to the poor who are loosely connected to or wholly disconnected from the labor market—encompassing most of the people below the federal poverty line. But the term is applied to a smaller subset of the poor who are, it is assumed, bound to their impoverishment by personal characteristics or structural circumstance.

The underclass label often implies flawed character. The "conventional portrait" of the underclass, according to a *Washington Post* writer, links "extreme poverty, chronic joblessness, welfare dependency, out-of-wedlock births, female-headed households, [and] high dropout rates" (April 17, 1991). Many would have added crime to this list. Sociologist William J. Wilson (1987, 1991, 1996), one of the most influential writers on minority poverty, more or less accepts this grim portrait, but defines the underclass as having marginal economic position coupled with geographic isolation. Wilson has in mind the inner-city poor, living in areas with extremely high concentrations of poverty and caught in a postindustrial economic trap of shrinking job opportunities. But few poor people conform to the conventional portrait, though many exhibit some of its features. For example, only a third of the poor live in female-headed families.

Implicit in most discussions of the underclass is the notion of a "cycle of poverty"—of social pathologies so severe that poverty is inevitably passed from one generation to the next. Given what we know about social mobility,

---

[5] Poverty for this study was defined as income below the 20th percentile.

we would be surprised if there were not at least some truth to this (seldom examined) assumption. But how much? According to an analysis of PSID data for the years 1968 to 1993, the vast majority of children raised in poor families are not poor as young adults. This generalization holds for blacks as well as whites. Only 1 in 4 poor children grows up to be a poor adult. The risk of inherited poverty is much higher for blacks than whites. Nonetheless, two thirds of poor black children will not be poor as adults (Corcoran 2001:1313).

Restructuring Welfare[6]

The great entitlement programs enacted or expanded in the 1960s and early 1970s, such as Social Security, **Aid to Families with Dependent Children (AFDC)**, food stamps, and Medicaid, helped reduce poverty and improved the material lives of the poor. They also consumed a growing portion of the federal budget and evoked growing public opposition. Criticism focused on the means-tested "welfare" programs, especially AFDC, which, critics claimed, was "growing out of control" and "full of fraud and abuse." Political candidates promised to reform the system. Ronald Reagan's presidential campaigns featured dubious stories of "welfare queens" who had grown rich on public assistance. Bill Clinton courted votes in 1992 with a promise to "end welfare as we know it." His initial, relatively liberal reform plan was transformed by a Republican Congress into a more conservative bill, which President Clinton somewhat reluctantly signed in 1996.

The 1996 law, grandly titled the Personal Responsibility and Work Opportunity Act, transformed AFDC and cut back food stamp benefits.[7] Both were means-tested entitlements backed by open-ended funding that guaranteed assistance to anyone who qualified. Spending on these programs had automatically swelled with increasing need in economic bad times—giving the economy a useful boost—and shrank during boom periods. AFDC, the basic public assistance program for needy families with children, was a joint federal-state program, with benefits varying from state to state. Food stamps provided the broadest safety net protection, assisting almost anyone whose income did not ensure adequate nutrition, including the working poor. Under the 1996 law, the food stamp program remained an entitlement. Cuts to the program were subsequently reversed and access to benefits was liberalized. But AFDC lost its entitlement status and became the stricter **TANF (Temporary Assistance for Needy Families)**. Politicians and the public, it seemed, were more willing to "feed the hungry" than "hand out welfare."

For the first time since the passage of the Social Security Act in 1935, there was no federal guarantee of income assistance for impoverished children and their families. Under TANF, states would receive federal poverty funding in lump sums known as block grants, which they could spend as they wished, subject to two critical limitations: (1) Families could not

---

[6] This section draws on Blank 2007; Burtless, Weaver, and Wiener 1997; *Congressional Quarterly* 1996; DeParle 1996; Edelman 1997; Grogger and Karoly 2005; Haskins 2006; O'Neill 2006; and Parrott 2006.

[7] The law also cut back SSI, the program for low-income elderly, blind, or disabled people.

receive more than 5 years of assistance, whether consecutive or nonconsecutive ("temporary" is clearly the operative term in the program's new title); and (2) most adults benefiting from TANF would be required to begin work of some sort within 2 years of receiving assistance.

The central theme of the reform legislation was summed up in the oft-repeated phrase "from welfare to work." Conservatives who backed the legislation believed that they could end welfare dependency, and perhaps poverty itself, by simply compelling the poor to become self-supporting. There was, moreover, a moral dimension to their expectations. They were convinced that low-income, single mothers who escaped (or avoided) welfare dependency would be more likely to marry and would, if they became self-supporting, provide an example of responsibility that would encourage better behavior in their children. The first, they believed, would improve their chances of escaping poverty, and the second would improve the prospects for the next generation. They anticipated fewer out-of-wedlock births. Many liberals, including Clinton's own welfare experts, were certain that the law would be a disaster for the poor. Some anticipated an abrupt upsurge in childhood poverty. The late Senator Daniel Patrick Moynihan, known for his own expertise on welfare policy, predicted that the nation would soon see "children sleeping on grates" (Bane 2009:371).

The welfare reform became law at a propitious moment. In 1996, the country was moving into a period of economic expansion and declining unemployment. Under legislation signed by Clinton 3 years earlier, the benefit available to the working poor from the Earned Income Tax Credit (EITC) was substantially increased—making every dollar they earned more valuable. The minimum wage had just been raised. Under state programs, child care assistance for working parents was expanded (though still not available to all). In short, in the late 1990s, there were more jobs for the poor and stronger incentives to work.

A decade after the Personal Responsibility and Work Opportunity Act was enacted, the results seemed neither as dire nor as encouraging as critics or supporters had imagined. Researcher Ron Haskins (2006), who had worked on the 1996 legislation as a Republican congressional staff member, summed up the most notable outcomes of the new system when he told a congressional committee, "The pattern is clear: earnings up, welfare down. This is the very definition of reducing welfare dependency." The national welfare caseload had, in fact, plummeted in the late 1990s. Over the same decade, though less dramatically, the proportion of single mothers who were employed rose and the poverty rates, by the Census Bureau's alternative SPM measure, continued a downward trend that began several years before the reform. These developments confounded the grim expectations of the critics. On the other hand, the changes in social behavior that conservatives anticipated did not materialize. Marriage rates at lower class levels did not rise, and the proportion of out-of-wedlock births did not fall.

The Great Recession (2008–2012),[8] the worst economic slump since the depression of the 1930s, put the new regime to a severe test. The

---

[8] We are defining the recession by extreme levels of unemployment rather than the economists' declining GDP standard.

employment rate climbed from a comfortable 4.6 percent in 2007 to 10 percent by late 2009 and would remain above 8 percent for the next 3 years. Unemployment rates were even higher among the low-skilled working poor. TANF, the reformed public assistance program, unlike the old AFDC program, had little capacity to respond to the crisis. But the EITC, along with expansions of unemployment benefits and the food stamp program, boosted the disposable incomes of many households during the economic crisis. The poverty rate, measured by the SPM standard, rose but did not spike during the recession, as it had during earlier downturns. An additional 1 percent of the population, representing about 3 million people, was counted as poor.[9]

The Earned Income Tax Credit

The key to the relative success of welfare reform was the EITC. Originally a minor provision of the tax code designed to reduce the federal tax burden on the working poor,[10] it had quietly become the biggest cash transfer program for low income families, benefiting about 1 in 5 American households. With its colorless, forgettable name, the Earned Income Tax Credit functions as a stealth poverty program, unknown to most Americans and (unlike "welfare,") seldom the subject of public debate. Because it is a tax *credit,* the EITC allows low wage workers to claim a tax "refund" bigger than what they actually paid in payroll deductions.

The EITC has aptly been described as "a pay raise for the working poor." It is especially aimed at families with children. A parent with job earnings of $15,000 might receive a refund check for $5,000, a substantial boost to family income. The expanded EITC was intended, said President Clinton, "'to reward the work of millions of working poor Americans [so that] if you work 40 hours a week and you've got a child in the house, you will no longer be in poverty'" (Halpern-Meekin et al. 2015:104). In fact, the credit was calibrated so that, for example, a mother with two children, employed full time, year round at the minimum wage could get her family just above the poverty line. Of course, many low-wage workers cannot work full time, year round, even if they want to. They are employed in sectors where hours are erratic, layoffs frequent, and work may be seasonal. Most live on tight budgets and remain economically vulnerable.

The EITC differs, in consequential ways, from public assistance (AFDC or TANF) which it displaced as the main national program supporting poor families. Its potential benefits are bigger. Unlike public assistance, the EITC offers strong work incentives; it is based on employment and does not reduce payments as earnings rise until earnings are fairly substantial. Perhaps the biggest change was the least anticipated: The EITC altered the way the people it helped felt about themselves. Public assistance branded those who received

---

[9] See Moffitt 2012, Danziger et al. 2012, U.S. Census Bureau 2013, Short 2012, Short and Smeeding 2012, and Mishel et al. 2012.

[10] Low income households might owe little or no federal income taxes, but workers from such households are subject to payroll deductions for the Social Security and Medicare programs and "withholding" for potential federal, state, and local income tax liabilities.

it as social parasites. Even people who have depended on AFDC or TANF at some point in their lives share the popular notions of welfare recipients as indolent ("sitting home all the time . . . watching the same [TV] shows") and dissolute ("they take their check and spend it on drugs"). In interviews with researchers, they remember their own encounters with the welfare bureaucracy as stigmatizing. "It was horrible," recalled one woman. "I think [the caseworkers] look at you like you're no good because you are on assistance." Another described her experience as "just so degrading and just so disrespectful." In contrast, EITC does not taint those it serves. It does not even separate the poor from the nonpoor, since the credit is available, in decreasing amounts, to people with relatively comfortable incomes. It is claimed on the tax return, usually completed with the help of professional tax preparers, such as H&R Block. In their offices, the working poor know they are not supplicants but paying customers, like many others who are filing a tax return and expecting a refund check. Those who benefit from the EITC feel that they are supporting their families and providing a positive example for their children. "It's not like I'm poor," one of them told a researcher (Halpern-Meekin et al. 2015:115–118, 20). Her comment says something about the meaning of poverty, which, beyond material depravation, involves issues of self-respect.

Despite its obvious advantages, the new regime does not resolve the problems of poverty in America. The EITC moves the families of low wage workers closer to the poverty line or maybe a little beyond. At this level, economic life remains precarious. Families are likely to be juggling debts and choosing, for example, between paying the rent and fixing the car that gets them to work. A sick child, a spell of unemployment, or a disintegrating relationship may throw everything out of kilter.

Families at the very bottom of the income distribution are probably worse off than they were before welfare reform. With little or no income from jobs or public assistance, many are in deep poverty (below 50 percent of the poverty line). By the comprehensive SPM measure of poverty, 15.6 million Americans, including 3.6 million children were in deep poverty in 2015. A disquieting number seem to be living at levels of destitution normally associated with the developing world (Edin and Shaefer 2015; Renwick and Fox 2016:7; Shaefer and Edin 2013; Tach and Edin 2017).

Persistent Poverty

Why does poverty persist in the United States, a wealthy country with a growing economy? The per capita output of the American economy doubled from 1975 to 2015. But the poverty rate hardly budged, if measured by market income (that is, what people make at work or from other nongovernment sources). Whatever progress has been made against poverty is the result of programs like Social Security, the EITC, and food stamps. The SPM poverty rate, which accounts for these items, has been stuck near 15 percent since 2000. Why? The most important explanatory factors are economic change and shifting family patterns, matters we have dealt with in earlier chapters because they affect a population broader than the poor.

We know that there is a considerable turnover in the poverty population. Many manage to climb over the poverty line, but their places are taken by others, because many are vulnerable. In 2015, about 1 in 5 Americans were part of households with incomes between the SPM poverty line and twice the SPM line. They were, in other words, living at a standard somewhere between the equivalent of $25,000 and $50,000 for a family of four. This not-quite-poor stratum, which together with those below the poverty line makes up one third of the population, will inevitably provide most of the new recruits to poverty. The poor do not, after all, live on another planet and are not so very different from the rest of us. In an increasingly unequal society, in which the benefits of growth flow upward and economic security is hard to achieve without two incomes, the problems of the poor should be understood as an exaggerated form of what many Americans face.

Economic Trends

As seen from the bottom, the labor market turned sour in the Age of Growing Inequality. Wages sank or stagnated and became increasingly unequal, as we showed in Chapter 3. The new era saw the proliferation of low-wage service jobs and the loss of many of the better-paying blue-collar jobs. Unemployment fluctuated wildly, but tended to be higher on average than in the Age of Shared Inequality, as Figure 10.4 demonstrates. People in low-wage jobs are the most vulnerable in periods of high unemployment. Even short periods of unemployment (or for that matter of reduced hours) could push a family below the poverty line. With the transformation of AFDC into TANF in 1996, millions of families that had been shielded from an erratic labor market were now exposed to it.

Figure 10.4   Unemployment, 1947 to 2015

In percent

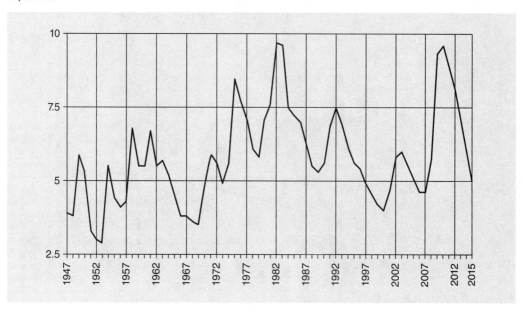

Changing Family Patterns

The negative effects of low wages and high unemployment have been reinforced by sweeping changes in family life. Figure 10.5 traces two key trends: In recent decades, the percentage of births to unwed mothers and the percentage of families with children headed by single females have risen steadily. Both conditions were rare in 1960. But by 2010, 40 percent of births were to unwed mothers and 25 percent of families with children were headed by single women. Divorces are also more frequent than they were in the 1960s, contributing to the numbers of female-headed families. As a result, the majority of American children will likely spend part of their childhood in a female-headed family, and most of the children who do will experience a period of poverty (Ellwood 1988:45–47, 67; Magnuson and Votruba-Drzal 2009:154).

These trends are quite pervasive in American society, affecting, in varying degrees, the poor and the nonpoor, and whites, blacks, and Hispanics. As our analysis in Chapter 5 showed, single motherhood varies with level of education. A wide gap separates those with college degrees from the rest of the population. Eighty-six percent of college-educated mothers are married, compared with 64 percent of those with high school diplomas and 60 percent of mothers with less than high school. This difference suggests that upper-middle-class people are relatively immune to single motherhood, while it is fairly common at mid-to-lower-class levels.

The changes in family life reflect both cultural and economic shifts. Since the 1960s, Americans have become much more accepting of both unwed motherhood and divorce. The once firm expectation that men would marry

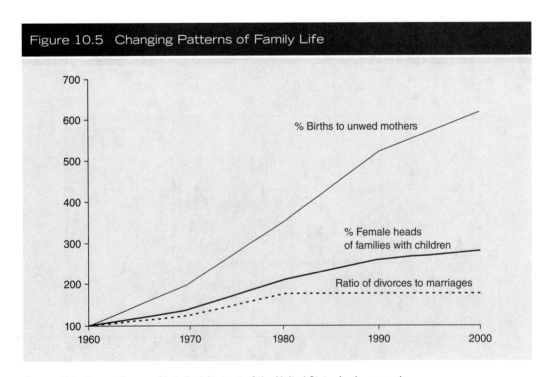

Figure 10.5 Changing Patterns of Family Life

Source: U.S. Census Bureau, *Statistical Abstract of the United States* (various years).

women they impregnate has been abandoned, along with the old-fashioned notion of "shotgun weddings." Women are now expected to be capable of supporting themselves. Job opportunities for women have broadened and the wage gap separating men and women has narrowed. At the same time, the economic prospects of men without special skills or advanced education have dimmed. As we have seen, fewer men now earn enough to lift a family above the poverty level. From the perspective of poor and working-class women, these men are less desirable marriage partners because they are less likely to become dependable family breadwinners.

If the range of choices facing young women has widened, the prospects for single mothers remain unenviable. As we noted in Chapter 4, custodial mothers receive modest child support at best. Employed women still make significantly less on average than employed men. The conflicts between the nurturer and provider roles, which all working mothers face, are even tougher for low-income, working single mothers, who generally bear the burdens of child-rearing alone.

In 2015, when the official poverty rate was 13.5 percent, 38 percent of female-headed families with children were counted as poor. The families of never-married mothers are, as might be expected, worse off than those of divorced mothers. An analysis of 2011 data found that the median income of families with children headed by never-married women was well below the poverty threshold for a three-person household. The median income of similar families headed by divorced, separated, or widowed mothers was substantially higher but still only half of the median for all families with children (Pew 2013:19).

Changes in family structure have made a substantial contribution to the persistence of high poverty rates. According to one careful analysis, the increasing portion of female-headed families from 1969 to 2006 added 2.6 percent to the poverty rate, expanding the poverty population by 7.7 million people (Cancian and Reed 2009:110).

Government Policy

How much can we blame government policy for persistent poverty? In a sense, not much. Fundamental changes in the economy and in patterns of family life, over which the government has only limited control, are the key factors, not changes in public policy. In the 1980s and 1990s, conservatives claimed that government promoted poverty by encouraging welfare dependency. But if there was anything to this argument, poverty should have vanished after the 1996 welfare reform. It didn't. The decline of the poverty rate in the 1990s, as we have seen, began before the reform, propelled by a booming economy and the EITC boost to the incomes of low-wage workers. Since 2000, the poverty rate has remained stuck at a fairly high level.

Government is not the cause of poverty, but perhaps it could be doing more to fight poverty. Consider this: The United States, as we show in the next section, has the highest or close to the highest poverty rates among the world's wealthy countries. We compete with these countries in a single global market. Presumably they employ similar advanced technologies to our own. They, like the United States, have increasing proportion of births to unwed mothers. Why then, do they have lower, in most cases much lower, poverty rates than the United States, especially among families with children? Two explanatory factors stand out: relatively higher wages toward the bottom of the labor market and more generous benefits aimed at nonelderly low-income households (Smeeding et al. 2001; Smeeding 2008).

These facts suggest that we may not be helpless against persistent poverty. At the very least, new policies might move the United States closer to the average among our international peers. The government could, for example, reduce poverty by making the EITC and the food stamp programs more generous; providing quality child care at low or no cost to working parents, especially single mothers; providing free postsecondary education; raising and indexing the minimum wage so that it keeps pace with inflation[11]; and strengthening labor unions. These policies would improve the prospects of the poor and near poor in the labor market and make it easier for them to survive on what they earn. They would also, inevitably, be expensive and politically problematic.

American Poverty in Comparative Perspective

Before concluding this chapter, we want to look at how the United States compares with other countries. The international Organization for Economic Co-Operation and Development (OECD) has calculated comparable poverty rates for its member nations, based on a relative standard. For each of the 14 countries in Figure 10.6, poverty was defined by household income below half the national median income, a level well below mainstream living standards in each country. The results indicate that relative poverty is more frequent in the United States than in comparable, high-income Western European and English speaking countries.[12]

The United States' weak showing in this comparison reflects the high level of inequality in American society and our relatively meager social support for low income households. The United States looks much better in a similar ranking of wealthy countries based on an absolute measure of market-income poverty; in that matchup, its market poverty rate is among the lowest. But the United States trails its peers once social benefits are added in; by a broad absolute standard similar to the Census Bureau's SPM alternative, only Italy, a notably less prosperous country, has a higher poverty rate than the United States (Gornick and Jantti 2016:16).

---

[11] The minimum wage, when last raised (to $7.25 in July 2009), provided just enough to allow a worker employed full time, year round, to keep a family of two above the poverty line, but by 2012, it would not even have achieved that modest goal. Since the minimum wage does not automatically increase with inflation, its purchasing power tends to erode over time. Some states have their own, higher minimum wages.

[12] The relative poverty rate for the United States in Figure 10.1 is slightly below the relative rate in Table 10.1 because it is based on a different definition of disposable income.

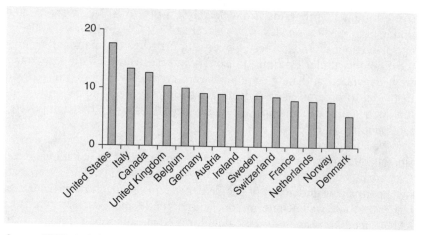

Figure 10.6   U.S. Poverty in Comparative Perspective, 2013

Percent Below Half the National Median Income

Source: OECD statistics from https://data.oecd.org/inequality/poverty-rate.htm.

Conclusion

This chapter on poverty has, perhaps inevitably, revolved around contentious issues. The first of these concerned the proper definition of poverty. Some writers favor an absolute definition based on a fixed material standard, which does not vary over time and place: Poverty means not having enough food, proper housing, and so forth. Critics of absolute definitions see them as subjective in practice and largely irrelevant to an affluent society like the United States. They prefer a relative definition: Poverty means a standard of living far below the mainstream standard of the larger society. The continuing debate about the important technical details of the definition also reflects differences over deeper political questions. As a practical matter, the choice of definition influences perceptions of the poverty problem and appropriate poverty policy.

The official definition adopted by the federal government in the 1960s and still widely used today is an absolute definition. This very dated measure of poverty is based on a minimum living standard that is much further from the average than when it was created in the early 1960s. It also fails to account for the effects of taxes and some key government benefits on disposable household incomes. By the official standard, 43 million Americans were poor in 2015. The Census Bureau has been developing an alternative poverty standard, the Supplemental Poverty Measure (SPM), which is based on a more reasonable measure of disposable income. The SPM does a better job of measuring long-term changes in the poverty rate, but it retains the weakness of an absolute measure. By the most commonly suggested relative measure, half the median household income, 67 million Americans were poor in 2015. The poverty rate, as measured by the SPM, declined significantly in the 1990s, but has changed little since 2000.

In this chapter, we repeatedly returned to the issues surrounding federal poverty programs. The federal government first took responsibility for the poor during the 1930s under the pressures of the sudden mass impoverishment brought on by the Depression. A series of protective entitlement programs, from Social Security to AFDC, were created under Franklin Roosevelt's New Deal. In the 1960s and early 1970s, an era of prosperity and protest, poverty returned to the national agenda, most notably under Lyndon Johnson's War on Poverty. Existing programs were expanded and new programs were created—some of them broad insurance programs like Medicare, and others, means-tested programs like food stamps. Rising Social Security benefits sharply reduced poverty rates among the elderly.

Welfare reform was another contentious issue. By the 1980s, the expansion of entitlement programs aimed at the poor had become a national issue. Conservatives found popular support for their claim that "welfare" was creating a permanent underclass of people dependent on government handouts. Under the 1996 welfare reform, AFDC lost its entitlement status and became TANF, a temporary assistance program for needy families with children, with stringent lifetime limits. The able bodied, nonelderly poor were expected to survive by their own labor, with only limited help from the government. But the incomes of low-wage workers did get a big boost from the EITC. The opponents of welfare reform had predicted a human disaster, while its supporters anticipated the moral transformation of the poor. The results fell short of the expectations of both sides.

The last pages of the chapter considered the paradox of persistent poverty in a wealthy country. For reasons we explored in detail in Chapter 3, the labor market has turned sour for those at the bottom, especially men with limited skills and education, though it has improved somewhat for women. Changing family patterns have also influenced poverty rates. The rising frequency of births to single mothers and the increase in the divorce rate have multiplied the numbers of female-headed families. Their poverty rate is 3 times the national average. The growing proportion of low-income, female headed households is, at the same time, a reflection of changing economic conditions. Many women remain single who might not have done so in the past because the men in their lives are unemployed or working at low-wage, unstable jobs and less able to support a family.

Conservatives contend that government policy contributes to persistent poverty by encouraging dependence and discouraging work. We concluded that any contribution of government policy to the persistence of poverty in recent decades is insignificant relative to these long-term economic trends and changes in family life. But we noted that U.S. poverty rates are very high by comparison with other wealthy capitalist countries and could obviously be reduced by policies designed to bolster the economic situation of low-income families, including a more generous EITC, affordable, quality child care for working parents, and free postsecondary education.

KEY TERMS DEFINED IN THE GLOSSARY

absolute poverty standards
(see poverty standards,
absolute and relative)
Aid to Families with
Dependent Children
(AFDC)
entitlement
in-kind benefits

market income
means-tested programs
poverty line
(see poverty threshold)
poverty rate
poverty standard,
federal (official)
poverty threshold

relative poverty standards
(see poverty standards,
absolute and relative)
risk of poverty (see poverty rate)
Supplemental Poverty
Measure
Temporary Assistance for
Needy Families (TANF)

SUGGESTED READINGS

Anderson, Elijah. 1999. *Code of the Street: Decency, Violence, and the Moral Life of the Inner City*. New York: Norton.

Highly regarded ethnographic study of the urban underclass.

Bailey, Martha and Sheldon Danziger, eds. 2013. *Legacies of the War on Poverty*. New York: Russell Sage Foundation.

Authoritative assessment of poverty programs since the 1960s, covering income support, education, housing and health care policies and outcomes.

Desmond, Matthew. 2016. *Evicted: Poverty and Profit in the American City*. New York: Crown Publishers.

How unaffordable, unstable housing undermines the lives of the poor.

Edin, Kathryn and Maria Kefalas. 2005. *Promises I Can Keep: Why Poor Women Put Motherhood Before Marriage*. Berkeley, CA: University of California Press.

A five-year study of 162 young, poor single mothers.

Halpern-Meekin, Sarah, et al. 2015. *It's Not Like I'm Poor: How Working Families Make Ends Meet in a Post-Welfare World*. Berkeley, CA: University of California Press.

The precarious economic lives of the working poor.

Kenworthy, Lane. 2011. *Progress for the Poor*. New York: Oxford University Press.

A short, revealing, comparative study of living standards of low-income households in twenty affluent countries, including the United States. The effects of economic growth, the changing labor market, and public policy since 1979.

Shipler, David. 2005. *The Working Poor: Invisible in America*. New York: Random House.

The lives of the working poor. A sprawling, insightful book by a former New York Times reporter that denies all simple explanations of poverty.

The American Class Structure and Growing Inequality

[We have seen] the triumph of upper America—an ostentatious celebration of wealth, the political ascendancy of the richest third of the population, and the glorification of capitalism, free markets, and finance. But while money, greed, and luxury [became] the stuff of popular culture, hardly anyone asked why such great wealth had concentrated at the top.

Kevin Phillips (1990)

In this final chapter, we synthesize what we have learned about the American class system and how it is changing. We review the evidence we have found of increasing inequality and reconsider the possible reasons for this trend. Readers may notice a shift of tone. In the preceding chapters, our overriding objective was to present the existing data and research as precisely and faithfully as possible. Here we are less constrained. We generalize broadly, emphasizing our own interpretations and, by and large, dispense with citations, numbers, and tables—to the relief, no doubt, of many readers.

How Many Classes Are There?

Those with good memories will recall our answer to this question from the first chapter: We found six classes, but there is no irrefutable answer. As we noted there, defining classes and specifying the dividing lines between them is as much art as science. The "raindrop" class model we developed in Chapter 1 (see Figure 1.1) reflects what we have learned researching this book, but it inevitably imposes a simplified pattern on a complicated, sometimes contradictory reality. Let's take a closer look at the model and how it was derived.

Drawing on Marx and Weber, we began with the assumption that the class structure develops out of the economic system. Our classes are based on economic distinctions—especially source of income and occupation—rather than the prestige distinctions that Lloyd Warner and his successors employed to develop their class models. But because prestige is generally rooted in economic differences, our map of the class system is broadly similar to Warner's prestige model for Yankee City or Coleman and Rainwater's model for Boston and Kansas City. There are two major differences: We do not employ their new money/old money distinction at the top, nor do we treat blue collar/white collar as the essential class distinction in the middle (Table 2.2 compares the three models).

As we learned in Chapter 4, three basic sources of income are available to households in this country: capitalist wealth, job earnings, and government transfers. The first source allows us to distinguish a top class that largely depends on income-generating assets. The third source points to a class that has minimal assets and limited labor force participation, but often depends on some form of help from the government. The great majority, who fall between these class extremes, rely on their jobs—ranked by the skill or education required, the judgment and authority exercised at work, and the level of earnings.

Taken together, these factors suggest a structure of six classes:

1. A *capitalist class of investors, heirs, and top executives*, whose income is derived largely from return on assets.

2. An *upper-middle class* of college-trained professionals and managers. At the very top of this class are the highly successful people we call the working rich.

3. A *middle class* whose members have significant skills and perform varied tasks at work, under loose supervision. They earn enough to

afford a comfortable, mainstream lifestyle. Most wear white collars, but some wear blue.

4. A *working class* of people who are less skilled than members of the middle class and work at routinized, closely supervised manual and clerical jobs. Their work provides them with a relatively stable income sufficient to maintain a living standard just below the mainstream.

5. A *working-poor class,* consisting of people employed in low-skill jobs, often at marginal firms. The members of this class are typically the lowest paid service, retail, and blue-collar workers. Their incomes leave them well below mainstream living standards. Moreover, they cannot depend on steady employment.

6. An *underclass,* whose members have limited or erratic participation in the labor force and do not have wealth to fall back on. Many depend on government programs.

The cutting points suggested by this schema are not equally significant or salient. The capitalist class is clearly separated from other classes by a crucial distinction: wealth as a primary source of income. The upper-middle class is set off from the classes below it by valuable credentials and the rewards that flow to them. The underclass is isolated from the classes above it by its weak connections with the world of work. But the other class boundaries are not so neatly defined. Even where boundaries appear well defined, we have learned that people often move back and forth across them due to economic fluctuations or changed personal circumstances. Within classes, family incomes vary widely, depending on the number of people employed, work experience, and other factors. As a result, households at the same income level may belong to different classes as we have defined them.

The hazy distinction between the middle and working classes, the two great classes at the center of the class structure, has long perplexed students of stratification. We have ignored the traditional blue-collar/white-collar distinction and emphasized differences of education, skill, and autonomy connected with particular occupations. Thus, the electrician is middle class, and the clerical worker doing routinized office tasks is working class, whatever the color of their shirt collars.

In summary, we are suggesting a model of the class structure based primarily on a series of qualitative economic distinctions. We emphasize the *source of income* and give limited attention to the amount of income. Our schema is summarized in Table 11.1, which provides fuller detail than the raindrop graphic in Chapter 1. As the table indicates, we think of the six classes as divided into three broader categories: the **privileged classes** (capitalist and upper middle), the **majority classes** (middle and working), and the **lower classes** (working poor and underclass).

The percentages in the table are rough estimates of the proportion of households in each class, based on the available occupation, education income, and wealth statistics. (Our rationale for conceiving of classes as groupings of households was presented in Chapter 1.) The classes are defined by the income sources and occupations listed in the second column.

Occupation here refers to the work of the highest-earning member of the household. The last two columns list education levels and incomes typical of each class. Of course, both will vary considerably in practice. Educational levels have risen in successive generations, so that a younger worker will tend to have more years of school than an older worker in the same class.

Let's take a closer look at the six classes.

The Class Structure

The Capitalist Class

The members of the tiny capitalist class at the top of the hierarchy have an influence on the economy and society far beyond their numbers. They make investment decisions that open or close employment opportunities for thousands of others. They also invest in politics and own media enterprises that allow them influence over the thinking of other classes.

The capitalist class strives to perpetuate itself: Assets, lifestyles, values, and social networks are all passed from one generation to the next. (In Bourdieu's terms, economic, cultural, and social capital are all vital parts of the inheritance.) The maintenance of family fortunes and cohesion among family members becomes more difficult as kin multiply and holdings are divided. Older families attempt to instill a sense of lineage in the young. Extended kin are drawn together by regular contact and by mutual dependence on their shared estate. Members of this class are active supporters of private schools and colleges for their children and for ambitious newcomers whom they expect to see socialized into their worldview. Educational "merit," certified by elite school credentials, provides this class and the working rich with an ideological justification for inherited privilege.

The richest, most powerful members of the capitalist class operate on the national and international scene. Some control major corporations. They donate large sums to election campaigns and other political projects. They fund foundations and public policy "think tanks." These national capitalists have less prominent counterparts in communities across the country—the people who own the local car dealerships, real estate empires, media outlets, and other major local businesses. They fund community nonprofit institutions and finance local politics. Their collective influence over national politics is significant because they are likely to have easy access to their own members of Congress (whose campaigns they help finance) and belong to politically potent local organizations like the Chamber of Commerce. At both the national and local levels, the political power of the capitalist class has grown since the late 1970s.

The capitalist class is defined by dependence on income-producing wealth. We include owners of substantial enterprises, investors with diversified wealth, heirs to family fortunes, and top-ranking executives of major corporations. Executives are included because their multimillion-dollar compensation typically includes a stake in the company they manage and permits the relatively rapid accumulation of sizable personal fortunes. Since the 1980s, finance and information technology have been the source of enormous new fortunes.

Class, Percent of Households	Source of Income, Occupation of Main Earner	Typical Education	Typical Household Income, 2015
Table 11.1	**Model of the American Class Structure: Classes by Typical Situations**		
Privileged Classes			
Capitalist 1%	Investors, heirs, top executives, and owners of substantial, closely held businesses.	Selective college or university. Often postgraduate degree.	$1.5 million
Upper-middle 14%	Upper managers and professionals, successful small-business owners, including the "working rich."	College, often postgraduate degree, including law and medicine.	$200,000 (Working rich: $500,000)
Majority Classes			
Middle 30%	Lower managers, semiprofessionals, nonretail sales workers, craftsmen.	At least high school, often some college, fewer with BA degree.	$85,000
Working 25%	Operatives, low-paid craftsmen, clerical workers, retail sales workers.	High school or some college.	$40,000
Lower Classes			
Working poor 15%	Low-paid service, retail, and blue-collar workers.	Most with high school or some college, but many without high school.	$25,000
Underclass 15%	Unemployed or part-time workers, many dependent on public assistance and other government transfers.	High school or some high school.	$15,000

The organization of wealth in this country has been changing for decades. Family-controlled enterprises still account for a large share of capitalist-class wealth and income. President Trump's family is a prominent example. Among the largest corporations, however, family control has, by and large, given way to a system of control by professional executives. As this happens, members of the capitalist class are diversifying their holdings. At the national level, families are less likely to be identified with a single enterprise. Local families sell the enterprises with which they established their fortunes to national corporations. Local banks, retail stores, newspapers, and television stations have been absorbed or displaced by national firms. The younger generation inherits diversified stock and bond portfolios. Local wealth becomes national wealth.

These changes create the basis for a more cohesive capitalist class, whose members are free from parochial identification with a particular firm, economic sector, or locality. In politics, this tendency has been reinforced since the 1970s by the business PACs, business lobby groups, and policy research organizations that defend the interests of the capitalist class as a whole rather than those of individual capitalists.

The Upper-Middle Class

Since the early decades of the twentieth century, the upper-middle class has grown in numbers and importance and its composition has changed. Increasingly, salaried managers and professionals have replaced individual business owners and independent professionals. The key to the success of the upper-middle class is the growing importance of educational certification in a society dominated by complex technology and large-scale organization. Weber, who died in 1920, saw this coming. He observed the spread of the bureaucratic form of organization, with its characteristic preference for formal credentials, in business, government, and elsewhere. Weber (1946) compared the "preferential social opportunities" available to the university-educated in modern societies to the privileges of the well born in earlier aristocratic societies (pp. 241, 301).

At the very top of the upper-middle class, we find a small but growing stratum that we call the *working rich*. Its typical members are very successful professionals (doctors, lawyers, finance professionals, dentists, CPAs, engineers), owners of profitable small businesses, and mid-level corporate executives—generally with incomes in the hundreds of thousands of dollars. We encountered them near the end of the income parade. Though rich, they cannot be considered members of the capitalist class because their incomes are not largely generated by income-producing assets, but by professional fees, executive salaries, or small business profits highly dependent on their own day-to-day efforts. Like the working poor, they have jobs and depend on them.

The upper-middle class exercises large and growing influence in American society. Because it seems to embody American achievement ideals and possesses vast collective purchasing power, its lifestyles and opinions are becoming normative for the whole society. The members of this class vote, volunteer, make campaign donations, and run for office. Their high level of political activity and organizational expertise amplify the influence of their political views and electoral choices. Congress is especially responsive to their policy preferences.

We have described the upper-middle class as one of the two "privileged classes." It is, however, a fairly porous class, open to ambitious people of modest origins who manage to earn the right credentials. But at the same time, it is increasingly separated from the rest of society. The income gap between the upper-middle class and the nonprivileged classes below it has widened. Upper-middle-class families are more likely to live in class-segregated neighborhoods and send their kids to class-segregated schools, public and private. We are convinced that the gap between this class and the rest of the population has replaced the traditional blue-collar/white-collar division as the most important cleavage in the American class structure.

The Middle Class

"The disappearing middle class" has become a recurrent theme among politicians, journalists, and pop sociologists. In fact, the middle class is probably growing and, given the occupational trends associated with postindustrial society, is likely to grow in the future. Of course, the middle class can be made to disappear and reappear by varying the way it is defined. But the very ambiguity of the concept is part of its appeal to politicians. By being for the middle class, they seem to be against no one. From our perspective, it is not the middle class but rather the middle-income group that is shrinking because of declining earnings of many working-class positions and the growth of family incomes toward the upper end of the distribution. At the same time that incomes stagnate at the bottom, the proportion of families with real incomes over $100,000 grows steadily.

The stratification hierarchy, as we have repeatedly observed, is clearest at the extremes. Toward the center, distinctions become blurred, people are more likely to move from one level to another, and status becomes ambiguous. This is particularly true at the point where the middle class and the working class meet—or, more precisely, overlap—so the reader should not expect precision of classification.

The changing character of work has largely eliminated the traditional differences between blue-collar and white-collar employment. The declining income differential between them, the increasing routinization of clerical tasks, and the corresponding drop in the prestige value of a white collar per se have all helped close the traditional gap between shop and office.

Viewed in terms of major occupational groupings, the problem of distinguishing the two majority classes centers on the sales, clerical, and craft categories. We distinguish jobs that require little preparation and are highly routinized, closely supervised, and typically not well paid from jobs that demand significant skill or knowledge and are fairly varied, autonomous, and well paid. On this basis, semiprofessionals (teachers or social workers, for example), low-level managers, most craft workers, and foremen are all middle class. Operatives, such as semiskilled factory workers and truck drivers, belong in the working class, along with routine clerical workers, whose jobs often have an assembly-line character and pay modest wages.

Sales occupations can be divided into retail and nonretail jobs, which we would categorize as working and middle class, respectively. The nonretail group includes insurance salespeople, real estate agents, and manufacturers' representatives. A few highly rewarded sales workers—stockbrokers, in particular—can be considered upper-middle class. On the other hand, we place the lowest-paid sales, clerical, and operative positions in the working-poor class.

By most definitions, the middle class is large and diverse. The first characteristic makes it a natural target of political campaigns; it is difficult, in most districts, to win elections without middle-class support. But the diversity of the middle class makes for ambiguous, if not conflicting, political interests. Although its numbers are larger, the middle class has less political influence than the upper-middle class, which is much more active politically and has a clearer sense of political direction.

The Working Class

The traditional core of the working class is easy to identify: semiskilled machine operatives, in factories and elsewhere, whose proportion of the labor force has been shrinking since the 1950s. Workers in routine white-collar jobs are, by our definition, also part of this class and their share has been growing. Working-class households often combine blue-collar, white-collar, and service jobs.

The long-term contraction of employment in manufacturing has powerfully affected the working class and the country as a whole. New high school graduates can no longer be assured of finding jobs that will enable them to support families. This is one of the factors contributing to rising rates of cohabitation, out-of-wedlock births, and single parenthood among working-class people. It has also propelled the decline of private sector union membership, which has, in turn, reduced the political influence of the working class and reinforced the conservative trend in national politics.

Members of the working class have low rates of political participation. With the decline of the urban political machines and labor unions that once mobilized them, they are less likely to vote than they were as recently as the 1960s.

The Working Poor

The working-poor class includes many service workers and the lowest-paid workers in other low-skilled occupations. Households in this class depend on food stamps and EITC to bolster their incomes. Aside from low pay, their jobs generally have other disadvantages, such as unpleasant or dangerous work, few benefits, erratic hours, and uncertain employment. The distinctions between this class and the classes below and above it are both problematic. Many jobs near the boundary between the working class and the working poor could be placed on either side. But the gap between average jobs in the two classes is quite large. Lifestyles also differ. The working poor tend to have less stable work histories—often for reasons beyond their control—and more personal and family problems. The lower boundary of this class, defined by more or less regular employment, is blurred by the tendency of some individuals to move back and forth across it—a pattern that might be described as oscillating mobility.

Many of the working poor are young workers who, with further training and experience, have traditionally managed to move up in the class hierarchy. It is not clear that they will find it as easy to do so in the future. Like the underclass beneath them, the working poor are generally alienated from political life and have minimal influence on the political process.

The Underclass

Low-income households with limited participation in the labor force form the underclass. Adult members of the underclass may work occasionally or at part-time jobs, but their lack of skills, incomplete education, spotty employment records, family responsibilities, and disabilities or substance abuse problems make it difficult for them to find regular, full-time positions, especially in periods of high unemployment. Many are single mothers, balancing nurturer and provider roles. But most are either individuals living on their own or members of families headed by married (or cohabiting) couples. A significant proportion of the underclass depends on government transfer programs, including food stamps, Social Security (if they are beyond retirement age), disability benefits, and to the extent that they have job income, the EITC. Before the 1996 welfare reform, many underclass families with children survived on public assistance, but their numbers have been radically reduced.

Both the working poor and the underclass tend to grow during and after periods of economic decline, such as the recent Great Recession.

Growing Inequality

A key theme in this book, announced in the title, has been the widening of class disparities in recent decades. The charts we previewed (Figure 1.2) in Chapter 1 trace a momentous shift, somewhere in the early 1970s, from increasing equality to rising inequality. On this basis, we distinguished two periods: the Age of Shared Prosperity (1946 to the early 1970s) and the Age of Growing Inequality (the period since the early 1970s). The date dividing these periods is imprecise because the exact timing depends on the indicator chosen, but the general pattern is unmistakable in the data on wealth, income, earnings, poverty, and other measures we have examined.

In the remaining pages of the chapter, we will summarize the trends we found and return to the question we have asked repeatedly: Why is this happening?

Occupational Structure

Around 1970, the United States completed the transition from an industrial to a postindustrial society—that is, from a society in which most workers were employed in predominantly goods-producing sectors of the economy to one in which most were employed in service-producing sectors (see Figure 3.1). We found that the postindustrial economy tends toward occupational polarization. It requires engineers, money managers, and physicians, but it also needs janitors, cashiers, and hospital orderlies. The demand for routine blue-collar and office workers shrinks in the postindustrial economy, reducing the opportunities for workers without strong educational credentials.

Earnings

Job earnings provide one of the best measures of the trends we have been discussing. During the Age of Shared Prosperity, rapid economic growth produced a steady rise in the median wage. But since the early 1970s, wages in the middle have more or less stagnated and the distribution of wages has become increasingly unequal (see Table 3.6). The change has been most dramatic at the top and bottom: Over the last 4 decades, the real compensation of CEOs grew 1,000 percent, while the proportion of workers earning poverty wages increased.

The trend toward earnings inequality is remarkably pervasive. Inequality has increased between the college and high school educated, between the skilled and the unskilled, between younger workers and older workers, but also among the college educated, among the high school educated, among doctors, among carpenters, among people employed in manufacturing, among those employed in the service sectors, and so on. Even among corporate executives, inequality has increased, as CEO earnings surged ahead of the rewards available to vice presidents and middle managers. There appears to be only one notable exception to this pattern: The earnings gap between men and women has narrowed. But at the same time, earning disparities have increased among women and among men.

Wealth

Inequality of wealth, measured by the concentration of net worth in the top 1 percent of the population, declined during the 1960s, only to rise sharply after the mid-1970s. By the 1990s, the top 1 percent controlled a larger share of private wealth than the bottom 90 percent. In a sense, wealth represents a deeper inequality than earnings or income: It can be passed from generation to generation perpetuating inequality; it can provide such life fundamentals as a college education or home ownership; and, in capitalist form, it can generate a stream of new income. The increased concentration of wealth suggests mounting inequalities in the future.

Poverty

At the very bottom of the class structure, homelessness and "food insecurity" reveal the persistence of material deprivation in a wealthy society. The poverty rate, measured by the Census Bureau's new and improved but still unofficial poverty standard, declined in the 1960s and 1970s and again in the late-1990s. But since 2000, it has been stuck in a narrow band. The government has clung to an absolute conception of poverty—that is, defining poverty by an unchanging material standard that was adopted in the 1960s and became an anachronism as living standards advanced.[1] Most sociologists would favor a relative standard that defines poverty in relation to mainstream living standards. By the most commonly suggested relative standard, half the median income, the U.S. poverty rate exceeds that of its peers among wealthy countries.

Income

Income provides the broadest and most continuous measure we have of economic inequality. Family income trends unambiguously reveal the differences between the Age of Shared Prosperity and the Age of Growing Inequality. During the first period, incomes at all levels rose swiftly and the distribution gradually moved toward greater equality. Remarkably, from 1950 to 1975, the real incomes of the poorest 40 percent of families almost doubled. In contrast, from 1975 to 2000, incomes grew very slowly at the bottom and in the middle, but soared at the top. In fact, the average income of the top 5 percent of families more than doubled (see Figure 4.7). The

---

[1] Both official standard and the unofficial SPM standard, as it has been used here for an analysis of historical trends are absolute standards. See Chapter 10 for details.

trend toward greater income inequality has continued unabated in the new century. While incomes have stagnated or worse in the lower half of the income distribution, many households have attained relative affluence. By 2015, 1 in 4 American households had incomes above $100,000. Twelve percent were above $150,000.

Social Life

Wealthy Americans have always been able to insulate themselves from the grimy realities of life at lower levels of the class structure. Has the increased economic inequality of recent decades meant increased social inequality? One important piece of evidence suggests that it has. Americans are more likely to be segregated by income into homogeneous neighborhoods than they were in 1970 (see Figure 5.2). This residential separation means more schools, malls, and athletic leagues that are class segregated, and fewer settings like the fictional neighborhood bar in the 1980s sitcom *Cheers,* where people of different classes encounter each other as equals.

Social Mobility

Intergenerational social mobility slowed in the Age of Growing Inequality. There was less upward and more downward mobility at the beginning of a new century than there had been a generation earlier. The decline was most evident among younger workers. Nonetheless, even among younger workers, upward occupational mobility was still more common than downward mobility. And even at the extremes of the class structure, position is not fixed at birth. For example, most young adults who were poor at birth are no longer poor (though their incomes typically remain below average). Remarkably, an increasing proportion of superrich Americans on the *Forbes* 400 list did not inherit significant wealth. In short, in the Age of Growing Inequality, it's harder to get ahead, but upward mobility is still pretty common. At the same time, international comparisons undermine our notion of the United States as a uniquely open society. The United States falls among the wealthy countries with the tightest correlation between the incomes of fathers and sons.

Does slowing mobility mean increasing inequality? Not necessarily. For example, if everyone moved down a notch (or up a notch), all would remain in the same relative position—inequality would not be affected. Recent studies do not suggest that a changing pattern of intergenerational mobility is contributing to increased inequality.

Political Power

In the Age of Growing Inequality, power has shifted away from the working class and working poor and toward the privileged classes—in particular, the capitalist class. Of course, power cannot be measured precisely like wealth or income. Moreover, classes are not conscious political actors— they are abstractions—so thinking of them as power players can be misleading. Yet we conclude that the class balance of power has shifted because the relative influence of institutions representing the interests of different social classes has changed and because national decision-making has become more favorable to the privileged.

In the early 1970s, national business leaders initiated a concerted drive to expand their influence in national affairs. With money from corporations and wealthy individuals, they organized to protect business interests, promote conservative ideas, and back pro-business, conservative candidates. Frequently, these candidates represented upper-middle-class constituencies, thus forging an implicit political link between representatives of the two privileged classes. During the same period, labor unions were in a steep decline, losing members, money, and political power. The unions had long spoken for a wider working-class constituency than their own members. The business political initiative and the decline of organized labor were among the key factors that contributed to a series of critical victories for conservatives from Ronald Reagan's election in 1980 to Donald Trump's in 2016 and to fiscal, social, and economic policies that tend to favor the privileged.

Why?

How, then, can we account for the Age of Growing Inequality? No one knows exactly, but here's a short, provisional answer: There were some big changes in the economy. The effects of these economic changes were amplified by the decisions of corporations, families, and political actors in and out of government.

The onset of the Age of Growing Inequality roughly coincided with the transition from an industrial to a postindustrial society. As we have seen, wage disparities of all sorts have widened. The new economy makes winners out of workers with advanced education and skills, and losers out of those who lack such training. In part, this is because of the effects of technological change and globalization. In the developed countries, advancing technology increases the demand for engineers, scientists, technicians, and those who manage them, while reducing demand for crafts workers, operatives, and laborers. The ease with which capital and goods now move around the globe favors the investor, the executive, the marketing expert, the financial professional, the aeronautical engineer, and the systems analyst, but undercuts the factory worker. Shoes, textiles, clothing, and consumer electronics products can be made by low-wage labor in Mexico, China, or Bangladesh. Manufacturing is still an important part of the U.S. economy, but computers and robots have sharply reduced the sector's need for unskilled labor.

Institutional mechanisms that once constrained wage differentials have weakened since the early 1970s. For example, fewer workers are protected by labor unions and collective-bargaining agreements. The value of the minimum wage has shrunk. Federal deregulation seems to have resulted in increased pay differentials in industries such as airlines and trucking.

Facing more competitive markets at home and abroad, corporations look for ways to cut labor costs. In the Age of Growing Inequality, corporations "downsize," "outsource," and move production abroad. They eliminate benefits, freeze wages, and create new classes of workers, including part-timers, temporary workers, second-tier new hires, and leased workers. They develop union-avoidance strategies and promote anti-union legislation. Although managers and professionals have not escaped the layoffs and wage reductions, the "meaner, leaner" labor practices have had their biggest impact at lower occupational levels. Corporations still offer generous competitive rewards to those whose talents are important to their success, from software designers to store managers—and, of course, CEOs.

Wage earners are family members, and the effects of economic change are refracted through the prism of changing family life. In the new era, Americans are less likely to marry, more likely to divorce, more likely to have children without marriage, and, as a result, much more likely to live in female-headed families. Because absent fathers typically pay limited child support and women generally earn less than men, female-headed families are concentrated on the low end of the income distribution. Among lower-class men and women, the failure to marry or stay married, reflects the reduced capacity of young men with limited education to provide for families as they might have in the past.

In the Age of Growing Inequality, more women are employed, they work longer hours, and they earn higher wages. Pay disparities among women have grown. The increased earnings of women have enabled many families to overcome the effects of erosion in men's earnings. But this trend is also contributing to inequality in family incomes. Families depending on one worker—male or female—usually fall well behind two-paycheck families. High-earning women tend to be married to high-earning men and experience faster growth in earnings. The net result of women's increased employment is greater inequality among families.

Government policy has enabled and amplified the growing inequality produced by the economy. The changed balance between labor and business has reinforced this tendency. We have already referred to the failure to sustain the purchasing power of the minimum wage and to the effects of deregulation. In the midst of the Great Recession, the federal government acted to prop up the major banks, but did little for the low- and middle-income families who were losing their homes. Presidents from both parties have promoted the elimination of barriers to international trade, a policy that has been injurious to the lowest-skilled workers, whatever its advantages to the economy as a whole. The decline of the labor movement is, in part, the result of weakened federal protection of union rights and of anti-union laws in states that provide a refuge for firms searching for cheap labor. All these policies allow greater freedom for market forces, which tend to produce unequal outcomes: rising rewards for some who are talented, well financed, or just lucky, and stagnant or declining rewards for many others.

In broad terms, public policy in the Age of Growing Inequality has become more responsive to the privileged classes and less sympathetic to other classes. Tax policy, for example, has zigged and zagged since the early 1970s, but the most significant net result has been sharply reduced federal taxation of high income households. This tendency has permitted increased concentration of wealth, which, given reduced estate taxes, assures the perpetuation of inequality from generation to generation.

Hard Times in the Age of Growing Inequality

Santa Claus noticed something different during the 2009 Christmas season, in the midst of the Great Recession. Children were lowering their expectations, especially those children who visited Santa in retail venues serving middle- to low-income neighborhoods. Santas in several states told *Wall Street Journal* reporters that they were hearing fewer pleas for Xboxes, iPods, and laptops and more for shoes, socks, and eyeglasses. One 5-year-old in Ohio asked Santa if he could turn her father into an elf. Asked why, she explained, "Because my daddy's out of work, and we're about to lose our house." But Santas who saw children in affluent settings reported that their requests were extravagant as ever (Woo 2009).

Like the family of the little girl in Ohio, many households were struggling with unemployment and the threat of foreclosure or eviction. At the time, nearly 1 in 5 workers was unemployed or underemployed, a level not seen in decades. But the burden of unemployment was not evenly distributed. Most affected were the working class and working poor; they got through the worst years with the help of expanded unemployment and food stamp benefits and the EITC. In contrast, upper-middle-class Americans were more worried about the plummeting value of their retirement accounts than about their jobs or their ability to put food on the table.

In the wake of the Great Recession, remarkably little had changed. By 2016, median income, unemployment, and the poverty rate were back to about where they had been in 2007, before the economic collapse. Real wages at the bottom and middle of the labor market had barely changed during the intervening years, while wages at the top had resumed their inexorable rise. The stock market, which had lost more than 50 percent of its value, bounced back, rising to unprecedented heights in 2016 and 2017. In early December 2017, Congress was on the verge of passing a tax bill whose biggest benefits would flow to business and wealthy households.

The end of the Age of Growing Inequality, it seemed, was nowhere in sight.

KEY TERMS DEFINED IN THE GLOSSARY

lower classes   majority classes   privileged classes

Glossary

Note: Terms in bold within definitions are listed separately in the glossary.

Absolute Poverty Standards See **poverty standards**.

Age of Growing Inequality The period beginning in the mid-1970s when inequality rose on multiple dimensions, including wages, income, and wealth. The growing inequality of this period is contrasted with the egalitarian tendency of the preceding **Age of Shared Prosperity**.

Age of Shared Prosperity The years from the end of World War II to the early 1970s when incomes at all levels grew at a healthy pace and economic and social inequalities were declining. Contrasted with the subsequent **Age of Growing Inequality**.

Agricultural Society See **postindustrial society**.

Aid to Families with Dependent Children (AFDC) The means-tested cash assistance program designed to aid needy, typically female-headed, families with children. Replaced in 1996 by **Temporary Assistance for Needy Families (TANF)**.

Association Patterns of interpersonal contact, such as in shared leisure activities, friendship, and marriage, especially among members of the same class. Class subcultures, marked by common values and lifestyles, can emerge when people of similar class position associate more often with one another than with persons of lower or higher classes. See Chapter 5.

Blue-Collar Workers Manual workers, including crafts workers, operatives, and laborers. Sometimes used as shorthand for the **working class**. Distinguished from **white-collar workers** and **service workers**.

Bourgeoisie Marx's term for the class that owns the means of production and controls the **superstructure** in a capitalist society.

Capital The funds, goods, machinery, land, and so on, invested in an enterprise by its owners. Bourdieu (see Chapter 5) extended this traditional conception to encompass three forms of capital: *economic capital*, the basic monetary form, institutionalized as property rights; *cultural capital*, knowledge in its broadest sense, institutionalized as educational credentials, but encompassing such matters as table manners and how to swing a tennis racket; and *social capital*, mutual obligations embodied in social networks such as kinship, friendship, and group membership.

Capitalism An economic system based on private ownership of business and controlled by markets in which capital, labor, goods, and services are freely bought and sold.

Capitalist Class In the **Gilbert-Kahl model**, the very small top class composed of people whose income is largely derived from return on assets. In Marx, same as bourgeoisie.

Chain of Causation A series of successive causal influences, especially in occupational achievement. For example, father's education may influence son's education, which in turn influences son's occupational attainment.

Chief Executive Officer (CEO) Highest ranking executive in a corporation.

Circulation Mobility Mobility made possible by movement within the existing occupational structure. For example, if some offspring of men with high-status jobs take lower status jobs, they create opportunities for the offspring of lower status job-holders to move up. See **structural mobility** and Chapter 6.

Class Consciousness The recognition by the members of a class of their common identity and shared interests. Marx saw class consciousness as a precursor to class conflict and revolution. Modern social scientists are more interested in class consciousness as an influence on political opinion, electoral preferences, and labor militancy. See Chapter 9.

Class Identification The class label people choose for themselves, particularly in response to some variant of the standard survey question: Do you consider yourself upper class, middle class, working class, or lower class? Responses consistent with **objective class position** are indicative of an important aspect of **class consciousness**. See Chapter 9.

Class Perspective A theoretical approach based on the idea that power is usually concentrated in the hands of the class that dominate the economy. See **elite, pluralist perspective**, and Chapter 8.

Class Position, Objective Position in the class structure as determined by objective economic criteria such as occupation, wealth, or income selected by the analyst. Contrasted with the subjective consciousness individuals have of their own class position.

Correlation, Simple A coefficient indicating how accurately the value of one variable can be predicted from another. A coefficient of 0.0 indicates that there is no relationship between the variables. A coefficient of +1.0 or −1.0 indicates that the value of one variable can be perfectly predicted by knowing the value of the other, because the two values move up and down (or in opposite directions) in unison. In the social sciences, most correlations are intermediate. For example, the correlation between father's education and son's education is 0.45, suggesting very significant, but not consistently decisive, influence of the first on the second.

Cultural Capital See **capital**.

Cutting Consistency The degree of community consensus about the points at which a hierarchy of individuals, families, or occupations should be divided into social classes. Studies have shown there is greater consensus about rankings than division into classes. See **ranking consistency** and Chapter 2.

Dividend A portion of a company's profits periodically paid to its shareholders in proportion to the number of shares each owns.

Downsizing Large-scale layoffs by corporations to lower costs and boost profits. Notable in the United States since the 1980s.

Earned Income Tax Credit (EITC) A provision of the federal tax code reducing taxes for low-income families with job earnings. Those who qualify, but owe little or no federal income tax, may receive the credit as a cash payment. An important supplement to the incomes of the working poor, especially families with children.

Earnings Money received as wages or salary for a job or as profit from a small business or professional practice. One of the components of **income**.

Economic Capital See **capital**.

Effective Tax Rates The proportion of income actually paid in taxes after various deductions, exceptions and credits. Sometimes refers to the combined effect of all taxes (income tax, payroll taxes, estate tax, etc.). Since taxes vary considerably in their incidence at different income levels, effective tax rates provide a useful measure of class differences in total tax burden. Often, effective tax rates are computed for each income **quintile** and the top 1 percent of households. See Chapter 4.

Elite A top-ranked group, especially one that exercises **power** by virtue of organizational position; for example, the military elite and the corporate elite. Properly used as a collective noun referring to a group, rather than to individual members of a group. An elite perspective on power makes a sharp distinction between an organized minority that rules and an unorganized majority that is ruled. See **elite cohesion**, **pluralist perspective**, and Chapter 8.

Elite Cohesion The degree to which members of a hypothesized **elite** band together in pursuit of common objectives and in opposition to other groups. The greater the degree of elite cohesion, the more likely it will be able to impose its will on others. See Chapter 8.

Elite Perspective See **pluralist perspective**.

Entitlement A government benefit program, available to all who meet specified prerequisites and supported by open-ended government funding. Entitlements can either be **means-tested**, such as the food stamp program, or available to people at any income level, such as Social Security.

Establishment, the An informal network of wealthy, powerful men drawn from the upper class. During the first three-quarters of the twentieth century, members frequently filled important government positions and influenced national policy, especially in international and economic affairs.

Family In studies of income, two or more related individuals residing together. The most common type of **household**.

Gilbert-Kahl Model of the Class Structure The authors' model of the American class structure. Based on economic distinctions, particularly source of **income** (assets, jobs, and government transfers) and occupation, rather than on prestige distinctions. The model divides the American class system into six classes: the **capitalist class**, the **upper-middle class**, the **middle class**, the **working class**, the **working poor**, and the **underclass**. See Figure 1.1.

Government Transfers Payments to individuals, such as Social Security, veterans benefits, and public assistance, that are not directly in exchange for goods or services provided.

Gross Assets A measure of **wealth** that is equal to the total value of the assets someone owns, without regard to debt. See **wealth**.

Household In studies of income, a domestic unit consisting of **families**, individuals residing alone, or unrelated persons residing together.

Ideology Term used by Marx to refer to the dominant ideas of a society, especially those that justify the *status quo*, including the privileges and power of the ruling class. Ideology may be explicitly political or subtly, even unconsciously, embedded in conceptions of religion, the family, education, law, and so forth. Marx argued that a society's ideology is controlled by the dominant class through its power over the institutions that create and disseminate ideas, such as schools, mass media, churches, and courts.

Income The inflow of money over a *period of time* (e.g., $500 a week or $50,000 in 1999). Distinguished from **wealth**, which refers to assets owned at a *point in time*. The primary source of income for most households is job **earnings**. Others include **government transfers**, such as Social Security benefits and public assistance; interest on bank accounts or bonds; dividends from corporate stock shares; profits from a business or professional practice; and profits from the sale of assets. See Chapter 4.

Industrial Society See **postindustrial society**.

Inflow Mobility Table See **outflow mobility table**.

In-Kind Benefits Noncash government benefits, such as health care, food stamps, and subsidized housing.

Intergenerational Mobility See **social mobility**.

Investor Class See **wealth classes**.

Joint Marital Relationships Marital relationships that focus on companionship and deemphasize the sexual division of labor. Husbands and wives in joint relationships share the planning of family affairs, carry out many household duties interchangeably, and value common leisure activities. More frequent at higher class levels. Contrasted with **segregated marital relationships**.

Life Chances Aspects of an individual's future possibilities that are shaped by class membership, from the infant's chances for decent nutrition to the adult's opportunities for worldly success. First used by Max Weber to emphasize the extent to which economic position shapes each person's chance of attaining the good things in life.

Lifestyle Introduced by Weber to describe distinctive patterns of social interaction, leisure, consumption, dress, language, and so on, associated with a social group—in particular, a prestige class or, in Weber's terminology, a "status group."

Lower Classes The working poor and underclass, as defined in this book.

Majority Classes The middle class and the working class, as defined in this book.

Market Income Pre-tax household income less government transfers like Social Security or public assistance.

Mean The mathematical average (sum of all values divided by the number of cases). Along with **median**, a measure of central tendency used to compare groups or measure change in a particular group over time.

Means of Production In Marx, the implements and physical structures that are necessary for production such as land, machines, mines, or factories. Marx argued that a person's social relationship to the means of production defines his or her class position. He defined the **bourgeoisie** as the class that owns the means of production in a capitalist society and the **proletariat** as the class of workers compelled to sell their labor to the owners in order to survive.

Means-Tested Programs Government benefits available only to people with incomes and/or assets below a specified level. See **entitlement**.

Median One way of measuring the average. More precisely, the midpoint in any distribution dividing the top 50 percent from the bottom 50 percent. Often used to make income comparisons among groups or over time periods. Unlike the **mean**, the median income figure is not distorted by extreme incomes at the high end of the distribution.

Middle Class One of the two largest classes in the **Gilbert-Kahl model**. Located below the **upper-middle class** and above the **working class**. Composed of lower managers, semiprofessionals, crafts workers, foremen, and nonretail salespeople. A higher level of skill or knowledge and independence required on the job distinguishes the middle class from the working class below. More loosely, middle class is sometimes used to refer to the upper part of the class hierarchy in contrast to the working class or lower part.

Minimum Wage The legal minimum that employers in most fields must pay. Important because the earnings of low-wage workers who receive more than the minimum are influenced by it. Set every few years by federal legislation, but has tended, especially since the 1980s, to lag behind inflation and thus lose purchasing power. States and cities may establish their own minimums, as long as they exceed the federal standard.

Mode of Production Marx's term for a society's basic socioeconomic system. Encompasses both the technology with which the society meets its economic needs and the social organization of production. Feudalism and capitalism are distinctive modes of production.

Multiple Causal Pathways Causation through two or more channels. For example, father's occupation may influence daughter's education, which in turn influences her own occupation. But father's occupation may also influence daughter's occupation later on, in a separate way, when the father directly influences the daughter's chances of finding a good job.

Nearly Propertyless Class See **wealth classes**.

Nest-Egg Class See **wealth classes**.

Net Worth See **wealth**.

New Middle Class/Old Middle Class C. Wright Mills' distinction between an old middle class of small entrepreneurs, farmers, shopkeepers, and independent professionals and a new middle class of salaried white-collar workers, including managers, employed professionals, office workers, and salespeople. The first is distinguished by its dependence on entrepreneurial property, the second by its dependence on marketable skills and salaried employment. They have long coexisted, but the first has been shrinking since the late nineteenth century, while the second has been growing. Changes in the economy after the initial stage of industrialization favor the growth of the new middle class. See Chapter 3.

Occupational Prestige The status or respect accorded an occupation. Measured by occupational prestige scores derived from opinion surveys. Occupational prestige influences personal **prestige**, especially when people do not have detailed knowledge of each other's income, family background, lifestyle, associations, and so on. See **socioeconomic status** and Chapter 2.

Occupational Structure The proportional distribution of workers in the different occupational categories. The occupational structure shifts with changes in the economy. For example, when the United States changed from an agricultural society to an industrial society, the proportion of farmers decreased and the proportion of operatives increased. See Chapter 3, especially Table 3.2.

Outflow Mobility Table/Inflow Mobility Table Cross tabulations of father's occupation in the past and son's or daughter's current occupation. The outflow table conceptually groups fathers into occupational categories and examines the occupational distributions in percent of their sons or daughters.

For example, such a table might include a row showing the occupations of all sons or daughters of upper-white-collar men. An outflow table suggests the extent to which careers are influenced by class background. The inflow table groups sons or daughters into occupational categories and examines the corresponding percentage distributions of their fathers. Inflow tables indicate the diversity of class origins among people in each occupational category. The outflow table asks, "Where did they go?" The inflow table asks, "Where did they come from?" Outflow tables typically show percentages across the rows; inflow tables, down the columns. See Chapter 6, especially Tables 6.1 and 6.2.

Outsourcing Corporate strategy to lower labor costs by purchasing services, components, or finished products from low-wage companies at home and abroad. Especially common among large American companies since the 1980s.

Path Analysis A method of causal analysis that uses formal path diagrams and related calculations to sort out the influences of a series of variables on one another and on an ultimate dependent variable. Used especially to examine the factors responsible for career success or failure. Such a model might, for example, be used to explore how a variety of social background variables and education influence each other and ultimate occupational achievement. See Chapter 7.

Pink-Collar Occupations Occupations that are largely female. With important exceptions (for example, registered nurses), these fields offer lower pay, less prestige, and slimmer opportunities for advancement than male-dominated occupations requiring similar levels of education and training. Examples: secretaries, cashiers, hairdressers, nurses, and elementary school teachers.

Pluralist Perspective A theoretical perspective that regards **power** as typically diffused rather than concentrated. Pluralists find multiple bases of power representing the interests of competing groups, such that no powerful minority can easily impose its will. Contrasted with the **elite perspective** that emphasizes the power of a ruling minority, and the **class perspective**, which associates power with a dominant social class, such as the capitalist class. See **elite** and Chapter 8.

Political Action Committee (PAC) A group formed, under the provisions of the campaign finance laws, to raise and contribute money for the campaigns of political candidates.

Postindustrial Society As defined in this book, a society in which most workers are employed in the **service-producing sectors**, like law, education, finance, and retail, rather than the goods-producing sectors of the economy. The United States has evolved from an *agricultural society*, in which most workers were farmers (1776 to 1900); to an *industrial society*, in which the majority of workers were employed in manufacturing or related fields such as mining, transportation, and utilities (1900 to 1970); to a *postindustrial society* (since 1970). See Chapter 3, especially Figure 3.2.

Poverty Line See **poverty threshold**.

Poverty Rate The percentage of people, families, households, or members of a specified group (e.g., Hispanics) who are poor by some standard (usually the official federal standard). Also referred to as the risk of poverty.

Poverty Standard, Federal (Official) Standard established in the 1960s to measure poverty rates and numbers of poor people or poor households. Originally based on the cost of feeding an average family and the proportion of the family budget devoted to nonfood expenses. Takes household size into account. The federal standard is an absolute poverty measure. It is adjusted annually for inflation, but not for changes in the general standard of living. See **poverty standards, absolute and relative**, and Chapter 10.

Poverty Standards, Absolute and Relative Absolute poverty standards define poverty as not having enough food, adequate housing, and so on. They represent a fixed material standard. Relative standards define poverty as having significantly less than the average member of the society. They change over time as a society's standard of living changes. The official poverty measure is an absolute standard. A commonly proposed relative standard is half the **median** family income. Critics of the official standard who favor a relative poverty standard see absolute standards as irrelevant to an affluent society like the United States. See **poverty standard, federal**, and Chapter 10.

Poverty Threshold The income below which a household of a given size is classified as poor. Federal poverty statistics are calculated using a series of such thresholds, which are based on the **federal poverty standard**, periodically adjusted for inflation. Also referred to as the poverty line.

Power The capacity of individuals or groups to carry out their will even over the opposition of others,

especially in broad political and economic contexts. For example, the power of the capitalist class over national economic priorities. See Chapter 8.

Prestige Social esteem or honor. Expressed in attitudes of respect or deference in social interaction. Sometimes used interchangeably with **status**. When a group of people or families in a community share a common position of prestige, they may be described as a prestige class. See Chapter 2.

Privileged Classes The **capitalist class** and **upper-middle class**, as defined in this book.

Productivity Output per worker per hour worked.

Progressive Tax A tax that takes higher proportions of income at higher income levels. The federal income tax, with its escalating marginal tax rates, is the most important progressive tax. See **regressive tax**.

Proletariat Marx's term for the working class, defined as people who must sell their labor power to business owners to survive in a capitalist society.

Quintile A ranked fifth of the population being studied. Comparisons of earnings, income, and wealth are often made among quintiles of households, ranked from the richest quintile to the poorest.

Ranking Consistency The degree of community consensus about rankings in a hierarchy of individuals, families, or occupations. Studies show greater consensus about rankings than about division of the hierarchy into classes. See **cutting consistency** and Chapter 2.

Real Income (also real earnings, wages, etc.) Income adjusted for inflation so that comparisons over long periods can be made. Always denominated in dollars of a specific year. Similar to conversion of prices from one national currency into another. For example, incomes from the 1970s restated in 2000 dollars would be several times higher while representing the same purchasing power.

Regressive Tax A tax that takes higher proportions of income at lower income levels. The retail sales tax, though charged at a flat rate, is regressive because low-income households spend a higher proportion of their income on retail items than do high-income households. See **progressive tax**.

Relative Poverty Standards See **poverty standards**.

Risk of Poverty See **poverty rate**.

Segregated Marital Relationships Marital relationship in which there is clear differentiation of concerns and responsibilities that minimizes the husband's involvement with household matters and the wife's with the world of the husband's work. Segregated marital relationships are most common at lower class levels. Contrasted with **joint marital relationships**.

Service Sectors (also service-producing sectors) Economic sectors, including retail, finance, law, hotels, health care, and education, that produce services. Contrasted with goods-producing sectors like agriculture, manufacturing, and construction. The service-producing sectors grow rapidly in a **postindustrial society**.

Service Workers The occupational category of workers who provide a service, including waiters, janitors, child care workers, domestic servants, police, and firefighters—generally, but not always, low-skill, low-pay occupations. Employment in service occupations expands in a **postindustrial society**. Not all service workers are employed in the **service sector** of the economy. (There are janitors in manufacturing, for example.) Not all service sector jobs are performed by service workers. (Doctors and lawyers work in service sectors, but are not considered service workers.)

Social Capital See **capital**.

Social Class A large group of families approximately equal in rank and differentiated from other families with regard to characteristics such as **occupation**, **prestige**, or **wealth**. See Chapter 1.

Social Clique According to W. Lloyd Warner, an intimate nonkin group with no more than 30 members. Warner found that most social cliques are composed of people of the same or adjacent classes.

Social Mobility The extent to which people move up or down in the class system, typically measured by occupational status. Intergenerational mobility is the movement of individuals relative to their parents' position. Social succession is the inheritance of parents' position. Intragenerational mobility is movement in the course of an individual's own career. See Chapters 6 and 7.

Social Status See **status**.

Social Strata See **strata, social**.

Social Stratification Ranking of individuals or families based on characteristics such as occupation, income, wealth, and social prestige. The hierarchy may be continuous or divided into a series of discrete **social classes**, consisting of people of roughly equal rank. Thus, class is a special case of stratification.

Social Succession See **social mobility**.

Socialization The process through which people learn the skills, attitudes, and customs needed to participate in the life of the community. Class-specific socialization reinforces distinctive class attitudes and lifestyles and encourages individuals to assume the class position of their parents. See Chapter 5.

Socioeconomic Status (SES) Social standing or prestige, especially as measured by the occupational prestige scores.

Status Synonym for social **prestige**. Also, used more generally in sociology to refer to any distinctive social condition or position. Weber wrote about "status groups," which he described as social communities of people who share a common position of social honor (or dishonor). Weber distinguished status groups from economically defined classes. His use of the concept established the idea of separate social and economic dimensions of stratification systems. See Chapter 1.

Strata, Social Levels in a stratified hierarchy, especially those based on prestige.

Structural Mobility Mobility made possible by changes in the occupational structure. A relative expansion of middle- or upper-level jobs, for example, would allow upward mobility from lower positions. See **circulation mobility** and Chapter 6.

Superstructure Marx's term for the dominant political institutions and **ideology** of a society. The means by which the ruling class controls a society. Marx distinguished between the superstructure and the socioeconomic base or foundation of a society.

Supplemental Poverty Measure An alternative measure of poverty published by the Census Bureau.

Temporary Assistance for Needy Families (TANF) Replaced **Aid to Families with Dependent Children (AFDC)** in 1996 as the income assistance program for impoverished children and their families. Different from AFDC in that TANF is not an **entitlement**. Under TANF, families generally may not receive aid for more than a lifetime total of 5 years, and adults benefiting from TANF must start some sort of work within 2 years after assistance begins. See Chapter 10.

Two-Tier Wage Systems The practice of paying new employees less than employees with longer job tenure. Used by some American corporations to reduce labor costs, especially since the 1980s.

Underclass The bottom class in the **Gilbert-Kahl model**. Low-income families with a tenuous relationship to the job market, whose incomes often depend on government programs. See Chapter 10.

Upper-Middle Class In the **Gilbert-Kahl model**, the class below the capitalist class and above the middle class, consisting of well-paid, university-trained managers and professionals.

Variance Explained An indicator of the accuracy with which a series of antecedent variables can predict the values of a dependent variable. For example, how accurately can a son's occupation be predicted from knowledge of his education, his father's occupation, and his father's education? Stated as a percentage of total variance. Because outcomes are always affected by chance factors that are difficult to take into account and our measurements are never perfectly accurate, the variance explained seldom exceeds 50 percent. The difference between 100 percent and the variance explained is the unexplained variance.

Wage-Setting Institutions Institutions, such as labor unions, internal labor markets within corporations, and minimum wage legislation, that shield workers from market forces by influencing decisions that would otherwise be determined by supply and demand.

Wealth The value of assets owned by an individual or family at a *point in time* (e.g., $150,000 on Dec. 31, 2018). Distinguished from **income**, which refers to value received over a *period of time*. Typical forms of wealth are homes, automobiles, bank accounts, and business or financial assets, including commercial real estate, small enterprises, stocks, and bonds. An important distinction is made between wealth held for personal use, such as a home, and wealth held in the form of income-producing assets such as stocks or commercial real estate. Wealth is typically measured as net worth, the value of assets owned less the amount of debt owed.

Wealth Classes Three classes, conceptualized by the authors, that describe the distribution of wealth in the United States. The **nearly propertyless** class, about 40 percent of the population, has little or even negative net worth. The **nest-egg class**, about 50 percent of the population, typically has significant equity in homes and cars, plus a thin cushion of interest-earning assets, such as bank accounts, and modest holdings of stocks or mutual funds. The **investor class**, 10 percent of the population, owns most of the privately held investment assets and typically controls large diversified portfolios.

White-Collar Workers Office workers, including the traditional U.S. Census categories of managers, professionals, clerical workers, and sales workers. Sometimes used to refer to the middle class. Distinguished from **blue-collar** and **service workers**.

Winner-Take-All Markets Term used by economists Frank and Cook (1995) to describe markets in which the rewards are heavily concentrated in the hands of a few top performers who are just slightly better than their closest competitors. Common in entertainment and professional sports but, according to these authors, also increasing across the economy. Important example: rise of corporate CEO compensation to multimillion-dollar levels in recent years.

Working Class One of the two largest classes in the **Gilbert-Kahl model**. Located below the middle class and above the working poor. Composed of low-skill manual workers, clerical workers, and retail salespeople. Commonly, the term is used to refer to the lower portion of the class structure or all blue-collar workers.

Working Poor In the **Gilbert-Kahl model**, the class below the working class and above the underclass, consisting of people who hold low-wage, low-skill, often insecure jobs typically involving menial blue-collar, sales, or service work.

Working Rich A small stratum at the top of the **upper-middle class**, consisting of very successful professionals (notably, lawyers, doctors, dentists), workers in finance, small-business owners, and ranking (but not top) corporate executives, with incomes typically in the hundreds of thousands. Distinguished from members of the capitalist class because their incomes are largely dependent on salaries, professional fees, or small business profits rather than rents, interest, dividends, and so forth, from assets. Like the working poor, they depend on their jobs.

Bibliography

Abramson, Paul R., John H. Aldrich, and David W. Rohde. 1995. *Change and Continuity in the 1992 Elections.* Rev. ed. Washington, DC: Congressional Quarterly Press.

Acemoglu, Daron, David Autor, David Dorn, Gordon Hanson, and Brendan Price. 2016. "Import Competition and the Great US Employment Sag of the 2000s." *Journal of Labor Economics* S141–S198.

Acker, Joan. 2006. *Class Questions: Feminist Answers.* Lanham, MD: Rowman & Littlefield.

Aldrich, Nelson W., Jr. 1988. *Old Money: The Mythology of America's Upper Class.* New York: Vintage.

Aleks, R. 2015. "Estimating the Effect of 'Change to Win' on Union Organizing." *Industrial & Labor Relations Review* 68:584–605.

Allan, Graham. 1989. *Friendship: Developing a Sociological Perspective.* Boulder, CO: Westview.

Allen, Frederick Lewis. 1952. *The Big Change.* New York: Harper & Row.

Alvarez, Louis and Andrew Kolker. 1999. *People Like Us: Social Class in America* [Video]. Public Broadcasting Service.

Anderson, Dewey and Percy Davidson. 1943. *Ballots and the Democratic Class Struggle.* Palo Alto, CA: Stanford University Press.

Anderson, Elijah. 1992. *Streetwise: Race, Class, and Change in an Urban Community.* Chicago, IL: University of Chicago Press.

Anderson, Elijah. 1999. *Code of the Street: Decency, Violence, and the Moral Life of the Inner City.* New York: Norton.

Applebaum, Benjamin and Robert Gebeloff. 2012. "Tax Burden for Most Americans Is Lower Than in the 1980s." *New York Times.* November 29.

Argyle, Michael. 1994. *The Psychology of Social Class.* New York: Routledge.

Arrow, Kenneth, Samuel Bowles, and Steven Durlauf, eds. 2000. *Meritocracy and Economic Inequality.* Princeton, NJ: Princeton University Press.

Atkinson, Anthony. 2015. *Inequality. What Can be Done?* Cambridge, MA: Harvard University Press.

Auletta, Ken. 1982. *The Underclass.* New York: Random House.

Autor, David. 2010. "The Polarization of Job Opportunities in the U.S. Labor Market: Implications for Employment and Earnings." Brookings Institution. The Hamilton Project.

_____. 2014. "Skills, Education and the Rise of Earnings Inequality Among the 'Other 99 Percent.'" *Science* 344:843–851.

_____. 2015. "Why Are There Still So Many Jobs? The History and Future of Workplace Automation." *The Journal of Economics Perspectives* 29:3–30.

Autor, David, David Dorn, and Gordon Hanson. 2016. "The China Shock: Learning From Labor Market Adjustment to Large Changes in Trade." National Bureau of Economic Research. NBER Working Paper Series 21906.

Bachrach, Peter and Morton S. Baratz. 1974. *Power and Poverty: Theory and Practice.* New York: Oxford University Press.

Baltzell, E. Digby. 1958. *Philadelphia Gentlemen.* New York: Free Press.

Bane, Mary Jo. 2009. "Poverty Politics and Policy." In *Changing Poverty, Changing Policies,* edited by M. Cancian and S. Danziger. New York: Russell Sage Foundation.

Bane, Mary Jo and David Ellwood. 1994. *Welfare Realities: From Rhetoric to Reform.* Cambridge, MA: Harvard University Press.

Barnouw, Erik. 1978. *The Sponsor: Notes on a Modern Potentate.* New York: Oxford University Press.

Bartels, Larry. 2008. *Unequal Democracy: The Political Economy of the Gilded Age.* Princeton, NJ: University Press.

Bartels, Larry. 2016. *Unequal Democracy: The Political Economy of the Gilded Age.* Second edition. Princeton, NJ: Princeton University Press.

Beeghley, Leonard. 1996. *The Structure of Social Stratification in the United States.* 2nd ed. Needham Heights, MA: Simon & Schuster.

Beeghley, Leonard and John K. Cochran. 1988. "Class Identification and Gender Role Norms Among Employed Married Women." *Journal of Marriage and the Family* 50:546–566.

Bell, Daniel. 1976. *The Coming of the Post-Industrial Society.* New York: Basic Books.

Beller, Emily and Michael Hout 2006. "Intergenerational Social Mobility: The United States in Comparative Perspective." *The Future of Children* 10:19–36.

Bendix, Reinhard and Seymour Martin Lipset, eds. 1953. *Class, Status, and Power.* 1st ed. Glencoe, IL: Free Press.

Bendix, Reinhard and Seymour Martin Lipset, eds. 1966. *Class, Status and Power: Social Stratification in Comparative Perspective.* 2nd ed. New York: Free Press.

Bennett, James and Bruce Kaufman, eds. 2007. *What Do Unions Do? A Twenty-Year Perspective.* New Brunswick, NJ: Transaction Publishers.

Berle, Adolf A., Jr. and Gardiner C. Means. 1932. *The Modern Corporation and Private Property.* New York: Commerce Clearing House.

Berman, Paul. 1991. "A Union Man From Harvard." *New York Times Book Review.* August 11.

Bernstein, Peter W. and Annalyn Swan, eds. 2007. *All the Money in the World: How the Forbes 400 Make—and Spend—Their Fortunes.* New York: Alfred A. Knopf.

Bianchi, Suzanne. 1995. "Changing Economic Roles of Women and Men." In *State of the Union: America in the 1990s, Volume 1: Economic Trends,* edited by R. Farley. New York: Russell Sage Foundation.

Birmingham, Stephen. 1987. *American's Secret Aristocracy.* Boston, MA: Little, Brown.

Birnbach, Lisa, ed. 1980. *The Official Preppy Handbook.* New York: Workman.

Blank, Rebecca M. 1997. *It Takes a Nation.* Princeton, NJ: Princeton University Press.

Blank, Rebecca M. 2007. "What We Know, What We Don't Know, and What We Need to Know About Welfare Reform." Paper presented at the conference Ten Years After: Evaluating the Long-Term Effects of Welfare Reform on Children, Families, Work and Welfare. University of Kentucky, Center for Poverty Research.

Blank, Rebecca M. 2009. "Family Structure and the Structure of Opportunity for Less-Skilled Workers." In *Changing Poverty, Changing Policies,* edited by M. Cancian and S. Danziger. New York: Russell Sage Foundation.

Blau, Francine and Lawrence Kahn. 2009. Inequality and Earnings Distribution. In *The Oxford Handbook of Economic Inequality.* Edited by Wiemer Salverda, et al. New York: Oxford University Press.

Blau, Peter M. and Otis Dudley Duncan. 1967. *The American Occupational Structure.* New York: Wiley.

Bloch, Fred. 1977. "The Ruling Class Does Not Rule: Notes on the Marxist Theory of the State." *Socialist Revolution* 7(1):6–28.

Blumberg, Paul M. and P. W. Paul. 1975. "Continuities and Discontinuities in Upper-Class Marriages." *Journal of Marriage and the Family* 37:63–77.

Blumenthal, Sydney. 1986. *The Rise of the Counter Establishment.* New York: Times Books.

Blumenthal, Sydney and Thomas Byrne Edsall, eds. 1988. *The Reagan Legacy.* New York: Pantheon.

Boston, Thomas D. 1988. *Race, Class, and Conservatism.* Cambridge, MA: Unwin Hyman.

Bott, Elizabeth. 1954. "The Concept of Class as a Reference Group." *Human Relations* 7:259–286.

Bott, Elizabeth. 1964. *Family and Social Network.* London: Tavistock.

Bottomore, Tom. 1966. *Elites in Modern Society.* New York: Pantheon.

Bourdieu, Pierre. 1984. *Distinction: A Social Critique of the Judgment of Taste.* Cambridge, MA: Harvard University Press.

Bourdieu, Pierre. 1986. "The Forms of Capital." In *Handbook of Theory and Research for the Sociology of Education,* edited by John Richardson. New York: Greenwood Press.

Bowen, William G. and Derek Bok. 1998. *The Shape of the River: Long-Term Consequences of Considering Race in College and University Admissions.* Princeton, NJ: Princeton University Press.

Bowen, William G., Martin A. Kurzweil, and Eugene M. Tobin. 2005. *Equity and Excellence in American Higher Education.* Charlottesville, VA: University of Virginia Press.

Bowen, William, Matthew Chingos, and Michael McPherson. 2009. *Crossing the Finish Line: Completing College at America's Public Universities.* Princeton, NJ: Princeton University Press.

Bowles, Samuel and Herbert Gintis. 1976. *Schooling in Capitalist America.* New York: Basic Books.

Bowles, Samuel, Herbert Gintis, and Melissa Osborne Groves, eds. 2005. *Unequal Chances: Family Background and Economic Success.* New York: Russell Sage Foundation.

Bowser, Benjamin P. 2007. *The Black Middle Class: Social Mobility—and Vulnerability.* Boulder, CO: Lynne Rienner.

Boyer, Richard and Herbert Morais. 1975. *Labor's Untold Story*. 3rd ed. New York: United Electrical Workers.

Bradburn, Norman. 1969. *The Structure of Psychological Well-Being*. Chicago, IL: Aldine.

Bradbury, Katherine and Jane Katz. 2002. "Issues in Economics." *Regional Review* Q4:2–5.

Braverman, Harry. 1974. *Labor and Monopoly Capital*. New York: Monthly Review Press.

Brewer, Mark D. and Jeffrey M. Stonecash. 2007. *Split: Class and Cultural Divides in American Politics*. Washington, DC: CQ Press.

Bricker, Jesse, et al. 2014. "Changes in U.S. Family Finances from 2010 to 2013: Evidence from the Survey of Consumer Finances." *Federal Reserve Bulletin*. 100:1–41.

Brody, David. 1980. *Workers in Industrial America: Essays on the 20th Century Struggle*. New York: Oxford University Press.

Brody, David. 1993. *Workers in Industrial America: Essays on the 20th Century Struggle*. 2nd ed. New York: Oxford University Press.

Bronfenbrenner, Kate. 2009. "No Holds Barred: The Intensification of Employer Opposition to Organizing." *Economic Policy Institute Briefing Paper No. 235*.

Bronfenbrenner, Urie. 1966. "Socialization Through Time and Space." In *Class, Status, and Power*, 2nd ed., edited by R. Bendix and S. M. Lipset. New York: Free Press.

Brooks, David. 2000. *Bobos in Paradise: The New Upper Class and How They Got There*. New York: Simon & Schuster.

Brooks, Thomas. 1971. *Toil and Trouble: A History of American Labor*. 2nd ed. New York: Dell.

Brown, Clifford, et al. 1995. *Serious Money: Fundraising and Contributing in Presidential Nominational Campaigns*. New York: Cambridge University Press.

Brunner, Borgna, ed. 2001. *Time Almanac 2002*. Boston, MA: Information Please.

Bucks, Brian, Arthur Kennickell, and Traci L. Mach. 2009. "Changes in U.S. Family Finances from 2004 to 2007: Evidence from the Survey of Consumer Finances." *Federal Reserve Bulletin* 95:A1–A56.

Bucks, Brian, Arthur Kennickell, and Kevin Moore. 2006. "Recent Changes in U.S. Family Finances: Evidence from the 2001 and 2004 Survey of Consumer Finances." *Federal Reserve Bulletin* 92:A1–A38.

Burch, Philip H., Jr. 1980. *Elites in American History: The New Deal to the Carter Administration*. New York: Holmes and Meier.

Burke, Vee. 2001. *Welfare Reform: TANF Trends and Data. CRS Report for Congress*. Washington, DC: Congressional Research Service.

Burke, Vee, et al. 2001. *Welfare Reform Briefing Book*. Washington, DC: Congressional Research Service.

Burman, Leonard and Joel Slemrod. 2013. *Taxes in America: What Everyone Needs to Know*. New York: Oxford University Press.

Burnham, James. 1941. *The Managerial Revolution*. New York: John Day.

Burtless, Gary. 1987. "Inequality in America: Where Do We Stand?" *Brookings Review* 5(Summer):9–16.

Burtless, Gary. 1990. *A Future of Lousy Jobs*. Washington, DC: Brookings Institution.

Burtless, Gary. 1995. "International Trade and the Rise in Earnings Inequality." *Journal of Economic Literature* 32:800–816.

Burtless, Gary, R. Kent Weaver, and Joshua Wiener. 1997. "The Future of the Social Safety Net." In *Setting National Priorities: Budget Choices for the Next Century*, edited by R. Reishauer. Washington, DC: Brookings Institution.

Cameron, Juan. 1978. "Small Business Trips Big Labor." *Fortune* 98(July):80–82.

Campbell, Angus, Gerald Gurin, and Warren E. Miller. 1954. *The Voter Decides*. Evanston, IL: Row, Peterson.

———. 1960. *The American Voter*. New York: Wiley.

Cancian, Maria, et al. 1993. "Working Wives and Family Income Inequality Among Married Couples." In *Uneven Tides: Rising Inequality in America*, edited by S. Danziger and P. Gottshalk. New York: Russell Sage Foundation.

Cancian, Maria and Sheldon Danziger, eds. 2009. *Changing Poverty, Changing Policies*. New York: Russell Sage Foundation.

Cancian, Maria and Deborah Reed. 2009. "Family Structure, Childbearing and Parental Employment: Implications for the Level and Trend in Poverty." In *Changing Poverty, Changing Policies*, edited by M. Cancian and S. Danziger. New York: Russell Sage Foundation.

Cantril, Hadley. 1951. *Public Opinion*. Princeton, NJ: Princeton University Press.

Caplow, Theodore. 1980. "Middletown Fifty Years After." *Contemporary Sociology* 9:46–50.

Caplow, Theodore and Bruce Chadwick. 1979. "Inequality and Life Styles in Middletown, 1920–1978." *Social Science Quarterly* 60:366–368.

Caplow, Theodore, et al. 1985. *Middletown Families: Fifty Years of Change and Continuity*. Minneapolis, MN: University of Minnesota Press.

Card, David and Alan B. Krueger. 1992. "School Quality and Black–White Relative Earnings: A Direct Assessment." *Quarterly Journal of Economics* 107:151–200.

Carnes, Nicholas. 2013. *White Collar Government: The Hidden Role of Class in Economic Policy Making*. Chicago, IL: University of Chicago Press.

Carnevale, Anthony P. and Stephen J. Rose. 2004. "Socioeconomic Status, Race/Ethnicity, and Selective College Admissions." In *America's Untapped Resource: Low-Income Students in Higher Education*, edited by R. D. Kahlenberg. New York: The Century Foundation Press.

Center on Budget and Policy Priorities. 2001. "Poverty Rates Fell in 2000 as Unemployment Reached 31-Year Low." Press Release, September 26. Washington, DC: Author.

Centers, Richard. 1949. *The Psychology of Social Classes: A Study of Class Consciousness*. Princeton, NJ: Princeton University Press.

Cerrato, et al. 2016. Trump Won in Counties That Lost Jobs to China and Mexico. *Washington Post. Monkey Cage*. https://www.washingtonpost.com/news/monkey-cage/wp/2016/12/02/trump-won-where-import-shocks-from-china-and-mexico-were-strongest/?utm_term=.a2e6db040112

Chaison, Gary. 2006. *Unions in America*. Thousand Oaks, CA: SAGE.

Charles, Kerwin Kofi and Erik Hurst. 2003. "The Correlation of Wealth Across Generations." *The Journal of Political Economy* 111:1155–1182.

Cherlin, Andrew. 2014. *Labor's Love Lost: The Rise and Fall of the Working-Class in America*. New York: Russell Sage Foundation.

Chetty, Raj, et al. 2017. "The Fading American Dream. Trends in Absolute Income Mobility Since 1940." *Science* 398–406.

Citizens for Tax Justice. 2016. "Who Pays Taxes in American in 2016?" Washington, DC.

Cohen, Jere. 1979. "Socio-Economic Status and High School Friendship Choice: Elmtown's Youth Revisited." *Social Networks* 2:65–74.

Colclough, Glenna and E. M. Beck. 1986. "The American Educational Structure and the Reproduction of Social Class." *Sociological Inquiry* 56:456–476.

Coleman, Richard P. and Lee Rainwater, with Kent A. McClelland. 1978. *Social Standing in America: New Dimensions of Class*. New York: Basic Books.

Coleman-Jansen, Alisha, et al. 2016. *Household Food Security in the United States in 2015*. Washington, DC: U.S. Department of Agriculture.

Collier, Peter and David Horowitz. 1976. *The Rockefellers: An American Dynasty*. New York: Holt, Rinehart & Winston.

Collins, Chuck and Felice Yeskel, with United for a Fair Economy and Class Action. 2000. *Economic Apartheid in America: A Primer on Economic Inequality & Insecurity*. New York: New Press.

Congressional Budget Office. 2016. "The Distribution of Household Income and Federal Taxes, 2016." Washington, DC.

Congressional Quarterly. 1976. *Guide to Congress*. 2nd edition. Washington, DC: Congressional Quarterly Press.

Congressional Quarterly. 1996. "Welfare Overhaul Law." Sept. 21:2696–2705.

Conley, Dalton. 1999. *Being Black, Living in the Red: Race, Wealth, and Social Policy in America*. Berkeley, CA: University of California Press.

Cookson, Peter and Caroline Hodges Persell. 1985. *Preparing for Power: America's Elite Boarding Schools*. New York: Basic Books.

Corak, Miles 2013a. "Income Inequality, Equality of Opportunity, and Intergenerational Mobility." *Journal of Economic Perspectives* 27:79–102.

Corak, Miles. 2013. "Inequality for Generation to Generation. The United States in Comparison." In *The Economics of Inequality, Poverty and Discrimination in the 21st Century*, edited by Robert Rycroft.

Corcoran, Mary. 1995. "Rags to Rags: Poverty and Mobility in the United States." *Annual Review of Sociology* 21:237–267.

Corcoran, Mary. 2001. "Mobility, Persistence and the Consequences of Poverty for Children: Child and Adult Outcomes." In *Understanding Poverty*, edited by Sheldon H. Danziger and Robert H. Haveman. New York: Russell Sage Foundation.

Corey, Lewis. 1935. *The Crisis of the Middle Class*. New York: Covici-Friede.

Corey, Lewis. 1953. "Problems of the Peace: The Middle Class." In *Class, Status, and Power,* edited by R. Bendix and S. M. Lipset. Glencoe, IL: Free Press.

Corrado, Anthony, Thomas E. Mann, Daniel R. Ortiz, and Trevor Potter. 2005. *The New Campaign Finance Sourcebook*. Washington, DC: Brookings Institution Press.

Coser, Lewis. 1978. *Masters of Sociological Thought*. 2nd ed. New York: Harcourt Brace Jovanovich.

Coverman, Shelly. 1988. "Sociological Explanations of the Male–Female Wage Gap." In *Women Working: Theories and Facts in Perspective,* 2nd ed., edited by A. Stromberg and S. Harkess. Mountain View, CA: Mayfield.

Crompton, Rosemary. 1998. *Class and Stratification: An Introduction to Current Debates*. 2nd ed. Cambridge, MA: Polity.

Crompton, Rosemary. 2008. *Class and Stratification: An Introduction to Current Debates*. 3rd ed. Cambridge, MA: Polity.

Croteau, David. 1995. *Politics and the Class Divide: Working People and the Middle-Class Left*. Philadelphia, PA: Temple University Press.

Cruciano, Therese. 1996. "Individual Tax Returns: Preliminary Data, 1994." *SOI Bulletin: A Quarterly Statistics of Income Report* 15(Spring):18–24.

Current Biography. 1982–1988. New York: W. W. Wilson.

Curtis, Richard F. and Elton F. Jackson. 1977. *Inequality in American Communities*. New York: Academic.

Dahl, Robert A. 1961. *Who Governs? Democracy and Power in an American City*. New Haven, CT: Yale University Press.

Dahl, Robert A. 1967. *Pluralist Democracy in the United States*. Chicago, IL: Rand McNally.

Danziger, Sheldon, Koji Chavez, and Erin Cumberworth. 2012. *Poverty and the Great Recession*. Stanford, CA: Stanford Center on Poverty and Inequality.

Danziger, Sheldon and Peter Gottschalk. 1995. *America Unequal*. New York: Russell Sage Foundation.

Danziger, Sheldon and Robert Haveman, eds. 2001. *Understanding Poverty*. Cambridge, MA: Harvard University Press.

Davidson, James D., Ralph E. Pyle, and David V. Reyes. 1995. "Persistence and Change in the Protestant Establishment, 1930–1992." *Social Forces* 74(1):157–175.

Davis, Allison, Burleigh B. Gardner, and Mary R. Gardner. 1941. *Deep South: A Social-Anthropological Study of Caste and Class*. Chicago, IL: University of Chicago Press.

Davis, Mike. 1980. "The Barren Marriage of American Labour and the Democratic Party." *New Left Review* 124:45–84.

DeCarlo, Scott. 2007. "Big Paychecks." *Forbes* May 21.

De Luca, Rita Caccamo. 2001. *Back to Middletown: Three Generations of Sociological Reflections*. Palo Alto, CA: Stanford University Press.

Demerath, N. J., III. 1965. *Social Class in American Protestantism*. Chicago, IL: Rand McNally.

Dent, David. 1992. "The New Black Suburbs." *New York Times Magazine* June 14.

DeParle, Jason. 1996. "Welfare: Progress Hijacked." *New York Times Magazine* December 8.

DeParle, Jason. 2004. *American Dream: Three Women, Ten Kids and a Nation's Drive to End* Welfare. New York: Penguin.

DeParle, Jason and Robert Gebeloff. 2009. "Food Stamp Use Soars, and Stigma Fades." *New York Times* November 29.

Desmond, Matthew. 2016. *Evicted: Poverty and Profit in the American City*. New York: Crown Publishers.

DiTomaso, Nancy. 2013. *The American Non-Dilemma: Racial Inequality Without Racism*. New York: Russell Sage Foundation.

Domhoff, G. William. 1967. *Who Rules America?* Englewood Cliffs, NJ: Prentice-Hall.

Domhoff, G. William. 1970. *The Higher Circles: The Governing Class in America*. Englewood Cliffs, NJ: Prentice Hall.

Domhoff, G. William. 1974. *The Bohemian Grove and Other Retreats*. New York: Harper & Row.

Domhoff, G. William. 1975. "Social Clubs, Policy Planning Groups, and Corporations." *Insurgent Sociologist* 5(3):173–195.

Domhoff, G. William. 2006. *Who Rules America? Power, Politics and Social Change*. 5th ed. Boston, MA: McGraw-Hill.

Domhoff, G. William and Hoyt B. Ballard, eds. 1968. *C. Wright Mills and the Power Elite*. Boston, MA: Beacon.

Dotson, Floyd. 1950. "The Associations of Urban Workers." Unpublished doctoral thesis, Yale University.

Dubofsky, Melvyn. 1980. "The Legacy of the New Deal." *Executive* 6(Spring):8–10.

Duhigg, Charles and Keith Bradsher. 2012. "How the U.S. Lost Out on iPhone Work." *New York Times* January 22.

Duncan, Otis Dudley. 1961. "A Socio-Economic Index for All Occupations" and "Properties and Characteristics of the Socioeconomic Index." In *Occupations and Social Status*, edited by A. Reiss. Glencoe, IL: Free Press.

Duncan, Otis Dudley. 1966. "Methodological Issues in the Analysis of Social Mobility." In *Social Structure and Mobility in Economic Development*, edited by N. Smelser and S. M. Lipset. Chicago, IL: Aldine.

Duncan, Otis Dudley, Archibald O. Haller, and Alejandro Portes. 1968. "Peer Influences on Aspirations: A Reinterpretation." *American Journal of Sociology* 74:119–137.

Dye, Thomas R. 1976. *Who's Running America? Institutional Leadership in the United States*. Englewood Cliffs, NJ: Prentice Hall.

———. 1995. *Who's Running America? The Clinton Years*. 6th ed. Englewood Cliffs, NJ: Prentice Hall

———. 2002. *Who's Running America? The Bush Restoration*. 7th ed. Englewood Cliffs, NJ: Prentice Hall.

———. 2016. *Who's Running America? The Obama Reign*. 8th ed. New York: Routledge.

Dye, Thomas R. 2016. *Who's Running America? The Bush Restoration*. 7th ed. Englewood Cliffs, NJ: Prentice Hall.

Edelman, Peter. 1997. "The Worst Thing Bill Clinton Has Done." *Atlantic Magazine* March.

Edin, Kathryn and Maria Kefalas. 2005. *Promises I Can Keep: Why Poor Women Put Motherhood Before Marriage*. Berkeley, CA: University of California Press.

Edin, Kathryn and Laura Lein. 1997. *Makin' Ends Meet. How Single Mothers Survive: Welfare and Low-Wage Work*. New York: Russell Sage Foundation.

Edin, Kathryn and H. Luke Shaefer. 2015. *$2.00 a Day: Living on Almost Nothing in America*. Boston, MA: Houghton Mifflin.

Edsall, Thomas B. 1984. *The New Politics of Inequality*. New York: Norton.

Edsall, Thomas and Mary Edsall. 1991. *Chain Reaction: The Impact of Race, Rights, and Taxes on American Politics*. New York: Norton.

Edwards, Alba M. and U.S. Bureau of the Census. 1943. *U.S. Census of Population 1940: Comparative Occupational Statistics, 1870–1940*. Washington, DC: U.S. Government Printing Office.

Ehrenreich, Barbara. 1989. *Fear of Falling: The Inner Life of the Middle Class*. New York: Pantheon.

Ehrenreich, Barbara. 2001. *Nickel and Dimed: On (Not) Getting by in America*. New York: Henry Holt.

Eismeier, Theodore and Philip Pollock. 1996. "Money in the 1994 Elections and Beyond." In *Midterm: The Elections of 1994 in Context*, edited by P. Klinkner. Boulder, CO: Westview.

Ellwood, David. 1988. *Poor Support: Poverty in the American Family*. New York: Basic Books.

Ellwood, David and Mary J. Bane. 1985. "The Impact of AFDC on Family Structure and Living Arrangements." In *Research in Labor Economics* 7, edited by R. Ehrenberg. Greenwich, CT: JAI Press.

Ellwood, David and Mary J. Bane. 1994. *Welfare Realities: From Rhetoric to Reform*. Cambridge, MA: Harvard University Press.

Elmelech, Yuval. 2008. *Transmitting Inequality: Wealth and the American Family*. New York: Rowman & Littlefield.

Erikson, Robert and John Goldthorpe. 1992. *The Constant Flux: A Study of Class Mobility in Industrial Societies*. New York: Oxford University Press.

Esping-Andersen, Gosta. 2007. Sociological Explanations of Changing Income Distributions. *American Behavioral Scientist* 50:639–658.

Farley, Reynolds. 1984. *Blacks and Whites: Narrowing the Gap?* Cambridge, MA: Harvard University Press.

Farley, Reynolds, ed. 1995a. *State of the Union: America in the 1990s, Volume 1: Economic Trends*. New York: Russell Sage Foundation.

Farley, Reynolds, ed. 1995b. *State of the Union: America in the 1990s, Volume 2: Social Trends.* New York: Russell Sage Foundation.

Faux, Jeff. 2006. *The Global Class War: How America's Bipartisan Elite Lost Our Future and What It Will Take to Win It Back.* New York: John Wiley.

Featherman, David. 1979. "Opportunities Are Expanding." *Society* March/April:4, 6–11.

Featherman, David L. and Robert M. Hauser. 1978. *Opportunity and Change.* New York: Academic.

Ferguson, Thomas. 1995. *Golden Rule: The Investment Theory of Party Competition and the Logic of Money Driven Political Systems.* Chicago, IL: University of Chicago Press.

Fine, Michelle and Lois Weis. 1998. *The Unknown City: The Lives of Poor and Working-Class Young Adults.* Boston, MA: Beacon.

Fisher, Claude, et al. 1996. *Inequality by Design: Cracking the Bell Curve Myth.* Princeton, NJ: Princeton University Press.

Fiske, Susan and Hazel Rose Markus, eds. 2012. *Facing Social Class: How Societal Rank Influences Interaction.* New York: Russell Sage Foundation.

Forbes. 1996. "The Forbes 400." October 14.

Forbes. 1998. "Family Fortunes: The 50 Wealthiest Families in America." October 12.

Forbes. 2001a. "The Forbes 400." October 8.

Forbes. 2001b. "The 500 Largest Private Companies." November 26.

Forbes. 2006. "The Richest People in America." October 9.

Forbes. 2009. "The 400." October 19.

Forbes. 2012. "The Forbes 400." October 8.

Fortune. 1937. "The Industrial War." 14(November):105–110, 122, 156, 160, 166.

Fortune. 1940. "The Fortune Survey: XXVII." February.

Frank, Robert. 2007. *Richistan: A Journey Through the American Wealth Boom and the Lives of the New Rich.* New York: Crown.

Frank, Robert H. and Philip J. Cook. 1995. *The Winner-Take-All Society.* New York: Simon & Schuster.

Fraser, Douglas. 1978. "UAW President Fraser Resigns From Labor-Management Group." *Radical History Review* 18(Fall):117–121.

Frears, John. 1988. "Liberalism in France." In *Liberal Parties in Western Europe,* edited by E. Kirchner, 124–150. Cambridge, UK: Cambridge University Press.

Freeman, Richard B. 1996. "Labor Market Institutions and Earnings Inequality." *New England Economic Review.* Special Issue(May/June):157–181.

Freeman, Richard B. 2004. "What, Me Vote?" In *Social Inequality,* edited by K. M. Neckerman. New York: Russell Sage Foundation.

Frieden, Jeffry A. 2006. *Global Capitalism: Its Fall and Rise in the Twentieth Century.* New York: Norton.

Furman, Jason. 2017. "Reducing Poverty: The Progress We have Made and the Path Forward." Center on Budget and Policy Priorities. January 17.

Fussell, Paul. 1983. *Class: A Guide Through the American Status System.* New York: Ballantine.

Galbraith, John Kenneth. 1958. *The Affluent Society.* Boston, MA: Houghton Mifflin.

Galbraith, John Kenneth. 1967. *The New Industrial State.* Boston, MA: Houghton Mifflin.

Garfinkel, Irwin and Sara McLanahan. 1986. *Single Mothers and Their Children.* Washington, DC: Urban Institute.

Garrett, R. Sam. 2016. *The State of Campaign Finance Policy: Recent Developments and Issues for Congress.* Congressional Research Service.

Gecas, Viktor. 1979. "The Influence of Social Class on Socialization." In *Contemporary Theories About the Family,* Vol. I., edited by W. R. Burr et al. New York: Free Press.

Geoghegan, Thomas. 1991. *Which Side Are You On: Trying to Be for Labor When It's Flat on Its Back.* New York: Farrar, Straus & Giroux.

Giddens, Anthony. 1973. *The Class Structure of the Advanced Societies.* New York: Harper & Row.

Gilens, Martin. 2012. *Affluence and Influence: Economic Inequality and Political Power in America.* Princeton, NJ: Princeton University Press.

Ginsberg, Benjamin and Martin Shefter. 1990. *Politics by Other Means: The Declining Importance of Elections in America.* New York: Basic Books.

Gittleman, Maury. 1994. "Earnings in the 1980s: An Occupational Perspective." *Monthly Labor Review* 117:16–27.

Glenn, Norval D. and Jon P. Alston. 1968. "Cultural Distances Among Occupational Categories." American Sociological Review 33:365–382.

Glenn, Norval D. and Jon P. Alston. 1975. "The Contribution of White Collars to Occupational Prestige." Sociological Quarterly 16:184–189.

Golden, Daniel. 2007. The Price of Admission: How America's Ruling Class Buys Its Way Into Elite Colleges and Who Gets Left Outside the Gates. New York: Three Rivers Press.

Goldin, Claudia and Lawrence Katz. 2007. "Long-Run Changes in Wage Structure: Narrowing, Widening and Polarizing." Brookings Papers on Economic Activity.

Gornick, Janet and Markus Jantti, eds. 2013. Income Inequality: Economic Disparities and the Middle Class in Affluent Countries. Stanford, CA: Stanford University Press.

Gornick, Janet and Markus Jantti. 2016. "Poverty. Pathways. The Poverty and Inequality Report." Stanford Center on Poverty and Inequality.

Graetz, Michael J. and Ian Shapiro. 2005. Death by a Thousand Cuts: The Fight Over Taxing Inherited Wealth. Princeton, NJ: Princeton University Press.

Graham, Lawrence Otis. 1999. Our Kind of People: Inside America's Black Upper Class. New York: HarperCollins.

Green, Mark. 1979. Who Runs Congress? 3rd ed. New York: Bantam.

Greene, Bert. 1978. Pity the Poor Rich. Chicago, IL: Contemporary.

Greenstone, J. David. 1977. Labor in American Politics. Chicago, IL: University of Chicago Press.

Grogger, Jeffrey and Lynn A. Karoly. 2005. Welfare Reform: Effects of a Decade of Change. Cambridge, MA: Harvard University Press.

Grusky, David, ed. 1994. Social Stratification: Class, Race, and Gender in Sociological Perspective. Boulder, CO: Westview.

Grusky, David, ed. 2001. Social Stratification: Class, Race, and Gender in Sociological Perspective. 2nd ed. Boulder, CO: Westview.

Grusky, David, ed. 2008. Social Stratification: Class, Race, and Gender in Sociological Perspective. 3rd ed. Boulder, CO: Westview.

Grusky, David, ed. 2014. Social Stratification: Class, Race, and Gender in Sociological Perspective. 4th ed. Boulder, CO: Westview.

Hacker, Jacob and Paul Pierson. 2010a. Winner-Take-All Politics: How Washington Made the Rich Richer and Turned Its Back on the Middle Class. New York: Simon & Schuster.

Hacker, Jacob and Paul Pierson. 2010b. "Winner-Take-All Politics: Public Policy, Political Organization and the Precipitous Rise of Top Incomes in the United States." Politics & Society 38:153–204.

Hacker, Louis. 1970. The Course of American Economic Growth and Development. New York: Wiley.

Halberstam, David. 1972. The Best and the Brightest. New York: Random House.

Halle, David. 1984. America's Working Man: Work, Home, and Politics Among Blue-Collar Property Owners. Chicago, IL: University of Chicago Press.

Halpern, Sarah, et al. 2015. It's Not Like I'm Poor: How Working Families Make Ends Meet in a Post-Welfare World. Berkeley, CA: University of California Press.

Hamilton, Brady, Joyce Martin, and Stephanie Ventura. 2009. "Births: Preliminary Data for 2007." National Vital Statistics Reports 57:12.

Hamilton, Richard. 1972. Class and Politics in the United States. New York: Wiley.

Hamilton, Richard. 1975. Restraining Myths: Critical Studies of United States' Social Structure and Politics. Beverly Hills, CA: SAGE.

Harding, David. 2005. "The Changing Effect of Family Background on the Incomes of American Adults." In Samuel Bowles, et al. eds.

Harrington, Michael. 1962. The Other America: Poverty in the United States. New York: Macmillan.

Harrison, Bennett and Barry Bluestone. 1988. The Great U-Turn: Corporate Restructuring and the Polarizing of America. New York: Basic Books.

Haskins, Ronald. 2006. Hearings on 1996 Welfare Overhaul. U.S. House of Representatives. Statement. Committee on Ways and Means. July 19.

Haveman, Robert and Barbara Wolf. 1994. Succeeding Generations: On the Effects of Investments in Children. New York: Russell Sage Foundation.

Herman, Edward S. 1981. Corporate Control, Corporate Power. New York: Cambridge University Press.

Heymann, Jody. 2000. The Widening Gap: Why American Working Families Are in Jeopardy and What Can Be Done About It. New York: Basic Books.

Hicks, Michael and Krikant Devaraj. 2017. "The Myth and Reality of Manufacturing in America." Center for Business and Economic Research. Ball State University.

Hochschild, Arlie Russell. 2016. *Strangers in Their Own Land*. New York: The New Press.

Hodge, Robert W. and Donald Treiman. 1968. "Class Identification in the United States." *American Journal of Sociology* 73:535–547.

Hodge, Robert W., Donald Treiman, and Peter H. Rossi. 1966. "A Comparative Study of Occupational Prestige." In *Class, Status and Power*, 2nd ed., edited by R. Bendix and S. M. Lipset. New York: Free Press.

Hodges, Harold M. 1964. *Social Stratification: Class in America*. Cambridge, MA: Schenkman.

Hoffman, Saul. 1977. "Marital Instability and the Economic Status of Women." *Demography* 14:67–76.

Hollingshead, August B. 1949. *Elmtown's Youth*. New York: Wiley.

Hollingshead, August B. 1950. "Cultural Factors in the Selection of Marriage Mates." *American Sociological Review* 15:619–627.

Hollingshead, August B. and Frederick Redlich. 1958. *Social Class and Mental Illness: A Community Study*. New York: Wiley.

Hout, Michael. 1988. "More Universalism, Less Structural Mobility: The American Occupational Structure in the 1980s." *American Journal of Sociology* 93:1358–1400.

Hout, Michael. 2001. "Social Mobility." In *Oxford Companion to Politics of the World*, 2nd ed., edited by J. Krieger. New York: Oxford University.

Hout, Michael. 2004. "How Inequality May Affect Intergenerational Mobility." In *Social Inequality*, edited by Kathryn M. Neckerman. New York: Russell Sage Foundation.

Hout, Michael, et al. 1995. "Class Voting in the U.S. 1948–92." *American Sociological Review* 60:802–828.

In the Vanguard. 2011 (Summer). A Veteran Economist Discusses Why This Isn't a Normal Recovery.

Irwin, Neil. 2017. "The Great American Janitor Test," *New York Times*. Sept. 2.

Isaacs, Julia. 2008. "International Comparisons of Economic Mobility." Economic Mobility Project. An Initiative of the Pew Charitable Trusts.

Jackman, Mary. 1979. "The Subjective Meaning of Social Class Identification in the United States." *Public Opinion Quarterly* 43:443–462.

Jargowsky, Paul. 1996. "Take the Money and Run: Economic Segregation in U.S. Metropolitan Areas." *American Sociological Review* 61:984–998.

Jefferson, Thomas. [1821] 1944. "Autobiography." In *The Life and Selected Writings of Thomas Jefferson*, edited by A. Koch and W. Peden. New York: Modern Library.

Jencks, Christopher, et al. 1972. *Inequality: A Reassessment of the Effect of Family and Schooling in America*. New York: Basic Books.

Jencks, Christopher, et al. 1979. *Who Gets Ahead?* New York: Basic Books.

Jencks, Christopher, et al. 1991. "Is the American Underclass Growing?" In *The Urban Underclass*, edited by C. Jencks and P. Peterson. Washington, DC: Brookings Institution.

Jencks, Christopher and Paul Peterson. 1991. *The Urban Underclass*. Washington, DC: Brookings Institution.

Judis, John B. 1991. "Twilight of the Gods." *Wilson Quarterly* 5(Autumn):43–57.

Kahl, Joseph A. 1953. "Educational and Occupational Aspirations of Common Man Boys." *Harvard Educational Review* 23:186–203.

Kahl, Joseph A. 1957. *The American Class Structure*. 1st ed. New York: Rinehart.

Kahl, Joseph A. and James A. Davis. 1955. "A Comparison of Indexes of Socio-Economic Status." *American Sociological Review* 20:317–325.

Kahlenberg, Richard D., ed. 2004. *America's Untapped Resource: Low-Income Students in Higher Education*. New York: The Century Foundation Press.

Kane, Thomas. 2004. "College Going and Inequality." In *Social Inequality*, edited by K. Neckerman. New York: Russell Sage Foundation.

Kanter, Rosabeth. 1977. *Men and Women of the Corporation*. New York: Basic Books.

Karabel, Jerome. 2005. *The Chosen: The Hidden History of Admission and Exclusion at Harvard, Yale, and Princeton*. New York: Houghton Mifflin.

Karabel, Jerome and A. H. Halsey, eds. 1977. *Power and Ideology in Education*. New York: Oxford University Press.

Karoly, Lynn and Gary Burtless. 1995. "Demographic Change, Rising Earnings Inequality, and the Distribution of Personal Well-Being, 1959–1989." *Demography* 32:379–405.

Kassalow, Everett. 1978. "How Some European Nations Avoid U.S. Levels of Industrial Conflict." *Monthly Labor Review* 101(April):97.

Kaus, Mickey. 1992. *The End of Equality*. New York: Basic Books.

Kaysen, Carl. 1957. "The Social Significance of the Modern Corporation." *American Economic Review* 47:311–319.

Keister, Lisa A. 2005. *Getting Rich: America's New Rich and How They Got That Way*. New York: Cambridge University Press.

Kelly, Kitty. 2004. *The Family: The Real Story of the Bush Family*. New York: Doubleday.

Kendall, Diana. 2008. *Members Only: Elite Clubs and the Process of Exclusion*. Lanham, MD: Rowman & Littlefield.

Kennickell, Arthur. 2006. "Currents and Undercurrents: Changes in the Distribution of Wealth, 1980–2004." *Federal Reserve Working Paper No. 2006–13*.

Kennickell, Arthur. 2009. "Ponds and Streams: Wealth and Income in the U.S., 1989 to 2007." *Federal Reserve Working Paper No. 2009–13*.

Kennickell, Arthur, Douglas A. McManus, and R. Louise Woodburn. 1996. "Weighting Design for the 1992 Survey of Consumer Finances." Federal Reserve. Available at http://www.federalreserve.gov/Pubs/oss/oss2/papers/weight92.pdf

Kerr, Clark and Abraham Siegel. 1954. "The Interindustry Propensity to Strike— An International Comparison." In *Industrial Conflict*, edited by A. Kornhauser et al. New York: McGraw-Hill.

Khan, Shamus. 2011. *Privilege: The Making of An Adolescent Elite at St. Paul's School*. Princeton, NJ: Princeton University Press.

Kichen, Steve, et al. 1996. "The Private 500." *Forbes* December 2.

Kingston, Paul W. 2000. *The Classless Society*. Palo Alto, CA: Stanford University Press.

Klinkner, Philip, ed. 1996. *Midterm: The Elections of 1994 in Context*. Boulder, CO: Westview.

Klinkner, Philip. 2017. "Understanding Support for Trump: It's Not the Economy, Stupid." Unpublished analysis. Hamilton College, November.

Kodrzycki, Yolanda K. 1996. "Labor Market and Earnings Inequality: A Status Report." *New England Economic Review* May/June 1996:11–25.

Koenig, Thomas. 1980. "Corporate Support for Political Contribution Disclosure." Unpublished paper presented at the American Sociological Association, New York.

Kohn, Melvin L. 1969. *Class and Conformity: A Study in Values*. Homewood, IL: Dorsey.

Kohn, Melvin L. 1976. "Social Class and Parental Values: Another Conformation of the Relationship." *American Sociological Review* 41:538–545.

Kohn, Melvin L. 1977. *Class and Conformity*. 2nd ed. Chicago, IL: University of Chicago Press.

Kohn, Melvin L. and Carmi Schooler. 1983. *Work and Personality: An Inquiry Into the Impact of Social Stratification*. Norwood, NJ: Ablex.

Komarovsky, Mirra. 1946. "The Voluntary Associations of Urban Dwellers." *American Sociological Review* 11:689–698.

Komarovsky, Mirra. 1962. *Blue Collar Marriage*. New York: Vintage.

Kosman, Barry A. and Seymour P. Lachman. 1993. *One Nation Under God*. New York: Harmony Books.

Koten, John. 2013. "A Revolution in the Making." *Wall Street Journal* June 11.

Krugman, Paul and Robert Lawrence. 1994. "Trade, Jobs, and Wages." *Scientific American* April:44–49.

Lamont, Michele. 1992. *Money, Morals and Manners: The Culture of the French and the American Upper-Middle Class*. Chicago, IL: University of Chicago Press.

Lamont, Michele. 2000. *The Dignity of Working Men: Morality and the Boundaries of Race, Class, and Immigration*. Boston, MA: Harvard University Press.

Landecker, Werner S. 1981. *Class Crystallization*. New Brunswick, NJ: Rutgers University Press.

Langerfeld, Steven. 1981. "To Break a Union." *Harpers* 262(May):16–21.

Langman, Lauren. 1987. "Social Stratification." In *Handbook of Marriage and the Family*, edited by M. Sussman and S. Steinmetz. New York: Plenum.

Lareau, Annette. 2003. *Unequal Childhoods: Class, Race, and Family Life*. Berkeley, CA: University of California Press.

Lassiter, Luke Eric, et al. 2004. *The Other Side of Middletown: Exploring Muncie's African American Community*. Walnut Creek, CA: Altamira Press.

Laumann, Edward O. 1966. *Prestige and Association in an Urban Community*. Indianapolis, IN: Bobbs-Merrill.

Laumann, Edward O. 1973. *Bonds of Pluralism: The Form and Substance of Urban Social Networks*. New York: Wiley.

Leahy, Robert. 1981. "The Development of the Conception of Economic Inequality." *Child Development* 52:523–532.

Leahy, Robert. 1983. *The Child's Construction of Social Inequality*. New York: Academic.

Leighley, Jan. 2006. Class Bias in the U.S. Electorate 1972–2004. *Annual Meeting of the American Political Science Association*, Philadelphia, PA.

Leighley, Jan and Jonathan Nagler. 2014. *Who Votes Now?* Princeton, NJ: Princeton University Press.

Lemann, Nicholas. 2000. *The Big Test: The Secret History of the American Meritocracy*. New York: Farrar, Straus & Giroux.

LeMasters, E. E. 1975. *Blue-Collar Aristocrats: Life-Styles at a Working-Class Tavern*. Madison, WI: University of Wisconsin Press.

Lenski, Gerhard. 1954. "Status Crystallization: A Non-Vertical Dimension of Social Status." *American Sociological Review* 19:405–413.

Lenski, Gerhard. 1966. *Power and Privilege: A Theory of Social Stratification*. New York: McGraw-Hill.

Lerner, Robert, Althea Nagai, and Stanley Rothman. 1996. *American Elites*. New Haven, CT: Yale University Press.

Leuchtenburg, William. 2015. *The American President: From Teddy Roosevelt to Bill Clinton*. New York: Oxford University Press.

Levine, Donald M. and Mary Jo Bane, eds. 1975. *The "Inequality" Controversy: Schooling and Distributive Justice*. New York: Basic Books.

Levitan, Sar A. 1990. *Programs in Aid of the Poor*. 6th ed. Baltimore, MD: Johns Hopkins University Press.

Levitan, Sar and Isaac Shapiro. 1987. *Working but Poor: America's Contradiction*. Baltimore, MD: Johns Hopkins University Press.

Levitan, Sar A. and Robert Taggart. 1976. *The Promise of Greatness*. Cambridge, MA: Harvard University Press.

Levy, Frank. 1995. "Incomes and Income Inequality." In *State of the Union: America in the 1990s,* Vol. 1, edited by R. Farley. New York: Russell Sage Foundation.

Levy, Frank and Richard J. Murnane. 1992. "U.S. Earnings Levels and Earnings Inequality: A Review of Recent Trends and Proposed Explanations." *Journal of Economic Literature* 30:1333–1381.

Levy, Frank and Peter Temin. 2007. "Inequality and Institutions in 20th Century America." *Massachusetts Institute of Technology Department of Economics Working Paper No. 07–17.*

Lewis, Neil. 1996. "This Mr. Smith Gets His Way in Washington." *New York Times* October 12.

Lewis, Sinclair. 1922. *Babbitt*. New York: Harcourt Brace Jovanovich.

Link, Arthur S. and William Cotton. 1973. *American Epoch*. Vol. 1. 4th ed. New York: Knopf.

Lipset, Seymour Martin. 1960. *Political Man*. New York: Doubleday.

Lipset, Seymour Martin. 1981. *Political Man*. Expanded ed. Baltimore, MD: Johns Hopkins University Press.

Litwack, Leon, ed. 1962. *The American Labor Movement*. Englewood Cliffs, NJ: Prentice Hall.

Liu, Yujia and David Grunsky. 2013. "The Payoff to Skill in the Third Industrial Revolution." *American Journal of Sociology* 118:1330–1374.

Lopata, Helena Z., et al. 1980. "Spouses' Contributions to Each Other's Roles." In *Dual-Career Couples,* edited by F. Pepitone-Rockwell. Beverly Hills, CA: SAGE.

Lord, Walter. 1955. *A Night to Remember*. New York: Henry Holt.

Lorwin, Lewis L. 1933. *The American Federation of Labor*. Washington, DC: Brookings Institution.

LTV Corporation. 1990. A Guide to the 102nd Congress: 1st Session Datebook/Calendar. Washington, DC: Author.

Lucas, Samuel Roundfield. 1999. *Tracking Inequality: Stratification and Mobility in American High Schools*. New York: Teachers College Press.

Lundberg, Ferdinand. 1968. *The Rich and the Super-Rich*. New York: Lyle Stuart.

Lundberg, Shelly, et al. 2016. "Family Inequality: Diverging Patterns in Marriage Cohabitation and Childbearing." *Journal of Economic Perspectives* 30:79–101.

Lynd, Robert S. and Helen Merrell Lynd. 1929. *Middletown*. New York: Harcourt Brace Jovanovich.

Lynd, Robert S. and Helen Merrell Lynd. 1937. *Middletown in Transition*. New York: Harcourt Brace Jovanovich.

Mackenzie, Gavin. 1973. *The Aristocracy of Labor: The Position of Skilled Craftsmen in the American Class Structure*. New York: Cambridge University Press.

Madison, James (with Alexander Hamilton and John Jay). [1787] 1961. *The Federalist Papers*. New York: New American Library.

Magnuson, Katherine and Elizabeth Votruba-Drzal. 2009. "Enduring Influences of Childhood Poverty." In *Changing Poverty, Changing Policies,* edited by Maria Cancian and Sheldon Danziger. New York: Russell Sage Foundation.

Makinson, Larry. 1990. *Open Secrets: The Dollar Power of PACs in Congress*. Washington, DC: Congressional Quarterly Press.

Makinson, Larry and Joshua Goldstein. 1996. *Open Secrets: The Encyclopedia of Congressional Money and Politics*. 4th ed. Washington, DC: Congressional Quarterly Press.

Malbin, Michael J., ed. 2006. *The Election After Reform: Money, Politics, and the Bipartisan Campaign Reform Act*. Lanham, MD: Rowman & Littlefield.

Manza, Jeff and Clem Brooks. 1999. *Social Cleavages and Political Change: Voter Alignments and U.S. Party Coalitions*. New York: Oxford University Press.

Manza, Jeff and Michael Sauder. 2009. *Inequality and Society. Social Science Perspectives on Social Stratification*. New York: Norton.

Marcus, Ruth and Charles Babcock. 1997. "The System Cracks Under the Weight of Cash." *Washington Post*. February 9.

Marx, Karl. 1978. *The Marx-Engels Reader,* edited by Robert C. Tucker. 2nd ed. New York: Norton.

Massey, Douglas. 1996. "The Age of Extremes: Concentrated Affluence and Poverty in the Twenty-First Century." *Demography* 33:395–412.

Massey, Douglas and Mary J. Fisher. 2003. "The Geography of Inequality in the United States, 1950–2000." In *Brookings-Wharton Papers on Urban Affairs 2003,* edited by W. G. Gale and J. T. Pack. Washington, DC: Brookings Institution.

Mayer, Jane. 2016. *Dark Money: The Hidden History of the Billionaires Behind the Rise of the Radical Right*. New York: Doubleday.

Mazumder, Bhashkar. 2005. "The Apple Falls Even Closer to the Tree Than We Thought." In *Unequal Chances: Family Background and Economic Success,* edited by S. Bowles, H. Gintis, and M. Groves. Princeton, NJ: Princeton University Press.

McCall, Leslie. 2001. *Complex Inequality: Gender, Class, and Race in the New Economy*. New York: Routledge.

McCarty, Nolan, Keith T. Poole, and Howard Rosenthal. 2006. *Polarized America: The Dance of Ideology and Unequal Riches*. Cambridge, MA: MIT Press.

McLeod, Jay. 2008. *Ain't No Makin' It: Leveled Aspirations in a Low-Income Neighborhood*. Revised ed. Boulder, CO: Westview.

Miller, Herman P. 1971. *Rich Man, Poor Man*. Revised ed. New York: Thomas Y. Crowell.

Mills, C. Wright. 1951. *White Collar*. New York: Oxford University Press.

Mills, C. Wright. 1956. *The Power Elite*. New York: Oxford University Press.

Mills, C. Wright. 1968. "Comment on Criticism." In *C. Wright Mills and the Power Elite,* edited by G. W. Domhoff and H. B. Ballard. Boston, MA: Beacon.

Mintz, Beth. 1975. "The President's Cabinet, 1897–1972." *Insurgent Sociologist* 5(3):131–149.

Mishel, Lawrence, Jared Bernstein, and Sylvia Allegretto. 2007. *The State of Working America, 2006/2007*. Ithaca, NY: Cornell University Press.

Mishel, Lawrence, Jared Bernstein, and Heidi Schierholtz. 2009. *The State of Working America, 2008/2009*. Ithaca, NY: Cornell University Press.

Mishel, Lawrence, Jared Bernstein, and John Schmitt. 2001. *The State of Working America, 2000/2001*. Ithaca, NY: Cornell University Press.

Mishel, Lawrence, Josh Bivens, Elise Gould, and Heidi Shierholz. 2012. *The State of Working America*. 12th ed. Ithaca, NY: Cornell University Press.

Moffitt, Robert. 2012. *The Social Safety Net and the Great Recession*. Great Recession Brief. The Russell Sage Foundation and The Stanford Center on Poverty and Inequality.

Morgenson, Gretchen. 2013. "An Unstoppable Climb in CEO Pay." *New York Times* June 29.

Mortenson, Thomas G. 1991. *Equity of Higher Educational Opportunity for Women, Black, Hispanic, and Low Income Students*. Iowa City, IA: American College Testing Program.

Mortenson, Thomas G. 2001. "Family Income and Higher Education Opportunity, 1970–2000." *Postsecondary Education Opportunity* October.

Moskowitz, et al. 2010. "Is the Census Bureau's Supplemental Poverty Measure a Relative Measure of Poverty?" The Brookings Institution. Center on Children and Families.

Murray, Charles A. 1984. *Losing Ground: American Social Policy*. New York: Basic Books.

Murray, Charles. 2012. *Coming Apart: The State of White America, 1960–2010*. New York: Crown Forum.

Nagle, John. 1977. *System and Succession: The Social Bases of Political Elite Recruitment*. Austin, TX: University of Texas Press.

Naimark, Hedwin. 1981. *The Development of the Understanding of Social Class*. Doctoral dissertation, New York University.

Nakao, Keiko and Judith Treas. 1990. "Revised Prestige Scores for All Occupations." Chicago, IL: National Opinion Research Center (unpublished paper).

National Center for Health Statistics. 2009. *Births, Marriages, Divorces, and Deaths: Provisional Data for April 2009*. Available at www.cdc.gov/nchs/data/nvsr/nvsr58/nvsr 58_09.htm

National Commission on Children. 1991. *Beyond Rhetoric: A New American Agenda for Children and Families*. Washington, DC: U.S. Government Printing Office.

National Opinion Research Center (NORC). 1953. "Jobs and Occupations: A Popular Evaluation." In *Class, Status, and Power*, edited by R. Bendix and S. M. Lipset. Glencoe, IL: Free Press.

Neckerman, Kathryn, ed. 2004. *Social Inequality*. New York: Russell Sage Foundation.

Neckerman, Kathryn and Florencia Torche. 2007. "Inequality: Causes and Consequences." *Annual Review of Sociology* 33:335–337.

Newman, Katherine S. 1988. *Falling from Grace: The Experience of Downward Mobility in the American Middle Class*. New York: Free Press.

New York Times. 1984. "How Senators View the Senate: What Has Changed and What it Means." *New York Times* November 24.

Noah, Timothy. 2002. "The Mobility Myth." *The New Republic* March 1.

Noguchi, Yuki. 2013. "50 Years After the Equal Pay Act Gender Gap Endures." National Public Radio. Morning Edition.

Nunn, James and Jeffrey Rohaly. 2013. Tax Provisions in the American Taxpayer Relief Act of 2012. *Tax Policy Center* January 9.

Oakes, Jeannie. 1985. *Keeping Track: How High Schools Structure Inequality*. New Haven, CT: Yale University Press.

Obama, Barack. 1995, 2004. *Dreams From My Father: A Story of Race and Inheritance*. New York: Three Rivers Press.

Oliver, Melvin and Thomas Shapiro. 1995. *Black Wealth/White Wealth: A New Perspective on Racial Inequality*. New York: Routledge.

O'Neill, June. 2006. *Hearings on 1996 Welfare Overhaul. U.S. House of Representatives*. Statement. Committee on Ways and Means. July 19.

Ornati, Oscar. 1966. *Poverty Amidst Affluence*. New York: Twentieth Century Fund.

Orshansky, Mollie. 1974. "How Poverty Is Measured." In *Sociology of American Poverty*, edited by J. Huber et al. Cambridge, MA: Schenkman.

Ossowski, Stanislaw. 1963. *Class Structure in the Social Consciousness*. New York: Free Press.

Ostrander, Susan. 1984. *Women of the Upper Class*. Philadelphia, PA: Temple University Press.

Page, Benjamin, Larry Bartels, and Jason Seawright. 2013. "Democracy and Policy Preferences of Wealthy Americans." *Perspectives on Politics* 11:51–73.

Page, Benjamin and Lawrence Jacobs. 2009. *Class War? What Americans Really Think About Economic Inequality*. Chicago, IL: University of Chicago Press.

Pakulski, Jan and Malcolm Waters. 1996. *The Death of Class*. Thousand Oaks, CA: SAGE.

Parrott, Sharon. 2006. Statement. *Hearings on 1996 Welfare Overhaul. U.S. House of Representatives*. Committee on Ways and Means. July 19.

Pell Institute. 2017. *Indicators of Higher Education Equity in the United States: 2017 Historical Trend Report*.

Pen, Jan. 1971. *Income Distribution*. London: Allen Lane.

Persell, Caroline Hodges. 1977. *Education and Inequality*. New York: Free Press.

Pew Research Center. 2010. The Decline of Marriage and the Rise of New Families. Nov. 18.

Pew Research. 2013. "Breadwinner Moms." www .pewsocialtrends.org/2013/05/29/breadwinner-mom/

Phillips, Katherin. 2001. "The Earned Income Tax Credit: Knowledge Is Money." *Political Science Quarterly* 116:413–424.

Phillips, Kevin. 1990. *The Politics of Rich and Poor: Wealth and the American Electorate in the Reagan Aftermath.* New York: Random House.

Phillips, Kevin. 2002. *Wealth and Democracy: A Political History of the American Rich.* New York: Broadway Books.

Pianin, Eric. 1997. "How Business Found Benefits in Wage Bill." *The Washington Post* February 11.

Piketty, Thomas and Emmanuel Saez. 2003. "Income Inequality in the United States, 1913–1998." *Quarterly Journal of Economics* 118:1–39. Updated files accessed at www.Elsa.Berkeley.edu/~saez

Piven, Frances Fox and Richard A. Cloward. 1971. *Regulating the Poor: The Functions of Public Welfare.* New York: Pantheon.

Polsby, Nelson. 1970. "How to Study Community Power: The Pluralist Alternative." In *The Structure of Community Power,* edited by M. Aiken and P. E. Mott. New York: Random House.

Rainwater, Lee. 1965. *Family Design: Marital Sexuality, Family Size, and Contraception.* Chicago, IL: Aldine.

Rainwater, Lee. 1974. *What Money Buys.* New York: Basic Books.

Ramsey, Patricia. 1991. "Young Children's Awareness and Understanding of Social Class Differences." *Journal of Genetic Psychology* 152:71–82.

Rank, Mark and Thomas Hirschl. 2015. "The Likelihood of Experiencing Relative Poverty over the Life Course." PLOS (http://dx.doi.org/10.1371/jour nal.pone.o133513)

Reardon, S.F. and K. Bischoff, 2011. "Growth in the Residential Segregation of Families by Income, 1970–2009." Report prepared for the Russell Sage US2010 project. www.s4.brown.edu/us2010/Data/ Report/report111111.pdf

Reich, Robert. 2007. *Supercapitalism: The Transformation of Business, Democracy, and Everyday Life.* New York: Random House.

Reischauer, Robert. 1997. *Setting National Priorities: Budget Choices for the Next Century.* Washington, DC: Brookings Institution.

Reiss, Albert. 1961. *Occupations and Social Status.* Glencoe, IL: Free Press.

Reissman, Leonard. 1954. "Class, Leisure and Participation." *American Sociological Review* 19:74–84.

Renwick T. and Liana Fox. 2016. "The Supplemental Poverty Measure: 2015." U.S. Census Bureau. Current Population Reports. P60–258 (RV).

Resignation letter from National Committee of Labor-Management Group, July 17, 1978. Published in: *North Country Anvil,* Nr. 28, (1778) p. 22.

Rieder, Jonathan. 1985. *Canarsie: The Jews and Italians of Brooklyn Against Liberalism.* Cambridge, MA: Harvard University Press.

Riesman, David. 1953. *The Lonely Crowd: A Study of the Changing American Character.* New Haven, CT: Yale University Press.

Ritter, Kathleen and Lowell Hargens. 1975. "Occupational Positions and Class Identifications of Married Women." *American Journal of Sociology* 80:934–948.

Ritzer, George. 1996. *The McDonaldization of Society: An Investigation Into the Changing Character of Contemporary Social Life.* Thousand Oaks, CA: Pine Forge.

Rodrik, Dani. 2011. *The Globalization Paradox: Democracy and the Future of the World Economy.* New York: Norton.

Rose, Stephen J. 2014. *Social Stratification in the United States: The American Profile Poster.* New Edition. New York: New Press.

Rosen, Ellen Israel. 1987. *Bitter Choices: Blue-Collar Women In and Out of Work.* Chicago, IL: University of Chicago Press.

Ross, Howard. 1968. "Economic Growth and Change in the United States Under Laissez-Faire: 1870–1929." In *The Age of Industrialization in America,* edited by F. C. Jaher. New York: Free Press.

Rossi, Peter H. 1989. *Down and Out in America: The Origins of Homelessness.* Chicago, IL: University of Chicago Press.

Rothman, Stanley and Amy Black. 1999. "Elites Revisited: American Social and Political Leadership in the 1990s." *International Journal of Public Opinion Research* 11:169–195.

Rubin, Lillian Breslow. 1976. *Worlds of Pain: Life in the Working-Class Family.* New York: Basic Books.

Rubin, Lillian Breslow. 1994. *Families on the Faultline: America's Working Class Speaks About the Family, the Economy, Race, and Ethnicity.* New York: HarperCollins.

Rubin, Z. 1968. "Do American Women Marry Up?" *American Sociological Review* 5:750–760.

Ryscavage, Paul, et al. 1992. "The Impact of Demographic, Social, and Economic Change on the Distribution of Income." In U.S. Census Bureau, *Studies in the Distribution of Income.* Washington, DC: U.S. Government Printing Office.

Sachs, Jeffrey and Howard Shatz. 1994. "Trade and Jobs in U.S. Manufacturing." *Brookings Papers on Economic Activity No. 1.*

Saez, Emmanuel and Gabriel Zucman 2014. "Wealth Inequality in the United States Since 1913: Evidence From Capitalized Income Tax Data." National Bureau of Economic Research. Working Paper 20625.

Sassler, Sharon and Amanda Miller. 2011. "Class Differences in Cohabitation Processes." *Family Relations* 60:173–177.

Sawhill, Isabel. 1989. "The Underclass: An Overview." *The Public Interest* 96(Summer):3–15.

Schlesinger, Arthur J., Jr. 1945. *The Age of Jackson.* Boston, MA: Little, Brown.

Schreiber, E. M. and G. T. Nygreen. 1970. "Subjective Social Class in America: 1945–1968." *Social Forces* 45:348–356.

Schwartz, Christine. 2013. "Trends and Variation in Assortative Mating: Causes and Consequences." *Annual Review of Sociology* 39:451–470.

Schwartz, Christine and Robert Mare. 2005. "Trends in Educational Assortative Marriage, From 1940 to 2003." *Demography* 42:621–646.

Schwartz, Michael, ed. 1987. *The Structure of Power in America: The Corporate Elite As a Ruling Class.* New York: Holmes & Meier.

Seefeldt, Kristin. 2016. *Social Service Review* 90:156–163.

Sewell, William H. and Robert M. Hauser. 1975. *Education, Occupation, and Earnings.* New York: Academic.

Sewell, William H. and Vimal P. Shah. 1977. "Socioeconomic Status, Intelligence, and the Attainment of Higher Education." In *Power and Ideology in Education,* edited by J. Karabel and A. H. Halsey. New York: Oxford University Press.

Shaefer, H. Luke and Kathryn Edin. 2013. "Rising Extreme Poverty in the United States and the Response of Federal Means-Tested Transfer Programs." *Social Service Review* 83:250–268.

Shapiro, Thomas. 2004. *The Hidden Cost of Being African American: How Wealth Perpetuates Inequality.* New York: Oxford University Press.

Shipler, David. 2005. *The Working Poor: Invisible in America.* New York: Random House.

Short, Kathleen. 2012. *The Supplemental Poverty Measure: Examining the Incidence and Depth of Poverty in the U.S. Taking Account of Taxes and Transfers in 2011.* U.S. Census. Housing and Household Economic Statistics Division.

Short, Kathleen and Timothy Smeeding. 2012. "Understanding Income-to-Threshold Ratios Using the Supplemental Poverty Measure: People With Moderate Income." *SEHSD Working Paper No. 2012-18.* U.S. Census.

Shostak, Arthur and William Gomberg, eds. 1964. *The Blue Collar World: Studies of the American Worker.* Englewood Cliffs, NJ: Prentice Hall.

Simkus, Albert. 1978. "Residential Segregation by Occupation and Race." *American Sociological Review* 43:81–93.

Simmons, Robert G. and Morris Rosenberg. 1971. "Functions of Children's Perceptions of the Stratification System." *American Sociological Review* 36:235–249.

Smeeding, Timothy. 2008. "Poverty Work and Policy: The United States in Comparative Perspective." In *Social Stratification: Class, Race and Gender in Sociological Perspective,* 3rd ed, edited by David Grusky. Boulder, CO: Westview.

Smeeding, Timothy, Lee Rainwater, and Gary Burtless. 2001. "U.S. Poverty in Cross-National Context." In *Understanding Poverty,* edited by Sheldon H. Danziger and Robert H. Haveman. New York: Russell Sage Foundation.

Smith, David H. and Jacqueline Macaulay. 1980. *Participation in Social and Political Activities.* San Francisco, CA: Jossey-Bass.

Smith, Hedrick. 2012. *Who Stole the American Dream?* New York: Random House.

Smith, James P. and Finis R. Welch. 1989. "Black Economic Progress After Myrdal." *Journal of Economic Literature* 27:519–564.

Smith, Tom W. 1987. "That Which We Call Welfare by Any Other Name Would Smell Sweeter: An Analysis of the Impact of Question Wording on Response Patterns." *Public Opinion Quarterly* 51:75–83.

Snow, David and Leon Anderson. 1993. *Down on Their Luck: Homeless Street People.* Berkeley, CA: University of California Press.

Solomon-Fears, Carmen. 2014. "Nonmarital Births: An Overview." Congressional Research Report.

Sorauf, Frank. 1992. *Inside Campaign Finance: Myths and Realities.* New Haven, CT: Yale University Press.

Sorensen, Annemette. 1994. "Women, Family, and Class." *Annual Review of Sociology* 20:27–47.

Statesman's Yearbook. 1979–1990. New York: St. Martin's.

Stendler, Celia Burns. 1949. *Children of Brasstown: Their Awareness of the Symbols of Social Class.* Urbana, IL: University of Illinois Press.

Stevens, Mitchell. 2007. *Creating a Class: College Admissions and the Education of Elites.* Cambridge, MA: Harvard University Press.

Stolberg, Sheryl Gay. 2013. "Pugnacious Builder of the Business Lobby." *New York Times* June 1.

Substance Abuse and Mental Health Services Administration (SAMHSA). 2011. "Current Statistics on the Prevalence and Characteristics of People Experiencing Homelessness in the United States." Available at http://homeless.samhsa.gov/ResourceFiles/hrc_factsheet.pdf

Sussman, Marvin and Suzanne Steinmetz. 1987. *Handbook of Marriage and the Family.* New York: Plenum.

Sweezy, Paul. 1968. "Power Elite or Ruling Class?" In *C. Wright Mills and the Power Elite,* edited by G. W. Domhoff and H. B. Ballard. Boston, MA: Beacon.

Szymanski, Albert. 1978. *The Capitalist State and the Politics of Class.* Cambridge, MA: Winthrop.

Tach, Lalura and Kathryn Edin. 2017. "The Social Safety Net after Welform: Recent Developments and Consequences for Household Dynamics." *Annual Review of Sociology.* Forthcoming.

Teixeira, Ruy. 1992. *The Disappearing American Voter.* Washington, DC: Brookings Institution.

Teixeira, Ruy and Joel Rogers. 2000. *America's Forgotten Majority: Why the White Working Class Still Matters.* New York: Basic Books.

Terkel, Studs. 1974. *Working: People Talk About What They Do All Day and How They Feel About It.* New York: Avon.

Thompson, E. P. 1963. *The Making of the English Working Class.* New York: Vintage.

Treas, Judith and Ramon Torrecilha. 1995. "The Older Population." In *The State of the Union: America in the 1990s, Volume 2: Social Trends.* New York: Russell Sage Foundation.

Treiman, Donald. 1977. *Occupational Prestige in Comparative Perspective.* New York: Academic.

Treiman, Donald and Patricia Roos. 1983. "Sex and Earnings in Industrial Society: A Nine-Nation Comparison." *American Journal of Sociology* 89:612–650.

Truslow Adams, James. 1931. *The Epic of America.* Boston, MA: Little, Brown.

Tuchman, Gaye, ed. 1974. *The TV Establishment: Programming for Power and Profit.* Englewood Cliffs, NJ: Prentice Hall.

Tutor, Jeannette. 1991. "The Development of Class Awareness in Children." *Social Forces* 49:470–476.

United for a Fair Economy, ed. 2004. *The Wealth Inequality Reader.* Cambridge, MA: Dollars & Sense, Economic Affairs Bureau.

U.S. Census. 1973–2011. *Statistical Abstract of the United States.* Various editions.

U.S. Census. 1975. *Historical Statistics of the United States.* Bicentennial ed. 2 Parts.

U.S. Census. 1976. *Bicentennial Statistics,* Pocket Data Book, USA.

U.S. Census. 1980. "The Social and Economic Status of the Black Population in the United States: An Historical View, 1790–1978." *Current Population Reports,* Special Studies Series P-23, No. 80.

U.S. Census. 1984. *1980 Census of Population,* United States Summary, Section A: United States. Characteristics of the Population. Series PC80–1-D1-A.

U.S. Census. 1990a. *Trends in Income, by Selected Characteristics: 1947 to 1988.* Current Population Reports. Series P-60, No. 167.

U.S. Census. 1990b. *Transition in Income and Poverty Status: 1985–86.* Series P-70, No. 18.

U.S. Census. 1991. *Transition in Income and Poverty Status: 1987–88.* Series P-70, No. 24.

U.S. Census. 1992. *Workers With Low Earnings: 1964–1990.*

U.S. Census. 1994. *Dynamics of Economic Well-Being: Labor Force and Income, 1990 to 1992.* Series P-70–40.

U.S. Census. 1996. "A Brief Look at Postwar U.S. Income Inequality." *Current Population Reports.* Series P-60–191.

U.S. Census. 2001. *Experimental Poverty Measures: 1999.*

U.S. Census. 2003. *Net Worth and Asset Ownership of Households 1998 and 2000.* Washington, DC: U.S. Census Bureau.

U.S. Census. 2011. *Custodial Mothers and Fathers and Their Child Support: 2009.*

U.S. Census. 2013. *Income, Poverty, and Health Insurance Coverage in the United States: 2012.*

U.S. Census. 2016a. *The Supplementary Poverty Measure: 2015.*

U.S. Census 2016. *Income and Poverty in the United States: 2015.*

U.S. Department of Education 2005. *Youth Indicators 2005: Trends in the Well-Being of American Youth.*

U.S. Department of Housing and Urban Development. 1999. *Homelessness: Programs and the People They Serve.*

U.S. Department of Housing and Urban Development. 2007. *The Annual Homeless Assessment Report to Congress.*

U.S. Department of Housing and Urban Development. 2009. *The 2008 Annual Homeless Assessment Report.*

U.S. Department of Housing and Urban Development. 2012. *The 2012 Point-in-Time Estimates of Homelessness: Volume I of the 2012 Annual Homeless Assessment Report.*

U.S. Department of Justice. 2001. *Intimate Partner Violence and Age of Victim, 1993–99.*

U.S. Department of Labor. 1984–2013. *Employment and Earnings.* January.

U.S. Department of Labor. 2001a. *Consumer Expenditures in 1999.* May.

U.S. Department of Labor. 2001b. *Employment and Earnings.* January.

U.S. House of Representatives, Committee on Ways and Means. 1991a. *Overview of the Federal Tax System.* WMCP-102–7.

U.S. House of Representatives, Committee on Ways and Means. 1991b. *Background Material and Data on Programs Within the Jurisdiction of the Committee on Ways and Means.*

U.S. House of Representatives, Committee on Ways and Means. 1992. *Overview of Entitlement Programs: Background Material and Data on Programs Within the Jurisdiction of the Committee on Ways and Means.* May 15.

U.S. House of Representatives, Committee on Ways and Means. 2000. *Background Material and Data on Programs Within the Jurisdiction of the Committee on Ways and Means.*

U.S. Internal Revenue Service. 1988–2009. *Statistics of Income.* Fall.

U.S. Senate. 1912. *"Titanic" Disaster: Report of the Committee on Commerce.*

Useem, Michael. 1996. *Investor Capitalism: How Money Managers Are Changing the Face of Corporate America.* New York: Basic Books.

Vanfossen, Beth Ensminger. 1977. "Sexual Stratification and Sex-Role Socialization." *Journal of Marriage and the Family* 39:563–574.

Veblen, Thorstein. [1899] 1934. *The Theory of the Leisure Class.* New York: Modern Library.

Venkatesh, Sudhir Alladi. 2000. *American Project: The Rise and Fall of a Modern Ghetto.* Cambridge, MA: Harvard University Press.

Verba, Sidney, Kay Lehman Schlozman, and Henry E. Brady. 2004. "Political Equality: What Do We Know About It?" In *Social Inequality,* edited by K. M. Neckerman. New York: Russell Sage Foundation.

Vornovitsky, Marina, et al. 2016. "Distribution of Household Wealth in the U.S.: 2000–2011." U.S. Census Working Paper.

Warner, W. Lloyd and Paul S. Lunt. 1941. *The Social Life of a Modern Community.* New Haven, CT: Yale University Press.

Warner, W. Lloyd, et al. 1949a. *Democracy in Jonesville.* New York: Harper & Row.

Warner, W. Lloyd, et al. 1949b. *Social Class in America.* Chicago, IL: Science Research Associates.

Warner, W. Lloyd, et al. 1973. *Yankee City.* Abridged ed. New Haven, CT: Yale University Press.

Wattenberg, Ben J. 1974. *The Real America.* Garden City, NY: Doubleday.

Weber, Max. 1946. *From Max Weber: Essays in Sociology,* edited by H. H. Gerth and C. W. Mills. New York: Oxford University Press.

Weissman, Stephen and Ruth Hassan. 2006. "527 Groups and BCRA." In *The Election After Reform: Money, Politics, and the Bipartisan Campaign Reform Act,* edited by Michael J. Malbin. Lanham, MD: Rowman & Littlefield.

Wessel, David 2012. *Red Ink: Inside the High-Stakes Politics of the Federal Budget.* New York: Crown Business.

Wetzel, James R. 1995. "Labor Force, Unemployment, and Earnings." In *State of the Union: America in the 1990s, Volume 1: Economic Trends,* edited by R. Farley. New York: Russell Sage Foundation.

Wilson, Valerie and William Rodgers III. 2016. Black-White Wage Gaps Expand with Rising Wage Inequality." Economic Policy Institute. Report.

Winters, Jeffrey 2011. *Oligarchy.* New York: Cambridge University Press.

Winters, Jeffrey and Benjamin Page. 2009. "Oligarchy in the United States?" *Perspectives on Politics* 7:731–751.

Who's Who in America. 1980. 41st ed. Chicago, IL: Marquis.

Who's Who in American Politics. 1979. 7th ed. New York: Bowker.

Whyte, Martin King. 1990. *Dating, Mating, and Marriage.* New York: Aldine de Gruyter.

Whyte, William H. 1952. *Is Anybody Listening?* New York: Simon & Schuster.

Wilcox, W. Bradford. 2010. *The State of Our Unions.* The National Marriage Project, University of Virginia.

Wilson, William J. 1980. *The Declining Significance of Race.* 2nd ed. Chicago, IL: University of Chicago Press.

Wilson, William J. 1987. *The Truly Disadvantaged: The Inner City, the Underclass, and Public Policy.* Chicago, IL: University of Chicago Press.

Wilson, William J. 1991. "Public Policy Research and the Truly Disadvantaged." In *The Urban Underclass,* edited by C. Jencks and P. Peterson. Washington, DC: Brookings Institution.

Wilson, William J. 1996. *When Work Disappears: The World of the New Urban Poor.* New York: Knopf.

Wilson, William J. 2009. *More Than Just Race: Being Black and Poor in the Inner City.* New York: W.W. Norton & Company.

Wilson, William Julius and Kathryn Neckerman. 1986. "Poverty and Family Structure: The Widening Gap Between Evidence and Public Policy Issues." In *Fighting Poverty: What Works and What Doesn't,* edited by S. Danziger and D. H. Weinberg. Cambridge, MA: Harvard University Press.

Wimer, Christopher, et al. 2016. "Progress on Poverty? New Estimates of Historical Trends Using an Anchored Supplemental Poverty Measure." *Demography* 53:1207–1218.

Wolfe, Tom. 1987. *The Bonfire of the Vanities.* New York: Farrar, Straus & Giroux.

Wolff, Edward. 1993. "The Structure of Wealth Inequality: A Report to the Twentieth Century Fund." Unpublished paper.

Wolff, Edward. 1996. "Trends in Household Wealth, 1983–1992." Report Submitted to the Department of Labor. Unpublished paper.

Wolff, Edward. 1998. "Recent Trends in the Size Distribution of Household Wealth." *Journal of Economic Perspectives* 12:131–150.

Wolff, Edward. 2002. *Top Heavy: The Increasing Inequality of Wealth in America and What Can Be Done About It.* New York: The New Press.

Wolff, Edward. 2014. "Household Wealth Trends in the United States, 1962–2013. What Happened Over the Great Recession." National Bureau of Economic Research. Working Paper 20733.

Wolff, Edward. 2016. "Deconstructing Household Wealth Trends in the United States, 1983–2013." National Bureau of Economic Research. Working Paper 22704.

Wolff, Edward. Forthcoming. "Changes in Household Wealth in the 1980s and 1990s in the U.S." In *International Perspectives on Household Wealth,* edited by E. N. Wolff, Cheltenham, UK: Elgar Publishing Ltd.

Wolfinger, Raymond E. 1973. *The Politics of Progress.* Englewood Cliffs, NJ: Prentice Hall.

Woo, Stu. 2009. "For America's Santas, It's Hard to Be Jolly With the Tales They're Hearing." *Wall Street Journal* December 14.

Wood, Thomas. 2017. "Racism Motivated Trump Voters More Than Authoritarianism." *Washington Post.* Monkey Cage. April 17. (https://www.washingtonpost.com/news/monkey-cage/wp/2017/04/17/racism-motivated-trump-voters-more-than-authoritarianism-or-income-inequality/?utm_term=.0899d4086686)

Wool, Harold. 1976. *The Labor Supply for Lower-Level Occupations.* New York: Praeger.

Wright, James. 1989. *Address Unknown: The Homeless in America.* New York: Aldine de Gruyter.

Wright, John, ed. 2007. *The New York Times Almanac.* New York: Penguin.

Zeitlin, Maurice. 1980. *Classes, Class Conflict and the State.* Cambridge, MA: Winthrop.

Zweigenhaft, Richard L. and G. William Domhoff. 1998. *Diversity in the Power Elite: Have Women and Minorities Reached the Top?* New Haven, CT: Yale University Press.

Note on Statistical Sources

Most of the statistics cited in the text and analyzed in tables and graphs come from the U.S. Census Bureau or the Bureau of Labor Statistics (BLS). In recent years, both agencies have placed mountains of information on the Web, while reducing their publication programs. In a gesture shocking to millions of librarians, journalists, and researchers, the Census Bureau ceased publication, in any form, of the *Statistical Abstract of the United States*, an invaluable, popular compendium of current economic and social statistics, which had been published continuously since 1878.[1] Government agencies have not, however, ceased collecting the relevant data.

To avoid cluttering the text with endless website and publication references, we have eliminated most citations for statistics derived from the Census Bureau's "March Current Population Survey" (the main source of income, poverty, and occupation data) and other standard series administered by the Census Bureau and the BLS. We have done the same for other standard statistical series regularly prepared by government agencies. However, information drawn from special publications of government agencies, rather than their regular series, are cited in the text and listed in the bibliography. Where necessary, government websites are usually cited by the agency's name (Census Bureau, Department of Justice, and so forth). Most were accessed in 2017. The Census Bureau site (www.census.gov) has links to other relevant sites, including the important Bureau of Labor Statistics site.

For statistics on jobs, wages, incomes, and related topics, the website of the Economic Policy Institute (EPI) is very helpful. EPI makes many key series available in downloadable format. See http://www.epi.org/data/. Another useful source of economic data is the St. Louis Federal Reserve at https://fred.stlouisfed.org/.

A few years ago, the Census Bureau radically recast the occupational categories it uses to describe the labor force. The Bureau has made modest adjustments to these categories in the past to accommodate economic change, but this recategorization clouded their meaning and, as the Bureau acknowledges, made comparisons with the past impossible. Previously, the basic occupational categories (managers, professionals, and so on) represented more or less homogeneous levels of skill, education, or authority. Now these concepts are mixed with notions of economic sector. Lawyers and judges, for example, are placed in the same category as paralegals, and teachers are lumped with teacher assistants, and all are categorized as professionals.

In order to describe the occupational structure in a coherent way for the purposes of Chapter 3, the more than 500 occupations defined by the Bureau for the 2010 census were resorted into 10 homogeneous, stratified categories which are fairly congruent with earlier series. These revised categories are used consistently throughout the chapter. Readers interested in a more detailed account should contact Professor Gilbert (dgilbert@hamilton.edu).

---

[1] Currently, there is a new electronic version of *The Statistical Abstract* published now by a private company that makes it available at prices aimed at libraries with ample budgets. Older years of the *Statistical Abstract*, going back to the nineteenth century, can be accessed at the Census Bureau website.

Index

Pages followed by (figure) indicate an illustration; followed by (table) indicate a table.

Truman, Harry, 178
Trump, Donald J.
  cabinet positions filled by, 178
  as *Forbes* 400 member, 169, 170 (table)
  Hacker and Piersons' findings as explanation for
    election of, 215
  income level of voters favoring, 201, 201 (table)
  political power shifts contributing to election
    of, 254
  pre-election media celebrity of, 215
  racist rhetoric and appeal of, 193, 202–203
  working to repeal Obamacare and Dodd-Frank
    Act, 186
Turner, Ted, 168
Tutor, Jeannette, 101
TV networks, 187–188
Two-tier wage systems, 65, 262

Underclass
  "conventional portrait" of, 230
  cycle of poverty notion associated with, 230–231
  definition of, 263
  description of the, 245, 247 (table), 250–251
  Gilbert-Kahl model description of, 14 (figure),
    32 (table)
  measuring transitory poor and the, 229–231
  Social Standing in America on, 28–32 (table)
  See also Lower classes; Poverty; Working poor
Unemployment
  Great Depression (1930s) rates of, 184,
    220–221
  Great Recession (2010) rates of, 89–90, 210,
    215, 232–233, 256
  loss of manufacturing jobs overseas causing,
    53–54 (figure), 210, 254
  rates from 1947 to 2015, 235 (figure)
  See also Labor; Poverty
United Auto Workers, 209, 211
United States
  comparative international and poverty in the,
    238–239 (figure)
  comparative international and social mobility in
    the, 136–138
  increasing segregation by social class in the,
    124–125
  loss of manufacturing jobs in the, 53–54 (figure),
    210, 254
  transformation from agricultural to postindustrial
    society, 51–53, 254
  transformation of the occupational structure in
    the, 49–51
  See also Occupation structure
United Textile Workers labor strike (1934),
    207–208

University of Michigan
  Panel Study of Income Dynamics (PSID) of,
    230, 231
  Survey Research Center (SRC) of, 35
University of Virginia, 140
*The Unknown City: The Lives of Poor and Working-Class
  Young Adults* (Fine and Weis), 116, 118
Upper-class
  C. Wright Mills on the history of the, 43–44
  Deep South report on, 25–28, 32 (table)
  Domhoff's argument on ties of corporate elites
    and, 164–165, 174–175
  Establishment made up of the, 174–176
  the "400" list of New York society, 44
  Gilbert-Kahl model description of the, 13,
    14 (figure), 32 (table)
  "preppies" of the, 173–174, 176–177
  Social Standing in America study on, 28–32 (table)
  Yankee City study on, 24, 32 (table)
Upper-lower class
  Deep South report on, 25–28, 32 (table)
  Social Standing in America study on, 28–32 (table)
  Yankee City study on, 24, 32 (table)
Upper-middle class
  association patterns of students bound for
    selective college, 109 (table)
  Deep South report on, 25–28, 32 (table)
  definition of, 263
  description of the, 244, 247 (table), 248
  Gilbert-Kahl model description of the, 13,
    14 (figure), 32 (table)
  joint marital relationships of the, 110–113,
    115–116
  language as main mechanism of discipline,
    106–107
  as privileged class, 15
  Rubin's study on behaviors of sons in, 113
  sense of entitlement cultivated in children of,
    107–108
  sex-role expectations in dual-career, 111–112
  Social Standing in America study on,
    28–32 (table)
  study findings on trends and changes in, 15–17
  teaching children to embrace institutions, 107
  traditional expectations of wives in the, 111
  Yankee City study on, 24, 32 (table)
  See also Privileged classes
Upper-upper class
  Deep South report on, 25–28,
    32 (table)
  Gilbert-Kahl model on capitalist or, 13, 14 (figure),
    32 (table)
  Social Standing in America study on, 28–32 (table)
  Yankee City study on, 24, 32 (table)

U.S. Census Bureau
    on custodial parents (2009) as primarily
        women, 85
    income distribution data collected by the,
        78 (table)–79
    "low-wage worker" as defined by the, 60–61
    major occupational groups with examples (2011),
        49 (table)
    measuring duration of individual poverty,
        229–230
    occupation system data collected by the, 48–51
    occupational structure of the U.S. (1870–2000),
        50 (table)
    poverty standard used by the, 225
    service workers category of the, 51
    statistics on increasing residential segregation, 125
    Supplemental Poverty Measure (SPM) of the,
        225, 226, 227, 232, 233, 238, 239
U.S. Chamber of Commerce, 185, 189, 211, 215
U.S. Congress
    Bartels' study on voting by senators of, 205–206
    professional and income of House members of
        the, 178–180
    white vote for (2012 and 2016) House members
        of, 202 (table)
    See also Government
U.S. Steel, 208

Vandenberg, Arthur, 209
Variance explained, 140, 141, 263
Veterans benefits, 74, 77, 80
Violence
    domestic, 116–118
    labor movement, class conflict, and, 206–207
    "union-busting" services coordinating, 207
    United Textile Workers labor strike (1934), 207–208
Voting
    Brewer and Stonecash's class differences study on,
        199–200
    class differences and participation in, 206–207
    class identification, political opinion, and, 197
    democratic class struggle, elections, and, 197–199
    party preferences by household income difference
        (1952–2004), 200 (table)
    party preferences in presidential elections by
        income (2012 and 2016), 201 (table)
    in 2014 elections by family income, 206 (table),
        206–207
    See also Politics

Wage inequality
    between blacks and whites, 58
    Frank and Cook on winner-take-all markets
        on, 66–67

Harrison and Bluestone study on corporate
        strategies to increase, 64–66
    between Hispanics and blacks, 58–59
    increasing rates of, 59–64, 251–252
    productivity in nonfarm business sector
        (1947–2010) and, 60 (figure)
    reasons for increasing, 62–64
    See also Earnings; Economy; Occupational
        structure
Wage inequality factors
    deregulation, 64
    economic restructuring, 49 (table), 62
    education levels, 63–64
    globalization, 63
    technological change, 63
    weakened wage-setting institutions, 64
Wage-setting institutions, definition of, 263
Wagner Act (National Labor Relations Act),
        208, 209
Wall Street Journal, 187, 256
Warner, W. Lloyd, 22–25, 28, 32 (figure), 121, 244
Washington Post, 187, 230
WASPs social class (Establishment), 20, 174–176
Watergate reform laws, 181–182
Weakened wage-setting institutions, 64
Wealth
    average net worth of households (2013), 87 (table)
    definition of, 86, 263
    gross assets and net worth measures of, 87
    growing inequality of, 252
Wealth classes
    decline of the old-money, 171
    definition of, 263
    efforts to reassert political power of the, 188–190
    emergence of corporate, 168–172
    Forbes 400 wealthiest Americans list, 169,
        170 (table)–171, 178, 180, 215
    investor class, 88
    nearly propertyless class, 87
    nest-egg class, 87–88
    political campaign contributions by, 181–184
    residential segregation of the, 125–126 (figure), 253
    See also Capitalist class
Wealth distribution
    concentration of key assets (2013), 89 (table)
    concentration of wealth (2013), 88 (table)
    Great Recession (2010) impact on, 89–90,
        210, 215
    growing inequality of, 252
    growing shift in, 89–90
    share of net worth held by top 1% of
        (1950–2010), 91 (figure)
    wealth classes and, 86–88
    See also Income distribution

domestic violence in the, 116–118

economic changes impacting marriages, 115–116, 255

Gilbert-Kahl model description of, 13–14 (figure)

industrialization and transformation of the, 44–46

joint marital relationships of the, 110–113

Marx's proletariat, 3–4, 6

parental values and occupational experience and patterns of, 102–105

Rubin's study on behaviors of sons in, 113

Social Standing in America study on, 28–32 (table)

study findings on trends and changes in, 15–17

teaching children to be intimidated by, 107

See also Blue-collar workers; Majority classes; Proletariat (working class)

Working poor

definition of, 263

description of the, 245, 247 (table), 250

Gilbert-Kahl model description of, 14

Social Standing in America study on, 28–32 (table)

study findings on trends and changes in, 15–17

Yankee City study on, 22–25, 32 (table)

See also Lower classes; Poverty; Underclass

Working rich

definition of, 263

Gilbert-Kahl model description of, 13, 14 (figure)

study findings on trends and changes in, 15–17

World Trade Organization, 53

Yankee City study

description of Yankee City, 23

Warner's prestige focus of the, 22–25, 32 (table), 244

Zuckerberg, Mark, 169, 170 (table)